REPRESENTATIVE DEMOCRACY IN THE CANADIAN PROVINCES

Allan Kornberg
William Mishler
Harold D. Clarke

Prentice-Hall Canada Inc., Scarborough, Ontario

To Dot

Canadian Cataloguing in Publication Data
Kornberg, Allan, 1931-
  Representative democracy in the Canadian
provinces

Includes index.
ISBN 0-13-773754-8

1. Provincial governments — Canada.*
2. Representative government and representation —
Canada. I. Mishler, William, 1947-
II. Clarke, Harold D., 1943- III. Title.

JL198.K67   324'.0971   C82-094330-4

Prentice-Hall, Inc., Englewood Cliffs, *New Jersey*
Prentice-Hall International, Inc., *London*
Prentice-Hall of Australia, Pty., Ltd., *Sydney*
Prentice-Hall of India Pvt., Ltd., *New Delhi*
Prentice-Hall of Japan, Inc., *Tokyo*
Prentice-Hall of Southeast Asia (PTE.) Ltd., *Singapore*

ISBN 0-13-773754-8

Production Editor: Charles Macli
Typesetting by: Compositor Associates Limited
Printed and bound in Canada by: Webcom Limited
1 2 3 4 WC 85 84 83 82

Contents

Preface

This book attempts to describe and explain the operation of provincial political systems and to evaluate their performance. Our analysis is organized around and informed by the theory of representative democracy, a hybrid of the principles of classical democracy and the pragmatism of representative government which provides a challenging yet practical standard for evaluating provincial political systems. Even if these were ordinary times the importance of understanding provincial politics would require little justification. Among the major federal systems of the world Canada is one of the most decentralized. Although the British North America Act established a federal system with weak provinces and a strong central government, over time the former have evolved into full partners with the latter. Collectively, provincial spending currently exceeds that of the federal government. The provinces enact more legislation, impose more regulations and employ a considerably larger number of civil servants. Indeed, the size and scope of provincial governments are such that few aspects of our daily lives are unaffected by their decisions. These are far from ordinary times, however. Federal and provincial leaders currently are engaged in a fundamental debate over the nature of Canadian federalism. The recent Quebec referendum on sovereignty-association, the protracted controversy over patriation of the constitution and continuing federal–provincial conflict in areas as different as language rights and natural resources are only its most visible manifestations.

Underlying this debate are varying perspectives on representation and democracy. Proponents of a decentralized federal system with even more powerful provinces frequently take the position that provincial governments are better able to represent their citizens because they are "closer" to them and thus can more easily identify and respond to their needs and demands. Similarly, because provincial governments are smaller and less complex than their federal counterpart, citizens are able to enjoy greater and more effective opportunities to participate in provincial politics and to influence the content of public policy. Understandably, advocates of a federal system in which the central government would enjoy enhanced powers hold quite different views. They argue, *inter alia*, that the size and relative homogeneity of the provinces makes them susceptible to control by special interests and less responsive to the needs and demands of disadvantaged groups in society. In contrast, the federal arena, because of the number and variety of interests represented there, encourages greater political competition and a more equitable distribution of governmental resources. Provincial governments are criticized as well for being too small and, in some instances, too poor to respond effectively to major public problems. Many of these transcend provincial boundaries and can be ameliorated by concerted, large-scale efforts which only the federal government is capable of mounting.

Despite the intensity with which these and a host of related positions have been argued, little evidence has been adduced to support conflicting claims. For example, almost no attention has been given to carefully assessing the character of political representation in Canada although that is, or ought to be, what the debate largely is about. Moreover, with respect to the provinces, we still have only a rudimentary understanding of the functioning of provincial political institutions and we know even less about mass political behaviour and its impact on the dynamics of provincial government. Scattered through the scholarly literature is a substantial body of empirical findings that could inform these matters but to date no one has attempted to integrate them in a systematic and relatively comprehensive fashion. The present volume addresses this neglect. It combines a synthesis and, in some instances, a reinterpretation of existing research with substantial new data in a description and explanation of the institutions and processes of provincial governments, their political cultures and the political behaviour of their citizens. The theory of representative democracy provides a critical perspective for evaluating the performance of provincial political systems and for gauging their future prospects.

* * *

Representative Democracy in the Canadian Provinces provides the student with an introduction to provincial politics, but one with a difference. Underlying our approach are a number of assumptions about the most appropriate ways of studying and presenting information on government and politics, an explication of which may contribute to a greater understanding of the content and organization of this book. First, we assume that a genuine understanding of government and politics, provincial or otherwise, requires more than an accumulation of facts about history, culture and institutions. Knowing these facts certainly is important but, like pieces of a jigsaw puzzle, they illuminate any subject only when they are properly interpreted and viewed as parts of an integrated whole. One of the reasons the theory of representative democracy is employed to inform the organization of this book is that we judge that it facilitates a student's ability to "make sense" of the facts presented. Second, although our perspective may appear quite critical at times, this appearance in great part is a consequence of an attempt to provide the student with a "balanced" book. The desire for balance is reflected in a tendency to note the weaknesses as well as the strengths of the provincial political systems and to present the varying positions that have been taken on controversial or problematic issues such as the character and future of federalism.

Third, this is in some sense an unorthodox book because it focusses on the commonalities rather than on the unique attributes of the provinces. Obviously, there are important differences among them: in their social and economic environments, the structure of their party systems and the extent to which their governments have been responsive to public needs, to cite but a few. However, their similarities are both more numerous and fundamental — well-educated populations, mixed economies, predominantly liberal value systems, a full panoply of civil rights and liberties, numerous organized interest groups, universal suffrage, political parties competing in regular, free elections, and, of course, a common federal government. We believe that overlooking commonalities and emphasizing the unique features of provincial societies and governments overlooks the fact that *all* of the provinces are members of the very small community of political systems which can be described as both representative and democratic in some sense of these terms. Given this perspective, our emphasis throughout this book is on the identification of common patterns and the development of theoretically relevant and empirically verified generalizations. At the same time, our desire for balance also has led us to note important provincial variations when these occur and to combine generalizations with considerable illustrative detail.

Finally, we have tried to achieve balance by combining an emphasis on political institutions, their procedures and the public policies they generate, with a concern for how people in these institutions and in the public at large behave politically. This fusion of institutional, public policy and behavioural perspectives reflects the view that political institutions cannot be comprehended apart from their environments. Provincial governments exercise considerable influence over many aspects of their environments but, in turn, they are profoundly influenced by them because, as democracies, they are expected — almost by definition — to be responsive to citizen needs and demands and to provide extensive opportunities for articulating them and for influencing public policy. As the final product of the political process, the content and direction of public policy are important indicators (perhaps the *most* important indicators) of the character of representative democracy in the provinces. Our analyses of the extent to which provincial public policies during the post-World War Two period have been congruent with the needs of their citizens lead to the conclusion that all of the provinces fall short of the democratic ideal. Nonetheless, over the years there has been significant movement towards this goal and suggestions are offered which could facilitate further advances.

* * *

This book is the product of a genuinely collaborative and equal effort by the three authors. Although the initial draft of each chapter was an individual responsibility, these were revised and rewritten by the co-authors. Consequently, the final product reflects a balance of various ideas, styles and perspectives, and should not be attributed to any single author.

Allan Kornberg
William Mishler
Harold Clarke

Acknowledgments

We wish to take this opportunity to thank all those individuals and organizations who helped to make this book possible. Generous financial assistance was provided by Duke University's Canadian Studies and Faculty Research programs. Valuable allotments of computer time were provided by the College of Arts and Sciences at Virginia Polytechnic Institute and State University, the State University of New York at Buffalo and Duke University. Especially important were research grants from the Social Sciences and Humanities Research Council of Canada. These enabled us to conduct much of the original research upon which this book is based. We owe a special debt to the late Frank Hintenberger of Prentice-Hall who encouraged us to undertake this project. After Frank's tragic death, Marta Tomins, Dick Hemingway and Chuck Macli steered the manuscript through its final preparation and into print. We also are indebted to Keith Archer, Mary Ellen Bernard, Jim Bruton, Euel Elliott, Ezio Di Emanuele, John Hogan, Henry Kramzyk, Lewis Kornberg, Tim Lomperis, Jim Minicozzi, John Moeller, John Shields and Mora Tobin for their data-gathering and processing work. Invaluable typing assistance was provided by Doris Linkous, Bea Martin, Debbie Moran and Bev Richards. Lisa Archer helped by preparing the index.

We were fortunate in being able to draw upon the previous research of a large number of students of Canadian government and politics. Their contributions are recognized throughout the text and in footnotes. Especially important for our efforts was access to data on political attitudes and behaviour. The Inter-University Consortium of Political and Social Research provided us with copies of the 1965 and 1968 Canadian national election studies conducted by John Meisel and his associates. The Institute for Behavioural Research at York University made their 1977 Quality of Life Study data available to us. Ms. Hélène Robillard-Frayne of the CBC provided us with the results of studies on trends in public attitudes toward Confederation in Quebec. We are indebted, as well, to our colleagues, Colin Campbell, David Falcone, Jane Jenson, Kai Hildebrandt, Lawrence LeDuc, Jon Pammett, Joel

Smith and Marianne Stewart, with whom we have collaborated in previous studies, some findings of which have been incorporated in the current text. Robert Drummond and Richard Van Loon made their data available and shared valuable insights with us. Although we are grateful to all of these organizations and persons for their assistance and many helpful recommendations, we naturally absolve them of responsibility for any errors of fact or interpretation. These are ours alone.

Finally, Dorothy Weathers typed numerous drafts of portions of the manuscript with grace and good humour and helped in so many other ways, they defy cataloguing. The dedication of this book to her cannot begin to express our deep appreciation for the friendship, loyalty and assistance she has given us over the years.

1
On Representative Democracy

The national interest is represented not just by the majority view of the House of Commons but requires a majority of regional wills . . . through provincial governments.

PREMIER ALLAN BLAKENEY,
Montreal Gazette, Sept. 15, 1980

There is a national interest which transcends regional interests. In a conflict between the national and provincial interests, the national interest must prevail.

PRIME MINISTER PIERRE TRUDEAU,
Toronto Globe and Mail, Sept. 15, 1980

INTRODUCTION

Democracy and representation are highly valued and extremely popular concepts. The great value that people ascribe to these concepts makes them ideals against which the character and performance of provincial political systems may be judged. Given their popularity, they have acquired a multitude of diverse and sometimes contradictory meanings. As terms such as participatory democracy, elitist democracy, representative government, responsible government, accountability, and authorization have become part of everyday speech, important distinctions among them have become blurred and much of their meaning distorted or entirely lost. Thus, before we can make an evaluation of the provincial political systems as representative democracies, the meaning of the concepts democracy and representation must be clarified. Accordingly, this first chapter outlines some of the principal conceptions of democracy and representation in political theory and Canadian political practice. The first section delineates the basic assumptions and values underlying these concepts, discusses their similarities and differences, and proposes that representative democracy is a desirable model to use when evaluating the governments and politics of the provinces. A second section considers some of the social and economic preconditions for achieving representative democracy and describes some of the

1

obstacles the provinces have encountered in moving toward this goal. The final section provides an overview of the remaining chapters and explains their relationship to the central purpose of this volume: an evaluation of how closely the provincial political systems approximate the ideal of representative democracy.

DEMOCRACY AND REPRESENTATION

Literally translated from its Greek roots, *demos* and *kratia*, democracy means, "rule by the people." "We are called a democracy," Pericles proclaimed in his funeral address to the citizens of ancient Athens, "because the government is in the hands of the many and not of the few." Reduced to its essential elements, democracy is a system of government by and for the people, in which political authority derives from citizen participation in governmental decisions.[1] In the classical theory of democracy — sometimes called direct democracy or participatory democracy — government and the governed are identical.[2] No distinctions are made between rulers and ruled, because citizens participate directly and continuously in all important political decisions which affect their lives. Decisions are made by majority rule based on principles of political equality and respect for minority rights. Underlying the emphasis on citizen participation is a fundamental belief in the intrinsic worth, dignity, and rationality of individuals, and the value of their involvement in public affairs to themselves and to the political system as a whole. For individuals, direct participation is the best means of ensuring the protection of their interests. Moreover, participation contributes to their moral and intellectual development and self-fulfillment. The political system benefits because participation nurtures within citizens the kind of public-spirited personality that a democracy requires if it is to survive and serve as a stable and effective means of governance.

Representation has a different meaning than democracy. Literally, it is a process in which an individual or group "stands in the place of others."[3] As it is currently employed, representation refers to a process in which political authority is transferred from citizens at large to public officials who are their "representatives." Although the average Canadian with more than a passing interest in politics probably considers representation and democracy logically inseparable, in fact, the marriage of these ideas occurred relatively recently. The grafting of representative principles on to the classical theory of democracy usually is credited to certain 18th and 19th century philosophers, notably Jeremy Bentham, Edmund Burke, James Mill and John Stuart Mill. Although there are important differences among these (and other) representational theorists, the views of John Stuart Mill and Edmund Burke may be regarded as illustrative of the liberal and conservative perspectives on representation and provide the theoretical bases for two important hybrids of classical democracy: representative and, for convenience, what may be termed "elitist democracy."[4]

For Mill, direct participation by all citizens in the affairs of state was the "ideally best" form of government. He strongly endorsed the classical democratic belief that participation has a salutary effect on both citizens and society and argued that "the only government which can satisfy all of the exigencies of the modern state is one in which the whole people participate."[5] Mill recognized, however, that practical constraints such as the size of modern states and the requirement that most people spend the bulk of their time earning a living prohibit the direct and continuous involvement of average citizens in public affairs. Consequently, he incorporated representative principles into democratic theory as a means of reducing the burdens of participation while preserving most of its individual and collective benefits. Although committed to the classical ideal, he defended "representative democracy" as the best form of government *in practice* since it recognized the necessity for a division of political labour between governors and governed but ensured that "the whole people . . . exercise through deputies . . . the ultimate controlling power . . . in all its completeness."[6]

Unlike Mill, Burke regarded classical democracy as anathema. He opposed direct participation by the great mass of the public because he was convinced that political inequality was both natural and desirable. Most citizens, he believed, were poorly equipped by temperament to play an active role in public affairs.[7] Believing in the existence of a natural aristocracy or ruling class, he advocated a form of "elite democracy" in which direct participation in governmental decisions would be reserved for those few good men of "unbiased opinion, mature judgment, and enlightened conscience" — men, in short, like himself. Ordinary citizens, which for Burke meant upper-middle and upper class men, would retain the right to participate in the selection of political leaders who would represent them, but participation in other forms of political activity would be discouraged. Unlike Mill, Burke favoured representation as a substitute for most forms of citizen participation and advocated it as a process that would promote the stability of a political system by insulating political leaders from undue and potentially disruptive public intrusions.

Today, most democratic theorists agree that classical democracy is an anachronism, applicable only to very small communities. However, the representative and elite theories of democracy have retained their intellectual vitality and continue to fuel a lively debate in Canada and elsewhere regarding the proper form of government and the appropriate role of citizens in the political process.[8] Contemporary proponents of the representative and elitist perspectives share a fundamental belief that in any society only a minority can govern. They also agree that the governors should be popularly elected and guided in their decisions by a conception of the public interest. They differ, however, on a wide range of equally important matters, including who is best suited to govern, the proper extent and nature of citizen participation and appropriate relationships between citizens and their representatives. To a substantial degree, their differences are reflected in the varying conceptions of representation which they hold.

In her insightful analysis of theories of representation, Hanna Pitkin distinguishes several meanings of the concept, of which three — formal, descriptive, and responsive[9] — are particularly germane. Formal conceptions of representation are concerned with the establishment of a system of *laws, institutions and procedures* designed either to transfer political authority from citizens to their representatives or to hold the latter accountable for actions taken on the former's behalf. Authorization and accountability theories of representation both argue that it is of paramount importance that citizens be provided with regular, constitutionally sanctioned opportunities to particpate in the selection of those who govern. The most important vehicle to be employed for this purpose is an open, competitive election. Descriptive theories of representation, in contrast, focus on *who* governs. Accepting the classical democratic argument that "in the absence of its natural defenders the interest of the excluded is always in danger of being overlooked,"[10] advocates of descriptive representation argue that a government is representative to the extent that the social and economic backgrounds of governmental leaders reflect politically relevant social and economic cleavages in the general public. Finally, the responsive theory of representation focuses on the *activities* and *outputs* of government. Proponents of this theory maintain that a government is representative if and when it demonstrates through its actions that it is responding to public needs and demands.

The representative and elitist theories of democracy differ over which of these conceptions of representation is most important. Elite theorists primarily are concerned with procedural devices and thus emphasize formal mechanisms of authorization and accountability. They are unconcerned with or explicitly oppose the idea of "democratizing" the social composition of government. They argue that establishing appropriate representative institutions and procedures (rather than selecting governmental officials whose social backgrounds and current statuses mirror the distribution of politically relevant characteristics in the public) is what ensures that government will be in the public interest. Thus, the classical statement of elitist democracy, provided by Joseph Schumpeter, defines the "democratic method" as "that institutional arrangement for arriving at political decisions in which [political elites] acquire the right to decide by means of a competitive struggle for the peoples' vote."[11]

Advocates of representative democracy acknowledge that formal institutions and processes and a government composed of officials similar in certain respects to the general public are important. They argue that widespread and extensive citizen participation is required to make these institutions and processes work to the public's advantage and to ensure that public officials will be selected who are concerned with furthering the public interest. Nevertheless, representative democrats contend that all of the above are essentially means to an end whereas political responsiveness — government action in the public interest — is, or should be, what government is finally about. Accordingly, one may define representative democracy as a political system in which citizens continuously exercise a diverse set of meaningful and relatively equal opportunities to influence the making of political decisions responsive to public needs and demands.

In distinguishing between representative and elitist theories of democracy, their differing conceptions of the public interest and how it is discovered should be underscored. Basically, for representative theorists, the public interest is what the public says it is; citizens are uniquely qualified to determine and articulate their needs and demands. Although representatives should consider their own judgment and experience when making political decisions, ultimately they must heed the public's directives, even if these conflict with personal beliefs. For elite theorists, the public interest transcends the sum of citizen demands and is likely to be recognized by individuals of superior education, talent and experience. Consequently, representatives must be freed from the particularistic requests of constituents and entrusted to employ their conscience and "enlightened good judgment" in responding to the needs of the country as a whole. Table 1.1 presents a summary of some of the principal differences among the classical, elitist and representative theories of democracy.

Given the richness and diversity of the Canadian political heritage, it is not surprising that elements of both representative and elitist theories of democracy and of the formal, descriptive and responsive conceptions of representation have found their way into the theory and practice of government in this country. The formal conception of representation is apparent, for example, in provisions of the British North America Act which establish the conditions of appointment and tenure of provincial Lieutenant Governors and regulate the apportionment of seats in the Senate and the House of Commons, as well as the frequency and duration of parliamentary sessions. The formal approach also provides the basis for laws governing the conduct of elections and the establishment of constituency boundaries. Moreover, it provides the justification for certain informal customs, such as the tradition of loyal opposition, that are deeply rooted in the political culture of every province. Similarly, the descriptive conception of representation is reflected in the constitutional doctrine of federalism and the geographic distribution of

TABLE 1.1

Comparisons of the Essential Features and Underlying Assumptions of the Classical, Elitist and Representative Theories of Democracy

	Classical Democracy	Elitist Democracy	Representative Democracy
Distribution of political power	Equality of power	Sharp inequality of power	Limited inequality of power
Nature and extent of participation	Universal and direct	Limited and indirect	Primarily limited and indirect but with opportunities for more extensive and direct participation
Who governs?	All equally; no distinction between rulers and ruled	Relatively small, homogeneous and closed group(s)	Relatively large, diverse and open groups
Prevailing concept of public interest	Sum of individual preferences	Collective good	Balance between individual preferences and collective good
How public interest is discovered	Citizens express demands directly	Representatives use own judgement	Representatives heed both citizen demands and own judgement, but give greater weight to citizen demands
Principal end of government	Individual self-development	Political stability	Both stability and self-development
Assumptions about human nature	Optimistic about individual rationality and tolerance	Skeptical of general public, optimistic about elites	Skeptical about present condition of elites and general public, but optimistic about their democratic potential
Prevailing concept of representation	None: representation is unnecessary given universal participation	Formal accountability	Political responsiveness

seats in both Houses of Parliament. It also underlies the recent concern with increasing the number of women, native peoples, and minorities in Parliament and the several provincial legislative assemblies. It is further reflected in the processes by which federal and provincial cabinets are constructed. Thus, first ministers try to achieve regional representation in their cabinets and attempt to include representatives of various ethno-linguistic, religious and occupational groups.

As for the belief that representatives ought to be responsive to public needs and demands, one need only read Hansard, listen to the radio, watch the evening news on television, or peruse a newspaper to be confronted with literally dozens of illustrative examples of the popularity this perspective enjoys among politicians and ordinary citizens alike. One finds that: provincial party leaders defend their positions on policy issues because they are in the "interests of the province"; local officials call for more federal or provincial funds on the grounds that local governments are "closest" to the people; pollsters report that public trust in government is eroding because elected officials are viewed as being more interested in their own than the public's interests; and candidates for provincial legislatures repeatedly promise during election campaigns that, if elected, they will heed the wishes of constituents more closely than their opponents and thereby force government to fulfill unmet needs. Indeed, most Canadians probably would find it strange if politics at any level of government ceased to be discussed in terms of governmental responsiveness.

Clearly, government in Canada at all levels is both democratic and representative in some sense of these terms. But which conceptions of representation and democracy are most desirable in the Canadian context and how well do provincial political systems conform to them? The appeal of classical democracy with its emphasis on human dignity and individual self-development is compelling. As noted, however, the problem is a practical one: namely, the size and complexity of a modern state place severe limits on the number of citizens who can participate directly in most governmental decisions.[12] The representative and elitist hybrids of democracy both recognize this problem but respond to it quite differently. For elite theorists, the problem of size is reinforced by a deep-seated suspicion of human nature. Consequently, they oppose classical democracy on philosophical as well as practical grounds and advocate a form of government in which formal institutions minimize the participatory role of citizens and provide maximum freedom to political leaders in their capacity as public officials.[13]

Proponents of representative democracy, in contrast, acknowledge that few citizens presently conform to the classic democratic ideal but they also are skeptical of the wisdom, integrity and competence of elites. Moreover, they remain optimistic about the democratic potential of most citizens and argue that both the quality of democratic citizenship and the responsiveness of political leaders would be enhanced if there were additional, more genuine opportunities for people to exercise political influence. Consequently, they advocate a system of government which conforms as closely to the classical ideal as possible. In such a system responsiveness to public needs and demands is paramount. Responsiveness can be ensured only by extensive citizen participation in the political process, the existence of political institutions open to citizen influence and capable of holding public officials accountable, and the selection of public officials sensitive to public needs and demands.[14] In our view, the ideas of representative democrats, with their emphasis on the individual and their concern with political responsiveness, embody the essential features of classical democracy. Because they do, they provide an appropriate standard against which the actual conduct of government in the several provinces can be examined and evaluated. This is the principal task of this volume.

TOWARD REPRESENTATIVE DEMOCRACY IN CANADA: AN OVERVIEW

The achievement of representative democracy is the result of an extended process. It is unlikely that representative democracy can be established and maintained in every society.[15] The growth of democratic institutions and procedures occurs gradually, sometimes over centuries and depends at every stage of development on the existence of particular configurations of social, economic and cultural conditions.[16] The emergence of representative democracy requires, *inter alia*, that a substantial body of citizens share certain fundamental values and perspectives. Among the most important are a sense of political community, a spirit of civic activism, a willingness to act rationally and to tolerate the political views and rights of others. Although the demands it makes are less severe than those of classical democratic theory, representative democracy places heavy burdens on political leaders and ordinary citizens alike.[17] At a minimum, the leaders must be willing to pursue power by strictly legal means, eschew violence, and accept political defeat peacefully. The great majority of citizens must be at least minimally politically informed, interested and think of themselves as participants in the political system, rather than as mere objects bound by laws and subject to the capricious whims of political elites over whom they have no control.

The establishment of democracy also is facilitated by the existence of conditions such as secularism, literacy, substantial affluence, a sizable middle class, and a fairly well-developed system of transportation and communication. These conditions are important, in part, because they contribute to the development of an appropriate political culture marked by cooperation, flexibility, accommodation and the feeling that change is normal and can result from individual initiatives. The shared perception that they have the ability to change their environment leads citizens to believe that at least in this respect they are equals. More importantly, it instills within them confidence that they are the ultimate source of political authority. Citizens convey authority to government through their participation, but the grant of that authority is limited and conditional and can be withdrawn. As noted above, representative democracy further requires open and effective political institutions. These must be sufficiently strong and endowed with enough resources to identify public needs and demands and to respond to them promptly and effectively. At a minimum, however, they must be subject to public scrutiny, participation and, ultimately, to public control.

Many of the preconditions for representative democracy were absent at the time of Confederation. Perhaps not surprisingly, therefore, the emergence of democratic government in Canada has followed an evolutionary rather than a revolutionary course,[18] and a highly elitist political system has developed into one with substantial *formal* opportunities for citizen participation. During the course of development, a number of difficult problems were faced and overcome. Four were especially vexing. The first was a problem of population and territory. Very simply, the former was too small for the latter, even in the most populous provinces, Ontario and Quebec. Vast areas were virtually uninhabited and the territories west of Ontario were not linked by systems of transportation and communication to the eastern half of the country. Second, in keeping with mercantilist practice, the resources of the provinces had been exploited for the benefit of Great Britain during the colonial period. In each province a small, indigenous elite exercised very substantial economic and political control. So small were these elite groups and so tight was their control that in derision the labels "Family Compact" and "Chateau Clique" were applied to them in Ontario and Quebec, respectively. Third, the existence of two distinct ethno-linguistic and religious communities made political cooperation difficult, especially since Quebec was a more traditional and less secular society than Ontario. Indeed, the entire struggle for responsible government during the first half of the 19th century was exacerbated by ethno-religious cleavages, in part reflected in the somewhat different character of the aborted rebellions that shook Upper and Lower Canada in 1837. Fourth, after Confederation, a large, militarily formidable and potentially hostile neighbour to the south and the Riel uprising in the Northwest threatened to detach what were to become the prairie provinces and to throw these territories and British Columbia into the lap of the United States, then under the sway of an expansionist, nationalist ideology of its own, "Manifest Destiny."[19]

Given these and other problems, how was Canada able to survive, let alone prosper, while simultaneously establishing and strengthening the democratic and representative character of its political institutions and processes? The answer is that even before Confederation the existing provinces possessed some formidable advantages and were blessed with a large measure of good fortune. Regarding the development of a political culture conducive to representative democracy, almost from the time Canada became British, the English-speaking portion of the population clamoured for representative political institutions. Moreover, when a legislative assembly was granted by the Constitutional Act of 1791, Quebecers were willing to accept it and ascribe it legitimacy. Similarly, at least some political leaders were willing and able to fulfill the principal duties and obligations which representative government imposed upon them. During the first half of the 19th century they learned the "rules of the game": to tolerate at least certain forms of political dissent and to respect those political opponents who are themselves "playing by the rules." Perhaps most importantly, during the 1860s, political elites from Upper and Lower Canada, Nova Scotia and New Brunswick were willing to make the often painful political accommodations and the structural–institutional changes that laid the groundwork for the British North America Act and the political system which, although changed in various ways over the years, continues to this day. In short, in each of the existing provinces, basic political institutions and processes — parliament, the cabinet form of responsible government, an independent judiciary, the rule of law, a civil and military bureaucracy accountable and subordinate to elected public officials, political parties, free and reasonably competitive elections, peaceful transitions of executive power, a loyal opposition, and the tradition of settling political conflicts by processes of negotiation and mutual accommodation — were largely in place and legitimized by 1867.

In the century since Confederation, these institutions and processes have grown in size and complexity. A continuously increasing population, changes in public expectations with respect to the proper role of government and the expansion of government's jurisdiction over new or emerging subject-matter fields are the principal reasons for this growth. Although both the size and powers of federal and provincial governments have increased over time, more recently the latter have grown more rapidly than the former. One estimate is that the size of the federal government has doubled since the end of the Second World War whereas the size of provincial governments has increased by a factor of seven. Their rapid growth helps to explain the enhanced power and influence of provincial governments *vis-à-vis* Ottawa.[20] Reasons for their expansion will be considered in considerable detail in several chapters of this book.

For the present, it may be noted that another important factor helping the new country to establish itself after Confederation was the absence of widespread debilitating health problems in the population. The latter may have been small, but in every province people were energetic, not to mention relatively well-nourished. Further, although existing educational systems were far from comprehensive, many people in the several provinces were literate. Ontario, Nova Scotia, New Brunswick and, to a lesser extent, Quebec, were essentially secular societies which were open to and capable of accommodating major changes in their social and economic environments. By way of illustration, we may note the rapid growth that took place within the nascent and protean industrial base of Ontario during the last two decades of the 19th and first decade of the 20th century.[21] Under Macdonald, the federal government had promulgated policies aimed at developing that base, as well as a transportation network which would link Manitoba, the Western Territories and British Columbia with the eastern half of the country. Although these policies generated bitter opposition at the time, the Canadian Pacific Railway was in place by 1885. The West was linked to the East, and the foundations were laid that were to make Ontario the industrial as well as territorial heartland.

Insofar as the security of the country was concerned, after the stifling of the Northwest Rebellion and the end of the Fenian raids, neither secession nor invasion from the United States posed serious threats to Canada's territorial integrity. Relatedly, the populating of the western provinces by means of policies designed to encourage large-scale immigration from Eastern and Central Europe not only helped ensure that these provinces would remain Canadian, but also stimulated their agricultural economies, provided a market for Ontario's manufactured products and helped provide an abundant and relatively cheap supply of food for consumption in every province.

The political system's development also can be attributed to relatively rapid and successful economic development. Social theorists long have contended that economic affluence is a major precondition for the emergence of democracy. Briefly, the contention is that economic prosperity and a reasonably equitable distribution of wealth create a middle class with a stake in the society and the ability and desire to participate in the conduct of public affairs. Economic affluence also makes politics less of a "life and death" struggle. Elites are willing to admit a substantial measure of citizen participation and to abide by the rules of a competitive democratic process — willingly relinquishing power when required to do so. Political defeats are not judged to be disastrous to incumbent politicians since there are alternative routes to social and economic advancement. Citizens, for their part, develop a measure of trust in political leaders and an understanding of the political process. They too are willing to abide by the "rules of the democratic game." Moreover, many citizens acquire the economic and educational resources needed to give at least some informed attention to political matters and the skills needed for effective, informed and rational participation. As a consequence, they are better able to demand that political leaders be accountable to them for actions taken on their behalf.

Over the years economic growth has been facilitated by a judicious application and pragmatic blending of the ideas of classical liberalism and tory paternalism. This blending has legitimized both the primacy of private property and the intervention of government whenever the owners of that property, Canadians and foreigners alike, appear to need a helping hand.[22] By way of illustration, provincial governments have cooperated with private investors to develop primary industries in nonrenewable resource areas such as coal, minerals and fossil fuels, as well as in renewable resources such as timber, fisheries and hydro-electric power. Provincial and local governments also have used a variety of inducements to attract and develop secondary industries (e.g., automobiles, textiles).

This strategy of providing a secure and cooperative sociopolitical environment has enabled the provinces to attract substantial foreign investment. The availability of foreign investment capital has had fairly obvious immediate and long-term benefits and less obvious but significant disadvantages.[23] In the post-World War Two period foreign investment helped to create the wealth necessary for the expansion of the welfare state and the quantitative and qualitative improvements in the educational structures of the several provinces. These in turn significantly increased the size of the middle class, particularly its professional and technical-managerial components. However, continued reliance on direct foreign investment and heavy foreign borrowing for capital formation has led to competition among the provinces, unbalanced economic development, with some provinces achieving much higher and more rapid rates of development than others, and a continuing reliance on primary as opposed to the development of secondary and tertiary industry. It also has produced a condition in which important segments of the economy of every province either are substantially foreign owned or influenced. A possible political–cultural consequence is the development of a collective sense of insecurity and political impotence that is destructive of the democratic personality. A second and equally serious consequence is that decisions that should be made in provincial capitals are made instead outside the country in the board rooms of multinational corporations. To the extent that they are, the ability of citizens to hold provincial political leaders accountable and the ability of leaders to respond effectively to citizen needs and demands are substantially impaired.

Yet another factor affecting the movement of provinces toward representative democracy has been the relative ease with which political development and change have occurred over time. The achievement of universal adult suffrage at the federal level and in most provinces by the early 1920s helped democratize the country, as well as organize and articulate opposition to the policies of the two older parties, the Liberals and the Conservatives. The first three decades of this century witnessed the rise of political protest movements, notably farmers' parties, Social Credit and the Cooperative Commonwealth Federation (CCF). Subsequently, the Union Nationale, Bloc Populaire, Parti Québécois and smaller political movements arose to articulate the needs and demands of the people of Quebec. By giving such needs and demands expression and representation, these essentially provincially or regionally based political parties helped to manage conflict, reduce societal tensions and promote peaceful political change. The latter, in turn, has facilitated the maintenance of an open and competitive process capable of representing divergent and sometimes sharply antagonistic interests.[24]

Also facilitating the representation of group interests has been the ability and general willingness of both federal and provincial political elites to be flexible, pragmatic and accommodating.[25] Historically, elites have been willing to recognize and tolerate the existence of a multiplicity of interests. They have ascribed them at least some legitimacy and ultimately invited the presentation of their claims upon the resources of society. Although such claims have not been invariably or immediately satisfied, gradually both the number of groups recognized as legitimate and the ways in which they could express their demands have expanded. For example, the 1960s witnessed the rise of native peoples' and women's groups as important actors on the federal and provincial political scenes. Although both types of groups made claims that were novel, these were accorded a respect and legitimacy they hitherto had not received. In making their claims, women and native peoples engaged in activities such as sit-ins, demonstrations in public buildings and picketing and protest marches that in the past might have been viewed as disturbances of public order and, hence, grounds for arrest and incarceration. By ascribing legitimacy to such tactics, political elites significantly expanded the repertoire of acceptable political action. It is important to note that women and native peoples joined rather than displaced recognized interest groups such as business, labour and farmers on the political stage. Moreover, the new methods of interest articulation employed by such groups were additions to rather than replacements for traditional means of making claims upon the political system. In addition to their protest marches, picketing and sit-ins, women and native peoples also worked for and supported candidates for public elective office, wrote letters, made personal representations to elected public officials and tried to mobilize the support of fellow citizens through personal solicitations and appeals in the mass media.

It can be argued that the ability of these and other groups to articulate their demands has been facilitated by the federal system, which provides a large number of access points to which claims can be addressed.[26] This argument regarding the facilitative character of multiple access points provided by different levels of government is in accord with a theoretical assumption underlying the choice of a federal system for a socially heterogeneous state such as Canada. A federal system supposedly takes cognizance of such heterogeneity by dividing jurisdiction between a national government and a number of constituent units. Such a division of authority minimizes societal conflict by assuring particular groups that interests which are especially important to them will be represented and protected by one or the other level of government. Certainly, a federal arrangement must have been compelling to the Fathers of Confederation, faced as they were with the task of designing a political system which could provide a responsible, effective and majoritarian national government, while accommodating the needs and interests of the new country's two major ethno-linguistic communities.

In a number of respects federalism might be judged a great success. For example, federalism has increased the number of formal opportunities members of the general public have to participate in the political system because positions in the ten provincial legislatures are filled by popular election. Federalism also has increased the size of the political elite by making available a variety of important appointive positions in the several provincial bureaucracies and judiciaries. Opportunities for participation in political party organizations also have been expanded by the presence of two levels of government, with parties playing important roles in structuring political conflict. Moreover, federalism has provided a number of unifying symbols around which provincial identities have been formed and fostered — identities which, for the most part, have complemented national identity rather than displaced it. In these respects, federalism could be argued to have contributed to the provinces' movement toward representative democracy.

However, it also is arguable that federalism has had a number of deleterious consequences for the achievement of representative democracy.[27] For one thing, federalism has been identified as a factor that contributes to the maintenance of continuing interprovincial inequities in the extent to which provincial governments have responded to the needs and demands of their citizens. The claim is that the various grants the federal government makes to the provinces encourage them to initiate or expand programs simply because funds are available, rather than respond to demonstrated public needs and demands. Conversely, federal programs may lead provincial governments to neglect needs because funds for them are unavailable.[28] Similarly, although federalism may facilitate the representation of group interests, numerous scholars have observed that some groups are much more favoured than others.[29] Groups representing major business interests, for example, not only are able to affect both the content and direction of policies pursued by the federal government, they are said to have an even greater influence on provincial policies, especially those of smaller provinces. It also has been argued that federalism has weakened one of the major mechanisms of representation, namely the political parties. By its very nature, federalism decentralizes political power and authority and makes it more difficult for party leaders to formulate and support policies and issues which transcend particularistic interests circumscribed by provincial or regional boundaries.[30] The resulting weaknesses of party organizations — and the fact that despite numerous formal opportunities to do otherwise, large numbers of people are only marginally involved in the political process[31] — have enhanced the ability of what have been termed "institutionalized" interest groups to have their way with government.

Progress toward the achievement of representative democracy has been hindered by other factors as well. There is evidence, for example, that people are ambivalent in their attitudes toward political authorities and skeptical about their own ability to influence the operation of government.[32] More generally, it is claimed that the Canadian political culture is at best a quasi-participative one[33] which limits the extent to which average citizens develop the kind of "democratic personality" Mill and other theorists have judged essential for the continuing good health of a democratic political order.

It is apparent even from this very brief overview that Canada and the several provinces have come a long way since Confederation in developing many of the social, economic, and cultural prerequisities of democratic politics. As a result, the provinces have moved toward representative democracy and, in comparative perspective, are much closer to this goal than are a great majority of the world's political systems. It also is apparent, however, that they have not yet gone far enough. They have not established fully democratic and representative institutions and processes capable of generating and implementing policies responsive to public needs and demands. In the chapters which follow we will delineate in detail how closely the provinces conform to the ideals of representative democracy. A brief description of how we will proceed follows.

ORGANIZATION OF THE VOLUME

Chapter Two: **Federalism**
Provincial governments do not operate in splendid isolation. Rather, they are embedded in and profoundly influenced by the federal structure of the political system. The changing nature of this structure and, more particularly, the distribution of political power and authority between the federal government and the provinces have been sources of continuing political tensions. Underlying the recurring tensions in

Canadian federalism are fundamental questions of representative democracy; specifically, which level of government is most attuned to public needs and demands and which is best able to respond to them promptly and effectively? Accordingly, we begin our evaluation of provincial political systems by considering the origins, development and current operation of the federal system. We attempt to explain the ebb and flow of federal and provincial power and authority since Confederation, examine the images of federalism held by citizens and assess public support for federal and provincial governments. In so doing, we delineate crucial features of the political system which condition the provinces' capacities to achieve representative democracy.

Chapter 3: **Provincial Societies and Political Cultures**
Theorists long have recognized the importance of political culture as a factor that can enhance or impede the establishment and effective performance of a democratic government. They also have contended that certain social and economic conditions such as generally high levels of formal education, affluence and urbanization contribute to the development of such a culture. As noted above, most provinces have achieved many of these social and economic preconditions. However, debate continues over whether there are significant differences in provincial cultures which affect the character of political life. Drawing upon historical studies, interpretive essays, and contemporary survey research this chapter sketches significant features of the social, economic and cultural environments of the provinces. We also investigate interprovincial differences in political culture and discuss how provincial political cultures facilitate or impede the development of representative democracy.

Chapter 4: **Participation and Elections**
Extensive citizen participation in political life is a hallmark of representative democracy. Consequently, its evaluation entails an inquiry into the nature and extent of political participation in the provinces. How politically active are citizens? Who participates and who abstains, especially in activities other than voting in periodic elections? What is the relative importance of party leaders, local candidates and political issues as forces influencing electoral decisions? How rational are electoral choices? This chapter addresses these and other important questions and in so doing illuminates the character of provincial political participation. Information from official election returns and recent surveys of the attitudes and behaviour of voters in every province are used to describe and explain variations in political participation.

Chapter 5: **Political Parties and Interest Groups**
It is conventional wisdom that political parties and interest groups are the principal institutional links between citizens and governments in contemporary democracies. Standing between individuals and their

governments, parties and interest groups either facilitate or inhibit the ability of average citizens to influence the political process. Data derived from several surveys and other studies of parties and interest groups inform our examination of these two linkage mechanisms. We discuss the origins and development of provincial parties, delineate the structures and activities of legislative and extralegislative party organizations and examine the characteristics of their identifying publics. Interest groups are examined in terms of their operation, leadership and patterns of public participation. A concluding section evaluates the relative contributions parties and interest groups make to the representation of citizens in provincial governmental processes.

Chapter 6: Legislatures, Bureaucracies and Judiciaries

This chapter describes the major institutions of provincial governments, with emphasis on the growth of government in the post-World War Two period. Recognizing the key role ascribed to legislatures in the representational process, attention is focused on the activities of provincial premiers, cabinets and private members in carrying out the tasks traditionally attributed to legislative bodies in parliamentary democracies. Also of concern are the growth and functions of provincial bureaucracies, especially the conditions that affect the extent to which they can be held accountable to and by the public. Investigation indicates that the degree of their accountability and the publics to whom they are most attuned vary both with the types of policies being administered and the internal dynamics of the bureaucratic units themselves. An assessment of provincial judiciaries suggests, in contrast, that they are not really accountable to any segment of the public. Paradoxically, their relative immunity from public or governmental control facilitates their ability to act as guardians of the legal rights and privileges of the entire political community and, in this sense, the judiciary represents us all.

Chapter 7: The Policy Process

Friends and foes of representative democracy long have debated whether democratic systems are capable of generating public policies that meet the needs and respond to the demands of citizens. This chapter begins our assessment of the responsiveness of provincial governments by examining the structure and operation of the policy process: the means through which governments attempt to identify and develop prompt and effective solutions to public problems. We define public policy and sketch the principal stages of the policy process. This is followed by a description and explanation of some of the principal dimensions of the complex interactions which determine policy development. An in-depth study of the origins and development of two major health programs in Saskatchewan is used to illuminate the provincial policy process, in practice as well as in theory.

Chapter 8: **Policy Responsiveness**

Responsiveness to public problems is the acid test of representative democracy. Consequently, this chapter considers provincial policy outputs and the degree to which they correspond to public needs. We begin by examining the changing pattern of provincial governmental expenditures since World War Two and attempt to explain shifting priorities in terms of several political, economic and constitutional factors. We then focus on the fields of education, health, and welfare, policy areas which consume some two-thirds of the expenditures of every provincial government. Investigation indicates that during the post-war period the provinces generally have overresponded to the health and underresponded to the educational and, especially, the welfare needs of their citizens. However, there are considerable interprovincial variations in responsiveness in different policy areas during particular time periods as well as in overall responsiveness during the entire post-war era.

Chapter 9: **Representative Democracy Reconsidered**

This chapter has a two-fold purpose. Highlighting and summarizing information considered in previous chapters, we again assess the extent to which the provinces approximate a model of representative democracy as conceptualized in this volume. Second, we consider certain suggestions for institutional and associated societal changes which conceivably could enhance the quality of democratic life in all provinces, today and in the future.

NOTES

1. Useful discussions of the many meanings of democracy are contained in C. B. Macpherson, *The Life and Times of Liberal Democracy* (Toronto: Oxford University Press, 1977); Macpherson, *The Real World of Democracy* (Oxford: Claredon Press, 1965); and Henry Mayo, *An Introduction to Democratic Theory* (New York: Oxford University Press, 1960).
2. Although there is considerable diversity among the political ideas of philosophers commonly associated with classical democracy, the ideas of John Stuart Mill are reasonably representative of classical democratic thought and provide the basis of our summary. Mill's ideas on democracy are most clearly set forth in two essays, "On Liberty," and "Considerations on Representative Government." See J. S. Mill, *Utilitarianism, Liberty and Representative Government* (New York: Dutton, 1951).
3. A comprehensive discussion of various meanings of representation is contained in Hanna F. Pitkin, *The Concept of Representation* (Berkeley: University of California Press, 1967).
4. The term "elitist theory of democracy" first appeared in Seymour Martin Lipset's introduction to Roberto Michels' study of oligarchic tendencies in political parties. See Roberto Michels, *Political Parties* (New York: Collier Books, 1962, paperback edition). Jack Walker has argued that there has been a concerted attempt on the part of social theorists such as Lipset, Henry Mayo, Joseph A. Schumpeter, Samuel Beer, Robert Dahl, Louis Hartz and others to revise the classical theory of

democracy and that their efforts can be subsumed under the label "elitist theory of democracy." He contends that this designation is "now employed in many contemporary books and articles . . . and is in fact becoming part of the conventional wisdom of political science." Not everyone who is familiar with the works of these theorists agrees that they are "elitists." Indeed, Dahl argues that as a group these theorists share little more than "a belief in the desirability of representative government." For the exchange between Walker and Dahl, see Jack L. Walker, "A Critique of the Elitist Theory of Democracy" and Robert A. Dahl, "Further Reflections on 'The Elitist Theory of Democracy'" in the *American Political Science Review*, 60 (1966), pp. 285–295, 296–305, and 391–392.

5. Mill, "Considerations on Representative Government," p. 291.

6. *Ibid.*, p. 305.

7. Burke's ideas on representation and democracy are scattered throughout his works and speeches, three of the most notable being "Reflections on the Revolution in France," "Appeal From the New to the Old Whigs" and "Speech to the Electors of Bristol." These are reprinted in *The Works of The Right Honorable Edmund Burke*, revised ed., (Boston: Little, Brown, 1965).

8. A concise summary of this debate is provided by Carole Pateman, *Participation and Democratic Theory* (London: Cambridge University Press, 1969). See also Henry S. Kariel, ed. *Frontiers of Democratic Theory* (New York: Random House, 1970).

9. Pitkin, *The Concept of Representation*, pp. 38–121.

10. Mill, "Considerations on Representative Government," p. 280.

11. Joseph A. Schumpeter, *Capitalism, Socialism and Democracy* (New York: Harper and Row, 1947), p. 269.

12. It should be noted that some theorists have argued that technological innovations now make it possible for citizens at large to record their political preferences continuously and almost instantaneously. See, for example, Macpherson, *The Real World of Democracy*, and Michael Margolis, *Viable Democracy* (London: Penguin Books, 1980). However, Macpherson himself has questioned the ability of these innovations to provide meaningful citizen participation. Macpherson, *The Life and Times of Liberal Democracy*, pp. 94–96. For a detailed discussion of relationships between the size of political systems and possibilities for democratic governance, see Robert A. Dahl and Edward Tufte, *Size and Democracy* (Stanford: Stanford University Press, 1973).

13. For an elaboration of this discussion see William Mishler, *Political Participation in Canada: Prospects for Democratic Citizenship* (Toronto: Macmillan, 1979), esp. pp. 10–14 and 153–163.

14. Pitkin, *The Concept of Representation*, pp. 234–240.

15. For example, Zevedei Barbu claims that: "Democracy grows out of its own soil . . . . It requires specific experiences and specific mental changes in a community before appearing as historical reality." Zevedei Barbu, *Democracy and Dictatorship: Their Psychology and Patterns of Life* (New York: Grove Press, 1956), p. 23.

16. See, for example, Seymour Martin Lipset, "Some Social Requisites of Democracy: Economic Development and Political Legitimacy," *American Political Science Review* 53 (1959), pp. 69–105; "The Value Patterns of Democracy: A Case Study in Comparative Analysis," *American Sociological Review*, 28 (1963), pp. 512–513; and "Anglo-American Democracy," in David L. Sills, ed., *International Encyclopedia of the Social Sciences*, Vol. 1 (New York: Macmillan and The Free Press, 1968), pp. 289–302. See also Lucien Pye, *Aspects of Political Development* (Boston: Little, Brown, 1966), pp. 71–88; Gabriel Almond and Sidney Verba, *The Civic Culture* (Boston: Little, Brown, 1965), pp. 337–374; and Charles F. Cnudde and Dean E. Neubauer, eds., *Empirical Democratic Theory* (Chicago: Markham, 1969).

17. See, for example, some of the points reviewed by Jeanne Kirkpatrick, "Dictatorship and Double Standards," *Commentary*, 68 (November 1979), pp. 36–38; and Almond and Verba, *The Civic Culture*, ch. 15.

18. See Seymour Martin Lipset, "Revolution and Counterrevolution: Canada and the United States," in Thomas Ford, ed., *The Revolutionary Theme in Contemporary America* (Lexington: University of Kentucky Press, 1965), pp. 21–64. See also the collection of essays in Richard Preston, ed., *Perspectives on Revolution and Evolution* (Durham: Duke University Press, 1979).

19. On the conditions affecting Canada both before and in the years after Confederation, see, *inter alia*, Donald Creighton, *The Road to Confederation* (Toronto: Macmillan of Canada, 1965); J. M. S. Careless, *Union of the Canadas: The Growth of Canadian Institutions, 1841–1857* (Toronto: McClelland and Stewart, 1967); William Whitelaw, *The Maritimes and Canada Before Confederation* (Toronto: Oxford University Press, 1966; William L. Morton, *The Critical Years* (Toronto: McClelland and Stewart, 1964); and Peter B. Waite, *Canada's First Century* (Toronto: Macmillan of Canada, 1970).

20. See Alan Cairns, "The Governments and Societies of Canadian Federalism," *Canadian Journal of Political Science*, 10 (1977), pp. 695–726.

21. See the collection of essays in D. S. Macmillan, ed., *Canadian Business History, Selected Studies, 1947–1971* (Toronto: McClelland and Stewart, 1972).

22. In this regard, the formation of the Canadian National Railway from a number of smaller rail lines (some of which were in serious financial straits) and the safeguarding of the interests of their stock and bond holders were governmental actions whose significance was not lost on future generations of investors. Nor were the actions of the federal government in this area unique. At different times the several provincial governments also have intervened and continue to intervene in various areas (e.g., hydroelectric power, transportation, and the exploitation of natural resources) to support, supplement or compete with the private sector of the economy.

23. There now is an enormous literature on the matter of foreign investment, especially that of U.S. nationals and corporations. Perhaps the most eloquent statement of the problem involved in maintaining the nation's independence in light of this investment is George Grant's *Lament for a Nation: The Defeat of Canadian Nationalism* (Toronto: McClelland and Stewart, 1965). Walter Gordon's book, *A Choice for Canada* (Toronto: McClelland and Stewart, 1966); and the "Watkins Report," more properly, *Foreign Ownership and the Structure of Canadian Industry* (Ottawa: Queen's Printer, 1968) also focussed attention on the problem and stimulated a number of additional investigations. See, for example, Government of Canada, *Foreign Direct Investment in Canada* (Ottawa: Information Canada, 1972); Patricia Marchak, *In Whose Interest: An Essay on Multinational Corporations in a Canadian Context* (Toronto: McClelland and Stewart, 1974); Abraham Rotstein and Gary Lax, eds., *Independence: The Canadian Challenge* (Toronto: Committee for an Independent Canada, 1974); and Wallace Clement, "Canada and Multinational Corporations: An Overview," in Daniel Glenday, H. Guindon and A. Turowitz, eds., *Modernization and the Canadian State* (Toronto: Macmillan, 1978). For a different perspective on the problem, see Harry G. Johnson, *The Canadian Quandary* (Toronto: McGraw-Hill, 1963); and "Problems of Canadian Nationalism," *International Journal*, 16 (1961), pp. 238–249; and "The Watkins Report: Toward a New National Policy," *International Journal*, 23 (1968), pp. 615–629.

24. On occasion, this process has broken down. For example, questions of justification aside, the federal government's imposition of the War Measures Act in October 1970 in response to terrorist acts by the FLQ resulted in serious violations of basic civil rights and liberties that undergird the democratic process.

25. Democracies that are characterized by these kinds of elite interactions have been termed "consociational" by Arend Lijphart. See *The Politics of Accommodation* (Berkeley: University of California Press, 1969). Robert Presthus has applied this theory, particularly as it relates to interactions between governmental officials and interest group leaders, to Canada. See his *Elite Accommodation in Canadian Politics*, (Toronto: Macmillan of Canada, 1973), especially pp. 3–98.

26. The conventional argument is that claims unsuccessfully pressed at one level of government, or upon one group of political actors, may well receive a sympathetic reception at or with another. See, for example, Dahl and Tufte, *Size and Democracy*, ch. 8 and "Epilogue." See also "Interest Group Demands and the Federal Political System," David Kwavnick's study of the efforts of the Canadian Labour Congress and the Quebec-based Confederation of National Trade Unions to influence the distribution of federal-provincial powers in Paul Pross, ed., *Pressure Group Behaviour in Canadian Politics* (Toronto: McGraw-Hill Ryerson, 1975), pp. 69–86. Various justifications of federalism are discussed in Garth Stevenson, *Unfulfilled Union* (Toronto: Macmillan of Canada, 1979), ch. 1.

27. In Canada, the classic critique of federalism from this perspective is John Porter, *The Vertical Mosaic* (Toronto: University of Toronto Press, 1965), pp. 379–385. For a more recent critique see Stevenson, *Unfulfilled Union*, pp. 44–48, 217–218.
28. These points are developed in more detail in our analyses in Chapter 8 of the direction provincial policies have taken during the post-World War Two period.
29. See, for example, Porter, *The Vertical Mosaic*, pp. 379–385; Presthus, *Elite Accommodation*, ch. 7; and Stevenson, *Unfulfilled Union*, ch. 4.
30. On the effects of federalism on Canadian political parties see, for example, Porter, *The Vertical Mosaic*, pp. 379–385; F. C. Engelmann and Mildred A. Schwartz, *Canadian Political Parties: Origin, Character, Impact* (Scarborough: Prentice-Hall, 1975), pp. 60–70; and John Meisel, "The Party System and the 1974 Election," *Canada at the Polls*, ed. Howard R. Penniman (Washington, D. C.: American Enterprise Institute for Public Policy Research, 1975), pp. 4–7; Stevenson, *Unfulfilled Union*, pp. 187–191.
31. See Mishler, *Political Participation in Canada*; and Allan Kornberg, Joel Smith and Harold D. Clarke, *Citizen Politicians — Canada* (Durham N. C.: Carolina Academic Press, 1979), ch. 3.
32. On these points, see Harold D. Clarke, Jane Jenson, Lawrence LeDuc and Jon Pammett, *Political Choice in Canada* (Toronto: McGraw-Hill Ryerson, 1979), ch. 1. See also Allan Kornberg, Harold Clarke and Marianne C. Stewart, "Public Support for Community and Regime in the Regions of Contemporary Canada," *The American Review of Canadian Studies*, 10 (1980), pp. 75–93.
33. See Presthus, *Elite Accommodation*, pp. 2–63; and "Evolution and Canadian Culture: The Politics of Accommodation" in Preston, ed., *Perspectives on Revolution and Evolution*, pp. 103–132.

FOR FURTHER READING

Bachrach, Peter. *The Theory of Democratic Elitism*. Boston: Little, Brown and Company, 1967. This book is an excellent critique of the elitist theory of democracy. The author examines the roots of this theory in the work of Mosca and Schumpeter and discusses how the findings of studies of mass political behaviour have been used to develop and buttress the theory.
Macpherson, C.B. *The Life and Times of Liberal Democracy*. Toronto: Oxford University Press, 1977, chs. 1–4. The author presents a brief, incisive analysis of three models of democracy. Particularly valuable is the discussion in Chapter 3 of how liberal economic theory has influenced conceptions of the role of the citizen in 20th century democratic theory.
Mayo, Henry B. *An Introduction to Democratic Theory*. New York: Oxford University Press, 1960. This work is a good example of the elitist theory of democracy.
Pitkin, Hanna. *The Concept of Representation*. Berkeley: University of California Press, 1967. In her classic analysis of the concept of representation, the author delineates the formalistic, descriptive and responsive meanings of this concept.
Porter, John. *The Vertical Mosaic*. Toronto: University of Toronto Press, 1965. Although published in 1965, this work remains "must reading" for anyone who wishes to understand the nature of Canada's society and political system.

2
Federalism

Before there was a Canadian state, there were provinces. On the one hand, their existence made Confederation possible. On the other hand, the presence of provincial communities with strong identities has been a contributing factor to some of the problems associated with the formation of a national identity and the maintenance of Canadian unity. Confederation, with its resulting federal system, has been a major institutional force in the environments of both national and provincial governments. The manner in which the system has been structured has borne heavily on the ability of both to move toward representative democracy. Historically, few issues have been the source of as much political conflict as the continuing controversy regarding the distribution of political power and authority between the two levels of government. At the center of this controversy are fundamental questions about political representation. Those who have argued for a federal system in which the provinces are "strong" have observed, *inter alia*, that strong provinces maximize governmental responsiveness in a socially and economically heterogeneous society. The needs and interests of Ontarians, for example, at times differ dramatically from those of residents of a Maritime province such as Prince Edward Island. Provincial governments are better able to discern and represent the differing needs and interests of their citizens because they are geographically and psychologically "closer" to them than is the national government. However, to represent their citizens most effectively provinces must have adequate power, resources, and freedom of action. Proponents of a federal system in which the national government is strong contend that a nation is more than an aggregation of geopolitical units. It is a political community. The principal agent of that community is the national government, which alone represents and safeguards the interests of the entire community and formulates and implements policies in pursuit of community goals. For example, only a national government can conduct foreign policy since treaties and agreements made with foreign powers must be implemented nationwide. To conduct foreign or other policies effectively, however, it must have the necessary power, authority and resources. In short, the proponents of strong provinces and their opponents who advocate a strong national government each argue that the unit they favour is most attuned and best equipped to respond to public needs and demands, but to do so effectively "their" government must have the requisite power and resources.

The manner in which these competing claims have been resolved at different times has substantially influenced the development of federalism. Consequently, in this chapter we will present an overview of the directions in which power has flowed in the federal system and consider some of the attempts that have been made to explain changes that have taken place. We also will examine images of federalism which underlie and condition public perceptions of the responsiveness and effectiveness of federal and provincial governments. Finally, we will consider the most recent positions of provincial and federal political leaders on the issue of "who speaks for Canadians" and suggest that the major contradictions in their positions will have to be resolved if current federal arrangements are ever to be "renewed" successfully.

FEDERALISM: ORIGINS AND DEVELOPMENT

Although there are almost an infinite number of variations, three themes appear in most definitions of federalism: governmental dualism, shared jurisdiction and legal autonomy. Thus, federalism may be defined as a form of political organization in which the activities of government are divided between a central government and a number of regional governments, each having jurisdiction over the same people and territory, and neither able to alter unilaterally the formal jurisdiction of the other.

Garth Stevenson contends that the event we call "Confederation" arose "from a convergence of internal and external circumstances."[1] The first of the major internal conditions was that government in the Province of Canada was approaching an *impasse* in 1857 because of the frequency with which cabinets were defeated in the legislature. What has been termed the "irrational pressure cooker"[2] of Canadian politics supposedly led the Cartier-Macdonald ministry of 1858 to propose a wider union of British North America and opponents of that proposal (principally, the politically powerful George Brown, leader of the "Clear Grits") ultimately to relent and, in June 1864, to accept the concept of a broader union.[3] A second and related circumstance was the energy and persistence of a single individual, John A. Macdonald, and the willingness of his colleagues to accede to his plans to build a new nation in the northern half of the continent.[4] A third factor was the desire of a number of Francophone political leaders to terminate their uneasy legislative union with Upper Canada and replace it with a structure which, conceivably, would give French Canadians greater political and cultural autonomy, at least within Quebec, the province in which the great majority then, as now, resided. A fourth motivating factor was the economic benefits that were expected to flow from provincial union. The most important of these, supposedly, were: 1) a transcontinental railway could be built which would join Canada with the Maritimes, the Western territories and British Columbia; 2) the railway could facilitate interprovincial trade between the Maritimes and Canada and help populate the West; and 3) the railway could make possible the marketing of Canada's industrial products in the West and Maritimes and enable the central and eastern provinces to exploit western natural resources such as timber and minerals.[5]

With regard to external circumstances, the principal one, as noted in the first chapter, was the threat posed by the United States to the security of the provinces. American political leaders were angry with Britain over the not-so-covert support her government gave the Confederacy during the Civil War. Provincial leaders feared that, unable to strike at Britain, large, battle-hardened Union armies might turn their wrath northward upon Britain's Canadian colonies.[6] The activities (more often, the threats) of the Fenians added to the sense of alarm felt by Canadian political leaders.[7] A second external factor was the pressure British officials exerted on a number of political leaders in the Maritimes because they expected that Britain would benefit economically and strategically from Canadian unity.[8]

As for the form the proposed Union would take, Macdonald proposed a "Confederation" in which the residual powers of government (i.e., those not specifically allotted the provinces) would be vested in the national government.[9] Such an arrangement, he believed, would make it difficult for the provinces to claim the kind of "States' Rights" which, in his view, were largely responsible for the American Civil War.[10] Perusal of parliamentary debates preceding Confederation indicates that not all Macdonald's colleagues shared his fears of internecine struggle or his interpretation of the proper distribution of powers within a confederation. Francophone MPs, in particular, were concerned with the nature of the federal principle and were considerably less sanguine that Confederation really would facilitate the maintenance of their French and Catholic identities.[11]

The British North America Act (hereafter referred to as the BNAA) established parliamentary and cabinet government at both the national and provincial levels. Because of disparities in population among the four provinces initially joining in Confederation, adjustments were made in the representation allocated them in the new bicameral national parliament: an appointed Senate and a popularly elected House of Commons. The Maritime provinces, despite their smaller populations, were allotted the same number of Senators (24) as Quebec and Ontario. In the House of Commons, provision was made for Quebec to retain a minimum of 65 members, regardless of the outcome of the 1871 census, or any subsequent decennial censuses.

The provisions made in the BNAA for representing the people of the several provinces in both the federal and provincial parliaments reflect a basic principle of both federalism and the formalistic conception of representation. A person is a citizen of both the country and the constituent unit (province, state, canton, or however named) in which he or she resides. On matters of concern to the entire country, the interests of residents of different provinces will be represented by the members elected to the national parliament. Collectively, the latter body is accountable to the country as a whole. On matters of concern only to the residents of a particular province, citizens will look to their provincial legislative representatives who are accountable only to the citizens of their province.

The initial division of jurisdiction between the federal government and the provinces (Sections 91 and 92, respectively, of the BNAA) indicates the expectation was that Parliament would be called to account more forcefully because people would rely upon their representatives in Ottawa far more than they would their representatives in provincial capitals. Thus, in addition to a general grant of power to make laws for the "Peace, Order, and Good Government of Canada," the preamble to Section 91 of the BNAA assigns all powers not granted the provinces to the "exclusive Legislative Authority of the Parliament of Canada." Illustrative, but in no way restricting the latter, are 29 enumerated powers. These include jurisdiction over matters such as defence, trade and commerce, raising revenue by any mode of taxation, the incorporation of banks and the issuing of paper currency, as well as "such Classes of Subjects as are expressly excepted in the Enumeration of the Classes of Subjects by this Act assigned exclusively to the Legislatures of the Provinces." Among the powers exclusively assigned the provinces were jurisdiction over municipal institutions, property and civil rights within their boundaries, the management and sale of public lands, the administration of justice, the incorporation of companies with provincial objectives and, generally, "all matters of a merely local or private nature in the province." Although it would be incorrect to assume from the latter Article (92:16) that the provinces were regarded by the Fathers of Confederation as merely glorified local governments,[12] the relationship between central and provincial governments was to be one of superior and subordinate.

The thrust of the division of jurisdiction between federal and provincial governments runs opposite to that of the United States Constitution of which Macdonald was so critical. Although the BNAA assigns residual powers to the national government, the 10th amendment to the American Constitution stipulates that "powers not delegated to the United States by the Constitution nor prohibited by it to the states are reserved to the States, respectively, or to the people." Notwithstanding this provision, American states today are far less important political entities than are Canadian provinces. The enhancement of the American national government's powers is a consequence of judicial interpretation of the Constitution (specifically, the broad interpretation the Supreme Court has given to Congress's power to legislate under the interstate commerce, taxing, and spending for the general welfare powers) and the expansion of government that occurred because of participation in two world wars and the growth of a welfare state. Although similar forces have operated in Canada, the provinces have acquired more power *vis-à-vis* the federal government than have the states in the American federal system. A number of explanations have been offered to account for this difference in development. First, contrary to United States Supreme Court practice, the judiciary in Canada renders advisory opinions to elected public officials. This has helped provincial political leaders constrain the powers of the federal government by providing them with the opportunity to refer federal actions they regard as objectionable to the courts for decision as to their constitutionality. Second, for almost a century (1867–1949), the court of last resort in Canada was not the Supreme Court, but the Judicial Committee of the Privy Council of Great Britain. That august body (contrary to the general direction of the rulings of the United States Supreme Court) interpreted the federal government's power under the Trade and Commerce provisions of the BNAA (91:2) very narrowly.[13] The Committee acknowledged that Parliament could regulate both international and interprovincial trade and commerce, but it could not legislate in matters affecting trade and commerce *within* individual provinces. To do so, the Committee contended, almost invariably would infringe upon provincial jurisdiction over "property and civil rights." Moreover, because the Judicial Committee found so many instances in which in its view *only* provincial interests in property and civil rights obtained,[14] the growth of federal government powers was effectively restricted.

Although it attempted to carefully distinguish between relevant cases in order to project an image of consistency, over time the Judicial Committee also substantially altered its interpretation of the federal government's right to legislate under the Peace, Order, and Good Government provision of Section 91 of the BNAA. After initially recognizing the federal government's broad powers under this clause,[15] the Committee subsequently decided that the 29 articles enumerated in Section 91 were not simply illustrative examples of parliament's broad powers to legislate, but an enumeration of the extent of its explicit powers.[16] A quarter of a century later it gave a narrow construction to these powers, restricting their application to periods of "unusual emergency."[17] In another series of cases,[18] the Committee recognized the national government's sole authority to make and implement treaties and international agreements and then proceeded to set limits on the power, ruling that the implementation of treaties and international agreements could not infringe upon the powers reserved to the provinces under Section 92.[19] The Committee also dealt a serious blow to the federal government's initial attempt to establish the foundation of a welfare state by declaring unconstitutional federal legislation intended to ameliorate some of the severe social and economic dislocations brought about by the Great Depression.[20]

A third reason offered to explain the direction federalism has taken is the absence of any real consensus among political leaders or constitutional scholars on the precise nature of the union that was forged in 1867. In addition to the general positions taken by those who advocate either strong provinces or a strong central government, a number of more specific interpretations, each of which has acquired substantial support, have been offered. Among the principal competing interpretations is the concept of the federal union as a "compact": a contractual arrangement entered into by the political leaders of the four original provinces. A variation of the compact theory is that Confederation brought together two ethno-religious communities, the Anglo-Celtic Protestant and French Catholic.[21] A third conception, termed "coordinate" or "classic" federalism,[22] holds that the two levels of government have equal status. Each is independent of the other and autonomous within the subject matter areas over which it has jurisdiction. The existence of these competing conceptions has contributed to the growth of provincial power in two ways: it has provided an ideological justification for the self-interested claims of generations of provincial politicians; and it has enabled them to organize a strong defence against federal officials advancing equally self-interested competing conceptions such as "cooperative," "administrative," and, more recently, "renewed" federalism. The reader should note that the assumptions underlying the compact theory are best explicated in the Tremblay Report[23] and the more recent Task Force on Canadian Unity.[24] Some of the assumptions upon which the coordinate federalism concept rests are outlined in certain of the Alberta and British Columbia governments' views on federalism.[25] Pierre Elliott Trudeau, in turn, has made the case for his version of federalism in a widely circulated federal government document titled, *A Time for Action*[26] and in the federal government's position at the September, 1980 Constitutional Conference. The diversity of views expressed in these and other reports and documents go far in explaining why, well over one hundred years after Confederation, both its form and future continue to be problematic.

A fourth explanation of the development of the respective powers of provincial and federal governments is cast in terms of their legitimacy and effectiveness and hence, the level of support they receive from the public. It is argued that the provinces enjoyed a substantial head start in developing legitimacy simply because they existed first. Recognizing this, Macdonald tried to establish the legitimacy of the new central government by demonstrating that it was more effective than the provinces in dealing with the economic problems of the day. However, he was not entirely successful and as a consequence there probably was more public support for the provinces than for the federal government during most of the 19th century.[27]

Public support for the provinces has continued to be strong in this century. Again, a number of reasons are offered in explanation. The interpretation the judiciary gave the respective powers of the two levels of government provided the legal justification for an expansion of provincial powers. Powers that were sanctioned, especially public works and property and civil rights, proved to be "growth industries"; much of the economic development that has taken place in this century has occurred in fields that fall within these two areas of provincial jurisdiction. This general economic development proceeded hand-in-hand with an increased public desire for new governmental services, many of which were within the jurisdictional scope of provincial governments.

Relatedly, the increased scope of provincial governmental activity required the provinces to expand their bureaucracies, which they did: so much so, that by the mid-1970s provincial governments (exclusive of British Columbia) employed over one-half million people, while their legal creatures, the municipalities, provided jobs for an additional one-quarter million.[28] If one adds dependents to those employed by provincial and municipal governments we have, in Alan Cairns' words, "an immense component of Canadian society directly tied to [provincial] government."[29] The implication is that people linked to provincial governments in this way will strongly support their continued existence. However, modern bureaucracies, Cairns observes, are not content simply to exist.[30] Typically, bureaucrats try to enlarge and redefine their jurisdiction because their status, perquisites and resources vary directly and positively with their level of activity. Therefore, unless they are strongly opposed, bureaucracies will expand. Enhancing the growth prospects of provincial bureaucracies is the fact that many organized interest groups have vested interests in their expansion. The policies of provincial governments can strongly affect the current and future good health of major interest groups. Consequently, powerful groups such as labour, business and agriculture not only cooperate with provincial bureaucracies they form *de facto* coalitions with them, thereby further enhancing the status and power of provincial governments.[31]

A somewhat different but complementary explanation of why provincial governments are powerful is offered by Garth Stevenson.[32] He stresses four factors: 1) the new national government of 1867 was established by a small coterie of politicians rather than by a majority of the population of the time; 2) the Canadian political process with its emphasis on relations between levels of government rather than among people lends itself to elite domination and the restriction of popular

participation in the making of important political decisions; 3) generations of provincial politicians have exploited the elitist character of the
political process to enhance their power and importance; and 4) the
shifting balance of political power favouring the provinces reflects
underlying economic forces and the current allegiance of economic elites
to provincial governments.

Regarding the origins of the national government and the elitism
characteristic of the political process, Stevenson observes that the
national government initially lacked legitimacy: not because it was
ineffective, but because it was the creation of few rather than many. Not
only did a small group of political leaders — the Fathers of Confederation
— make the decision to establish a new state and then supply the
necessary details, they also manipulated subsequent events to ensure
that only a minute proportion of the people of the four uniting provinces
ever had the opportunity to ratify Confederation: to vote "yea" or "nay"
on what they had done. The Fathers of Confederation, he wryly notes,
"were not supporters of democracy."[33]

Lack of popular participation in the process that established the
national government lends credence to the claim that Confederation was
a contractual arrangement entered into by provincial governments. In
turn, this has given succeeding generations of provincial leaders the
opportunity to restrict participation in important decisions on the
grounds that the issues in question were the prerogatives of the
"provinces": prerogatives, that is, of the *governments* which *they* led.
Thus, an elite style of political decision–making has persisted and,
buttressed by theoretical constructs such as "consociationalism" and
"executive federalism," has become more firmly entrenched over time.

With respect to the skills with which provincial politicians have been
able to play the political power game, Oliver Mowat and Honoré
Mercier, long-time 19th century premiers of Ontario and Quebec respectively, were especially adept at using the compact theory to justify and
expand provincial autonomy and (concomitantly) their own status and
authority. However, given the scope of provincial activities and the
limitations that were placed on their taxing powers by the BNAA,
provincial politicians frequently have had to pursue a second strategy.
They have had to argue that the provinces are the principal representatives of provincial interests and that in order to perform their representational functions they require ever-increasing financial resources. As a
corollary of this argument they have tried to increase their revenue base
by demanding and receiving more "tax room" (i.e., a greater share of
taxes collected on their behalf and redistributed by the national government). These efforts have been aided by the Judicial Committee's
interpretations of the BNAA and the success of Quebec political leaders
in identifying the interests of all French Canadians with those of the
province of Quebec.

The revenues initially available to the provinces largely were derived from subsidies paid them by the federal government. New provinces (Manitoba, British Columbia, Prince Edward Island, Alberta, and Saskatchewan) received roughly comparable financial assistance in the form of per capita and governmental housekeeping grants. These were increased periodically but they could not keep the provinces from falling into great financial difficulty during the Depression; the smaller and less prosperous ones simply lacked the financial resources to fund the programs and services for which they were responsible. The deepening crisis led to the establishment of a Royal Commission (the Rowell-Sirois Commission) charged with evaluating the status of the federal system and recommending solutions to the serious imbalance between the responsibilities of the provinces and the fiscal resources at their disposal. Although the Commission recommended a number of significant changes in the distribution of financial resources between the central and provincial governments, these were set aside during World War Two. In their place an arrangement was made whereby provincial governments agreeing not to tax personal or corporate incomes were compensated by federal contributions toward interest payments due on provincial debts.

The tax rental agreement was the principal form fiscal federalism took in the post-World War Two decade. Under this scheme the provinces agreed to "rent" their personal, corporate and succession taxes to the federal government for five-year periods in return for rental payments. In 1957 the rental payments that provinces received for their taxes were increased and further augmented by "equalization" grants. In 1962 pressure from Quebec's political leaders induced the federal government to abandon tax renting for tax sharing. The federal government collected direct taxes on behalf of the provinces while continuing to make equalization payments to the less prosperous ones. Since this change, the provincial governments, led by Ontario and Quebec, continually have asked for and received larger shares of the direct taxes collected from their individual and corporate residents. The practice has been to begin negotiating each five-year agreement some two years in advance. A series of federal-provincial meetings are held at which first and finance ministers of the provinces, accompanied by groups of advisers, stake out initial positions and then, following the lead of the largest and most prosperous provinces, adjust these positions until agreement is reached with the representatives of the federal government.

The process by which various federal-provincial agreements currently are negotiated, sometimes termed "executive federalism," places a premium on shrewdness, assertiveness, and determination: in short, on strong leadership. Provincial First Ministers such as Frost and Robarts of Ontario, Lesage of Quebec, Smallwood of Newfoundland,

Manning of Alberta, W.A.C. Bennett of British Columbia and, more recently, Davis, Lévesque, Blakeney and Lougheed have provided this leadership. It also is apparent that this arrangement tends to cast the federal government in the role of "bad guys" — the collector of taxes — and the provincial governments in the opposite role, the dispensers of social and economic benefits to their respective citizens. The ability of provincial political leaders to represent themselves to their electorates as good "providers," coupled with the tendency to extend federal-provincial negotiations to areas *other* than finance, have led to a significant increase in both the power and prestige of provincial first ministers and of the governments they lead.

The political acumen and strong leadership of provincial politicians and their advisers are not the only reasons they have been able to extract ever more favourable terms from their federal counterparts. Another reason is the underlying economic forces that currently favour the provinces. There have been three periods of relatively rapid change in the balance of federal-provincial power. The first began *circa* 1887 and lasted until approximately World War One when power shifted toward the provinces. The second, when power shifted back to the federal government, began in the mid-1930s and continued through the late 1950s. The most recent shift again favours the provinces. These shifts have been explained in terms of certain characteristics of the political economy. Some scholars argue that historically the principal function of government in Canada has been to assist economic growth by providing various guarantees and incentives to private sectors of the economy and by intervening directly to supply needed services and resources when, and, if, the private sector is unwilling or unable to provide them. Of course, business and other economic interests are not monolithic. In fact, they often conflict. Under the federal system conflicting economic interests can be articulated "through accommodation and compromise at the level of the central government . . . or through different governments, federal and provincial."[34] The latter course is frequently taken. By way of illustration, social groups or business interests who feel the central government is more sympathetic to opposing interests than to their own turn to provincial governments for succor, especially, if these groups and interests occupy a prominent position within a particular province. Frequently, they welcome increases in the taxing, spending and regulatory powers of provincial governments since enhancement of these will enable the particular provincial government to whom they look for assistance to better provide it. The opposite considerations obtain if a group or business interest perceives that the central government is the more sympathetic. These "group-government" alliances can last for long periods but they are not immutable. Changing circumstances have led those affected to transfer their allegiances from one level of government to another. When enough powerful groups make such a change, the government to which they have transferred their allegiance becomes the more powerful. In brief, the periodic shifts in the balance of power between the central government and the provinces reflect changes in alliances between major social and economic groups and the level of government which, in their view, best serves their purposes at any time.[35]

Other observers contend that the federal and provincial governments, *as governments*, have played a considerably more active role in effecting shifts in the power balance than the above analysis implies.[36] Provincial governments more often have manipulated than they have been manipulated by powerful social and economic forces. Illustrative of the supposed primacy assigned to the role of governments in inducing changes in the balance of power in the federal system are the labels applied to time periods[37] more or less coterminous with those arguing the primacy of social and economic forces. Thus, periods in which the balance of power favoured the central government have been termed "nation-building." Those in which the balance swung to the provinces have been labelled "province-building" and, more recently, "Quebec nation-building."

Somewhat differently, it has been argued that the ability of provincial government leaders to secure a favourable balance of power *vis-à-vis* the federal government has been greatly facilitated by the fact that they have a separate power base.[38] Since provincial politicians are responsible only to their own electorates, they are encouraged to pursue policies favourable to their residents and their own political status even if these are inimical to the interests of Canadians in other provinces or to a national interest as articulated by the federal government. The energy and natural resource policies advocated by the Lougheed government of Alberta and the Peckford government of Newfoundland exemplify this tendency, or so some would argue. First ministers conferences, because of their visibility and strategic importance, provide especially good opportunities for provincial leaders to advocate self-interested policies whose principal merit may be the "pay-off" they can have in a future election. Reinforcing this tendency is the tentative and "open-ended" nature of the federal system. Provincial leaders who fail to have their way on an issue are encouraged to keep pushing their position on the assumption that ultimately they may be successful. In federal-provincial negotiations, it has been asserted, "nothing has been settled definitely, nothing is above discussion, nothing can be assumed or taken for granted."[39]

To recapitulate, the Fathers of Confederation tried to establish a political system in which both the individual and collective interests of Canadians would be represented in and by the new national government. Although the provincial governments were assigned a secondary representational role at best, the power and importance of the provinces and their governments have increased enormously over the years. While there is disagreement about the relative importance of various causes of the growth of provincial power, all observers concur that provincial governments have become so powerful they affect the everyday lives of their citizens in ways that the architects of Confederation never anticipated.

PUBLIC IMAGES OF FEDERALISM

The character of a federal system is determined by more than a set of constitutional arrangements through which jurisdiction over various subject matter areas is divided between national and subnational units of government. Equally, perhaps even more, important is the degree of support these governments receive from citizens. No political arrangements, federal or otherwise, can long survive, let alone purport to represent and be responsive to the public, if they are not adequately supported by that public. The problem of securing adequate support is more difficult in a democracy than it is in an authoritarian or totalitarian state because political leaders in a democratic country normally cannot rely on massive applications of force to make people obey laws and regulations and support the political system. Instead, leaders must depend largely on unforced compliance with governmental edicts and voluntary rendering of support to public officials and to the political system more generally. To comprehend the character òf political support in Canada, we must know what its magnitude is and whether it varies significantly for different political objects, or among people in different parts of the country. Since support does not exist in a vacuum but rather is rooted in people's perceptions and evaluations of what a government does, how it does it, and how what it does affects them personally, we also must know something about the distribution of such orientations. Happily, a number of national opinion studies conducted since 1965 shed light on these matters. Regarding the magnitude and distribution of public support for the principal components of federalism, people taking part in the 1974 national election study were given a picture of a thermometer scaled from 0°–100°, with 50° designated as a neutral point and asked their feelings about a variety of political objects such as Canada, the government of Canada, their province and their provincial government. The public's ratings may be regarded as a measure of the support citizens ascribe these objects.

The ratings revealed a hierarchical ordering of support. It was highest (and highly positive) for the national and provincial political communities and lowest for political leaders, with support for the federal and provincial governments, as governments, falling in between. Within these categories there was more support for Canada than for the provinces and more support for the federal than for provincial governments.[40] The data also revealed that support for the federal government is partially affected by people's partisan identifications. In 1974, support for the federal government was higher, on average, among Liberal identifiers than among persons identifying with other parties or no party whatsoever. However, partisan attachments were *not* a significant correlate of support for Canada. Five years later, levels of public support for both the federal and provincial political communities also were not significantly affected by partisan attachments. However, in the five-year interval, Canadians' support for their national political community had decreased slightly (by four points), whereas support for the several provinces had risen marginally (by two points). In contrast to the 1974 study, the average level of support for provincial governments was slightly higher than for the federal government (see Table 2.1).

Closer inspection of the 1979 data indicates that support for the country as a whole eroded in each of the 10 provinces, the decline being greatest in Ontario and Saskatchewan and least in Newfoundland and Manitoba. Although the overall level of support for provinces as political communities remained virtually unchanged during the five-year period, it was maintained largely because Quebecers displayed more affection for their province in 1979 than they had five years earlier. Other than in Quebec (and Saskatchewan) support for provinces decreased slightly, with the greatest decline occurring in Manitoba and Newfoundland. With respect to support for governments, public affection for provincial governments declined sharply in Prince Edward Island and New Brunswick but increased markedly in British Columbia, Newfoundland, Saskatchewan, Ontario and Manitoba. Support for the federal government remained relatively constant in the western half of the country but declined rather sharply in Ontario, Quebec and New Brunswick.

Given the relatively continuous jurisdictional conflicts between federal and provincial governments (most recently dramatized in periodic first ministers conferences) it is possible that an increase in a person's level of support for one government might well result in a reduced level of support for the other. Consequently, a more precise indication of the affection Canadians display for their country and province and for the governments of each can be obtained by creating two four-fold typologies — one depicting support for country and province and a second depicting support for their governments. The first has been labelled a "political community" and the second a "regime" support typology. With respect to the typology of community support, the four categories are composed of persons who accord: (1) positive support to both the country and their province of residence; (2) positive support to the country but neutral or negative support to their province; (3) positive support to the province but neutral or negative support to the country; and (4) neutral or negative support to both. The regime support

TABLE 2.1
Levels of Support for Canada, Province of
Residence and Federal and Provincial Governments, 1974 and 1979
(measured using 100-point thermometer scale)

Province of Residence	Mean Support Score for Canada		Mean Support Score for Province	
	1974	1979	1974	1979
Newfoundland	76	75	82	78
Prince Edward Island	86	82	86	85
Nova Scotia	89	86	83	82
New Brunswick	82	78	70	69
Quebec	75	71	71	76
Ontario	91	85	80	79
Manitoba	87	85	79	73
Saskatchewan	86	81	81	81
Alberta	85	80	85	84
British Columbia	87	84	85	83
Residents of all provinces	84	80	78	79

Province of Residence	Mean Support Score for Government of Canada		Mean Support Score for Provincial Government	
	1974	1979	1974	1979
Newfoundland	65	59	50	61
Prince Edward Island	65	61	67	52
Nova Scotia	62	62	62	59
New Brunswick	65	56	59	47
Quebec	63	54	54	54
Ontario	65	56	54	61
Manitoba	58	59	53	58
Saskatchewan	59	58	57	67
Alberta	59	60	71	73
British Columbia	60	60	46	58
Residents of all provinces	63	57	55	59

typology is constructed in a similar fashion. For both typologies, the labels applied to the four groups are "federalists" (group 1), "nationalists" (group 2), "provincialists" (group 3), and "alienated" (group 4).[41]

As expected, comparisons of the sizes of these groups indicate that in both 1974 and 1979 substantially more positive support existed for the country and provinces as political communities than for their respective

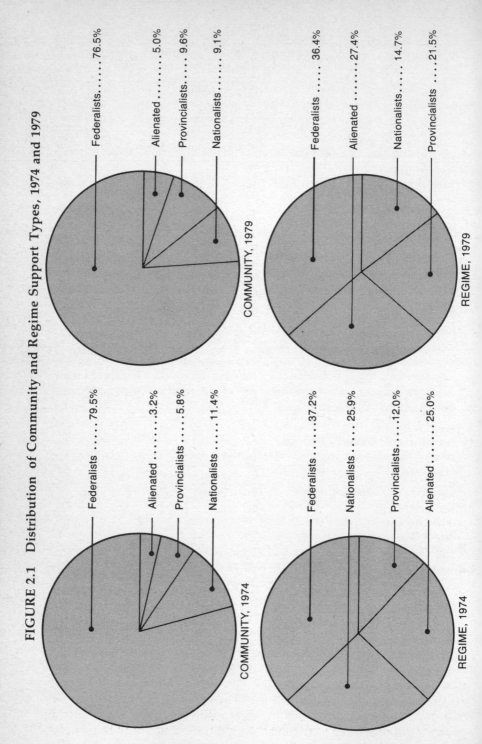

FIGURE 2.1　Distribution of Community and Regime Support Types, 1974 and 1979

COMMUNITY, 1979

Federalists......76.5%
Alienated........5.0%
Provincialists.....9.6%
Nationalists......9.1%

REGIME, 1979

Federalists 36.4%
Alienated 27.4%
Nationalists 14.7%
Provincialists 21.5%

COMMUNITY, 1974

Federalists 79.5%
Alienated 3.2%
Provincialists 5.8%
Nationalists 11.4%

REGIME, 1974

Federalists 37.2%
Nationalists 25.9%
Provincialists....12.0%
Alienated........25.0%

governments. In both years approximately three-quarters of the public ascribed positive support to both Canada and their province, more than twice as large as the group supporting both levels of government. Similarly, relatively miniscule proportions of people in each survey were "alienated" from both the country and their province, but more than a quarter were alienated from both levels of government. Examining these data by province, the most striking difference is that Quebecers display considerably more negative feelings toward both country and province than do people in other regions. The size of this group in Quebec diminished somewhat in the interim between the two surveys, but its decrease has been accompanied by an increase in the percentage of regime provincialists: people who view their provincial government favourably but their national government neutrally or negatively. In fact, Quebec was the home of the largest group of such people — over one-half of all regime provincialists in the entire country were Quebecers.

Despite moderate erosion in support scores for both the federal and provincial political communities between 1974 and 1979, outside of Quebec support for country and province remained highly positive in all provinces. Collateral evidence supports this inference. For example, in a 1977 national survey conducted by scholars at York University (the Quality of Life Study) participants were asked whether their first identification was with Canada or the province in which they lived. A majority in every province but Newfoundland and Quebec replied that they thought of themselves as "Canadians first." The proportions whose first identifications were with Canada rather than their province ranged from 87% in Ontario to 31% in Newfoundland (see Figure 2.2).

The Quality of Life study also revealed that despite their identification with Canada most people have a strong affection for their province. Overwhelming majorities (from 80% in New Brunswick, Manitoba, and Saskatchewan to 100% in Prince Edward Island) stated they preferred living in the province where they currently resided and had no desire to live elsewhere. Further, in response to a question asked of people taking part in the 1979 national election study, "When you think of *your* government, which government comes to mind, the government of Canada or the government of (province)," although a majority mentioned the federal government, one of every three respondents designated their provincial government and an additional 11% said "both." The federal government was most popular among Ontarians, Manitobans and Nova Scotians; the provincial among residents of Newfoundland and Quebec.

Support for any government in part is grounded in a person's knowledge of what it does, how it does it and how what government does affects that person and his or her family. In these regards, there is considerable survey evidence indicating that provincial governments generally receive very good grades from their publics. In three of four national studies conducted between 1965 and 1979 larger proportions of people stated their provincial governments were more important than the federal government in determining how they and their family "get on." In 1979, for example, 37% and 33% of a national sample selected the provincial and federal governments respectively. (The remainder mentioned their local government or stated that all levels of government

FIGURE 2.2   Distribution of Public's Identifications with Canada and Province of Residence, 1977

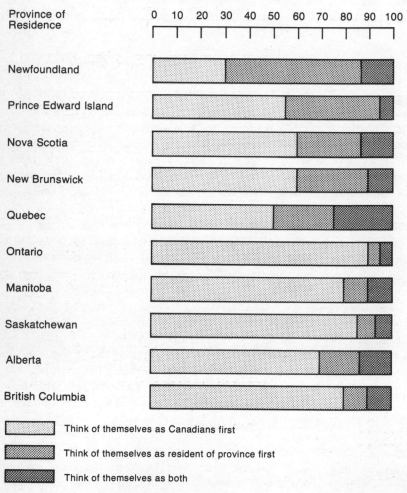

were equally important.) On a province by province basis, the 1979 data show that sizable groups in every province thought the provincial government had the greatest impact on their lives. Majorities or large pluralities in all four Western provinces, Quebec and Newfoundland selected their provincial government, while the federal government was chosen by pluralities in the other three Atlantic provinces and Ontario (see Figure 2.3).

FIGURE 2.3   **Public Perceptions of Which Level of Government Most Affects Their Lives, 1979**

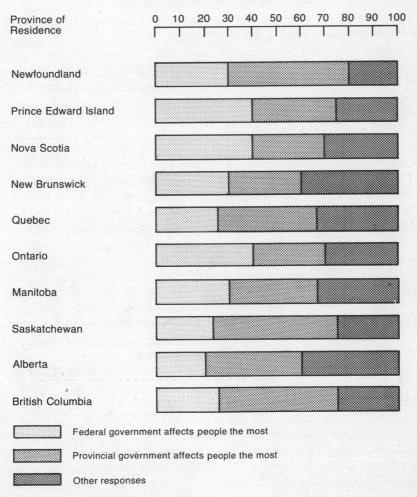

Other evidence indicates that many people in all parts of the country seem to have a high regard for the efficiency of their provincial governments. In the 1977 Quality of Life survey, residents of five of the 10 provinces (Prince Edward Island, Nova Scotia, Ontario, Manitoba, and Alberta) more often said in response to a question asking whether they were "satisfied" or "dissatisfied" with their provincial and federal governments that they were "satisfied" with their provincial government (from a high of 67% in Alberta to a low of 28% in New Brunswick). In only three provinces, Newfoundland, New Brunswick, and British Columbia, were the percentages of unsatisfied respondents greater than those of satisfied citizens. Two years later, in a study conducted by the CBC, majorities in every region of the country except Quebec (49%) stated that they were "very" or "fairly" satisfied with their provincial governments. In the CBC survey residents of every region but Quebec also more often reported that their provincial rather than their federal government "looked after their needs and interests the best." The differences favouring provincial governments over the federal ranged from a high of 50% in Alberta (66% vs. 16%) to a low, on average, of 7% in the Atlantic provinces.[42]

Satisfaction with the performance of provincial governments may help explain why, in the 1974 national election survey, majorities of respondents in every province but Ontario and Quebec, said they felt "closer" to their provincial than to the federal government.[43] It may also help explain why a significant proportion of the public in both the 1977 Quality of Life and 1979 CBC surveys indicated they would not be adverse to increasing the powers of the provinces. Thus, although 35% of the 1977 sample felt that the current distribution of power was "about right," 16% felt the provinces had "too little" power. Only 8% felt this way about the federal government and more than five times as many (42%) said the federal government exercised "too much" power. Only 29% said this of their provincial governments. In 1979, a third of all respondents (49% in Quebec) said they would increase the power of the provinces if the constitution were to be revised,[44] whereas only 15% favoured an increase in federal powers. (Four of every 10 people wanted to see the current balance of powers maintained.)

This is not to say that Canadians are overly enthusiastic about the operation of either the federal system or the status of their own province, *vis-à-vis* other provinces. A 1974 study of public perceptions of costs to, benefits from and the power exercised by the provinces in the federal system indicated that residents of each of the provinces tended more often than nonresidents to judge that their own province paid disproportionate costs whereas provinces other than their own benefited unduly. The tendency to feel disadvantaged by the operation of federalism was particularly sharp in three of the Western provinces (Manitoba, Alberta, and British Columbia) and in Ontario and Quebec. Relatively few people in any province perceived that provinces other

TABLE 2.2
Public Perceptions of the Costs and Benefits of Federalism, 1979

Province	Which Provinces Pay Undue Costs or Receive Less than Fair Share of Benefits			Which Provinces Receive Disproportionate Benefits or Bear Less than Fair Share of Costs		
	Residents	Non-Residents	Total*	Residents	Non-Residents	Total*
Newfoundland	23%	6%	6%	10%	14%	15%
Prince Edward Island	19	5	5	13	16	14
Nova Scotia	39	5	7	7	13	14
New Brunswick	34	5	6	7	13	14
Quebec	38	5	14	10	35	28
Ontario	46	20	29	12	25	21
Manitoba	48	7	8	5	6	6
Saskatchewan	43	8	9	1	7	7
Alberta	62	24	27	10	15	7
British Columbia	58	12	17	4	8	7

*percentages for whole country based on weighted national sample (N=2670).

than Ontario, Quebec and, to lesser extent, Alberta and British Columbia, were powerful.[45] The pattern of these findings largely was repeated when similar questions were asked in 1979. Most respondents again perceived Ontario, Quebec and Alberta as being powerful. And, as in 1974, people tended to see provinces other than their own receiving disproportionate benefits and paying less than a fair share of the costs of federalism (see Table 2.2). Overall, Ontario and Quebec were most frequently judged to be the provinces receiving disproportionate benefits from federalism whereas Alberta and Ontario were viewed as bearing disproportionate costs.

Another complaint many people voice about the operation of the federal system is that "Ottawa" (i.e., the federal government) does not treat their province "fairly." In the 1977 Quality of Life survey majorities in every province but Quebec and Ontario (and 48% of the latter) felt Ottawa "paid too much attention to Quebec." In contrast, over two-fifths of Quebec Francophones perceived the opposite (i.e., Ottawa "paid too little attention to them"). Again, many people complain that the federal government interferes in affairs that are properly the concern of provincial governments. Across the country as a whole 54% felt this way in 1979. The number of persons holding this view varied substantially by province, the highest percentages being 67% in Alberta and 68% in Quebec. Among Quebec Francophones 72% perceived federal government interference and 30% felt such interference could not be justified. The latter percentage was considerably larger than in any other province, save Alberta (27%).[46]

One very important consequence of Francophone Quebecers' perceptions of unjustified federal interference in provincial affairs may well be the increase in separatist sentiments that has occurred in that province since the early 1960s: from 8% in favour of separatism in 1962 to 28% in early 1980. The number in favour of the Parti Québécois' sovereignty-association scheme is even greater. In 10 surveys over the period August 1977 to April 1980, the percentage of Quebecers supporting sovereignty-association averaged 39%[47] (see Figure 2.4). The consistency of this support is indicated by the fact that on only one occasion did the proportion of respondents favouring sovereignty-association fall below one-third. That Canadians outside of Quebec are cognizant of these feelings is reflected in a concomitant increase in the proportion who thought Quebec would separate at some future time: from 19% in 1968 to 36% in 1977.

Regarding attitudes toward the possibility that Quebec might separate, in the 1977 Quality of Life study, only a minority (14%) felt that Quebec should be forceably prevented from separating, but only 11% of people residing in provinces *other* than Quebec were willing to have the federal government make "major" concessions to keep the province in Confederation. Another 38% said they would be willing to see "minor" concessions made, but an even larger group (43%) were unwilling to

FIGURE 2.4   Percentages of Quebecers Favouring
Sovereignty-Association and Independence, 1977–80

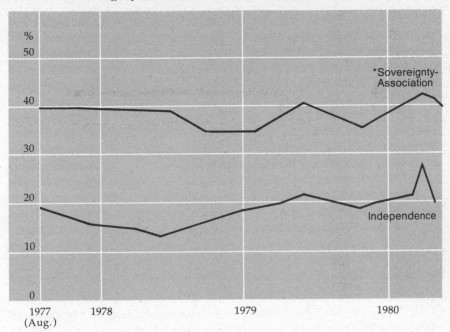

Source: Hélène Robillard-Frayne and Claude Gauthier, *Les Québécois et La Campagne Référendaire* (Montreal: Radio-Canada, le 9 mai, 1980), section IV, p. 13.

*Actual Vote in Quebec Sovereignty-Association Referendum

have Ottawa make *any* concessions! Similarly, in the 1979 CBC survey, only one-third of Quebecers (16% of Anglophones, 35% of Francophones) and only one-quarter of residents of other provinces felt that Quebec had the right to leave Confederation. In the 1977 Quality of Life survey, the great majority (93% outside and 75% within Quebec) felt that Quebec's economy would suffer if the province became independent. However, half of the people living in Quebec and almost two-thirds of the residents of the other provinces judged that the economy of the rest of Canada also would suffer if Quebec separated. Therefore — notwithstanding the significant resistance that existed in 1977 and subsequently to making concessions to keep Quebec in Confederation — some eight of 10 Quebecers and more than half of the rest of Canada agreed that, should Quebec ever become independent, appropriate economic arrangements should be made to minimize any deleterious consequences that might ensue.

On May 20, 1980 the Quebec electorate rejected the Parti Québécois' sovereignty-association proposal by a six to four margin. Analyses of the vote indicate that the result was not merely a product of overwhelming Anglophone opposition, but rather that a majority of Francophones rejected the Péquiste option. However, the referendum outcome should not be interpreted as indicating Québécois[48] are now content with the existing federal system. As Figure 2.4 shows, in every survey in the past four years large minorities have approved the idea of sovereignty-association. Even larger numbers in every survey (clear majorities in nine of 10 instances) during this period have approved the idea of "renewed federalism." Indeed, it can be argued that one of the principal results of the protracted PQ campaign for sovereignty-association has been to shift the ground of debate concerning Quebec's status *vis-à-vis* the federal system. No longer are the terms of reference constitutional change vs. the status quo, but rather the extent and nature of such change.

Two other facts support this interpretation. First, and most obvious, is the PQ's sound electoral victory in the 1981 Quebec provincial election. In this contest the PQ increased its popular vote from 41% to 49% and captured 80 seats, 11 more than in 1976. The only other party to capture any seats (42) in this election were the Liberals, the advocates of renewed federalism. Second, and less salient, are the demographic characteristics of persons supporting various constitutional options. Studies repeatedly have shown that sovereignty-association and out-right independence have their strongest appeal among younger, better-educated Québécois, whereas the status quo is favoured by older, less-educated elements in the Quebec population.[49] Figure 2.5 illustrates the relationship between age and political support. These data, taken from the 1980 national election study, show that support for Canada is lower among Québécois than persons living in other provinces. More-over, levels of support among the former are clearly age-related — mean thermometer scores rising from 62 among the youngest (18–25 years) to 79 among the oldest (56 and over) age group. What is potentially very significant about this finding is that over time, there will be fewer and fewer of the latter group in the population. Assuming the PQ continues to be successful in convincing many younger Québécois of the need for fundamental change, the long-term stability of the Canadian federal system is bound to be problematic.

FEDERALISM: RETROSPECT AND PROSPECT

As noted earlier, federalism is a form of political organization in which the powers and activities of government are divided. In comparison to the powers initially allotted the national government, the powers assigned the provinces in the BNAA were limited to a number of supposedly inconsequential subjects. Since 1867, the scope of both levels of government has increased substantially but the power and

FIGURE 2.5 Feelings for Canada by Age Group, 1980
(Mean Thermometer Scores)

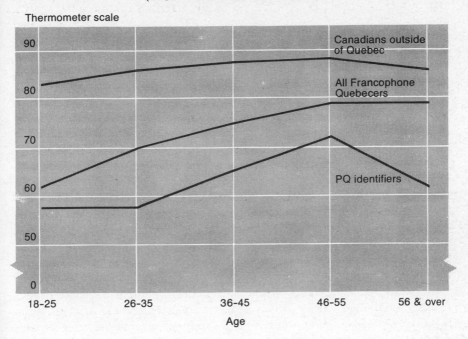

Thermometer scale

Age

authority of the provinces have expanded more than those of the federal government. Some observers would contend that they have expanded at the expense of the federal government. This has been attributed to a combination of circumstances including: the elitist origins of Confederation and continued elite domination of the political process; the inability of the new national government to establish its legitimacy and generate widespread public support for its activities in the generation after Confederation; decisions by the Judicial Committee of the British Privy Council that favoured the provinces; the increased importance in the 20th century of areas of provincial jurisdiction; the insistent claims of provincial political leaders that they are the best representatives of the interests of citizens in their provinces; the post-World War Two success of provincial political elites in securing federal revenues to support the expanded activities of their governments; the increased competence of provincial bureaucracies whose growth has been financed, in part, by revenues derived from provincially-controlled natural resources; the ability of provincial public officials to form coalitions with important economic interests in support of provincial claims; and the enhanced visibility of and public support for provincial political elites that are consequences of executive federalism and their own strong leadership.

Currently, Canadians enjoy a wide range of social services and one of the highest standards of living in the world. Nonetheless, there are substantial interprovincial differences in industrial development and notable variations in the magnitude and value of their natural resources. The federal government has tried to narrow interprovincial differences that result from variations in their industrial and natural resource bases by redistributing revenues derived from wealthier provinces to less prosperous ones through such vehicles as "equalization" payments and, more recently, DREE grants. In 1976, a reasonably typical year, the per capita value of federal transfer payments to Prince Edward Island was approximately 3½ times as great as the ones to Ontario and the transfers to Newfoundland approximately 2½ times as great as those to British Columbia. More generally, the Atlantic provinces, Manitoba, and Saskatchewan all received larger proportions of total federal funds than they would be entitled to on the basis of their populations. In contrast, Ontario, Quebec, Alberta, and British Columbia received smaller shares. However, disparities in provincial populations place limits on attempts to redistribute wealth in this way. Thus, given their much larger populations, Ontario and Quebec were allocated the lion's share of the transfers, some 55%. British Columbia and Alberta received 15%, leaving only 30% of the total funds to be shared by the six other provinces.

Given the current and projected distributions of provincial populations, it may be impossible for the latter ever to catch up. Any really significant attempt to achieve economic parity would require a much more radical redistribution of wealth than has been attempted to date. This is an unlikely undertaking for two reasons. First, the larger and wealthier provinces probably would not agree and, given their political muscle, it would be difficult for the federal government to coerce them. Second, federal governments have been unwilling to press the four largest and wealthiest provincial governments to accede to a more extensive redistribution. To the extent that there has been coercion, smaller and poorer provinces usually have been the objects of pressure. For example, Newfoundland has had to sell its Labrador-generated electrical power to Quebec "at an absurdly low price"[50] because Quebec has refused to permit the transfer of power across its territory. Similarly, because Ontario and Quebec have objected, no federal government has been willing to establish the kind of national power grid that could significantly further the industrialization of the Atlantic provinces, Manitoba and Saskatchewan.[51]

Some observers believe that increases in the power and importance of the provinces, particularly during the past two decades, have been advantageous to provincial political and economic elites, and in the short run, to the general populations of the larger and more prosperous provinces.[52] Arguably, these developments have not been advantageous to Canadians residing in the smaller and less prosperous provinces. Given their smaller populations, less abundant and/or valuable natural resources, and lower levels of industrialization, these provinces probably will continue to lag behind the wealthier provinces in rates of economic growth — and may become even less prosperous in an absolute sense. Nor can it reasonably be expected that future federal government policies will significantly narrow the differences between the "haves" and the "have nots." Some analysts have argued that ultimately these economic differences, rather than the aspirations of separatist elements in Quebec, may pose the most serious threat to Canada's long-term unity and continuity.

Although many students of Canadian federalism might not agree that interprovincial economic disparities pose the greatest threat to national unity, they might well agree that federalism — in combination with British model parliamentary government, a single member plurality electoral system and a population distributed in a manner such that approximately two-thirds reside in Ontario and Quebec with some four-fifths of French Canadians in the latter province — make it difficult for smaller and less prosperous provinces to represent their interests *vis-à-vis* the larger provinces and the federal government. Indeed, it can be contended that this combination of factors makes it difficult for minorities in general to have their interests effectively represented, which is why they have tried to utilize whatever institution or level of government is most receptive and accommodative to their perceived needs. To the extent that the representation of the interests of minorities is made more difficult by these factors, representative democracy, as we have defined it, is more difficult to achieve.

Conversely, it can be maintained that there are "trade-offs" in the sense that these same factors can enhance prospects for representative democracy. For example, a plurality electoral system makes it easier for political parties to obtain the parliamentary majority required to govern. Relatedly, the parliamentary system, with its disciplined and cohesive legislative parties, facilitates the generation of coordinated and integrated public policies and enhances the public's ability to hold governments accountable for these policies. Further, the concentration of population in the country's heartland has bolstered the growth of an industrial infrastructure, facilitated interprovincial trade and eased the development of transcontinental systems of transportation and communication. In subsequent chapters we will consider some of the ways in which these and other sociopolitical factors affect prospects for representative democracy.

In this chapter we have concerned ourselves largely with the ways in which the evolution of the federal system has affected and been affected by the competing claims of generations of federal and provincial leaders that *they* speak for Canada. Given the jurisdiction of both over the same population, there is a certain inevitability to such claims. This justification of provincial premiers from Mowat and Mercier to Lévesque to Lougheed has been that, collectively, their governments best represent the people because they are in some sense or other closest to them. The justification of prime ministers from Macdonald to Trudeau has been that Canada is a political community that is more than the sum of its parts and that its instrument, the federal government, represents all of the people of that community.

Provincial claims of "closeness" and greater responsiveness were given renewed impetus at the Confederation of Tomorrow Conference called by former Premier John Robarts of Ontario on the occasion of Canada's centennial celebrations in 1967. These claims underlie some of the positions taken by provincial first ministers at the Victoria Constitutional Conference in 1971 and at periodic federal-provincial and interprovincial conferences in the middle and late 1970s. They were reaffirmed at the Constitutional Conference of September, 1980.[53] The provinces' version of a renewed federation that would enhance their ability to respond to citizen needs incorporates the perspectives and objectives of more than one political actor. Nonetheless, the principal dimensions of the provincial package are reasonably clear. First, anachronistic vestiges of a federalism in which the national and provincial governments stand in a superior-subordinate position must be swept away. Consequently, the federal declaratory power and the power to disallow or reserve provincial legislation must be terminated. In addition, the federal government's ability to infringe upon provincial jurisdiction through its power to tax and spend must be curtailed. Second, primacy in the process of amending a patriated constitution must lie with the provinces. Premier Lougheed of Alberta has gone so far as to argue that each province must have the option of "opting out" of any amendment it regards as repugnant. Third, in any future constitution, provincial jurisdiction must be enhanced and a concomitant effort made to "provincialize" national policy-making. The principal vehicle for achieving such provincialization should be a reconstituted upper chamber of Parliament, however named. Some or all of the members of this body should be appointed by provincial first ministers and these members, under certain conditions, should act as instructed delegates of the provinces. Other major institutions such as the courts, including the Supreme Court, and key bureaucratic agencies such as Air Canada and the CBC also must be more sensitive and better reflect provincial interests. As with a reconstituted second parliamentary chamber, the enhanced sensitivity of such institutions to provincial interests can best be achieved by allocating to provincial cabinets major responsibility for the appointment of their officials.

Not surprisingly, the federal government's image of a renewed federalism more effectively serving the interests of all Canadians varies sharply from the perspective of the provinces. Since 1968, that image largely has reflected the views of Pierre Elliot Trudeau. Perhaps more than any of his predecessors as Prime Minister, Trudeau's principal goal has been to create an overarching Canadian political community that mitigates historic ethno-linguistic and regional cleavages. According to Trudeau this goal can only be attained by vigorously employing the powers available to a strong federal government. Such a government must extend French language and educational rights beyond the boundaries of Quebec. It must strengthen the role of the federal government in interprovincial trade and commerce. It must ensure the civil rights and liberties of all Canadians through a constitutionally entrenched Charter of Rights. It must have primacy in the constitutional amending process and, most important, its policies must continuously reflect the fact that the interests of a national political community transcend any particularistic interests bounded by the geography of region or province. Obviously, Trudeau's perspective on who speaks for Canadians and how the public's interests can best be represented are incompatible with — indeed, hostile to — the provincial perspective. Thus, it is hardly surprising that efforts during the past decade to construct a "new federalism" have been characterized by acrimony, deadlock and frustration. Equally clearly, given the realities of growing economic power in the Western provinces and the unsatisfied cultural and political aspirations of many Québécois, the problems of Confederation will continue to be difficult to resolve. To resolve them in a way that preserves the Canadian political community while providing effective and responsive governance at *both* the federal and provincial levels will be an even more arduous task.

SUMMARY

The existence of provincial communities and governments long before the passage of the BNAA made Confederation possible and the maintenance of national unity more difficult than it might have been. In this chapter we have traced the evolution of the federal system giving particular emphasis to arguments that have been offered to explain the very substantial increase in provincial powers over the years. We have examined public images of the federal system and considered the bases of the claims of provincial and federal political leaders that they speak for the people of Canada. In a political system in which two sets of political leaders have jurisdiction over the same population, claims of this kind are probably inevitable. Although the positions of federal and provincial leaders respecting the kind of structural and procedural arrangements that could best facilitate their ability to speak for Canada continue to differ, it is clear that the future of representative democracy in the provinces and the country as a whole will be strongly affected by the manner in which these differences ultimately are resolved.

50 *Representative Democracy in the Canadian Provinces*

NOTES

1. Garth Stevenson, *Unfulfilled Union* (Toronto: Macmillan of Canada, 1979), p. 28.
2. S.F. Wise, "Conservatism and Political Development: The Canadian Case," *South Atlantic Quarterly*, 69 (1970), pp. 226-243.
3. Donald G. Creighton, *A History of Canada* (Boston: Houghton Mifflin, 1958), p. 295.
4. Creighton is the best known of Macdonald's biographers. See Creighton, *John A. Macdonald, The Young Politician* Vol. 1 (Toronto: Macmillan, 1952) and *The Old Chieftain*, Vol. II (Toronto: Macmillan, 1955).
5. Legislature of Canada, *Parliamentary Debates on the Subject of the Confederation of the British North American Provinces* (Quebec: Queen's Printer, 1965), pp. 97-98.
6. See, for example, *Parliamentary Debates on the Subject of the Confederation of the British North American Provinces*, pp. 53-62 and 125-146. There also was concern that land-hungry Americans would push into the West, create incidents which could justify sending troops to protect them, and that these troops then would occupy the West and make it a part of the American empire. See Donald Creighton, *The Road to Confederation* (Toronto: Macmillan, 1965), pp. 16-19, 212-213, and 274-275.
7. C.P. Storey, "Fenianism and the Rise of National Feeling in Canada at the Time of Confederation," *Canadian Historical Review*, 12 (1931), pp. 238-261.
8. P.B. Waite, *The Life and Times of Confederation* (Toronto: University of Toronto Press, 1962), ch. 2.
9. Joseph Pope, *Correspondence of Sir John Macdonald* (Toronto: Oxford University Press, 1921), p. 11.
10. See, for example, *Parliamentary Debates on the Subject of the Confederation of the British North American Provinces*, pp. 33-145.
11. Allan Kornberg and Samuel M. Hines, "Parliament's Role in the Integration-Modernization of Canadian Society, 1865-1876," in Albert F. Eldridge, ed., *Legislatures in Plural Societies: The Search for Cohesion in National Development* (Durham N.C.: Duke University Press, 1977), pp. 213-214; Walter L. White, Ronald H. Wagenberg, Ralph C. Nelson and Walter C. Soderlund, *Canadian Confederation: A Decision-Making Analysis* (Toronto: McClelland and Stewart, 1979), pp. 51-55.
12. The provinces also were to exercise primary responsibility over education (Section 93) and to share jurisdiction with the central government over agriculture and immigration.
13. *Citizen's Insurance Company v. Parsons* and *Queen's Insurance Company v. Parsons* (1881).
14. *Attorney General of Canada v. Attorney General of Alberta* (1916); *Toronto Electric Company v. Snider* (1925); and *Proprietary Articles Trade Association v. the Attorney General of Canada* (1931).
15. *Russell v. the Queen* (1882).
16. *Attorney General of Ontario v. Attorney General of Canada* (1896).
17. *In Re: Board of Commerce Act* (1922); and *Fort Frances Pulp and Paper Company v. Manitoba Free Press* (1896).
18. *In Re: Regulation and Control of Aeronautics in Canada* (1932); and *In Re: Regulation of Radio Communication in Canada* (1932).
19. *Attorney General of Canada v. the Attorney General of Ontario* (Labour Conventions Case, 1937).
20. *Attorney General of Canada v. the Attorney General of Ontario* (Employment and Social Insurance Reference, 1937); and *Attorney General of British Columbia v. Attorney General of Canada* (Natural Products Marketing Act Reference, 1937).
21. See, for example, the discussions of Edwin R. Black, *Divided Loyalties: Canadian Concepts of Federalism* (Montreal: McGill-Queen's University Press, 1975); and Ramsey Cook, *Provincial Autonomy, Minority Rights, and the Compact Theory, 1867-1921*. Study No. 4 of the Royal Commission on Bilingualism and Biculturalism (Ottawa: Queen's Printer, 1969).
22. J.R. Mallory, "The Five Faces of Federalism" in P.A. Crépeau and C.B. Macpherson, eds., *The Future of Canadian Federalism* (Toronto: University of Toronto Press, 1965), pp. 3-15; Black, *Divided Loyalties*. See also, A.R.M. Lower, "Theories of Canadian Federalism — Yesterday and Today," in A.R.M. Lower, F.R. Scott, J.A. Corry, F.H. Soward, and Alexander Brady, eds., *Evolving Canadian Federalism* (Durham N.C.: Duke University Press, 1958), pp. 3-53.

23. See the analysis by David Kwavnick, ed., *The Tremblay Report: Report of the Royal Commission of Inquiry on Constitutional Problems* (Toronto: McClelland and Stewart, 1973).
24. See, for example, the Task Force on Canadian Unity, *A Future Together: Observations and Recommendations; Coming to Terms: The Words of the Debate* and *A Time to Speak: The Views of the Public* (Ottawa: Minister of Supply and Services, 1979). The dualistic view of Canada from which the compact theory derives also is set out in considerable detail in some of the reports produced by the Royal Commission on Bilingualism and Biculturalism. See, for example, Cook, *Provincial Autonomy, Minority Rights and the Compact Theory, 1867-1921*.
25. See, for example, *British Columbia Constitutional Proposals Presented to the First Ministers Conference on the Constitution* (Victoria: Province of British Columbia, 1978).
26. Pierre Elliot Trudeau, *A Time for Action: Towards the Renewal of the Canadian Federation* (Ottawa: Minister of Supply and Services, 1978). See also, *A Time for Action: Highlights of the Federal Government's Proposals for the Renewal of the Canadian Federation* (Ottawa: Minister of Supply and Services, 1978).
27. Edwin R. Black and Alan C. Cairns, "A Different Perspective on Canadian Federalism," *Canadian Public Administration*, 9 (1966), pp. 27-44.
28. Alan C. Cairns, "The Governments and Societies of Canadian Federalism," *Canadian Journal of Political Science* 10 (1977), pp. 695-726.
29. *Ibid.*, p. 703.
30. *Ibid.*
31. According to Cairns, the growth of bureaucracy and the symbiotic relationships that have developed between bureaucracies and interest groups have had a two-fold effect. On the one hand they have involved government in virtually every aspect of our daily lives. On the other, the general lack of public interest and involvement in politics coupled with the high level of activity of organized interest groups have significantly restricted the average citizen's — as opposed to interest groups' — ability to influence the content of governmental decisions. Cairns, "The Governments and Societies of Canadian Federalism," p. 707.
32. Stevenson, *Unfulfilled Union*, chs. 2,4,5.
33. *Ibid.*, p. 45.
34. *Ibid.*, p. 83.
35. *Ibid.*, pp. 83-102.
36. See, for example, J. Evenson and R. Simeon, "The Roots of Discontent" in *The Political Economy of Confederation* (Kingston: The Institute of Intergovernmental Relations, Queen's University, 1978), pp. 165-197; Alan C. Cairns, "Constitution-Making, Government Self-Interest and the Problem of Legitimacy in Canada," in Allan Kornberg and Harold D. Clarke, eds., *Political Support in Canada: The Crisis Years* (Durham: Duke University Press, 1982), forthcoming.
37. R. Durocher identifies two periods of central government dominance, 1867-1896 and 1939-1960, and two periods in which the balance of power swung to the provinces, 1896-1939 and 1960 to the present. The latter he terms a period of "confrontational federalism." See R. Durocher, "The Evolution of Canadian Federalism, 1867-1976," in *The Political Economy of Canada*, pp. 361-389.
38. Howard Cody, "The Evolution of Federal-Provincial Relations in Canada: Some Reflections," *The American Review of Canadian Studies*, 7 (1977), pp. 55-83. See also, Cairns, "The Governments and Societies of Canadian Federalism," p. 724.
39. Cody, "The Evolution of Federal-Provincial Relations in Canada," p. 76.
40. Allan Kornberg, Harold D. Clarke, and Marianne C. Stewart, "Federalism and Fragmentation: Political Support in Canada," *The Journal of Politics*, 41 (1979), pp. 889-906.
41. These labels are used largely for convenience and are not intended to convey any particular theoretical meanings. Easton, for example, has argued that non-support and alienation are not the same. See David Easton, "A Re-Assessment of the Concept of Political Support," *British Journal of Political Science*, 5 (1975), pp. 453-457.
42. The Quebec data reflect very sharp differences of opinion between Francophones and Anglophones about the provincial government. Thus, 55% of the former but only 24% of the latter are either "fairly" or "very" satisfied with their provincial

government. Similarly, 39% of the Francophones but only 11% of the Anglophones judged that the provincial government looked after their needs and interests best. See Hélène Robillard-Frayne, ed. *Confederation/Referendum* (Montreal: Radio Canada/CBC, March 1979), section 2, pp. 14-22.

43. Harold Clarke, Jane Jenson, Lawrence LeDuc, and Jon H. Pammett, *Political Choice in Canada* (Toronto: McGraw-Hill Ryerson, 1979), p. 72, Table 3.3.

44. Again, there is sharp disagreement between Francophones and Anglophones in Quebec — 56% of the former but only 21% of the latter wanted to expand the powers of the provincial governments. Robillard-Frayne, ed., *Confederation/Referendum*, section 2, p. 50.

45. Kornberg, Clarke, and Stewart, "Federalism and Fragmentation: Political Support in Canada" pp. 896-897.

46. Robillard-Frayne, ed., *Confederation/Referendum*, section 2, p. 30.

47. *Ibid.*, section 2, p. 66.

48. Throughout the text the term "Québécois" will be used to refer to Quebec residents of French ethnicity.

49. See Harold Clarke, "Partisanship and the Parti Québécois: The Impact of the Independence Issue," *The American Review of Canadian Studies* 8 (1978), pp. 37-38; Jon H. Pammett, Harold D. Clarke, Jane Jenson and Lawrence LeDuc, "Political Support and Voting Behaviour in the Quebec Referendum," in Allan Kornberg and Harold D. Clarke, eds. *Political Support in Canada: The Crisis Years* (Durham, N.C.: Duke University Press, 1982), ch. 12

50. Stevenson, *Unfulfilled Union*, pp. 106-109.

51. *Ibid.*, p. 110.

52. *Ibid.*, chs. 4, 5, cf., pp. 96-101.

53. For a detailed description and a comprehensive discussion of both the provincial and federal positions in recent constitutional debates see Alan Cairns, "Constitution-Making, Government Self-Interest, and the Problem of Legitimacy in Canada," in Allan Kornberg and Harold D. Clarke, eds., *Political Support in Canada: The Crisis Years*, ch. 14

FOR FURTHER READING

Cairns, Alan C. "The Governments and Societies of Canadian Federalism," *Canadian Journal of Political Science* 19 (1977), pp. 695-726. The author's analysis stresses the importance of the growth of provincial governments as a factor shaping provincial economies and societies and recent trends in federal-provincial relations.

Kornberg, Allan, Harold D. Clarke and Marianne C. Stewart, "Federalism and Fragmentation: Political Support in Canada," *Journal of Politics* 41 (1979) pp. 889-906. The authors examine how public perceptions of the costs and benefits of federalism influence support for the Canadian political system.

McRoberts, Kenneth, and Dale Posgate. *Quebec: Social Change and Political Crisis*. Toronto: McClelland and Stewart, 1980. In chapters 6-11 the authors present a cogent analysis of the social, economic and political development in Quebec since World War II.

Smiley, Donald V. *Canada in Question: Federalism in the Eighties* 3rd ed. Toronto: McGraw-Hill Ryerson Limited, 1980. This book is a basic text on Canadian federalism. Particularly valuable are chapter 4 which describes interactions between federal and provincial governments and chapter 6 on changing economic relationships between the two levels of government.

Stevenson, Garth. *Unfulfilled Union*. Toronto: Macmillan, 1979. In this analysis of the operation of the federal system, Stevenson argues that the balance of federal-provincial power reflects shifts in the balance of economic forces between and within provinces. See especially chapter 4.

3
Provincial Societies and Political Cultures

The political culture of a society consists of beliefs, attitudes and opinions about the political world that are widely shared by members of that society.[1] As a concept political culture holds a special fascination for many students of politics because they believe that political behaviour is strongly influenced by psychological orientations toward political objects. Cultural orientations may be classified as "cognitive," "affective," or "evaluative." Cognitive orientations involve beliefs about matters of fact — what *is* true. Affective orientations refer to feelings or preferences, to likes and dislikes. Evaluative orientations involve values, judgments and justifications — what *ought* to be done and why. Cognitive, affective and evaluative orientations may be directed toward individuals (e.g., party leaders, candidates for public office, the self as a political actor), political processes (e.g., the electoral, legislative or judicial systems), political institutions (e.g., political parties, interest groups, bureaucracies) or the political system as a whole. Taken together, these orientations are extremely important. They govern the range of political problems and the types of solutions that people of any society will consider and the kinds of political activity in which they will engage.

Many scholars have argued that a particular configuration of political culture is crucial for the development and maintenance of a democratic political system.[2] In a *representative* democracy extensive, informed citizen participation is vital. Accordingly, the representative democratic political culture is characterized by high levels of political knowledge, interest and efficacy. Many citizens are interested in and knowledgeable about crucial issues of the day, and they feel competent to influence the course of political events. They understand how their political system operates and recognize the need for active involvement in political life.

While appreciating the value of participation, citizens also realize the need for a division of political labour. They do not hesitate to entrust the day-to-day operation of government to a small group of public office-holders. At the same time, citizens retain the belief that ultimately they are the best judges of their own interests. Thus, their trust in public officials is limited and conditional. Acting responsively to public needs and demands is the "acid" test by which citizens select (and reject) persons aspiring to public office. Leaders, for their part, hold the same cultural orientations as other citizens. Because they do, they believe that they should act responsively and realize that their grants of political authority will be withdrawn should they fail to heed public needs and demands.

The political orientations which characterize a representative democracy are not formed or maintained in a vacuum, but rather are embedded in, and are products of, a more general matrix of cultural, social and economic conditions. Two crucial features of the broader culture are a strong allegiance to the overarching political community and a high level of trust in one's fellow citizens. Together, these moderate political conflicts and keep societal cleavages from becoming deep and irreconcilable fissures that could destroy the democratic political system. Social and economic conditions also are important. A democratic political culture is most likely to develop and be sustained in societies which have achieved relatively high levels of industrialization and urbanization and have developed efficient networks of transportation and communication. Additionally, levels of literacy will be high, many citizens will have substantial formal education, and there will be a reasonably equitable distribution of wealth.[3]

Are the several provinces characterized by the cultural, social and economic conditions that facilitate the development of a democratic political culture? Are there important differences among provinces in the extent to which such cultures have developed? To answer these questions is the task of this chapter. We will begin by discussing some of the central features of Canadian political culture as these have been revealed in previous studies. Then we will proceed to a detailed empirical examination of provincial societies and cultures.

THE CANADIAN POLITICAL CULTURE

In the past two decades substantial efforts have been made to delineate the principal dimensions of Canada's political culture. The methodologies of these inquiries have varied from inferential reconstructions based on examinations of historical data, to exegeses of the ideas of leading politicians and political thinkers, to attempts to identify "typical" response patterns in public opinion surveys.[4] Although there is less than perfect consensus about the nature of the country's political culture in these works, certain themes do recur. The conclusions they suggest about the extent of cultural support for representative democracy would appear to be mixed and somewhat contradictory. First, there is general agreement that Canada is characterized by some variant of a *liberal democratic* political culture.[5] The value placed on representative political institutions, the selection of representatives on the basis of formal political equality among voters ("one person, one vote") within the context of single- or multi-member plurality electoral systems, the use of the principle of majority rule within Parliament and provincial legislative assemblies, and concern and respect for the rights of minorities, are all indicative of the democratic dimension of the political culture. The liberal element is reflected in matters such as the value ascribed to freedom of speech and assembly, private property rights, a free market economy and other mechanisms of capitalism.[6]

Second, comparisons of Canada's political culture with the cultures of other Anglo-American countries, particularly that of the United States, have pointed to the presence of *conservative* and *socialist* as well as liberal elements in the former.[7] Conservatism emphasizes the significance of the community as opposed to the individual, deference to traditional and institutional sources of authority within a hierarchically-ordered society, and the desirability of gradual social and political change. Conservative beliefs and attitudes are said to be rooted in Canada's origins as a non- or counter-revolutionary "fragment" of British North America; the nation's subsequent development within the framework of the British Empire and Commonwealth; and the presence of a large French ethnic minority whose cultural heritage lies in pre-revolutionary absolutist France.[8]

The socialist element in the political culture, like the conservative, is said to differentiate it from that of the United States where liberalism constitutes a dominant, all-encompassing ideological framework.[9] Socialism in Canada, as elsewhere, emphasizes the desirability of not only political but also social and economic equality. Rather than advocating a revolutionary transformation of political, social and economic systems to achieve these goals, most Canadian socialists argue that it is possible to use the existing mechanisms of parliamentary government to effect desired changes.[10] The presence of such a non-revolutionary gradualist brand of socialism is another reflection of Canada's British cultural heritage which emphasizes the possibility and desirability of peaceful, gradual changes in major political, social and economic institutions. Relatedly, it has been maintained that the "respectability" of this type of socialism (because its origins are British rather than continental European), its advocacy of evolutionary rather than revolutionary change, and the catalytic effects provided by the "Tory touch" (i.e., the conservative component) made possible socialism's subsequent development as a significant protest movement and its institutionalization in an important political party, the CCF-NDP.[11]

A third theme, the "quasi-participative"[12] nature of Canadian political culture, is related to and rests on the presence of the conservative, liberal and socialist elements within it. Very briefly, although Canadians participate in politics, their participation is sharply limited. Citizens tend to be deferential to their "betters" and are content to be spectators rather than players in the "political game." They pay their admission to this game by voting in periodic elections. However, they then sit on the sidelines and confine themselves to occasionally cheering for their favorite "teams" (parties) or "players" (politicians). They rarely attempt to become active players themselves because they do not believe they can perform effectively. A perceived lack of competence coupled with willingness to ascribe it to those assumed to be their superiors are the kinds of attitudes one might expect in a country with a political culture having a strong conservative component.

A fourth and related theme is the preference for "elite accommodation" as the dominant mode of political decision-making.[13] Since Canadian society is characterized by deep-seated, reinforcing ethnolinguistic, religious and regional cleavages, the prospects for political stability are enhanced by the willingness of ordinary citizens in the various subcultures defined by these cleavages to remain largely uninvolved in the political process. This permits political elites from these subcultures to bargain with one another in processes of mutual accommodation. Elite accommodation as the operative political style is strengthened by the tendency of political leaders to define the most crucial aspects of the political process in terms of interactions between federal and provincial levels of government, by an emphasis on periodic elections as the primary form of citizen participation and, more generally, by the strength of conservative and quasi-participative elements in the political culture.

Fifth, the pervasiveness of elite accommodation processes notwithstanding, in recent years a number of studies have concluded that Canadian political culture varies significantly from one region or province to the next.[14] The strength of conservatism and traditional patron-client relationships[15] is said to be greatest in the Atlantic provinces and weakest in the West. In the latter region, support for radical ideologies and political movements is stronger than elsewhere. Attitudes conducive to citizen participation in politics are most pronounced in British Columbia and weakest among Québécois and residents of the Maritimes. Again, support for the existing federal system is strongest in Ontario and weakest in Quebec and the West. The emphasis accorded these or other specific differences in regional or provincial political cultures varies from study to study. What they have in common is their stress on the significance of regional and provincial cultural differences for understanding the conduct of politics within particular provinces and the larger political system.

This brief review of principal themes in descriptions of Canadian political culture indicates that the range of beliefs, attitudes and opinions which might be included in a study of provincial political culture is very great. Indeed, if one accepts the proposition that regional, provincial or other subgroup differences are significant, the task of fully delineating political cultural orientations in 10 provinces assumes Herculean proportions. Here, our inquiry is limited to cultural orientations which seem especially relevant for the development and maintenance of representative democracy and the extent to which these are present in various provinces. Before doing so, on the assumption that any political culture reflects certain underlying configurations of social and economic conditions that are products of the development of a society over time, we provide a brief overview of Canada's social and economic development. Particular attention will be paid to variations in the provinces' current levels of industrialization, the magnitudes and values of their natural resource bases, and the extent to which they have developed their respective educational systems.

Since political behaviour is affected by a variety of beliefs, attitudes and opinions, only some of which are manifestly political, several diverse but politically relevant aspects of provincial cultures also will be examined. First, we will consider social and political trust. Representative democracies are fragile entities resting on consensus rather than coercion. As noted above, therefore, trust in others is an important (perhaps *the* most important) factor facilitating popular acceptance of the "rules of the democratic game."[16] Trust in political leaders also is important. While this should be limited and conditional, its lower bound should be a measure of healthy skepticism rather than a generalized and corrosive cynicism. The second set of orientations to be examined concern the nature and origin of social classes. For well over a century many social and political theorists have argued that social class is the crucial politically relevant cleavage in advanced industrial societies.[17] Some theorists also have contended that class conflict is dangerous because it has the potential to destroy the societal consensus needed to make democracy work, while still others maintain that class conflict can play a vital role in enhancing the democratic character of existing political systems.[18] To the extent that class conflict revolves around questions pertaining to an equitable division of societal resources, it would appear that the latter argument has merit. As noted above, a reasonably equitable division of wealth and the provision of substantial educational and material resources to the vast majority of citizens are held to be important prerequisites for the achievement of representative democracy. Studying popular attitudes toward the existence, origins and political significance of social classes may facilitate an understanding of the present realities and future potential of class-based politics and, by extension, the prospects for representative democracy in the several provinces.

Since attitudes towards issues such as the distribution and redistribution of wealth in a society are at least partially affected by people's perceptions of their current economic status and future well-being, we next will present data on these matters, as well as on perceptions of whether governmental actions affect people's general and economic well-being. A fourth and related task will be to determine what people in each province think government should be doing. Knowledge of the public's priorities can help illuminate those aspects of political culture which direct and set limits on governmental involvement in social and economic affairs. Because their potential impact on the character of popular participation in politics is very great, we then will consider the degree of public interest in politics and the extent to which people in various provinces feel capable of making the system respond to their wishes and actions. We will conclude the chapter with an evaluation of the extent to which existing political cultures facilitate the operation of representative democracy in the provinces.

Our approach to studying political culture is quantitative, empirical and analytic. Data from nationwide surveys conducted in 1965, 1968, 1974, 1977 and 1979 are used to delineate cultural orientations, and census and other forms of aggregate data are employed in the overview of provincial economic and social development. Such an overview indicates that although each province has experienced a significant degree of social and economic development since Confederation, marked differences in population and wealth based on the possession of natural resources and an industrial infrastructure continue to characterize them. Analyses of the survey data indicate, in contrast, that in comparative perspective, provincial cultures are much more "alike" than "different." In no province does the political culture closely approximate the representative democratic culture described above. Moreover, in most instances, observed differences are better explained by variations in the socioeconomic and demographic characteristics of residents of the several provinces than by provincial residence *per se*. Thus, unlike previous studies which have emphasized *differences* in provincial political cultures, a major argument of this chapter is that the cultural basis for representative democracy varies only marginally across the country and is not fully established in any of the provinces.

PROVINCIAL SOCIETIES AND ECONOMIES

Since birth Canada has changed from a small, economically underdeveloped, largely rural society with a population of some three million, into an advanced industrial society with a population of some 24 million, the majority of whom reside in urban areas. The population has grown because of natural causes (i.e., births in excess of deaths) and immigration. With regard to the latter, it is estimated that over nine million immigrants have arrived since 1867, with immigration being heaviest during the decade before World War One and during the post-World War Two period. Immigration patterns have made the country an ethnic polyglot. The largest ethnic groups are the Anglo-Scottish-Irish and French. However, large numbers of Canadians and their forebearers came from Central and Eastern Europe. Immigration from these areas was especially heavy between 1890 and 1920. In fact, the three Prairie provinces were populated largely by these immigrants. The tendency of immigrants to move west is reflected in the current ethnic distribution of the population. Persons of other than Anglo-Celtic or French origins currently comprise slightly over one-quarter of the population but they constitute only 3% to 12% of the populations of the Atlantic provinces and Quebec. In contrast, a majority of the residents of Saskatchewan and approximately one-half of those living in Manitoba and Alberta are of other than Anglo-Celtic or French descent, as are two-fifths of the British Columbia and one-third of the Ontario populations. Language provides another indication of the ethnic diversity of the provinces. In total, some 7% of the population speak a language other than English or French at home. However, less than 1% of the residents of the Atlantic provinces and only 4% of the residents of Quebec do so. The number of such persons in other provinces varies from a low of 7% in British Columbia to a high of 13% in Manitoba.

Not only has the distribution of population been affected by immigration, it also has been influenced very strongly by internal migration. The most important patterns have been east to west and rural to urban-metropolitan. Regarding the east-west flow, in 1871 people in Prince Edward Island, Nova Scotia and New Brunswick made up 20% of the population. Quebec contributed 35%, Ontario 43%, and British Columbia, 2%. In 1976, people in the four Atlantic provinces constituted less than 10% of the population, Quebec 27%, Ontario 36%, the Prairies 16% and British Columbia 11%. These changes obscure the fact that in the post-World War Two period only three provinces, Ontario, Alberta and British Columbia, have experienced significant gains in population. In the mid-1950s the birthrate began to fall, particularly in Quebec. In addition, people leaving the Atlantic provinces, Quebec, Manitoba and Saskatchewan in search of greater economic opportunities usually found them in Ontario and the two westernmost provinces.

With respect to the rural to urban movement, in 1871 less than one-fifth of the people lived in urban areas. One hundred and five years later over three quarters of Canada was urban and only in Prince Edward Island did a majority of residents still live in rural areas. Moreover, and as might be expected, two-thirds of the people of Ontario and over half of those in Quebec, Manitoba and Alberta now live in metropolitan areas. This also is the case for almost half of the residents of British Columbia, a third of Nova Scotia, a quarter of Newfoundland and about a fifth of New Brunswick. Despite the concentration of population in 23 metropolitan areas, the average population density, even if the Yukon and Northwest Territories are excluded, is still among the lowest in the world.

Since many of the immigrants who came to Canada were men, the sex ratio until relatively recently has favoured males, reaching a peak of 113/110 in 1911. The proportion of females has risen steadily since then, and by 1976 it was greater than the proportion of males. With the decline of the birthrate and improved health care the proportion of the population under 15 has declined whereas that 65 and over has increased. Census figures show Newfoundland has the largest proportion of young people and Saskatchewan the largest proportion of older persons. In the 1970s Newfoundland had both the highest birthrate and the lowest deathrate. Overall, the average life expectancy of both men and women was highest in Saskatchewan and lowest in Quebec.

Perhaps the most dramatic change that has occurred over time is in the level of education Canadians enjoy. Prince Edward Island was the first (1852) to provide publicly supported education. After Confederation the provinces established departments of education, provided public funds for their support and passed legislation making school attendance compulsory. Higher education also had its beginnings before Confederation (e.g., Dalhousie, 1818; King's College of Toronto, 1817; and Laval, 1852) thanks to the efforts of several religious denominations. Over the years the increase in the number of people attending schools consistently has exceeded the general rate of population growth.[19] For the first 60 years of this century, for example, the population increased by 240%, the number attending school by 370%. During the 1960s growth in the proportions of the population enrolled in public and secondary schools in every province continued to be substantially higher than the rates of population increase (see Table 3.1). Moreover, during the 1950s and 60s there generally were even greater increases in university enrollments. For example, in Ontario, between 1960 and 1970, the population grew only half as fast as public school enrollments but the increase in full-time university enrollments exceeded population growth by fourteen fold. Other notable increases in university enrollments during that decade occurred in Newfoundland, Prince Edward Island and Alberta.

The decline in the birthrate after the post-World War Two "baby boom" and its impact on education also are reflected in Table 3.1. Although each province experienced a net increase in population during the past decade, public school enrollments declined over what they had been in the '60s in all but Alberta and British Columbia; Ontario's remained constant. University enrollments in the '70s continued to increase in six provinces, although in only three (Nova Scotia, Quebec and Ontario) did they exceed the rate of increase in the general population.

TABLE 3.1
Changes in General Population, Proportion Enrolled in Primary and
Secondary Schools, and Proportion Enrolled in Universities,
1950–1977 (in percent)

	1951–1961	1950–1960		1961–1971	1960–1971		1971–1976	1971–1977	
	Percent Change in Population	Percent Change in Primary and Secondary School Enrollments	Percent Change in Full-Time University Enrollments	Percent Change in Population	Percent Change in Primary and Secondary School Enrollments	Percent Change in Full-Time University Enrollments	Percent Change in Population	Percent Change in Primary School Enrollments	Percent Change in Full-Time University Enrollments
Newfoundland	+27%	+63%	+225%	+14%	+26%	+472%	+8%	-3%	-6%
Prince Edward Island	+6	+34	+108	+7	+29	+214	+8	0	-20
Nova Scotia	+15	+29	+43	+8	+20	+185	+6	-5	+10
New Brunswick	+16	+44	+98	+6	+12	+169	+8	-7	0
Quebec	+30	+71	+78	+15	+44	+66	+4	-11	+21
Ontario	+35	+81	+39	+24	+46	+318	+9	0	+19
Manitoba	+19	+47	+36	+7	+29	+177	+4	-1	+4
Saskatchewan	+11	+25	+106	0	+17	+162	+1	-8	-3
Alberta	+42	+69	+120	+22	+45	+302	+17	+5	+12
British Columbia	+40	+85	+91	+34	+63	+120	+14	+7	+9

Increases in public education have roughly paralleled the growth of industrialization in Canada. Although all the provinces have experienced some degree of industrialization, they differ markedly in the extent to which the industrial process has advanced. By way of illustration, in 1975 there were more than 12,000 individual manufacturing units in Ontario employing more than 600,000 people — some 18% of the provincial labour force. Quebec had over 9,000 units employing 18% of its labour force, whereas the next two most industrialized provinces, British Columbia and Alberta, had only some 3,000 and 2,000 manufacturing units employing, respectively, 11% and 7% of their labour forces. Another indication of interprovincial differences is data on the manufactured goods exported by the several provinces in 1961 and 1977. In both years, the value of goods exported by Ontario and Quebec was far in excess of the export value of goods manufactured by any of the other provinces. Further, although there was a three-fold increase in the value of goods exported by British Columbia, Nova Scotia and New Brunswick and a four-fold increase in the value of Alberta's manufactured exports over this 16-year period, Ontario's and Quebec's exports also showed handsome increases in value. Still another indication of interprovincial differences is "value added" to a product as a consequence of manufacturing. In this respect, there is an enormous gap between the value added to the goods manufactured in Ontario and Quebec and those manufactured in other provinces, an indication of the concentration of industrial strength in the former two provinces.

One should not conclude from the above discussion that British Columbia and Alberta are impoverished. It has been estimated that in 1971, when the effects of differences in the provinces' occupational structures were controlled (i.e., when, for example, the fact that Ontario has a larger number of high income-producing professionals than have other provinces is taken into account), the populations of only three provinces enjoyed above-average incomes: British Columbia residents with incomes 9% above the national average, Ontarians with incomes 6% above average and Albertans with incomes 0.5% above average.[20] At the other end of the income continuum, residents of Prince Edward Island had incomes that were fully 20% below the national average, with New Brunswick, Newfoundland, Nova Scotia, Saskatchewan, Manitoba and Quebec ranging between 16% and 5% below average. Five years later (1976), British Columbians enjoyed the highest and Albertans the second highest average weekly earnings in the country. That same year, Alberta ranked first and British Columbia third in terms of other indicators of economic well-being such as the number of telephones per 1,000 population and the per capita value of current construction projects. Data on gross annual provincial product in millions of dollars for each of the provinces for the period 1962-77 provide additional evidence of the increasing prosperity of Alberta and British Columbia. At the beginning of this period Ontario and Quebec had the highest gross provincial products. In 1961, the per capita value of the gross provincial product of Ontario was $2,860; British Columbia's was $2,693; Alberta's $2,550; while Quebec's was $2,180. In 1976 Alberta's provincial product was approximately $2,000 higher than British Columbia's, $2,200 higher than Ontario's and fully $4,000 higher than Quebec's. In great part, the latter figures reflect the increase in the value of Alberta's petroleum and natural gas products following the 1973 Arab oil embargo.

Historically, provincial governments have tried to use their resource wealth to develop or enlarge their industrial base. Ontario public officials used the province's forest and hydroelectric resources to generate revenue, increase provincial self-reliance, and create or enhance support for existing industries.[21] Currently, Quebec is pursuing a similar policy with respect to hydroelectric energy, Saskatchewan is exploiting its vast potash deposits, and Alberta, British Columbia and Newfoundland are developing their fossil fuel resources. Nonetheless, the fact remains that both with respect to their industrial bases and the amount and value of their natural resources, some provinces (Alberta, British Columbia, Ontario) are highly favoured, others (Manitoba, Quebec, Saskatchewan) somewhat less so, and still others (New Brunswick, Newfoundland, Nova Scotia, Prince Edward Island) not at all. Moreover, barring unforeseen new resource finds or dramatic increases in their industrial bases, the economic condition of these latter provinces is likely to remain relatively unchanged in the foreseeable future.

Although there are many economic differences among provinces, there are also important similarities. One of them is particularly noteworthy here, namely the populations of all provinces are characterized by sharp differences in levels of income and education and types of occupations pursued. Thus, for example, in 1975, on a cumulative distribution of annual family income the lowest one-fifth of the population received only 4% of all income; the upper one-fifth received 42%.[22] Regarding education, in 1971 10% of the population had attended a college or university while 37% had terminated their formal educations at the elementary school level.[23] As for occupation, in 1971 less than 20% of persons in the work force were classified as professional or managerial personnel but well over 50% were engaged in blue collar, service, sales or clerical work.[24] To reiterate, the relevance of these inequalities lies in the fact that levels of income and education and type of occupation pursued affect the amount and kinds of resources available for effective political participation. To the extent that some people have markedly fewer of these resources than others, full implementation of representative democracy in the provinces is inhibited.

The social and economic conditions of the several provinces and changes in them over time have heavily influenced the quality of people's lives and thus are important in their own right. As previously noted, however, they also are important because they constitute crucial aspects of the environments of the provincial political systems. In addition to affecting levels and kinds of resources citizens may utilize to facilitate their political involvements, one of the most important ways in which social and economic conditions influence politics is by affecting the beliefs, attitudes and opinions which, taken together, constitute the politically relevant elements of a society's culture. Such cultural elements, in turn, powerfully shape political behaviour and ultimately the possibilities for democratic governance. Here, we will begin our examination of provincial political cultures by determining whether differing levels of social and political trust distinguish the populations of particular provinces.

SOCIAL TRUST

A minimal level of social trust is a prerequisite for the existence of *any* type of political and social order because without it, conditions would approximate Hobbes' metaphoric "state of nature" — a "war of all against all: where life is nasty, brutish and short, solitary and poor." It is impossible to specify precisely how high levels of social trust must be to ensure the successful functioning of a representative democracy. Nonetheless, the general proposition that *substantial* trust in fellow citizens is a fundamental precondition for the maintenance of a democratic polity can be readily accepted. The willingness of people to abide by the principle of majority rule and accept the functional division of political labour implied by the notion of representative government is predicated on mutual trust. Gabriel Almond and Sidney Verba make this point forcefully when they observe that "the role of social trust and cooperativeness as a component of the civic culture cannot be overemphasized. It is, in a sense, a generalized resource that keeps a democratic polity operating."[25]

Data gathered in a 1977 national survey of Canadians' economic, social and political values (hereafter referred to as the "Quality of Life" study) enable us to investigate levels of trust among persons living in different provinces. In this survey respondents were asked the following three questions:

(1) Generally speaking, would you say that most people can be trusted or that you can't be too careful in dealing with people?
(2) Would you say that most of the time people try to be helpful or that they are mostly just looking out for themselves?
(3) Do you feel that most people would try to take advantage of you if they had the chance or would they try to be fair?[26]

Slightly less than half of the national sample judged that people could be trusted or try to be helpful, but about two-thirds said people do try to be fair. Altogether, nearly one-third of those surveyed offered two or more "trusting" responses to the three questions (see Table 3.2). Although it is difficult to make definitive judgments about the "highness" or "low-ness" of these figures in any absolute sense, some perspective may be gained by comparing them to responses to similar questions asked in surveys conducted in other countries. For example, in a 1976 survey of the American electorate slightly over one-half of the respondents thought people could be trusted or try to be helpful and just under two-thirds indicated that people try to be fair.[27] In an earlier study of political culture in five nations (the United States, Great Britain, West Germany, Italy, Mexico) the proportion of persons believing most people can be trusted ranged from approximately one-half in the United States and Great Britain to less than one-fifth in West Germany and Italy. Proportions believing most people are inclined to be helpful were approximately one-third in the former countries and less than one-fifth in the latter.[28] The available data do not permit firm conclusions, but levels of social trust in the Canadian provinces generally appear to be equivalent, or, in some instances, superior to those in many Western countries.

Perhaps the most interesting exception to the above generalization is Quebec where social trust is much lower than elsewhere. For example, Ontarians are twice as likely to find fellow citizens trustworthy; three times as likely to see them as being helpful, and half again as likely to judge them fair as are Quebecers (Table 3.2). Indeed, only 10% of Quebecers believe most of their fellow citizens possess any two of these traits. Low levels of social trust in Quebec are primarily attributable to

TABLE 3.2
Responses to Social Trust Questions, 1977

| Province | Percent Stating: | | | Percent Offering 2 or 3 "Trusting" Answers |
	People can Be Trusted	People Helpful	People Fair	
Newfoundland	43%	55%	77%	32%
Prince Edward Island	48	57	73	39
Nova Scotia	63	69	78	48
New Brunswick	51	69	79	42
Quebec	26	16	51	10
Ontario	50	58	70	35
Manitoba	59	62	77	46
Saskatchewan	62	75	83	50
Alberta	54	66	78	41
British Columbia	59	61	73	41
Canada	46	49	68	32

Francophones rather than Anglophones; the latter being approximately five times as likely as the former to offer at least two "trusting" responses. Other provinces also have varying levels of social trust, but these differences are considerably more modest, with the percentage of persons giving two or more trusting answers ranging from 32% in Newfoundland to 50% in Saskatchewan.

Analyzing social trust in terms of province of residence, ethnicity or language does not tell us much about the sources of such attitudinal differences. Differing levels of social trust are at least partially attributable to personality characteristics and early life socialization experiences that cannot be investigated thoroughly with available information. In a very general and indirect way, however, educational data can be used as a surrogate that reflects important socialization experiences. There are three reasons for making such an assumption. First, persons with higher levels of formal education generally develop cognitive skills and enjoy career advancement opportunities that may prompt them to see society as tractable and benign. Second, educational and career successes coupled with high levels of status attainment may reinforce positive societal images and trusting orientations toward fellow citizens. Third, as a result of extended formal education, people may well acquire an appreciation of the normative value of interacting with others on a basis of trust, equity and mutual assistance; they may have learned that it is a "good thing" to deal with others in this way. Given that level of formal education and socioeconomic status are positively associated, we may further hypothesize that social trust is class-related.

In fact, there are relatively strong relationships between social trust and educational level. The percentage of persons who believe that most people can be trusted is nearly two and one-half times greater among university graduates as among persons with elementary school educations. Similarly, social trust is markedly higher among persons with higher annual family incomes. However, one cannot conclude that variations in social trust are simply products of differences in formal education or social class more generally, because the relationship between trust and ethnicity among Quebecers (discussed previously) remains when educational and class differences are equalized. However, since the relationships between trust and education and income also persist when ethnicity is controlled, it appears that both social class and ethnic background have independent effects on the extent to which people are socially trusting.

TRUST IN POLITICAL ELITES

Representative democracy requires trust in those who govern since the very notion of representation implies a division of political labour between "the rulers" and "the ruled." Unless the general public is willing to trust political elites to be responsive to their needs and demands the long-term health of a democratic political order is problematic.[29] A pervasive lack of trust in party leaders, legislators, civil servants or other important political actors will erode support for governmental institutions such as legislative assemblies or the public service. In turn, lack of trust in political institutions may spread and deepen and the viability of the entire political community eventually may be threatened.[30] As noted, however, trust in political elites must be limited and conditional. Unquestioning faith in their leaders will keep citizens from actively involving themselves in political life to ensure that those who govern are responsive to public needs and demands.

Unfortunately, it is very difficult to establish precisely just what level of political trust is conducive to the effective functioning of a representative democracy. Also, measuring trust so that one may distinguish between feelings about governmental or other political actors as opposed to support for the political regime or the more general political community is a difficult and contentious issue.[31] The 1979 national election study attempted to tap feelings of trust in *governmental* elites by asking respondents if they agreed or disagreed with the following statements:

(1) Many people in government are dishonest.
(2) People in government waste a lot of the money we pay in taxes.
(3) Most of the time we can trust people in government to do what is right.
(4) Most of the people running government are smart people who usually know what they are doing.

Responses to these questions (see Table 3.3) reveal two important points. First, except for displaying an overwhelming belief that those in government waste the public's tax dollars, most persons manifest at least some trust in governmental elites. Overall, slightly over two-fifths of the respondents make three or more "trusting" responses to the four questions. This pattern is different from that of the United States where, in recent years, in response to very similar questions, citizens have demonstrated a pervasive lack of trust in specific political leaders as well as government more generally.[32] Second, at least moderate levels of trust in governmental elites are characteristic of every province including Quebec (which, it will be recalled, was markedly lower on *social* trust than other provinces). Even in Newfoundland, where the level of trust in governmental elites is lowest, over one-third of those surveyed offer three or more "trusting" responses. Also indicative of the modest provincial variations in trust in governmental elites is the fact that the mean number of trusting responses varies only slightly — from a low of 1.8 in Newfoundland to a high of 2.3 in Prince Edward Island, Quebec and Saskatchewan.

Trust in governmental elites also differs from social trust in that differences among socioeconomic groups are generally quite small. The differences between persons with elementary school educations and

TABLE 3.3
Trust in Governmental Leaders, 1979

Province	Many People in Government are Dishonest (% Disagreeing)	People in Government Waste a Lot of Money (% Disagreeing)	People in Government Do What's Right (% Agreeing)	People in Government are Smart (% Agreeing)	Percent Offering 3 or 4 "Trusting" Answers
Newfoundland	43%	10%	68%	59%	34%
Prince Edward Island	68	20	66	74	48
Nova Scotia	56	16	75	67	42
New Brunswick	51	23	61	68	40
Quebec	57	33	63	76	46
Ontario	64	15	70	67	43
Manitoba	55	13	67	76	41
Saskatchewan	66	20	79	64	45
Alberta	66	14	76	66	43
British Columbia	56	12	68	65	37
Canada	60	19	69	69	43

those with college or university degrees making three or more trusting responses is only 10%. Generally, most of the differences in trust among socioeconomic groups are attributable to their differing responses to the "people in government are dishonest" question. Nearly half again as many people who have attended or graduated from a college or university as compared to those with elementary school educations or less attest to the honesty of governmental elites. The pattern using a general measure of socioeconomic status (the Blishen scale of occupational prestige) instead of educational level is virtually identical.

Other intergroup differences in trust are even smaller. For five age groups in the population differences in the number of persons making three or more trusting answers never exceed 5%. As for ethnicity, considering the country as a whole, variations among major ethnic groups are less than 10%. Even in Quebec, where Québécois manifest higher levels of trust in governmental elites than do persons of Anglo-Celtic or other ethnic backgrounds, the observed differences do not exceed 15%.

In general, then, there are both similarities and differences between the pattern of trust in governmental elites and that for social trust discussed earlier. In both cases, levels of trust are quite similar throughout much of the country. Unlike social trust, however, trust in governmental elites is not lower in Quebec than elsewhere. Also, unlike social trust, trust in governmental elites has only very weak relationships with societal cleavage variables such as socioeconomic status and ethnicity. Given the weakness of these relationships, the sources of trust in governmental elites are not evident from our analyses.[33] Moreover, the current status of trust in governmental elites as a cultural resource for the sustenance of representative democracy in the provinces is unclear. Intuitively, overall levels of trust appear "moderate," but it is evident that perceptions of government waste are the principal reason that they are not higher. This, and the fact that responses to the trust questions do not unambiguously reveal *why* people said what they did, suggest that we should be cautious about concluding that people in the provinces manifest the "limited and conditional" trust in public officials that is conducive to the development and sustenance of representative democracy.

Governmental elites are only a subset of the broader category of political elites, and there is reason to believe that many Canadians perceive them as less than completely trustworthy. Questions about politicians in public opinion surveys have yielded many negative responses.[34] This phenomenon is not new. Data from surveys conducted in the 1960s and 70s illustrate its persistence and pervasiveness. For example, in 1974, when presented with a blank map of Canada and requested to write five comments about politics, slightly over two-fifths of all responses concerned the behaviour and performance of politicians.

Strikingly, 60% of these references to politicians were negative and only 13% were positive.[35] Considerable negative feeling for politicians also is present in the 1979 national survey responses concerning what comes to mind when the word "politics" is mentioned. In every province large numbers (from 41% to 58%) of persons answer by discussing politicians. Nearly two-fifths of these comments are distinctly negative in tone, three-fifths are neutral and only one in 20 is positive. Viewed in a somewhat different perspective, over two-thirds of all the negative comments made about *any* aspect of politics concerned politicians. These negative comments are prevalent in every province and among all major ethnic, educational and socioeconomic groups in the population.

The implications for political trust of the negative tone of the comments about politicians in surveys conducted over the past 20 years are not completely clear. Certainly, a negative comment about a particular politician and a generalized lack of trust in political elites are not the same thing. Still, the pervasiveness of such negative comments and the fact that they are made about many political actors and not just one or two *bête noirs* suggest that many citizens in every province may have a generalized propensity to distrust their political leaders. To the extent that this is true, prospects for representative democracy are inhibited.

SOCIAL CLASS

In many advanced industrial societies social class divisions have important political consequences. Since the middle of the 19th century political and social theorists repeatedly have hypothesized that divisions based upon social class differences will become the predominant bases of political conflict, replacing older pre-industrial cleavages such as ethnicity, religion and region. Contrary to this hypothesis, Canada provides an example of a contemporary industrialized society where social class has *not* replaced other societal divisions (e.g., ethnicity, region) as the basis of political conflict.[36] A note of caution is in order, however, since most existing research on relationships between societal cleavages and political behaviour has been conducted at the federal level. In provincial politics, class divisions may be considerably more important in at least some instances. Perhaps the most salient example is British Columbia, but Saskatchewan and, more recently, Manitoba and Ontario also are cited by some observers as having significant levels of "class politics."[37]

Certainly, in an objective sense, there is no doubt that social classes exist in every province. As noted above, using conventional sociological measures of social class (occupation, income, education), it is everywhere apparent that income is unequally distributed, educational attainment varies widely and the kinds of occupations pursued differ markedly. However, the objective reality of social class is one thing, perceptions of that reality are quite another. In order for class differences to affect political behaviour, at a minimum people must think of themselves as members of a class and assess their class positions correctly. John Porter and others have argued that in Canada the majority of people do not think of themselves in class terms or, if they do, they think (or, perhaps more accurately, have been led to believe) that they are members of the middle class.[38] As a result, class conflict is severely muted. Survey evidence strongly indicates, however, that many Canadians do think of themselves in class terms. Well over two-fifths of those interviewed in the 1979 national election survey thought of themselves as belonging to a social class (see Table 3.4). Nearly one-third felt "close" to "their" class. Regarding the content of those self-perceptions, either spontaneously or after being requested to do so, 11% of the 1979 sample placed themselves in the upper or upper-middle classes, approximately one-half (52%) chose the middle class and 35% selected the working or lower classes. Comparable 1974 figures are very similar, the largest difference being that 41% chose the working or lower classes. In both surveys only relatively small minorities flatly refused a class label (3% in 1979 and 1% in 1974).[39]

Social class perceptions are not perfectly uniform across the country. Most noticeably, Quebecers are considerably more likely (58%) to see themselves in class terms (Table 3.4). Elsewhere, the incidence of spontaneous class self-perceptions is very similar, ranging from a low of 31% in Prince Edward Island to a high of 39% in Newfoundland, Manitoba and British Columbia. Small provincial differences also are evident in feelings of "closeness" to members of one's own class — in every case only minorities have such feelings. Differences by province in the distribution of class self-image also are modest. In every province substantial numbers of people are willing to place themselves in the working or lower classes.

Finally, there are strong, if imperfect, correlations between characteristics such as occupation, education, and income and subjective class placements. The number of persons in the 1979 national sample placing themselves in the upper or middle classes increases from 47% to 87% as one moves from the lowest to the highest category of the Blishen measure of occupational prestige.[40] Likewise, 44% of those with elementary school education or less, as compared to 81% of persons who have at least one university degree, place themselves in these classes. Similar patterns obtain in all provinces. The nature and pervasiveness of these relationships between objective and subjective indicators of social class suggest, contrary to Porter's argument, that the subjective social class orientations in provincial political cultures frequently are rooted in the socioeconomic realities of provincial societies.

This finding notwithstanding, the translation of social class perceptions into a politically-relevant societal cleavage remains a complex

TABLE 3.4
Social Class Perceptions, 1979

Province	% Perceiving Self in Class Terms	% Feeling "Pretty Close" to Own Class	% Stating "There is Bound to be Some Conflict Between Different Social Classes"	Subjective Class Perceptions (horizontal %)			
				Upper and Upper Middle Class	Middle Class	Working, Lower Class	Denies Class
Newfoundland	39%	32%	43%	7%	46	47	0
Prince Edward Island	31	22	46	4%	57	38	1
Nova Scotia	33	28	56	8%	49	41	2
New Brunswick	32	28	42	5%	38	50	8
Quebec	58	37	41	11%	59	29	1
Ontario	38	26	48	13%	49	36	2
Manitoba	39	28	61	5%	42	48	5
Saskatchewan	34	27	52	5%	53	38	5
Alberta	36	27	48	9%	49	33	9
British Columbia	39	24	54	14%	49	34	4
Canada	43	29	47	11%	52	35	3

process because the politics of social class in part are grounded in conflicting beliefs people hold about an equitable distribution and redistribution of societal goods and services.[41] More specifically, beliefs about whether there are basic minimum shares of various societal resources to which every citizen in "entitled" and, if so, what the magnitudes of these entitlements are, as well as the conditions under which they may be claimed, play an important role in defining the extent to which class divisions achieve political relevance.

In the 1977 Quality of Life survey, people were questioned about their attitudes toward the redistribution of wealth and asked their opinions about the origins of social classes. With respect to the former, in all provinces, majorities of varying sizes (ranging from 53% in Prince Edward Island to 79% in Newfoundland) agreed that there was "too much difference between rich and poor in this country." Also, everywhere but in New Brunswick and Saskatchewan majorities (from 56% in Manitoba to 69% in Quebec) agreed that "people with high incomes should pay a greater share of the total taxes than they do now." Thus, the idea of redistributing wealth has substantial but far from unanimous support in all parts of the country, suggesting that there may be considerable potential in every province for politicizing class cleavages. However, opinions regarding the *origins* of class divisions indicate such an inference is problematic. Large majorities in all provinces agreed that "upper and lower classes exist because people are naturally unequal in character and ability." Nationally, 71% held this opinion, with levels of agreement ranging from a low of 61% in Quebec to a high of 77% in Alberta. Moreover, unlike opinions favouring the redistribution of wealth which are class-related (i.e., fewer wealthy people feel differences between rich and poor are too great, or want higher taxes for high income people), perceptions that class inequalities are an unavoidable outcome of natural differences in ability are widespread in all income and educational categories (e.g., between two-thirds and three-quarters of those in every income bracket share the perception that class differences are natural). The extent to which this view is shared among all social classes may sharply limit the ability of redistribution issues to stimulate class conflict.

ECONOMIC AND LIFE SATISFACTION

A departure point for many studies of Canadian politics is the observation that the country is characterized by persistent regional and provincial economic disparities. The extent of some of these differences in provincial wealth already have been documented in this chapter. It often has been argued that levels of economic well-being profoundly influence political behaviour at both the federal and provincial levels. Perhaps most notably, provincial economic disparities have been and continue to be a source of serious conflict in the federal system. Indeed, some observers believe they presently threaten the stability of the political order. Implicit in arguments about the importance of provincial economies is the assumption that the nature and volume of demands on the political system reflect, in part at least, the influence of economic conditions on people's levels of material and more general life satisfaction. Satisfied people make fewer and more moderate demands on government. But how satisfied are Canadians with economic or other aspects of their lives? Do satisfaction levels vary from one province to the next? To answer these questions the 1977 Quality of Life survey measured economic and more general life satisfaction using a ten point ladder scale.[42] Respondents were requested to rank their present level of satisfaction, that of the average person in Canada, what they expected in five years, and what they judged they deserved "right now."

Nationally, Canadians seem fairly satisfied with their general life situations (mean score = 7.2, maximum value = 10.0), and are optimistic about their future in that they expect conditions to be even better in five years (mean = 8.3). They also feel that they deserve better right now (mean = 8.2). However, they couple these feelings with widespread perceptions that they personally are better off than the "average" person (the average score ascribed to the latter is 6.0). These patterns obtain for the country as a whole and for every province considered separately. It also is noteworthy, despite substantial objective differences in living standards in various provinces, that provincial differences in the life satisfaction scores are slight.[43]

Scores on the economic ladders generally are somewhat lower than those for comparable life satisfaction measures (e.g., national means on the economic ladders are: present status = 6.0; five years hence = 7.4; deserve right now = 7.7; average Canadian = 5.6).[44] In every province people manifest ambivalent economic attitudes: they regard themselves as better off than the average person, they feel the future will bring improvements, but they deserve better right now. Finally, similar to the life satisfaction scores, provincial differences in economic satisfaction scores are slight. This is true not only of present economic satisfaction scores which range from averages of 5.8 in Newfoundland, Saskatchewan and British Columbia to 6.2 in Quebec and Manitoba, but also of perceptions of future conditions (range = 6.8 in Newfoundland to 7.4 in Ontario and British Columbia) and judgments of what is deserved right now (range = 7.2 in Prince Edward Island to 8.0 in Quebec). To reiterate, it would appear that economic disparities among provinces do not have strong effects on citizens' judgments about their personal life satisfaction and economic well-being.[45]

The political ramifications of these perceptions are difficult to specify without additional information. How judgments regarding economic well-being or more general life satisfaction are translated into demands on the political system depends upon beliefs about the proper scope and substance of governmental activity and the impact of ongoing government programs. The former will be considered in the section below. As for the latter, survey data suggest that many Canadians judge that governmental actions *do* affect their material and more general life satisfaction. In the 1979 national election study 29% perceived that government had "a great deal" of influence on their material well-being and a further 37% accorded "some" influence to government. On a provincial basis the percentage ascribing at least some influence on economic well-being to government varies from a low of 55% in New Brunswick to a high of 81% in Saskatchewan. Many persons also felt that government actions influenced their lives more generally. For the country as a whole, 16% and 35%, respectively, judged that government had "a great deal" or "some" impact on life satisfaction. Provincially, at least two-fifths of the populations of every province except Nova Scotia (35%) accorded government at least some influence on their life satisfaction.

These data on individual perceptions of economic and more general life satisfaction and government's impact thereon suggest that there is considerable "demand potential" for governmental action in all parts of the country. This is particularly true in the economic sphere since many people appear to be only moderately satisfied with their present situations, feel they deserve better and expect improvement in the years ahead. What converts these perceptions and judgments into politically relevant cultural orientations is a widely shared belief (by two of every three people) that government actions affect people's economic well-being. Together, these orientations establish conditions under which the federal and provincial governments are expected to make people's lives better and are judged on the basis of how well they do so. This being the case, it is important to inquire what people want from government in the way of programs.

DEMANDS ON GOVERNMENT

Data in the Quality of Life study can assist us in answering questions about what people expect of government. In this study people were asked to specify how much effort the government should put into several different areas and at the same time cautioned to keep in mind that "putting more effort into one of these areas would require a shift of money from other areas or an increase in taxes."[46] Perhaps the most striking aspect of responses to this question is the high level of demand expressed for increased governmental activity in *many different* areas. Over half of those interviewed wanted "more" or "much more" government effort in 12 of the 21 areas listed (see Table 3.5). Conversely, there were only three areas in which as many as one-quarter of those surveyed requested "less" or "much less" effort. Fully 86% of the public wanted the government to intervene to create more jobs and reduce inflation. Three of every four people wanted more environmental protection and almost as many wanted the government to do more about national unity. The only areas where as many as one person in four wanted *less* government activity were bilingualism, foreign aid and unemployment assistance.

Analyzing responses for each of the 21 areas of government activity in each province would be a labour of Sisyphus. Fortunately, a statistical technique (factor analysis) enables us to make this large amount of information more manageable. The analysis detects underlying general patterns or "factors" which govern responses to the 21 specific items. The first factor to emerge from this analysis is labelled "social welfare/economic." It is associated primarily with responses to such items as health care, job creation, increased assistance to retired people

TABLE 3.5
Distribution of Public Demands on Government, 1977
(horizontal percentages)

Area	Amount of Government Effort Desired				
	Much More	More	Some	Less	Much Less
Health care	14%	33	50	3	0
Native peoples' rights	11%	42	37	9	2
Assist unemployed	13%	24	31	21	5
Support business community	5%	30	47	16	3
Promote bilingualism	9%	25	28	23	15
Create jobs	40%	46	10	3	1
Maintain national unity	30%	42	23	4	1
Help poor	24%	42	30	4	1
Crime prevention	28%	43	28	1	0
Build public housing	15%	35	38	10	2
End discrimination against women	18%	34	37	9	3
Cut inflation	45%	41	12	2	0
Eliminate pornography	31%	27	28	10	4
Protect environment	31%	47	20	1	1
Provide daycare	13%	37	37	10	4
Foreign aid	4%	15	50	24	8
Education	19%	36	40	5	1
National defense	9%	28	49	11	4
Help retired people	27%	45	27	1	0
Workmen's compensation	15%	31	50	4	0
Decrease regional inequality	13%	43	38	6	1

and workmen's compensation. The second, "security/morality," is related most strongly to the elimination of pornography and the bolstering of national defense. Loading heavily on the third factor, designated "post-materialist,"[47] are the rights of native peoples, environmental protection, discrimination against women and efforts to lessen regional inequalities. The fourth and fifth factors, i.e., "bilingualism/national unity" and "foreign aid/economic," are associated primarily with responses to these specific items.[48] Using statistical information generated by the factor analysis we are able to create five indices (one for each factor) which reflect the emphasis a person places on each of the five areas of possible governmental action.[49]

Opinions regarding desired governmental activity differ from one province to the next. The call for greater effort in the social welfare/economic field is most pronounced in three of the Atlantic provinces (Newfoundland, Nova Scotia and New Brunswick) and in Quebec. Increased efforts to promote bilingualism and national unity are most desired by Quebecers and least wanted by residents of the Prairie provinces. Persons in the West also are least in favour of foreign aid. The post-materialist issues (rights of native peoples, discrimination against women, etc.) have their greatest appeal for people in Quebec and Newfoundland while the demand for action on morality and national defense is of approximately equal strength in every province.

Which demands on government a person emphasizes are related to characteristics other than province of residence. Consistent, for instance, with the argument that political orientations frequently are associated with socioeconomic status are correlations between the emphasis placed on social welfare/economic matters and income and educational levels. As might be expected, demand for more action in the social welfare areas is strongest among persons with the lowest levels of income and education. These attributes also are associated with an emphasis on morality and law and order issues. Additionally, education, but not income, is related to a stress on the post-materialist issues, such issues being accorded priority by persons with high levels of formal education.[50] Demographic characteristics such as ethnicity and age also are associated with differences in opinions about governmental priorities. Francophones tend to stress bilingualism/national unity and social welfare/economic issues; older people are more concerned with morality and law and order; and younger people give particular emphasis to post-materialist issues and foreign aid.

Are there distinct provincial political-cultural differences in the demands people place on government or can these be accounted for by variations in the sociodemographic characteristics of persons living in different provinces?[51] For example, can the emphasis placed on social welfare issues by Maritimers be explained by the fact that there are many poor people living in the area, or is there something about the political culture of this region which produces such an emphasis independently of the socioeconomic status of its residents? One method of answering this kind of question is to examine correlations between provincial residency and governmental priorities while holding constant people's socioeconomic and demographic characteristics (age, education and income). Such an examination reveals contrasting patterns for different areas of possible government action. The emphasis placed on social welfare/economic priorities is related to both provincial residence and sociodemographic characteristics, whereas the importance accorded bilingualism and national unity seems to be a product of provincial residence alone. Yet another pattern is that manifested for the post-materialist issues. The priority people assign to governmental action in this area is related, but very weakly, to both demographic characteristics and provincial residency. In sum, both sociodemographic characteristics and provincial residence are relevant for comprehending patterns of demand for different kinds of government action, but neither provide a complete explanation of these patterns.[52] Moreover, the importance ascribed to some governmental priorities — particularly those respecting issues involving the rights of women and minority groups or environmental protection — tends to cut across traditional socioeconomic and provincial/regional cleavages in the population.

POLITICAL EFFICACY

Several previous studies of provincial political cultures have emphasized the concept of political efficacy.[53] Political efficacy may be defined as "a sense that one can be personally influential in politics, can make one's voice heard, and can be effective."[54] As argued above, political efficacy is an important aspect of political culture in a representative democracy. Persons with a strong sense of political efficacy are more likely to participate in the political process. For their part, recognition by political elites that feelings of efficacy are widespread stimulates them to respond to public needs and demands and to try to anticipate citizen reactions to their behaviour.[55] By enhancing the sensitivity of elites to expressed and anticipated public problems, efficacy plays an important role in the operation of representational processes. Additionally, in the context of a political culture which emphasizes the appropriateness and utility of citizen participation, efficacy is important because of its relationship to the generation of supportive public attitudes for democratic institutions and processes. Indeed, in such a cultural context, the feeling of being able to exert political influence is perhaps the most important reason people have for regarding an existing political order as legitimate.[56]

Political efficacy traditionally has been measured using "agree/disagree" responses to statements such as the following:

(1) I don't think that the government cares much what people like me think.
(2) Sometimes politics and government seem so complicated that a person like me can't really understand what's going on.
(3) People like me don't have any say about what the government does.
(4) Generally, those elected to Parliament soon lose touch with the people.[57]

A close reading of these statements suggests that the second and third basically are measuring a person's sense of political *competence*, whereas the first and fourth are eliciting perceptions of governmental *responsiveness*.[58] For every statement, disagreement signifies the presence of politically efficacious feelings.

Provincial distributions of average political efficacy scores in 1977 (see Table 3.6) indicate that Ontarians are the most and Newfoundlanders the least likely to feel that government is responsive (statements 1 and 4 above). Newfoundlanders also have the lowest whereas British Columbians have the highest political competency scores (statements 2 and 3). On an overall efficacy index based on responses to all four statements, Ontarians rank highest, Newfoundlanders lowest. More generally, however, provincial differences in these scores are modest. The dominant impression derived from the data is that levels of political efficacy tend to be relatively low in all provinces. By way of illustration, on the overall index, in no province is the mean score as high as 2.0 (i.e., the score obtained by a person who gives efficacious responses to one-half of the efficacy items), and nowhere do as many as one-quarter of the 1977 respondents make three or more efficacious responses (see Table 3.6). Furthermore, the generally low levels of efficacy exhibited in 1977 are by no means unique. Analyses of identical political efficacy items in the 1965, 1968, 1974 and 1979 national surveys yield very similar results. In every instance provincial differences in efficacy are statistically significant but small.[59] In our view, rather than stressing such differences (as some observers have done), when evaluating provincial political systems as representative democracies, it is more important to emphasize that low levels of efficacy characterize citizens in every province.

Comparing levels of political efficacy over the past 15 years indicates there has been a modest decline in efficacy throughout most of the 1970s, with a slight upturn at the end of the decade. As Figure 3.1 illustrates, this is particularly true of the responsiveness dimension of efficacy. For example, the proportion of respondents disagreeing with the proposition that "those elected to Parliament soon lose touch with the people" declines from nearly two-fifths to less than one-quarter over the four surveys conducted between 1965 and 1977 and rebounds to one-third in 1979. Considering the responsiveness index, the national mean scores vary from .85 in 1965 to .61 in 1977 and then climb to .78 in

TABLE 3.6
Political Efficacy, 1977

Province	Responsiveness Index		Perceived Competence Index		Overall Efficacy Index	
	Mean Score	% Making 2 Efficacious Responses	Mean Score	% Making 2 Efficacious Responses	Mean Score	% Making 3 or 4 Efficacious Responses
Newfoundland	0.47	8	0.55	9	1.02	14
Prince Edward Island	0.69	24	0.59	16	1.27	24
Nova Scotia	0.65	19	0.65	16	1.30	20
New Brunswick	0.62	15	0.68	12	1.30	14
Quebec	0.57	15	0.80	23	1.36	21
Ontario	0.68	18	0.78	18	1.46	22
Manitoba	0.53	16	0.65	18	1.18	19
Saskatchewan	0.62	16	0.64	15	1.26	19
Alberta	0.61	16	0.72	16	1.33	16
British Columbia	0.58	14	0.87	22	1.45	19
Canada	0.62	16	0.76	19	1.38	20

1979. Competence scores, in contrast, show no consistent pattern. The proportion of the public who feels government is *not* too complicated to understand varies from a low of 27% (1965, 1968) to a high of 32% (1974, 1979) and the proportion who is unwilling to admit that they have no say in government ranges from 49% (1977, 1979) to 60% (1968) (see Figure 3.1). Competence index scores for the four surveys are virtually invariant, moving from .73 in 1965 to .74 in 1979.

Declining levels of political responsiveness throughout much of the 1970's were not evident in every part of the country. In 1965, perceptions of responsiveness were lower in Quebec and the Atlantic provinces than elsewhere. During the next 12 years responsiveness levels in Quebec remained virtually constant while fluctuating in the Atlantic provinces. In Ontario and the western provinces, however, responsiveness perceptions declined markedly, particularly in the post-1968 period. The net result of these contrasting patterns was to narrow interregional differ-

FIGURE 3.1   Trends in Political Efficacy, 1965–1979

% giving efficacious responses

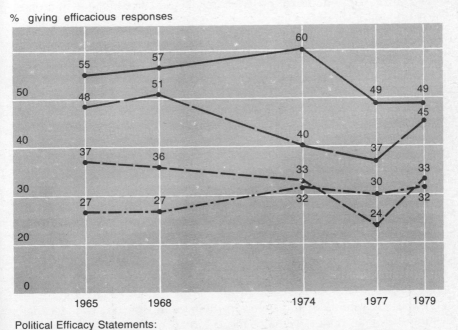

Political Efficacy Statements:

—————————— People like me don't have any say about what the government does.
—— —— The government doesn't care much what people like me think.
—— —— —— Those elected to Parliament soon lose touch with the people.
—·——·——·— Politics and government are too complicated to understand.

*disagreement with the statements indicates efficacious feelings.

ences and to increase the total number of persons across the country as a whole who perceived the political system as unresponsive. As noted, the trend was reversed in 1979, but even then, average levels of perceived responsiveness were lower in Ontario, the Prairies and British Columbia than they had been a decade earlier.

Differing regional trends in political efficacy should not obscure the basic point that levels of efficacy in all provinces and regions are quite low. In statistical terms, it is apparent that neither "province" nor "region" can explain a great deal of the variance in political efficacy. How then does one explain differences in levels of efficacy? We suggest two possible explanations. On the one hand, perceptions of responsiveness may be largely a rational response to *external* conditions. Governmental and other political institutions and the behaviour of political elites either may facilitate or inhibit the workings of representational processes and hence influence citizens' responsiveness perceptions. On the other hand, feelings of political efficacy, particularly a sense of competence, may be grounded in psychological and sociological characteristics of individuals. For example, persons with high levels of self-esteem and strong feelings of competence in non-political spheres of life may transfer or generalize these feelings about themselves when making judgments about the likely consequences of political involvement.[60] Additionally, high levels of political competence may reflect the possession of certain skills, resources and social statuses. In Canada and elsewhere the skills, resources and statuses conducive to effective political action are unequally distributed, being related to socioeconomic characteristics such as higher levels of education and income and to certain prestigious occupations (e.g., law) as well as to demographic factors such as age and sex.

Consistent with the latter explanation, persons with high levels of formal education and higher incomes *do* have higher levels of political efficacy (see Figures 3.2 and 3.3). As expected, these relationships are stronger for feelings of competence than for perceptions that government is responsive. Correlations between age and sex and efficacy are weaker, with younger people and men tending to feel more efficacious. Relationships between political efficacy and age controlling for education are virtually non-existent, suggesting that higher levels of efficacy among younger people largely reflect age-related differences in levels of educational attainment. As a result of the rapid expansion of the educational systems of the several provinces in the past two decades, younger people generally have more formal education than their elders.[61] The observation that men tend to feel more competent politically than do women is not unexpected in a society such as Canada which historically has discriminated against women's efforts to participate in politics and other areas of social and economic life. Such discrimination

FIGURE 3.2   Mean Political Efficacy Scores by Level of
Formal Education, 1979

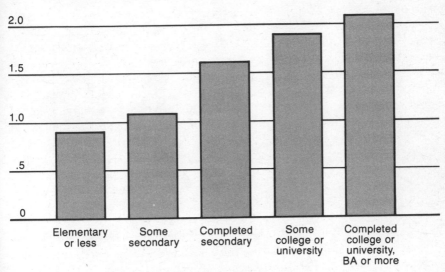

Mean political efficacy score

Level of formal education

has mutually reinforcing consequences. Women tend to have fewer of the resources (high levels of education and income, prestigious occupations) that facilitate effective political participation and as a result, culturally conditioned sex-role stereotypes inhibiting women's political participation have been sustained and reinforced over time.[62] Given the pervasiveness and durability of these stereotypes, it is surprising that the difference in political efficacy between the sexes is not larger.

The finding that socioeconomic and demographic characteristics rather than province or region of residence are the major correlates of political efficacy is buttressed by more sophisticated analyses of the national survey data. These analyses document that the statistical effects of province or region on efficacy are very small once other factors are controlled.[63] Simply stated, to the extent that one can explain levels of political efficacy, a person's demographic characteristics and socioeconomic status are more important than the province or region in which that person resides.

FIGURE 3.3   Mean Political Efficacy Scores by
Annual Family Income, 1979

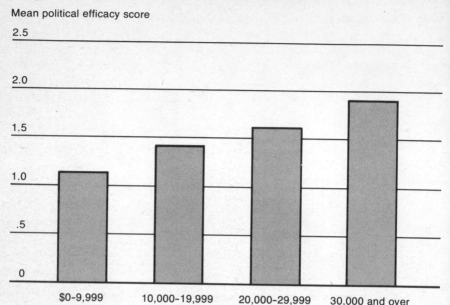

Mean political efficacy score

Annual family income

POLITICAL INTEREST AND MEDIA CONSUMPTION

Public interest in things political is crucial for the health of a democratic polity. Interest in political affairs bolsters levels of political knowledge and increases the likelihood of rational political action. In turn, rational political action on the part of an informed citizenry helps to ensure high levels of responsiveness by political elites to public needs and demands. Elite responsiveness, for its part, stimulates citizens' feelings of political efficacy and efficacy is positively related to both political participation and the legitimation of existing political institutions and processes. Political interest thereby plays a central role in a syndrome of attitudes and behaviour that influences the long-term effectiveness and stability of democratic polities.

There are a number of ways to measure political interest. One is the extent of public attention paid to news, because much of the news communicated through the mass media is at least implicitly political in content. Information regarding public attention to news in mass media is provided by the 1977 Quality of Life study. In this survey, three-quarters of the national sample stated that they watched news on TV "every day" or "several times a week," with the proportions doing so ranging

from slightly over two-thirds in Alberta to over four-fifths in Saskatchewan. Reading newspapers on a daily basis varied more widely — from
30% in Newfoundland to 70% in Prince Edward Island. Nationally,
slightly over one half of those surveyed in 1977 read a newspaper every
day and nearly two-fifths stated that they read newspaper editorials
"frequently." When asked to summarize their attention to news and
current events, 45% indicated they paid "a great deal" of attention, and
only 10% paid "very little" or "none at all." Provincial differences in
these percentages were modest, Ontario having the highest percentage
paying a "great deal" of attention and Prince Edward Island the lowest.

Notwithstanding these substantial levels of media attention, more
direct measures of political interest indicate that politics is not a
consuming passion for most Canadians. When queried in the 1979
national election study about how much attention they pay to politics on
a day-to-day basis, only 14% stated they followed politics "very
closely," 48% followed politics "fairly closely," and 38% said "not much
at all." Attention to politics was somewhat greater in British Columbia,
Ontario and Prince Edward Island than elsewhere, but again, the
general picture is decidely one of subtle rather than striking provincial
differences.

Similar to other analyses, socioeconomic and demographic characteristics have moderately strong relationships with political interest. Regarding socioeconomic status, the percentage of persons with high

FIGURE 3.4   Level of Political Interest by Socioeconomic Status
(Blishen Occupational Prestige Scale), 1979

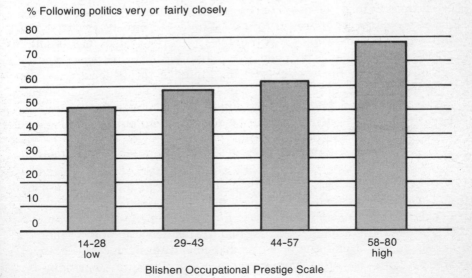

% Following politics very or fairly closely

Blishen Occupational Prestige Scale

levels of political interest increases steadily as levels of occupational prestige, income and education increase. The former relationship is illustrated in Figure 3.4. Age and sex are related to political interest as well. Predictably, in every province younger persons report lower levels of interest and, although the differences are seldom large, women consistently are less interested than men. Finally, when province of residence is used along with the socioeconomic and demographic variables as predictors of political interest, the latter account for nearly all of the explained variance. This result is similar to that for political efficacy and suggests there are few provincial differences in levels of political interest which are not attributable to socioeconomic and demographic differences in their populations.

SUMMARY: POLITICAL CULTURE AND REPRESENTATIVE DEMOCRACY

The answer to the question of whether or not provincial political cultures are conducive to representative democracy depends in part upon one's definition of representative democracy. Our definition goes well beyond the "democratic elitist" view that a system is democratic and representative if its members are provided with institutionalized opportunities to choose between or among competing candidates for public office. To maximize responsiveness, citizens in a representative democracy are provided with and utilize many different opportunities to influence political processes. During election campaigns they have opportunities to discuss political issues and the merits of candidates freely, to convince others of the correctness of their views, to participate in the selection of candidates for public office, to provide financial and other forms of assistance to candidates and political parties of their choice and to influence the policy positions adopted by parties and party leaders. Opportunities also exist to influence the actions of public officials and the content and administration of policy in the interim between elections. For their part, public officials must be attentive to both the expressed demands and the needs of their publics and try in a variety of ways to respond to them.

In the chapters that follow we will examine both the extent to which people participate politically and the responsiveness of major provincial political institutions and incumbent authorities to their publics. This chapter has examined aspects of provincial societies and economies deemed important prerequisites for the development of representative democracy. Attention then focussed on the incidence and distribution of certain values, attitudes and beliefs that constitute significant cognitive, affective and evaluative components of political culture. Regarding the former, since Confederation an ever-increasing population with few widespread debilitating health problems has been able to create an infrastructure of communications, transportation and educational facilities conducive to the operation of a complex, productive, urban-industrial society. Many social theorists have concluded that societies with these facilities and this kind of economy are best able to develop a political culture that enhances the prospects of attaining and maintaining a democratic political order. Although it can be argued that all of the provinces have reached or surpassed minimum "threshold" levels of social and economic development required to support democratic institutions and processes, problems remain. For one thing, in some provinces (e.g., Quebec and New Brunswick) important social cleavages (such as religion, language and ethnicity) strongly reinforce one another. Such a pattern of reinforcing cleavages may inhibit the operation of a democratic political system by stimulating feelings of group distinctiveness and "we-they" attitudes which increase the potential for serious inter-group conflict. Another problem is that the wealth based on the level of industrialization or the possession of natural resources is unequally distributed among the several provinces. To meet public needs and demands poorer provinces must rely heavily on the federal government for financial assistance which the latter provides by redistributing wealth from richer provinces. The resulting complexities in federal-provincial fiscal relations allow political elites in all provinces to avoid being held accountable by blaming the federal government and the operation of the federal system more generally for failing to redistribute resources in a more equitable fashion. A more general problem is that in every province wealth is distributed very unequally. The resulting class structures are such that many people lack the resources (high levels of formal education and income, prestigious occupations) which facilitate sustained and effective political participation. In sum, although provincial societies and economies differ in a number of important respects, none of them provide ideal bases for representative democracy.

Significant similarities and differences also characterize provincial political cultures. For example, Québécois have considerably lower levels of social trust than residents of other provinces. However, this is not true of their trust in governmental elites. One reason for Québécois' lower level of social trust may be their historic status as a minority. Nationalist elements in Quebec long have complained of being dominated by the English-speaking majority in other provinces in cooperation with Anglophone economic elites within Quebec itself. It has been argued that the perceived use of unnecessary or inappropriate power in relationships between two social groups of unequal strength invariably alienates the weaker actor from the stronger because the former comes to believe that the latter cannot be trusted. Distrust and the resulting negative sentiments which are generated eventually may lead the weaker actor to reject entirely any relationships with the stronger. Students of Quebec nationalism might well argue that the Parti Québécois program of independence is only the most recent manifestation of this kind of rejection.

There are other ways in which provincial similarities and differences complicate attempts to generalize about political culture. Quebecers are considerably more likely than residents of other provinces to think of themselves in class terms. People in the Atlantic provinces and Manitoba are the most likely to label themselves as "working" or "lower" class. Such provincial differences notwithstanding, the general conclusion suggested by the data examined in this chapter is that the cultural orientations of Canadians, regardless of province of residence, are more notable for their similarities than their differences. Moreover, variations in these orientations frequently can be better explained by socioeconomic and demographic factors than by provincial residency.

Consider again the data on social class orientations. They indicate that many people in every province see themselves in class terms. Relatedly, in virtually every province a majority of people feel that the gap between the rich and the poor is too great and wealth should be more equitably distributed. Notwithstanding these views, they maintain that classes reflect "natural" differences among individuals. Moreover, insofar as people differ in these beliefs, the differences are more closely related to socioeconomic status factors such as income than to province of residency. Analyses of differences in political efficacy and political interest yield similar results. In short, insofar as one is concerned with the set of beliefs, attitudes and opinions related to the generation and maintenance of representative democracy, there appears to be a genuine national political culture, some of whose principal components already have been accurately, albeit speculatively, described in previous studies.

For example, the finding that a majority of people feel that the gap between the rich and the poor is too great and that taxation should be used to narrow this gap can be interpreted as reflecting the position socialist tenets occupy in Canadian political culture. Relatedly, the finding that a majority of people also believe that social classes are natural because they reflect individual differences in ability and personality is a classic assumption of conservatism and can be interpreted as reflecting the presence in the culture of what Horowitz has called the "Tory touch".[64] Also consistent with socialist and conservative philosophic tenets is the widespread belief that government affects not only the economic well-being of people, but also the general quality of their lives. Moreover, in contrast to the laissez-faire liberal belief that government is best when it governs least, majorities in every province want government to do *more* of virtually everything — to expand activities in almost every policy area.

This latter finding is consistent with the argument that participation in the two great wars of this century and the growth of the welfare state with its attendant expansion of the scope of governmental activities have stimulated the development of feelings of "entitlement" among citizens in all Western countries. People feel they deserve, as a natural right, certain services which, until this century, have been regarded as privileges.[65] Also consistent with this argument is the observation that large numbers of people in every province are only moderately satisfied with the quality of their lives and their current economic well-being and feel they deserve *better, now*. At the same time, the impact of classical liberalism on provincial political cultures is evident in the optimism large numbers of people in every province express about their future prospects.

Proponents of the view that Canadian political culture is quasi-participative and deferential toward elites might point to the finding that most people, irrespective of province, have low levels of political efficacy — feeling incompetent to affect government and judging government to be unresponsive to citizen concerns. Those making such an argument might point to the additional fact that, except for widespread perceptions that governmental elites waste tax dollars, many persons in all parts of the country attested to the honesty, intelligence and probity of these elites. Before accepting these latter data as conclusive evidence of the pervasiveness of trusting and deferential orientations towards political elites, however, it should be remembered that other data indicate considerable cynicism and disdain for politics and politicians and the ability of the latter to manage the Canadian economy and society. Also, as noted in the previous chapter, in every province, people distinguish between government and the political community more generally, offering considerably more support to the latter than to the former. *In toto*, it seems that many persons in all parts of the country are *ambivalent* about their political system as a whole and political elites in particular. Such ambivalence suggests that a characterization of Canadian political culture as deferential is not entirely accurate.

There are a number of explanations *other* than the deference Canadians supposedly show toward elites that could explain their generalized lack of political efficacy. Political efficacy is related to socioeconomic status (i.e., education, income, occupation) and although many people in each province have high levels of education and income and prestigious occupations, many more do not. Relatedly, the operation of the federal system, particularly of federal financing, is extremely complex and may not be well understood by even the best-educated members of the public. The use of complicated financial transfer payments and tax-sharing agreements by the two levels of government in part may explain why so many Canadians seemingly ignore the truism that there is no "free lunch," even from government. Since both the federal and provincial governments are able to fund existing programs and periodi-cally to add new ones because of these transactions, average citizens may only dimly comprehend that a new program or an increase in activity in one programmatic area may result in decreased activity in another; and ultimately they pay for any and all governmental activity, regardless of area, because governments have no financial resources of their own.

Another possible explanation of the low political efficacy characteriz-ing large groups of people in every province may lie in their actual experiences with federal and provincial bureaucracies. These bureaucra-cies are large and often unwieldy and they *can* frustrate many of those seeking to obtain what are believed to be just entitlements. Ordinary citizens and politicians alike are frequently unable to get the "great doers" of government to do what they want done. Bureaucrats fre-quently appear to act as defenders of ongoing, status-quo-oriented policies. This frustrates efforts to institute new policies designed to make government more responsive to public needs. In any event, whatever the explanation, a generalized lack of political efficacy consti-tutes an element of political culture which inhibits movement toward greater representative democracy in every province.

In making this argument, we are *not* contending that persons living in different provinces hold identical beliefs, attitudes and opinions about all significant aspects of Canadian political life. Certainly, the data on class perceptions in this chapter as well as those on attitudes toward the operation of the federal system in Chapter 2, and on voting behaviour and support for political parties in Chapters 4 and 5 document impor-tant provincial differences, and may be interpreted as attesting to the reality of provincial political cultures.[66] Indeed, it might be argued that varying orientations toward federalism and political parties constitute *the* major differences in provincial political cultures. The point here is simply that such provincial differences in political culture should not be allowed to obscure the existence of broad trans-provincial similarities in how Canadians view and relate to their society and political system. As a result of these similarities, the cultural basis for representative democ-racy differs only by degree from one province to the next.

NOTES

1. On various conceptions of political culture, see the discussion by David J. Elkins and Richard E.B. Simeon, "A Cause in Search of Its Effect, or What Does Political Culture Explain?," *Comparative Politics* 2 (1979), pp. 127-146. See also the classic discussion of political culture in Gabriel Almond and Sidney Verba, *The Civic Culture* (Princeton: Princeton University Press, 1963), ch. 1; and Jon H. Pammett

and Michael S. Whittington, "Introduction: Political Culture and Political Socialization," in J. Pammett and M. Whittington, eds., *Foundations of Political Culture: Political Socialization in Canada* (Toronto: Macmillan, 1976), ch. 1.

2. Arguments regarding the content of such a political culture have been heavily influenced by varying conceptions of democracy held by different scholars. Compare, for example, Almond and Verba, *The Civic Culture*, ch. 15 with Christian Bay, "Behavioural Research and the Theory of Democracy," in Henry S. Kariel, ed., *Frontiers of Democratic Theory* (New York: Random House, 1970), pp. 327-352.

3. For arguments regarding the importance of social and economic development for establishing and maintaining a democratic political system see Seymour Martin Lispet, "Some Social Requisites of Democracy," *American Political Science Review* 53 (1959), pp. 69-105; Philips Cutright, "National Political Development: Its Measurement and Social Correlates," in Nelson W. Polsby, Robert A. Dentler and Paul A. Smith, eds., *Politics and Social Life* (Boston: Houghton Mifflin, 1963), pp. 569-582. The importance of social, economic *and* cultural conditions for democracy is argued in Deane E. Neubauer, "Some Conditions of Democracy," *American Political Science Review* 61 (1967), pp. 1002-1009.

4. Among the large number of relevant studies are the following: Kenneth D. McRae, "The Structure of Canadian History," in Louis Hartz, ed., *The Founding of New Societies* (New York: Harcourt, Brace and World, 1964), ch. 7; Gad Horowitz, "Conservatism, Liberalism, and Socialism in Canada: An Interpretation," *Canadian Journal of Economics and Political Science* 32 (1966), pp. 144-171; Tom Truman, "A Critique of Seymour M. Lipset's Article, 'Value Differences Absolute or Relative: The English Speaking Democracies'," *Canadian Journal of Political Science* 4 (1971), pp. 497-525; Seymour Martin Lipset, "Revolution and Counterrevolution: The United States and Canada," in O. Kruhlak, *et al.*, eds., *The Canadian Political Process*, 2nd ed. (Toronto: Holt, Rinehart and Winston, 1973), pp. 3-29; Robert Presthus, *Elite Accommodation in Canadian Politics* (Toronto: Macmillan, 1973); Kenneth McRae, ed., *Consociational Democracy* (Toronto: McClelland and Stewart, 1974); Richard Simeon and David J. Elkins, "Regional Political Cultures in Canada," *Canadian Journal of Political Science* 7 (1974), pp. 397-437; Mildred Schwartz, *Politics and Territory* (Montreal: McGill-Queen's University Press, 1974); John Wilson, "The Canadian Political Cultures: Towards a Redefinition of the Nature of the Canadian Political System," *Canadian Journal of Political Science*, 7 (1974), pp. 438-483; David J. Bellamy, *et al.*, eds., *The Provincial Political Systems* (Toronto: Methuen, 1976), chs. 1-7; Jon H. Pammett and Michael S. Whittington, eds., *Foundations of Political Culture* (Toronto: MacMillan, 1976); Richard J. Van Loon and Michael S. Whittington, *The Canadian Political System* (Toronto: McGraw-Hill, 1976), chs. 3,4; Stephen H. Ullman, "Regional Political Cultures in Canada: Part I," *The American Review of Canadian Studies* 7 (1977), pp. 1-22, and "Regional Political Cultures in Canada: Part II," *The American Review of Canadian Studies* 8 (1978), pp. 70-101; Martin Robin, ed., *Canadian Provincial Politics*, 2nd ed. (Scarborough: Prentice-Hall, 1978); David Bell and Lorne Tepperman, *The Roots of Disunity* (Toronto: McClelland and Stewart, 1979); Allan Kornberg, Harold D. Clarke and Marianne C. Stewart, "Public Support for Regime and Community in the Regions of Contemporary Canada," *The American Review of Canadian Studies*, 10 (1980), pp. 75-93.

5. Van Loon and Whittington, *The Canadian Political System*, pp. 77-80.

6. *Ibid*, p. 79.

7. See, for example, Horowitz, "Conservatism, Liberalism and Socialism;" Lipset, "Revolution and Counterrevolution;" Presthus, *Elite Accommodation*, ch. 2. The strength of these non-liberal elements in Canadian political culture has been disputed. Compare, for example, Horowitz's interpretation with that of McRae in "The Structure of Canadian History." See also the commentary on Lipset by Truman, "A Critique."

8. McRae, "The Structure of Canadian History," pp. 220-230.

9. Horowitz, "Conservatism, Liberalism and Socialism," pp. 51-52.

10. *Ibid.*, pp. 61-63. See also Walter D. Young, *The Anatomy of a Party: The National CCF* (Toronto: University of Toronto Press, 1969), *passim*.

11. Horowitz, "Conservatism, Liberalism and Socialism," p. 63.

12. The term "quasi-participative" is Presthus'. See *Elite Accommodation*, pp. 38-59. On a similar theme see Richard J. Van Loon, "Political Participation in Canada: The 1965 Election," *Canadian Journal of Political Science* 3 (1970), pp. 376-399.

13. S.J.R. Noel, "Consociational Democracy and Canadian Federalism," *Canadian Journal of Political Science* 4 (1971), pp. 15-18; Presthus, *Elite Accommodation, passim;* McRae, ed., *Consociational Democracy*, pp. 238-261.

14. See, for example, Simeon and Elkins, "Regional Political Cultures;" Schwartz, *Politics and Territory*, ch. 12; Wilson, "The Canadian Political Cultures;" Bell and Tepperman, *The Roots of Disunity*, ch. 6.

15. Noel has argued that the pervasiveness of various forms of clientelism is one of the most salient features of provincial political cultures. S.J.R. Noel, "Leadership and Clientelism," in D. Bellamy, *et al.*, eds., *The Provincial Political Systems*, ch. 14.

16. Almond and Verba, *The Civic Culture*, p. 490.

17. Although the argument has been made most forcefully by Marxists, many non-Marxists have espoused it as well. See, for example, Robert Alford, *Party and Society* (Chicago: Rand McNally, 1963); and Seymour Martin Lipset and Stein Rokkan, "Cleavage Structures, Party Systems and Voter Alignments: An Introduction," in Lipset and Rokkan, eds., *Party Systems and Voter Alignments* (New York: The Free Press, 1967), pp. 1-64.

18. See, for example, John Porter, *The Vertical Mosaic*: (Toronto: University of Toronto Press, 1965), ch. 12. In Canada, the further argument has been made that social class divisions have the potential to mute divisive cleavages by cutting across reinforcing regional, religious and ethno-linguistic divisions in the population. See, for example, John Wilson, "Politics and Social Class in Canada: The Case of Waterloo South," *Canadian Journal of Political Science* 1 (1968), pp. 307-309.

19. For an overview of changing levels of educational attainment in Canada see Warren E. Kalbach and Wayne W. McVey, *The Demographic Bases of Canadian Society*, 2nd ed. (Toronto: McGraw-Hill Ryerson, 1979), ch. 10.

20. David Bennett, "Income" in D. Michael Ray, *et al.*, eds., *Canadian Urban Trends: National Perspectives* (Toronto: Copp Clark, 1976), p. 157.

21. Garth Stevenson, *Unfulfilled Union* (Toronto: Macmillan, 1979), pp. 106-109.

22. Dennis Forcese, *The Canadian Class Structure* (Toronto: McGraw-Hill Ryerson, 1980), p. 63.

23. Kalbach and McVey, *The Demographic Bases of Canadian Society*, p. 251, Table 10.4.

24. *Ibid.*, p. 292, Table 11.13.

25. Almond and Verba, *The Civic Culture*, p. 490.

26. *Social Change in Canada: Trends in Attitudes, Values, and Perceptions* (Toronto: York University, Institute for Behavioural Research), p. 41.

27. *The CPS 1976 American National Election Study Codebook*, V. 1 (Ann Arbor: Inter-University Consortium for Political and Social Research, 1977), pp. 380-384.

28. Almond and Verba, *The Civil Culture*, p. 267.

29. *Ibid.*, ch. 15.

30. On this possibility in Canada see Allan Kornberg, Harold D. Clarke and Marianne C. Stewart, "Federalism and Fragmentation: Political Support in Canada," *Journal of Politics* 41 (1979), pp. 889-906.

31. See, for example, the debate between Arthur Miller and Jack Citrin. Arthur H. Miller, "Political Issues and Trust in Government: 1964-1970," *American Political Science Review* 68 (1974), pp. 951-992; Jack Citrin, "Comment: The Political Relevance of Trust in Government," *American Political Science Review* 68 (1974), pp. 973-988. On this issue in Canada see Michael M. Atkinson, William D. Coleman, and Thomas J. Lewis, "Regime Support in Canada: A Comment," *British Journal of Political Science* 10 (1980), pp. 402-409; and Allan Kornberg, Harold D. Clarke and Lawrence LeDuc, "Regime Support in Canada: A Rejoinder," *British Journal of Political Science* 10 (1980), pp. 410-416.

32. Everett C. Ladd, Jr., "A Nation's Trust," *Public Opinion* 2 (October/November 1979), pp. 27-37.

33. It should be observed, however, that trust in governmental elites is not simply a function of support for the government in power. The mean trust score for federal Liberal party identifiers is 2.2; PCs — 2.1; NDP — 2.2; Socreds — 2.2; non-identifiers — 2.0. For provincial party identifications the means are: Liberals — 2.2; PCs — 2.2;

NDP — 2.0; Socreds/Créditistes — 2.2; Péquistes — 2.5; non-identifiers — 1.7.

34. For a review of some of these findings see Allan Kornberg and Judith D. Wolfe, "Parliament, the Media and the Polls," in Harold D. Clarke, *et al.*, eds., *Parliament, Policy and Representation* (Toronto: Methuen, 1980), ch. 3.
35. Calculated from data in Harold D. Clarke, *et al.*, *Political Choice in Canada* (Toronto: McGraw-Hill Ryerson, 1979), p. 29, Table 1.9.
36. *Ibid.*, pp. 107-119.
37. See, for example, John Wilson, "The Canadian Political Cultures," *passim*; and Wilson, "The Decline of the Liberal Party in Manitoba," *Journal of Canadian Studies* 10 (1975), pp. 24-41.
38. Porter, *The Vertical Mosaic*, especially pp. 3-7.
39. To place these data in perspective, comparisons with other Western countries are useful. Information gathered in 1974 by Barnes, Kaase, *et al.*, on subjective social class perceptions in four European countries and the United States reveal that Canadians' class self-perceptions are generally similar to those of persons residing in countries where class conflict has been a salient feature of the political landscape. The most noteworthy difference involves the Canadian-British comparison. The latter is the only instance where a majority of the respondents (65%) placed themselves in the working class. However, in this respect, the British data differ not only from the Canadian, but also from continental European countries (The Netherlands, Germany, Austria) as well. One would not wish to argue the absence of class politics in these cases. See Alan Marsh and Max Kaase, "Background of Political Action," *Political Action*, ed. Samuel H. Barnes and Max Kaase (Beverly Hills: Sage Publications, 1979), p. 127.
40. A discussion of the construction of this measure may be found in Bernard Blishen and Hugh McRoberts, "A Revised Socioeconomic Index for Occupations in Canada," *Canadian Review of Sociology and Anthropology* 13 (1976), pp. 71-80. For the analysis described here, the Blishen scale is collapsed into four categories. This measure is described in Clarke, *et al.*, *Political Choice in Canada*, pp. 427-428.
41. Richard Rose and Guy Peters, *Can Government Go Bankrupt?* (New York: Basic Books, 1978), ch. 5.
42. The wording of the "ladder" questions can be found on pages 5 and 36 of the *Social Change in Canada* questionnaire.
43. For example, mean life satisfaction scores range from a low of 6.0 in Newfoundland and Manitoba to a high of 7.3 in New Brunswick, Quebec and Manitoba. It is also noteworthy that the Canadian scores differ only slightly from those for several other Western democracies. Scores (measured in 1974) for the Netherlands, Britain, the U.S.A., West Germany and Austria were 7.6, 7.3, 7.4, 7.1 and 7.1 respectively. See Barnes, *et al.*, "Personal Dissatisfaction," *Political Action*, p. 387.
44. The Barnes and Kaase data indicate that Canadians have slightly lower levels of economic satisfaction than citizens of some other Western democracies. Scores (measured in 1974) for the Netherlands, Britain, the U.S.A., West Germany and Austria were 7.6, 6.6, 6.9, 6.7 and 6.6 respectively. *Ibid.*
45. However, the complexities of relationships between objective economic conditions and subjective perceptions are illustrated by the fact that at the *individual* level income differences correlate fairly strongly with some of the ladder scores. For example, the average score for projected economic situation in five years increases steadily from 6.7 for persons with family incomes under $10,000 per annum to 8.1 for those earning $25,000 or more a year. A similar pattern exists for present economic conditions, but not for perceptions of what they deserve. Regardless of income level, however, people feel they deserve more *now*.
46. The wording of this question can be found on p. 8 of the *Social Change in Canada* questionnaire.
47. The term "post-materialist" is Inglehart's. See Ronald Inglehart, *The Silent Revolution* (Princeton: Princeton University Press, 1977).
48. Statistical details concerning the factor analysis are available from the authors upon request.
49. The method of constructing these factor score variables is described in Norman H. Nie, *et al.*, *Statistical Package for the Social Sciences*, 2nd ed. (Toronto: McGraw-Hill Ryerson, 1975), pp. 487-489.

50. In this respect the post-materialist issues complex resembles the post-materialist values identified by Inglehart in his analyses of political change in Western Europe. Ronald Inglehart, *The Silent Revolution*; and Inglehart, "Value Priorities and Socioeconomic Change," *Political Action*, ed. S. Barnes and M. Kaase, ch. 11. See also Kendall Baker, Russell Dalton and Kai Hildebrandt, *Germany Transformed* (Cambridge: Harvard University Press, 1981), chs. 6, 7.

51. The significance of controlling for the possible effects of such sociodemographic variables when offering cultural explanations for observed intergroup differences is argued in Elkins and Simeon, "A Cause in Search of Its Effect," pp. 135-136.

52. Statistical details concerning these analyses are available from the authors upon request.

53. See, for example, Presthus, *Elite Accommodation*, ch. 2; Simeon and Elkins, "Regional Political Cultures," *passim*; Schwartz, *Politics and Territory*, ch. 9.

54. Simeon and Elkins, "Regional Political Cultures," p. 404.

55. Carl Friedrich, *Man and His Government* (New York: McGraw-Hill, 1963), p. 203. See also Almond and Verba, *The Civic Culture*, pp. 485-486.

56. Kornberg, *et al.*, "Public Support for Regime and Community," p. 77.

57. These four efficacy statements are common to all of the national surveys. Hence, they are used here to permit cross-time analyses of changing levels of efficacy in the several provinces.

58. See Edgar Litt, "Political Cynicism and Political Futility," *Journal of Politics* 25 (1963), pp. 312-323.

59. The statistical basis for this conclusion is elaborated upon in Kornberg, *et al.*, "Public Support for Regime and Community," pp. 78-79.

60. Almond and Verba, *The Civic Culture*, ch. 12; Carole Pateman, *Participation and Democratic Theory* (London: Cambridge University Press, 1970), ch. 3.

61. Kalbach and McVey, *The Demographic Bases of Canadian Society* p. 254, Table 10.5.

62. Forcese, *The Canadian Class Structure* pp. 52-58; 77-79; Allan Kornberg, Joel Smith and Harold D. Clarke, *Citizen Politicians-Canada* (Durham, N.C.: Carolina Academic Press, 1979), ch. 9.

63. Statistical details may be found in Kornberg, *et al.*, "Public Support for Regime and Community," pp. 79-80.

64. Horowitz, "Conservatism, Liberalism and Socialism in Canada," *passim*.

65. Robert Nisbet, "The Fatal Ambivalence of an Idea," *Encounter* 47 (1976), pp. 10-21.

66. For a recent analysis of similarities and differences in provincial political cultures see David J. Elkins and Richard Simeon, eds., *Small Worlds* (Toronto: Methuen, 1980).

FOR FURTHER READING

Almond, Gabriel and Sidney Verba. *The Civic Culture*. Princeton: Princeton University Press, 1963, chs. 1, 2, 15. In the first two chapters Almond and Verba discuss the concept of political culture and methods used for studying political cultures. Chapter 15 analyzes relationships between political culture and the stability of democratic political systems.

Bellamy, David J., Jon H. Pammett and Donald C. Rowat, eds. *The Provincial Political Systems*. Toronto: Methuen, 1976, chs. 1-5. These five chapters present brief sketches of the political cultures of Canada's five major regions.

Elkins, David J. and Richard E.B. Simeon. "A Cause in Search of Its Effect, or What Does Political Culture Explain?," *Comparative Politics* 2 (1979), pp. 127-146. Elkins and Simeon analyze the concept of political culture and argue that one should attribute explanatory power to political cultural variables only after other types of explanations (e.g. social, economic, structural) have been exhausted.

Horowitz, Gad. "Conservatism, Liberalism and Socialism in Canada: An Interpretation," *Canadian Journal of Economics and Political Science* 32 (1966), pp. 144-171. In this classic analysis of the content and development of Canadian political culture, Horowitz explains the presence of socialism in Canada in terms of the interaction of liberal and conservative elements in the culture.

Kalbach, Warren E. and Wayne W. McVey. *The Demographic Bases of Canadian Society* 2nd ed. Toronto: McGraw-Hill Ryerson, 1971. This is a useful source book of data on several aspects of Canadian society and societal change over time. Much of the data is analyzed on provincial and/or regional bases.

Neubauer, Deane E. "Some Conditions of Democracy," *American Political Science Review* 61 (1967), pp. 1002-1009. The author argues that social and economic conditions provide "thresholds" for the development of democratic political systems, but that cultural factors are crucial for determining how democratic such systems will be.

4
Participation and Elections

Political participation is *the* key element in classical theories of democracy. According to these theories, citizen participation has numerous benefits for society and the individual. For society, participation is said to foster the development of public policies reflecting the interests of all citizens and the equitable distribution of government benefits among all social groups and classes. The result is a just and stable political order. For individuals, participation increases feelings of personal efficacy and self-esteem, bolsters political interest and understanding, and promotes tolerance, thus enhancing the quality of democratic citizenship. Classical democratic arguments regarding the benefits of citizen participation are well-known and have provided the impetus for considerable research on political behaviour in Canada and elsewhere over the past three decades. The results of this research have sparked lively controversies about the quantity, quality, and consequences of participation and the prospects for increasing citizen involvement in political life. Although these controversies are kaleidoscopic and include a number of divergent points of view, two general positions are prominent. The first, espoused by individuals belonging to the group identified as "elitist democrats," argues that widespread participation is neither possible nor desirable. In addition to the practical impossibility of involving citizens directly in all significant political decisions, elitist democrats point to substantial gaps between democratic ideals and empirical reality with respect to both the quantity and quality of citizen participation. Few citizens participate extensively in political life, and fewer still manifest high levels of political information, rationality and tolerance. Moreover, because non-participants possess fewer of the attributes of democratic citizenship than do those who participate extensively, elitist democrats maintain that mobilizing currently inactive citizens would exacerbate social tensions, undermine political stability, and threaten the democratic political order.

A second perspective on the controversy is provided by those who may be designated "participatory democrats." Acknowledging practical limits on the number of people who can participate directly in many governmental decisions, participatory democrats, nevertheless, contend that much higher levels of participation are possible and desirable. Recalling the classical democratic argument that political involvement is a means of civic education, they argue that apathy, alienation, ignorance and intolerance are consequences of limited opportunities for effective participation. In their view, increasing participation is likely to create the kind of rational, informed and tolerant citizenry which is essential for democracy. They believe that the cure for the ills of contemporary government in Canada and elsewhere is more participation, not less.[1]

We will not attempt to resolve the debate between elitist and participatory democrats. Instead, the opposing positions in the debate can provide a general theoretical context within which data regarding political participation in the provinces may be considered. The model of representative democracy presented in Chapter 1 postulates the requirement of extensive citizen participation. Although full-time political activity remains the preserve of a small group, the political elite is not juxtaposed against a broad, undifferentiated mass public which confines its political involvement to occasional sojourns to the polling booth. Giving vitality to the political process and enhancing its democratic character is a third, relatively large group of attentive citizens, who participate in a wide range of political activities on an occasional, part-time basis. In essence, the model of representative democracy stipulates levels of citizen participation which fall between those advocated by the elitist democrats on the one hand and their participatory antagonists on the other.

Measuring levels of political participation in the provinces is, then, an important step in evaluating the extent to which their political systems approximate representative democratic political orders. This will be the first task of the present chapter. The second will be a consideration of the correlates of political activity. What are the socioeconomic, demographic and attitudinal characteristics of persons who are politically active? Answering this question will help explain current participation levels and identify factors that would facilitate increased participation in the future. The chapter will conclude by examining processes of electoral choice in provincial elections. Although widespread voting in periodic elections is not sufficient for the achievement or maintenance of a democratic political order, it is a critically important form of political participation. At issue is not only how many citizens go to the polls, but also the nature of electoral choice. The model of representative democracy posits that citizens are confronted with meaningful alternatives when casting their ballots and that their electoral decisions reflect rational, informed judgments about the relative desirability of these alternatives. Determining whether electoral choices actually are made in this way is crucial for evaluating the extent to which provincial political systems approximate the model.

POLITICAL PARTICIPATION: SCOPE

"Political participation is activity by which citizens take part in, or attempt to influence, the distribution of values in society."[2] Clearly, this definition is applicable to many different types of behaviour. A moment's reflection suggests it encompasses several familiar electoral activities such as voting, working in a campaign for a party or candidate, and contesting or actually occupying a public elective office. To be sure, political participation in Canada and other Western political systems does not focus exclusively on the electoral arena. Other activities are also political. "Communal activities" and "particularized contacting" are labels that have been applied to additional modes of political participation.[3] The former refers to activities in which individuals work together in a non-electoral context for the achievement of certain collective benefits. Examples include ratepayers associations which are organized to impress municipal councils with the need to improve garbage collection and snow removal services in communities and senior citizens groups that mount letter-writing campaigns to convince provincial legislators to give tax relief to persons living on fixed incomes. Particularized contacts also are directed at public officials but are engaged in by individuals wanting to promote their own rather than the broader community's well-being. A classic example is the person who writes his or her MLA asking the legislator to persuade a recalcitrant bureaucracy to provide a particular good or service such as a hospital insurance cheque or information about a government program.

The above constitute what may be termed conventional and approved forms of political behaviour which are recognized as legitimate means of individual or collective involvement in the political process of a democracy such as Canada. Historically, other forms of political participation are less common in such systems and may not be accorded full legitimacy, either in law or in the minds of many citizens. Perhaps most salient are protest activities. Some of these are non-violent and may not contravene existing laws. Marches and picketing of government buildings are good examples. Others, such as sit-ins and wildcat strikes, are peaceful, but may be illegal. Still others involve violence and are clearly illegal. Street fights between opposing bands of political extremists, "trashing" government or private property and political assassinations are in this category. In sum, the range of activities constituting political participation is very broad. The following analysis, therefore, will consider several different activities with the attention given each reflecting the limits of available information and our more general theoretical concerns.

POLITICAL PARTICIPATION IN CANADA: EXTENT

Available information on political participation is largely confined to electoral activities, most notably voting. Official statistics on electoral behaviour are kept by the federal and provincial governments. These show that for the 1949–79 period, turnout in federal elections averaged 76% for the country as a whole.[4] Provincial differences in *federal* voting rates have generally been modest, with averages ranging from a low of 72% in Alberta to a high of 79% in Newfoundland, Nova Scotia and New Brunswick.[5] In *provincial* elections, turnout varies more widely. Since 1949 voting rates in excess of 75% have been common in Prince Edward Island, Nova Scotia, New Brunswick, Quebec and Saskatchewan. Lower levels of voting (less than 70%) have been typical in British Columbia, Alberta, Ontario, Manitoba and, until 1971, Newfoundland. In general, only in Ontario, Manitoba and Alberta have voting rates in provincial elections been substantially lower than in federal elections. Moreover, during certain historical periods, turnout in provincial elections in particular provinces (e.g., Quebec) has regularly exceeded that in federal contests.[6]

Official statistics on virtually every form of political participation other than voting are unavailable (candidacy for public elective office being a notable exception). However, information on at least some of these activities has been gathered in national surveys conducted over the past two decades. The 1974 and 1979 data are particularly useful in the present context because of the explicit distinction made in these studies between participation in federal and provincial politics. The frequencies with which respondents in the 1979 survey reported engaging in several activities at these two levels are contained in Tables 4.1 and 4.2.

Only relatively small minorities of citizens are engaged in most electorally-related activities other than voting. Approximately two-thirds of the respondents report they never have attempted to convince a friend how to vote or attended a campaign meeting or rally. Four-fifths or more never have worked in a political campaign or contributed money to a candidate or party and less than 5% report doing any of these four activities "often." As suggested by electoral turnout figures, voting is at the other end of the participation continuum. At both the federal and provincial levels, over 85% of those interviewed in 1979 stated that they had voted in at least "some" of the elections in which they were eligible. Federally, 66% reported voting in "all" elections; provincially, this figure is 58%. "Discussing politics with other people" and "reading about politics in the newspaper" are the only other items to which majorities respond positively. Approximately two-fifths and one-quarter respectively performed these activities frequently.

Three points about these data are in order. First, the sharp "fall off" in participation in activities other than voting is not peculiar to 1979. Other

TABLE 4.1
Provincial Political Participation, 1979

Voting Frequency	All Elections 58%*	Most 28	Some 9	None 4	(N) (2501) **

| | Frequency of Engaging in Various Activities | | | | |
	Often	Sometimes	Seldom	Never	(N)
Read about politics in newspaper	45%	28	16	11	(1310)***
Discuss politics	27%	36	21	17	(1307)
Try to convince friends how to vote	8%	12	13	67	(1307)
Attend political meeting or rally	3%	15	18	63	(1307)
Contact public officials or politicians	4%	14	17	65	(1307)
Work for party or candidate	3%	7	9	82	(1307)
Contribute money to party or candidate	3%	8	5	85	(1304)

*horizontal percentages
**weighted national sample, missing data removed
***weighted national half-sample, N varies slightly with missing data removed

TABLE 4.2
Federal Political Participation, 1979

Voting Frequency	All Elections 66%*	Most 24	Some 9	None 2	(N) (2310) **

| | Frequency of Engaging in Various Activities | | | | |
	Often	Sometimes	Seldom	Never	(N)
Read about politics in newspaper	43%	28	19	11	(1312)**
Discuss politics	25%	38	23	14	(1312)
Try to convince friends how to vote	8%	12	14	66	(1311)
Attend political meeting or rally	4%	13	22	62	(1312)
Contact public officials or politicians	3%	14	19	64	(1311)
Work for party or candidate	3%	7	10	80	(1309)
Contribute money to party or candidate	2%	7	5	85	(1309)

*horizontal percentages
**weighted national sample, missing data removed
***weighted national half-sample, N varies slightly with missing data removed

studies at the federal and provincial levels and detailed surveys of the populations of Vancouver and Winnipeg conducted in the late 1960s yield very similar results.[7] Other than voting, frequent involvement in politics, even in informal ways—such as discussing political affairs with a friend, neighbour or family member — is avoided by approximately three-quarters of the population. Sustained campaign activity and candidacy for public elective office are the preserves of minute fractions of the population.

Second, an overall scale of political activity measuring participation at least "sometimes" in four activities (voting, discussing politics, convincing friends or attending meetings and campaign activity), reveals that over two-fifths of the respondents in the 1979 survey not only voted but also discussed politics (see Figure 4.1). When one also considers that there is an additional 20% who periodically engage in attempts to convince friends or neighbours how to vote, it is clear that the Canadian public cannot be characterized as "non-participants" and "voters only." Frequent or sustained participation may be rare, but occasional informal involvement is fairly common.

Third, overall levels of participation in federal and provincial electoral politics are similar. For example, just under 10% said they often try to convince friends how to vote in provincial elections and an identical percentage reported lobbying their friends in federal elections. Similarly, four out of every five citizens admitted they never engage in either provincial or federal campaign activity. Indeed, except for voting, there is no indication that participation in federal politics significantly exceeds provincial participation. Even with respect to voting, federal–provincial differences in reported rates of participation are consistently less than 10%.

Because federal and provincial participation rates in electoral activities are very nearly equal does not mean that the *same* people are equally active at both levels, or that aggregate rates of electoral participation are equal in all provinces. In fact, however, most individuals *are* equally active (or inactive) at both levels. Correlating the summary provincial and federal participation scales described previously yields very high values for all provinces, the maximum being +.89 for Prince Edward Island, the minimum, +.76 for Quebec. Nationally, the figure is +.79.[8] Further, although the official statistics on turnout presented above document substantial interprovincial differences, there are only modest differences in other forms of political activity. Thus, the number of respondents with maximum scores on the overall provincial participation scale varies from a low of 4% in Ontario to a high of 10% in PEI. Provincial differences in the frequency of performing specific actions also are small, with the exception of vote frequency. Illustrative is the finding that the percentage reporting that they often engage in campaign work at the provincial level ranges from a low of 2% in New-

FIGURE 4.1   **Distributions on Overall Provincial and
Federal Electoral Activities Scale, 1979**

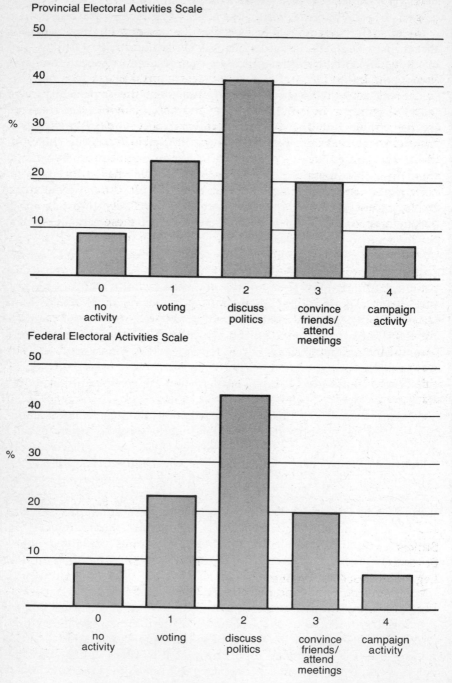

foundland, Ontario and British Columbia to a high of 5% in Saskatchewan. In contrast, the percentage voting in all provincial elections varies from 48% in Manitoba to 81% in PEI. Federally, the range is from 53% (Newfoundland) to 79% (PEI).

Information regarding citizen participation in non-electoral types of activity (i.e., particularized contacting, communal activity and protests) is less readily available. That which is suggests levels of participation are even lower. In the 1979 national survey less than 20% said they often or sometimes contacted public officials and about the same percentage reported working in community affairs. Again, provincial differences are discernible but not dramatic. National survey data on political protests are unavailable, but in a study conducted in Toronto in the early 1970s, 6% claimed to have particpated in "an authorized protest rally or march," 7% had disobeyed "an unjust law," and 2% had been involved in "a non-authorized protest rally or march."[9] Since these data were gathered during a period characterized by unusually high levels of political unrest, there is reason to believe that even these relatively small percentages may be inflated indicators of typical levels of protest activity.

Regarding the *potential* for political protest, the 1977 Quality of Life study asked a national sample how frequently various types of protest activities could be justified. The results (see Table 4.3) indicate that many Canadians approve of some forms of protest on at least an occasional basis and that they distinguish sharply between legal and illegal, and peaceful and violent protests. Three-quarters of those surveyed thought that peaceful rallies or marches can be justified at least "sometimes," but only 10% thought this of violent protest. Provincial differences in these attitudes are modest with greatest agreement existing on the illegitimacy

TABLE 4.3
Attitudes Toward Political Protest Activities, 1977

Activity	Activity Can Be Justified			
	Often	Sometimes	Never	(N)
Strikes	10%*	66	24	(3180)
Boycotts	15%	57	29	(3049)
Legal and peaceful demonstrations, e.g. marches, rallies and picketing	20%	57	24	(3147)
Illegal but peaceful demonstrations, e.g. sit-ins	7%	39	54	(3095)
Violent protests	2%	8	90	(3183)

*horizontal percentages

of violent protests. The largest provincial differences concern illegal but peaceful protests with the percentage judging that such activities frequently are justified ranging from a low of 4% in Alberta to a high of 16% in Newfoundland.

In summary, available information on political participation seems to conform, in general outline at least, to findings reported for other Western countries.[10] Large majorities of people vote on a fairly regular basis, some will occasionally discuss politics with their friends and neighbours or try to convince them how to vote, but other electoral activities are the preserve of small groups of inveterate political activists. Similarly, involvement in non-electoral activities is not widespread. In Canada, the pattern of minimal involvement beyond the voting level obtains for both federal and provincial politics with people tending to be equally active (or better, equally inactive) at each level. Finally, although there are provincial differences in participation, both in an overall sense and with regard to specific activities, with the exception of vote frequency, these differences are modest. As anticipated by the discussion of political culture in Chapter Three, when it comes to citizen involvement in the political process, the provinces are more alike than different.

WHO PARTICIPATES?

Research on political participation in Western countries has repeatedly found that certain socioeconomic, demographic, attitudinal and family background characteristics are associated with political activism.[11] Although the strength of these relationships varies from one country to the next, their ubiquity and persistence suggest that similar relationships will obtain in Canada. Regarding socioeconomic characteristics, the pattern is for persons with higher incomes, extensive formal education and more prestigious occupations to participate more frequently than those with lower socioeconomic statuses. As for demographic characteristics, men and middle-aged people have the highest participation rates. Attitudinally, persons with higher levels of political interest and efficacy, individuals who believe that it makes a difference which party forms the government and those with strong psychological attachments to political parties are more likely to be frequent participants. Activists also are more likely to have been reared in families in which parents or other relatives were either active or at least very interested in politics. This finding holds not only for famous political families such as the Kennedys and the Churchills but also for thousands of others whose members are involved in less influential and less glamorous aspects of political life.

That high levels of socioeconomic status are associated with political activity is not surprising since political participation requires resources of various kinds. Money is perhaps the most obvious. The observation that political involvement can be expensive may be trite, but, nonetheless it is true, particularly if one is interested in mounting a serious candidacy for federal or provincial elective office. Educational and occupational resources often are relevant as well. Well-educated persons with prestigious occupations frequently have the leisure time required for participation in politics and in at least some cases (the classic example is law), the demands on one's time created by the pursuit of such occupations are sufficiently flexible to permit lengthy periods of full-time political involvement. More generally, there is considerable truth even today to Woodrow Wilson's famous aphorism "the profession I chose was politics, [therefore], the profession I entered was law." Well-educated persons practicing law or other high-status "brokerage" occupations, in addition to possessing the time and money needed for sustained political participation, develop a valuable armory of verbal and forensic skills. In the contemporary era of "media politics" skillful symbol manipulation is one of the major weapons of virtually every political gladiator. Even if one's political pursuits are strictly avocational, they are nonetheless *social* activities. As such, techniques of effective communication and persuasion frequently are of the utmost importance.

Relationships between demographic characteristics and political participation are understandable given the cultural context of politics in contemporary Western societies. For example, until very recently politics has been considered "a man's game." Attitudes about the inappropriateness of political activity for women have been reinforced by more general societal norms which effectively have discriminated against political participation by women by inhibiting access to those resources (higher levels of education and income, prestigious occupations) discussed above.

To explain age-related differences in participation, many scholars again have argued the importance of social structure and culturally conditioned attitudes. Although socioeconomic status and age are positively correlated, more important for explaining the relatively high levels of participation by middle-aged persons is their sense of a "stake" in society. Unlike younger or older people, middle-aged citizens tend to be enmeshed in a complex set of social relationships which enhance their awareness of the personal relevance of politics. The "fall off" in participation rates among older citizens has other sources as well. Older people generally have less formal education and Western societies have tended to force older persons to disengage themselves from important areas of social life (forced retirement at age 65 being perhaps the most obvious example). In addition to reducing their sense of the personal relevance of politics, disengagement from important areas of economic and social life creates a generalized sense of powerlessness and incompetence which is transferred to the political arena. For the oldest citizens, physical incapacities may also play a role in restricting their ability to participate in at least some types of political activities.

Finally, the tendency for "politics to run in the family" can be explained in two ways. First, in terms of political socialization, in most cases children reared in families where parents, siblings or other relatives are politically active will learn that such activities are "natural and desirable." Overlaying these positive orientations toward political involvement will be unusually well-developed levels of knowledge about the political system and its access points. Second, it also is likely that membership in a "politicized" family has important implications for political recruitment. Persons in such families are more apt than others both to know and to be known by political activists. Placement in socio-political networks of this kind facilitates eventual entry into the political world.

Regarding attitudinal correlates of participation, certain aspects of the liberal democratic political cultures of contemporary Western countries (e.g., freedom of speech and assembly, respect for minority rights, the rule of law, an emphasis on the peaceful resolution of social conflict) permit positive orientations toward political action to be translated relatively easily into actual behaviour. Persons with high levels of political interest, regardless of sex, race, ethnic background, age or socioeconomic status, are not formally prohibited from participating in politics. There remain few legal barriers to participation, and there are few, if any, serious sanctions (legal or otherwise) associated with the decision to cease participating. Also, for many conventional forms of political activity, the financial costs are relatively low. (As noted, a major exception is candidacy for public elective office.) Moreover, participatory opportunities of some sort are relatively widespread. For example, political parties usually try to attract new workers at election time. In societies such as Canada where most citizens work for 40 hours or less per week, party work and some other forms of political activity such as contacting a public official or joining a community action group easily can be accommodated as a leisure-time pursuit. Of course, many of these opportunities for political participation may be judged less than satisfactory for the exercise of political influence or the achievement of particular policy goals. Such negative judgments about the instrumental value or intrinsic rewards of political action may be valid. We will defer consideration of this important question until later. The point here is simply that Canada's liberal democratic culture and the relatively high level of material well-being enjoyed by many of its citizens provide a low risk, low cost environment conducive to the translation of psychological dispositions toward political involvement into actual activity.

Empirically, the correlates of participation in provincial politics conform to most of the patterns described above. Regarding socioeconomic and demographic variables, however, it is apparent that one must distinguish carefully between various forms of political activity. Data on federal MPs, provincial MLAs and party officials to be presented in Chapters 5 and 6 clearly show that these forms of political participation are virtually monopolized by middle-aged, upper-middle class men with representation of the "charter" ethnic groups (Anglo-Celtic, French) being roughly proportional to percentages of persons in these groups in the population as a whole. Socioeconomic and demographic correlates of electorally related activities such as voting, discussing politics, attending rallies and part-time campaign work are much weaker. Middle-aged people, men and individuals with upper socioeconomic status are more active than others, but none of these differences is large. Similarly, with only minor exceptions, relationships between socioeconomic and demographic variables and other kinds of participation (e.g., contacting public officials, communal activity, protests) also are quite weak.

With regard to family background, studies of federal MPs, provincial MLAs and party activists support the proposition that those heavily involved in politics are considerably more likely than are persons with lesser levels of involvement to have parents or other relatives who were themselves politically active. In a survey of local party officials and members of the general public in Vancouver and Winnipeg, for instance, four times as many party officials had fathers or mothers who had been active in party work. Additionally, party officials from politicized families reported patterns of political socialization different from and more conducive to early and sustained political involvement than did other citizens.[12] Finally, this study indicates that being a member of a politically active family leads to the development of social ties which facilitate eventual political recruitment. These people tend to know and to be known by persons already politically active. Such social grids frequently constitute the "pathways to politics."[13]

Attitudinal correlates of participation are much stronger than most of the socioeconomic and demographic patterns examined above. This point can be illustrated using the provincial electoral activity scale (see Table 4.4). Political interest, strength of party identification, the personal competence dimension of political efficacy (see Chapter 3), and judgments regarding how much difference it makes which party controls the provincial government, all have stronger relationships with electorally related forms of participation than do any of the socioeconomic or demographic variables. These attitudes also have relatively strong relationships with other forms of participation such as contacting public officials and communal activity, but not with protest activities.

Thus far, we have considered relationships between political participation and socioeconomic, demographic and attitudinal characteristics one at a time. To ascertain the effects of these variables more precisely, multivariate analyses are required. These also enable us to determine

TABLE 4.4
Provincial Political Participation Scale by Selected
Attitudinal Variables, 1979

	Provincial Participation Scale				
	low				high
	0	1	2	3	4
Interest in Politics					
Follow politics: Not much at all	20%*	44	24	10	2
Fairly closely	4%	27	41	21	7
Very closely	2%	12	31	37	18
Political Efficacy					
Government responsiveness — Low	11%	38	30	17	5
— Moderate	10%	29	34	21	6
— High	8%	21	37	23	11
Political Efficacy					
Personal Competence — Low	13%	39	31	13	3
— Moderate	9%	27	35	21	8
— High	4%	21	33	31	12
Strength of Provincial Party Identification					
No identification	23%	41	27	9	0
Not very strong	19%	36	32	12	2
Fairly strong	7%	31	37	19	6
Very strong	3%	24	29	31	14
Party Differences					
Party in power in provinces makes:					
No difference	14%	42	29	12	3
Some difference	10%	30	38	17	5
A great deal of difference	5%	23	32	28	12

*horizontal percentages

the extent to which there are regional and provincial differences in participation over and above those that can be accounted for by the effects of the socioeconomic, demographic and attitudinal variables.[14] Measuring the magnitude of such regional and provincial effects is relevant to a more general comparison of the status of the provinces as representative democracies. The results of these analyses show that political interest, political efficacy, strength of party identification, age and ethnicity have statistically significant effects on frequency of voting in provincial elections and other electoral activities. For the electoral activities scale (but not for vote frequency), perceptions of social class location and orientation to provincial politics have significant effects. It also is noteworthy that even with the effects of other variables controlled, French/non-French differences in provincial participation rates remain substantial. Francophones participate more.

Three additional observations about these analyses are in order. First, the attitudinal variables (political interest, orientation toward provincial politics, strength of party identification, political efficacy) have much stronger effects on the overall electoral activities scale than on provincial vote frequency. In the latter analysis, French ethnicity is the dominant variable. Second, the inclusion of regional residency in the analyses does not enhance our ability to understand differences in provincial participation. For both measures of participation regional residency increases the explanatory power of the analysis by only 1%. Third, the total explanatory power of the several socioeconomic, demographic and attitudinal variables is less than perfect, a finding characteristic of other studies of political participation in Canada and elsewhere. Although there are several possible reasons for this finding, it reminds us that our understanding of why people participate in politics is incomplete.

It is useful to conduct analyses similar to those described above for other types of provincial political participation such as contacting public officials and campaign activity. Briefly, the results are similar to those for the overall electoral activities scale in that political interest and political efficacy are relatively strong predictors. Strength of partisanship enhances the likelihood of campaign activity, but is not related to contacting officials. As for demographic characteristics, younger people again are found to participate less than middle-aged persons, but French ethnicity does not have significant effects. Sex, an insignificant variable in the analyses of electoral activities, has a small effect on contacting officials (men are more likely to do so). The measures of socioeconomic status (income, subjective social class) have very weak effects, with only social class perceptions having a significant influence on the likelihood of contacting officials. Finally, for neither campaign activity nor contacting officials are regional effects significant once other variables are controlled.

The general weakness of regional effects on levels of participation in provincial politics is consonant with the arguments presented in Chapter 3 regarding similarities across the several provinces in attitudes toward political participation and related aspects of democratic government and politics. The inquiry into regional effects can be pressed somewhat further by conducting multivariate analyses of political participation within each region. These additional analyses produce similar results, however. In every region the attitudinal variables are strong predictors when considered as a group. Considered individually, orientations toward provincial politics have relatively strong effects only in Quebec, while political interest and strength of party identification have marked effects in all regions. Political efficacy has significant effects in three regions (Quebec, Ontario and British Columbia) and just fails to achieve significance in the Atlantic and Prairie provinces.

Regarding the demographic characteristics, age has significant effects in three regions (Quebec, Ontario, British Columbia) with younger people consistently participating less. Also, differences in the electoral participation rates of men and women are small in every region. As for the measures of socioeconomic status, only subjective social class achieves statistical significance, and then only in the Prairies. The weakness of provincial differences *within* regions is suggested by the fact that in neither the Atlantic provinces nor in the Prairies is residency in a particular province associated with one's score on the electoral activities scale.

VOTING AND ELECTIONS

In every province large numbers of citizens avail themselves of the opportunity to vote in provincial elections. Indeed, voting is by far the most popular form of participation in provincial politics. Yet, by itself, the fact that many people regularly troop to the polls in provincial elections does not warrant the conclusion that representative democracy has been achieved. For elections to serve as truly effective instruments of democratic governance several conditions must be met. Voters must be presented with authentic choices. Only if parties and their candidates take differing positions on issues of concern to the electorate can "real" choice be said to exist. In addition, voters must be cognizant of the alternatives confronting them. The ability to choose wisely when casting one's ballot is contingent upon having accurate information about available choices. Voters also must make their decisions on the basis of the issue positions of the parties and do so in such a way that the party selected is the one which articulates an issue position closest to the voters' own preferences. Lastly, if elected to office, a party must attempt to implement policies congruent with the issue positions it assumed during the election campaign. Only if these conditions are met is it possible to conclude that elections are functioning as they should in a representative democracy.

The above conditions are simply stated. Much more difficult is an evaluation of the extent to which they are met in practice. For example, scholars have debated at length whether or not Canadian parties offer meaningful alternatives to the electorate.[15] There is even considerable disagreement over what constitutes a "real" or "meaningful" alternative. The nature of voting choice also has been hotly contested. Some analysts have argued that most voters are essentially irrational and ignorant, subject to group prejudices and the pre-packaged personality appeals of "charismatic" party leaders, the latter being merchandised and sold to the electorate by slick media campaigns.[16] Others maintain that voters act as intelligently as can be expected, their choices reflecting essentially rational responses under conditions of very imperfect information.[17] Nor is there agreement about how parties perform once they capture power. Whether parties behave differently once in office, and if so, whether their behaviour is predicated upon accurate perceptions of their electoral mandates remain subjects of lively debate.[18]

These controversies are indicative of the acute difficulties involved in accurately measuring how voting and elections contribute to the achievement of representative democracy. Some of these difficulties arise because of a lack of adequate information. Others are products of divergent interpretations of the same "facts." These problems notwithstanding, we can investigate several relevant features of provincial electoral processes. In particular, we will consider the impact of issue perceptions on electoral choice and explore relationships between individual voting behaviour and election outcomes. By so doing we will lay the groundwork for a more general evaluation of how closely the provincial political systems approximate the ideals of representative democracy.

PATTERNS OF ELECTORAL CHOICE

The most striking fact about provincial elections is the tendency for voters to behave differently in different provinces. As is evident from the results of recent elections (Table 4.5), no party is able to obtain large proportions of the vote in every province. Liberal voting strength is

TABLE 4.5
Results of Recent Provincial Elections
(percentage of popular vote)

Province	Liberal	PC	NDP	SC/Créd.	UN	PQ	Other
Newfoundland (1979)	41%*	50	8	—	—	—	—
Prince Edward Island (1979)	46%	53	—	—	—	—	—
Nova Scotia (1978)	39%	46	15	—	—	—	—
New Brunswick (1978)	45%	45	6	—	—	—	5
Quebec (1981)	46%	—	—	—	4	49	1
Ontario (1981)	34%	45	21	—	—	—	—
Manitoba (1977)	12%	49	39	—	—	—	—
Saskatchewan (1978)	15%	38	48	—	—	—	—
Alberta (1979)	6%	57	16	20	—	—	1
British Columbia (1979)	—	5	46	49	—	—	—

*horizontal percentages

substantial in Ontario, Quebec and the Atlantic provinces, but in the Prairies and British Columbia no more than one voter in seven chooses this party. For the NDP, this pattern is largely reversed — weakness in the Atlantic provinces coupled with strength in Manitoba, Saskatchewan, and British Columbia. Similar to the Liberals, the NDP obtains the support of 20 to 35% of the Ontario electorate. Social Credit voting is largely concentrated in British Columbia and Alberta, and Union Nationale and Parti Québécois support is, of course, confined to Quebec. At present, the party with the broadest appeal is the Progressive Conservatives, which received at least one-third of the vote in eight of the provinces in the most recent provincial elections. Nevertheless, PC strength in British Columbia is minimal and the party does not even field candidates in Quebec provincial elections.

Such differences in provincial voting patterns are not new, but rather have existed throughout the post-World War Two period. As a result, patterns and levels of competition among different parties have varied greatly from one province to the next for many years. This point can be appreciated by considering the data in Table 4.6. These data show that the Liberals have held power provinciallly for 76% of the post-war period in Prince Edward Island, but have never formed a government in Ontario. In contrast, the PCs have been in office continually since 1943 in the latter province, but have failed to win a single election in Saskatchewan. The NDP has never won an election east of Manitoba, but has formed governments in all of the western provinces except Alberta. Such examples could be multiplied, but it is abundantly evident that patterns of individual voting behaviour, party competition and election outcomes have varied sharply across the provinces.

Two additional points about relationships among voting behaviour, party competition and election outcomes are noteworthy. In several provinces voters have given very strong support to particular parties for lengthy periods, producing marked tendencies toward one-party dominance in these provinces. In Newfoundland, Prince Edward Island, Ontario, Saskatchewan, Alberta and British Columbia a single party has held office for over 70% of the post-war period. Further, in no province have as many as half of the elections produced a change in government. Relatedly, the tendency for a single party to remain in office for long periods has not been solely the product of patterns of individual voting choice. Rather, this is a tendency which is accentuated by the operation of provincial electoral systems. With the exception of two elections in British Columbia (1952, 1953), votes have been translated into seats through the use of either single- or multi-member plurality electoral systems.[19] The candidate or candidates receiving the largest share (not necessarily a majority) of the popular vote in a constituency win(s) the seat(s). As a result, the allocation of seats only imperfectly reflects parties' electoral strength; the party with the greatest number of votes

TABLE 4.6
Interparty Competition in Provincial Elections, 1945–1979

Province	Number of Elections	Number of Government Turnovers	Number of Parties Forming Government	Percentage of Period Governing Parties Held Office	Average Percentage of Seats Won by Governing Party	Average Difference in Percentage of Seats and Votes Won by Governing and Largest Opposition Party	
						Seats	Votes
Newfoundland	10	1	2	Lib = 73 PC = 27	76	54	22
Prince Edward Island	10	3	2	Lib = 76 PC = 24	72	45	8
Nova Scotia	10	3	2	Lib = 56 PC = 44	70	44	9
New Brunswick	9	3	2	Lib = 45 PC = 55	63	26	6
Quebec	9	4	3	UN = 52 Lib = 39 PQ = 10	71	41	12
Ontario	10	0	1	PC = 100	66	47	11
Manitoba	10	3	3	Lib = 38 PC = 53 NDP = 24	55	27	9
Saskatchewan	9	2	2	Lib = 23 CCF/NDP = 77	67	36	10
Alberta	9	1	2	SC = 74 PC = 26	84	74	29
British Columbia	12	3	4	Lib } 21 PC } NDP = 9 SC = 71	65	38	8

tends to win a disproportionate number of seats. Table 4.6 documents this tendency. In all provinces but Manitoba the governing party, on average, has won at least three-fifths of the seats. In seven provinces, it has won at least two-thirds. A comparison of the last two columns of the table shows how the electoral system has influenced these results. In all provinces, percentage differences in seats between governing and opposition parties greatly exceed percentage differences in votes.

Clearly, although plurality electoral systems may have several virtues,[20] they do not accurately reflect electoral preferences. By the same token, it is noteworthy that these distortions are matters of degree. It is not the case that plurality electoral systems totally pervert the will of provincial electorates. The party preferred by a plurality or majority of voters is very likely to receive a plurality or majority of seats and hence is able to form a government.[21] Moreover, less popular parties, if they receive more than a modicum of support, usually will be able to elect at least some of their candidates. Since votes do count, it is necessary to investigate how electoral choices are made.

DETERMINANTS OF ELECTORAL CHOICE

Sociodemographic Characteristics: Traditionally, studies of voting in Canada have emphasized the importance of ethno-linguistic, religious and regional divisions in the population.[22] One might assume that these societal cleavages have such long-term salience and significance that voters in particular social groups simply cast ballots *en bloc* for parties perceived as representing their interests. One might go further and argue that for most people the act of voting is nothing more than a symbolic affirmation of primordial group loyalties. Certainly, there is conventional wisdom consistent with such interpretations. Perhaps most familiar are the clichés that French Canadians and Roman Catholics consistently give overwhelming support to the Liberals, Anglo-Saxon Protestants traditionally vote Conservative and blue-collar workers favour the NDP.[23]

If such bloc voting were descriptive of reality, how would one evaluate the contribution of provincial electoral processes to representative democracy? Would one conclude that most voters were unthinking automatons, prisoners of irrational group prejudices? Such an interpretation might seem plausible, particularly when one is assessing the effects of societal divisions such as religion that have few if any linkages with present-day political issues. On the other hand, cleavages such as ethnicity, language, region and social class *are* related to debates that have both historic and contemporary resonance for many voters. Accordingly, strong and enduring correlations between such social divisions and electoral choice might reflect essentially rational commitments by many voters to parties they think will best defend and advance their long-term interests. Thus, the interpretation of strong correlations between societal cleavages and voting is problematic. Of course, the very existence of such correlations is a prior empirical question.

Inspection of correlations between several sociodemographic characteristics (sex, age, ethnicity, religion, and socioeconomic status) and voting for the winning party in the most recent provincial election in each province suggests two important conclusions. With few exceptions, most of the relationships are quite weak, indicating that differences in the voting behaviour of various social groups are not overwhelming. Further, the signs (+, −) of the correlations reveal that the party preferences of the same group can vary in different provinces. Religion provides a good example of this point. The strength of the correlation between religious affiliation and voting is −.25 in Ontario and +.29 in Newfoundland. These two correlations are of approximately equal size, but the signs are different even though the Conservatives won the election in both cases. In Newfoundland, Roman Catholics tend to support the Tories, in Ontario they do not. Correlations between ethnicity and voting are equally instructive. In Newfoundland, Nova Scotia and New Brunswick, the relationships are of virtually equal strength. In the first of these provinces, however, Anglo-Celtic voters tended to oppose the victorious PCs, whereas in the latter two they supported the Conservatives.

Not all of the stronger correlations involved religious and ethnic cleavages. For example, age differences in voting were significant in Quebec, Ontario and British Columbia. In Quebec, older voters favoured the Liberals, whereas in Ontario and British Columbia they opted for the PCs and the Socreds, respectively. Conspicuous by their absence were correlations involving sex and socioeconomic status. In each case such relationships were significant in only one province. In Quebec, men were somewhat more likely than women to favour the PQ; in British Columbia, persons of higher socioeconomic status tended to vote Social Credit.

The weak correlations between socioeconomic status and voting deserve additional comment. As indicated in Chapter 3, social class typically is one of the most important, if not the primary, politically relevant social cleavage in advanced industrial societies.[24] Blue-collar workers and other lower status persons provide strong support for various left-of-centre parties (e.g., social democratic, socialist and communist parties) committed to redistributing wealth from the upper and middle to the working and lower classes and the more general leveling of economic, social and political hierarchies. Middle and upper class persons, in contrast, tend to support centre or right-of-centre parties advocating no or only moderate incremental change. Research at the federal level in Canada indicates that this country is an exception since — given Canada's high levels of industrialization and urbanization — correlations between measures of socioeconomic status and federal voting are surprisingly weak in virtually every province.[25] The present analysis indicates that such weak correlations typify provincial voting patterns as well.

The weakness of these correlations is further illustrated in Table 4.7. Displayed in this table are indices of class voting computed by subtracting the percentages of subjectively identified middle or upper class persons voting for left-of-centre parties from the percentage of subjectively identified working or lower class persons choosing such parties.[26] These indices range from −100 to +100, with values greater than zero indicating that working or lower-class persons differentially favour the left-of-centre political alternatives. As Table 4.7 shows, the tendency for working-class persons to favour these parties is relatively weak in every province except British Columbia. This is true at both the federal and provincial levels with class voting being slightly stronger in provincial elections in most cases. Moreover, the weakness of the class-voting relationship holds for analyses in which the NDP is considered the only left-of-centre party as well as for those where the Liberal party also is classified as a left-of-centre option.[27] To place these findings in comparative perspective, it is useful to note that similar analyses in countries such as Great Britain and Australia regularly have produced indices of class voting varying from +30 to +50.[28] Only at the provincial level in British Columbia does one find even roughly comparable levels of class polarization.

In general, relationships between sociodemographic characteristics and provincial voting behaviour are neither strong nor uniform across the country. Certain social groups in particular provinces do strongly favour particular parties, but these tendencies cannot fully explain, either statistically or substantively, how people vote in provincial elections. Thus, if many voters do make their choices on an issue basis, these issues are not tied in any straightforward way to voters' group memberships. It is necessary, therefore, to press beyond simple sociological criteria if we are to understand how people make their electoral choices.

Partisanship: Political parties are highly salient objects on the electoral landscape and so it can be argued that popular orientations toward parties provide a key to understanding voting behaviour and election outcomes. In every province overwhelming proportions of the electorate report psychological attachments to federal and provincial political parties. Great majorities of these voters are not formal members of party organizations. Rather, in some sense or other, they think of themselves as Liberals, Conservatives, New Democrats, Péquistes and so forth, or at least as being "close" to a party. Moreover, in every province, whenever an election is held, partisan identifications are very reliable guides to voting choice. Considering the most recent provincial elec-

TABLE 4.7

Indices of Class Voting in Provincial and Federal Elections

Province	NDP Voting		NDP & Liberal Voting	
	Last Provincial Election	1979 Federal Election	Last Provincial Election	1979 Federal Election
Newfoundland	−12	−13	− 6	−26
Prince Edward Island	*	− 2	− 8	−11
Nova Scotia	+ 3	− 8	+11	0
New Brunswick	+ 7	+ 8	+14	− 3
Quebec	− 5†	− 2	− 4†	+ 1
Ontario	+12	+11	+13	+10
Manitoba	+16	+ 8	+11	+10
Saskatchewan	+11	+ 7	+11	+10
Alberta	+ 5	+ 1	+ 3	+12
British Columbia	+25	+11	+21	+20
Canada	+ 5	+ 4	+ 4	+ 4

*cannot be computed, no NDP voters in sample
†substituting Parti Québécois for NDP

tions, 90% of a national sample of provincial party identifiers interviewed in 1979 reported voting for "their" party, a percentage that was typical of the results in each province considered separately.

Given such extremely strong relationships it is important to inquire about the nature of partisanship.[29] How partisan attachments are formed and the conditions under which they change are crucial for comprehending the act of voting. If these attachments develop early in life as a result of non-rational socialization processes and are resistant to change as a result of experiences in later life, then it follows that voting choice is not the result of conscious deliberation about party stands on salient contemporary issues. At most, current partisan attachments may reflect the echoes of great issues from bygone days that mobilized and crystallized the partisanship of earlier generations.

If, in contrast, voters' partisan attachments are not immutable, but rather are subject to change in response to present-day political issues, personalities and events, then an alternative conception of partisanship is possible. According to this conception, partisan feelings reflect the results of "rough and ready" calculations about party stands on important issues or perceptions of the relative competence of parties and their leaders to implement widely desired policy goals. This does not necessarily mean that partisan preferences are reconsidered in every election and are simply another way of expressing current vote intentions. Rather, the adoption of partisan attachments may constitute a "standing decision" to support a particular party as the one that, generally speaking, seems to serve one's interests best. To reduce the costs of acquiring sufficient political information and obviate the necessity of making an informed choice *de novo* at each successive election, the voter adopts a partisan attachment. This attachment serves as a convenient, cost-effective guide for making voting choices and simplifying the "buzzing and booming" confusion of political life. In a sense, such attachments and the behaviour they evoke represent "investments" by voters.[30] As such, partisan ties are flexible. Presented with evidence that they no longer serve their best interests, voters can be expected to divest themselves of their present partisan attachments and invest their political capital elsewhere.

These two conceptions of partisanship and voting, for sake of convenience, can be labelled the "socialization" and "investment" models. How many voters actually conform to either model is an empirical question. Existing evidence suggests that electorates in the several provinces contain a mix of partisan types — some people seem to conform to the first model (socialization), whereas others manifest characteristics suggestive of the second (investment). Let us consider some pertinent data. First, regarding the initial development and long-term stability of partisanship, intergenerational (i.e., parent-child) agreement in partisan preferences is very imperfect: from 22% in

Alberta to 43% in Prince Edward Island report having the same partisan preferences as their fathers. For mothers, comparable figures are 17% (Alberta) and 39% (Nova Scotia). Aggregating all provincial electorates the figures are 27% (fathers) and 22% (mothers). If one considers only those voters who recall that their parents had partisan preferences, the relevant percentages are substantially greater, but still only slightly over half of all voters state that their current partisanship is the same as that of one or both of their parents. Thus, although initial partisan attachments are frequently acquired as a result of parent-child socialization processes,[31] in many cases these party ties are changed later in life.

There are other, more direct indicators of the mutability of partisanship. Most simply, when asked if they had ever felt closer to any other political party, large numbers of voters in every province respond affirmatively. In the 1979 election study, 29% of all those interviewed reported that they had previously felt closer to another provincial party. On a province by province basis, the percentage indicating that they have altered their provincial partisan preferences varied from a low of 19% in New Brunswick to a high of 47% in Manitoba. Additional evidence of partisan change in provincial politics derives from direct comparisons of the partisanship of persons interviewed in both 1974 and 1979. (Such comparisons avoid biases that might possibly be introduced by asking voters to recall previous partisan ties.) For the country as a whole, 38% reported different provincial partisan allegiances in these two surveys. For 16%, change involved moving to or from the status of "nonidentifier," (i.e., describing oneself as not having a partisan attachment). However, fully 22% actually changed their provincial party identifications (e.g., from Liberal to New Democrat). Again, differences in reports of provincial partisanship between 1974 and 1979 can be detected in every province, with the percentage changing their identifications varying from a low of 19% in Prince Edward Island to a high of 40% in Newfoundland, Ontario, Saskatchewan and Alberta.

Isolating factors that induce people to change their partisan preferences is important if we wish to understand the nature of voting decisions. If such changes are stimulated by reactions to parties' issue positions, or actual or anticipated performance in office, rather than responses to non-rational "personality" appeals by party leaders or local candidates, one could conclude that partisanship is not merely an affective attachment but rather has an instrumental quality. Although a thoroughgoing analysis of factors associated with partisan change remains to be conducted, it does appear that such changes often are reactions to policy or party performance considerations. When asked why they changed their provincial party identifications, 12% of the 1979 national sample mentioned specific policies and 17% cited more general issue concerns. An additional 23% made reference to the performance of the party in office. More detailed analyses suggest that there are many voters in every province who cite policy and/or party performance reasons for partisan change. The weight given to policies versus party performance does vary across provinces, but everywhere there are large numbers of persons for whom partisanship seems to be a contingent and instrumental tie rather than a deep-seated, non-rational attachment.

Further evidence supporting this interpretation is provided by data on the positive or negative tenor of reasons for switching partisan allegiances and the timing of such changes. Regarding the former, many voters indicate that they abandoned an earlier partisan tie because of *negative* evaluations of their previous party. Nationally, in 1979, 42% cited such negative reasons, 35% mentioned a positive attraction to a new party and the remaining reasons could not be classified in these terms. These figures are indicative, in a gross sense at least, of the kinds of reasons for partisan change offered by electorates in every province. That many people evidently are prompted by negative evaluations to abandon an "old" party rather than being positively attracted by a "new" one can be interpreted as further evidence of the contingent nature of partisan allegiances.

The timing of partisan change is also suggestive. Of those interviewed in 1979 who had changed their partisanship 39% indicated that they did so in or after 1976, 29% cited 1970 to 1975, and 31% mentioned a date prior to 1970 or gave vague answers such as "a long time ago." A relatively large incidence of recent partisan change can be found in all provinces with the percentages switching since 1976 varying from a low of 24% in British Columbia to a high of 62% in Prince Edward Island. Overall, data on the timing of partisan change suggests the existence of an ongoing process. While the unhinging of partisan allegiances may be triggered by traumatic socioeconomic or political events such as wars and depressions, it is not confined to the occurrence of crises. Rather, it appears that many voters are willing to alter their partisan allegiances in response to less dramatic features of social and political life.

There are two other aspects of the party identification data which reinforce the idea that partisanship is not necessarily a blind affective tie. First, many persons do not identify with the same party at the federal and provincial levels of government. For the country as a whole, 40% of those interviewed in 1979 did not have consistent partisan ties at both levels. Twenty-two percent actually identified with different parties at the two levels, and the remainder identified at one level only or had no partisan ties whatsoever.[32] The number of inconsistent partisans varied widely across the several provinces, but nowhere was it less than 18% (Newfoundland). In two provinces (Quebec and British Columbia), more than half of the electorate failed to display consistent partisan ties. Second, many persons indicated that they did not identify strongly with a provincial party. Considering the entire 1979 electorate, only 29% stated that they were "very strongly" attached to their provincial parties. The frequent weakness of partisan attachments may well reflect their tentative, instrumental character.

In sum, there are several indications that partisan ties frequently are instrumental and contingent rather than non-rational products of early life socialization experiences. It is, in fact, likely that provincial electorates contain both types of individuals. How many are of the former type? This is difficult to estimate precisely, but if one includes all those who (a) report changing their partisan ties, or (b) do not identify with the same party at both levels of government, or (c) are not strongly identified with a provincial party, the total approaches 60% of all those interviewed in recent national election studies. Although the number of such persons, whom we will designate as *flexible* partisan to distinguish them from persons with *durable* partisan allegiances, varies discernibly from one province to the next, in every case it is sufficiently large to influence election outcomes.

The large number of flexible partisans suggests that at least some voters may make their decisions on the basis of political issues. However, for voters to react rationally to issues, it is necessary for them to perceive the existence of issues and to have sufficient information to make an informed judgment about which party will best serve their interests. As an indicator of the extent of the electorate's exposure to political information it may be noted that 14% of those interviewed in 1979 stated they follow politics "very closely" and a further 48% placed themselves in the "fairly closely" category.[33] Together these two groups constitute nearly two-thirds of the national electorate. Further, many of these people (39% of the entire 1979 sample) indicate that they are at least as interested in provincial as in federal or local politics.[34] Large numbers of such provincially oriented persons — from a minimum of 29% in Ontario to a maximum of 54% in British Columbia — can be found in every province.

Data on partisanship and political interest may be employed to develop a typology of provincial electorates.[35] Such a typology will show how many voters are flexible partisans with at least moderate levels of political interest. These are persons most likely to base their electoral decisions on issue-related considerations. In constructing such a typology it also is useful to think of the electorate as being composed of four groups of political participants. First, there is what may be termed the *permanent* electorate, (i.e., persons who vote in every provincial election for which they are eligible). Second, there are persons who cast ballots occasionally, whom we may call *transient* voters. The flow of transient voters into and out of the active electorate may well determine the outcome of a particular electoral contest. Third, in every election, there is a group of *new* voters, persons eligible to cast a ballot for the first time.

Fourth, there are the *permanent non-voters*, persons who either have chosen or been forced to disenfranchise themselves. This group, by consistently not participating, is not responsible for producing differences in election outcomes over time. Thus, it may be ignored when constructing a typology of provincial electorates.

Table 4.8 presents such a typology. The typology, based on the 1979 survey data, indicates that there is a sizable group of persons who are apt to react rationally to political issues and who are regular participants in provincial elections. These are the flexible high and flexible moderate interest partisans in the permanent electorate. On a national basis they constitute nearly 30% of the entire active electorate and they can be found in large numbers in each province, with percentages varying from 21% (Nova Scotia) to 41% (British Columbia). Flexible high and moderate interest partisans also constitute approximately one-third and one-fourth of the transient and new voters respectively. In sum, even though in every province flexible high and moderate interest partisans constitute minorities of the electorate, their numbers are sufficiently large in all cases to permit issues to play important roles in determining election outcomes.

ISSUES AND VOTING

Thus far, this discussion of provincial electoral behaviour has not directly considered the impact of issues on voting. Rather, it has attempted to identify groups of voters who might make their electoral decisions on the basis of informed assessments of the issue positions of parties. Determining more precisely the effects of issues on voting is difficult given constraints imposed by available data. Nonetheless, the 1979 national election survey does permit us to make some headway. In this study respondents were asked which factor, party leaders, local candidates or parties as a whole, was most important in affecting their voting decision in the most recent provincial election.[36] They then were asked if there was an issue basis for their selection of that particular factor. The results indicate that large proportions of those selecting any of the three options (i.e., party leaders, local candidates, parties as a whole) designated an issue or issues as the basis for their vote. In total, self-identified issue voters constitute 33% of the 1979 national sample, with their presence in various provinces ranging from a low of 23% in Prince Edward Island to a high of 41% in Quebec and Alberta (Table 4.9, last column).

Voters' reports of their reasons for casting a ballot admittedly are not definitive evidence of the reality of issue voting. Some self-identified issue voters may *rationalize* decisions made on other grounds in issue terms, judging that reporting an "issue reason" for voting is the

TABLE 4.8

A Typology of Provincial Electorates, Based on Partisanship, Political Interest and Vote History[a]

		The "Permanent" Electorate[b] Partisanship		The "Transient" Electorate[c] Partisanship		The New Voters[d] Partisanship	
		Durable	Flexible	Durable	Flexible	Durable	Flexible
Political Interest	High	5.7	7.4	0.7	1.5	0.2	0.2
	Moderate	17.4	22.4	2.5	5.3	1.4	1.5
	Low	9.4	13.7	2.5	4.5	1.8	2.1
		32.5	43.5	5.7	11.3	3.4	3.8

[a]Total N for all types = 2281 (national weight)
[b]Persons who vote in "all" or "most" provincial elections and who voted in last two provincial elections
[c]Persons who vote in "some" provincial elections or who voted in one but not both of the last two provincial elections
[d]Persons newly eligible to vote in last provincial election

TABLE 4.9
Most Important Factor in Voting Decision,
Last Provincial Election

Province	Party Leaders	Local Candidates	Parties as a Whole	Percentage With Issues Basis* for Vote
Newfoundland	28%	33	39	34
Prince Edward Island	28%	41	31	23
Nova Scotia	27%	25	48	29
New Brunswick	31%	38	31	29
Quebec	38%	21	41	41
Ontario	25%	35	40	29
Manitoba	26%	24	50	26
Saskatchewan	23%	27	50	32
Alberta	42%	21	37	41
British Columbia	23%	15	63	34
Canada	30%	27	44	33

*combined "party leader," "local candidate" and "parties as a whole" groups

"appropriate" response. Others may *project* their personal issue preferences onto parties favoured for non-rational reasons. Certainly, one would not wish to include such rationalizations and projections in an estimate of the true magnitude of issue voting. However, two additional types of information are available to buttress the conclusion that issues really do have resonance for many voters.

The first is relatively simple and concerns the kinds of issues identified by persons offering issue responses to the party-leader-candidate question sequence. Those signifying that there was an issue basis for their vote were asked to identify specific issues. Most were able to do so and selected issues that have been subjects of lively controversy among the parties. The Quebec data provide a good example. Fully 65% of the self-identified issue voters in this province mentioned some aspect of the relationship between Quebec and the rest of Canada as the issue determining the direction of their vote in 1976. More generally, large numbers of voters in every province (29% across the entire country) mentioned economic and related issues such as inflation, unemployment, or energy shortages. Other frequently cited issues were social welfare and the performance of governing parties. The fact that many of the issues cited referred to important social and economic problems rather than to idiosyncratic matters removed from the substance of current political debate, suggests that in many cases expressed issue concerns *did* genuinely motivate persons mentioning them.

A second type of evidence may be derived from analyses of federal voting behaviour using a typology of partisanship and political interest similar to the one presented above. Employing a battery of information on voters' issue preferences, the intensity of their feeling regarding specific issues and perceptions of which party was closest to them on these issues,[37] it is possible to analyze the impact of issues on the vote while controlling for several other factors such as feelings about party leaders and local candidates. These analyses (conducted using data gathered in 1968, 1974 and 1979) consistently indicate the existence of significant issue effects concentrated among the flexible partisans, particularly those with higher levels of political interest.[38] The similarity of the typologies used to classify voters at the federal and provincial levels and the fact that a large majority of persons classified as flexible moderate or high interest partisans in federal politics also are so categorized in the provincial typology discussed above, strongly suggest the reality of issue effects on provincial voting.

There is also evidence that flexible partisans who are sensitive to political issues when making their voting decisions can influence election *outcomes*. Although the amount of vote switching in provincial elections in different provinces varies, in every case the numbers are sufficiently great to dramatically affect election results, *if* all those switching were to move in the same direction. The 1979 survey data, for example, reveal that the percentage of voters casting their ballots for different parties in two successive provincial electoral contests varies from 11% in British Columbia to 29% in Newfoundland. Moreover, as Figure 4.2 illustrates, voter migration is heavily concentrated among flexible partisans. On average, for all provinces, 28% of flexible partisans as opposed to only 6% of durable partisans switched their votes in the two most recent provincial elections. This pattern obtains in every province.

In general, the impact of vote switching on election outcomes is problematic. Much depends on directions of voter migration and the way voters are distributed across the several constituencies. Regarding the latter point, we already have seen how the electoral system operates to distort the relationship between parties' vote and seat totals. In the present context, it may be readily appreciated that the effect of vote switching might be very different if it were concentrated in only a few constituencies where pre-existing voting patterns heavily favoured one party, as opposed to being more evenly divided across a number of constituencies where differences in support levels for various parties were small. Under the latter condition, even a small amount of vote switching, provided the movement was concentrated in a particular direction, could be decisive.

Earlier, it was noted that several provinces have been characterized by lengthy periods of one-party dominance. Since these provinces also

FIGURE 4.2   **Incidence of Vote Switching in Provincial Elections by Partisan Type**

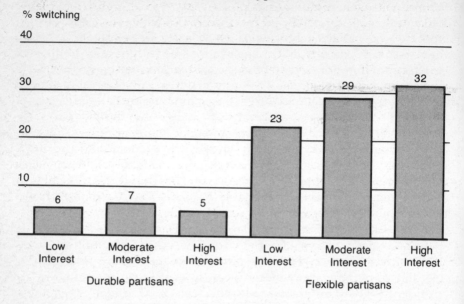

manifest substantial amounts of vote switching in successive elections, it may be inferred that very often patterns of switching in such provinces were countervailing — parties exchanged approximately equal numbers of voters and the net effect on the election outcome was small.[39] Occasionally, however, elections do result in a change of government. Historically, the balance of political forces in certain provinces has been drastically and permanently altered in a single election. Frequently, such dramatic reversals of political fortune not only have swept a previous opposition party into power but also have signalled the onset of a new period of one-party dominance. To reiterate, the two types of elections, one in which a long-term governing party remains in office and the other in which a party captures power, either for the first time or after a lengthy sojourn in the political wilderness, can both be characterized by substantial vote switching. It is the *net effects* of such switching which differ greatly.

The 1976 Quebec and the 1977 Ontario elections illustrate the importance of contrasting patterns of vote switching on provincial election outcomes. In the former contest, the Parti Québécois, formed only eight years previously, increased its vote and seat totals by 11% and 59% respectively and swept the Liberals out of office. In the latter, the PCs, in power in Ontario continuously since 1943, added 3% to their vote total and won seven additional seats. As a result, they maintained their status as a minority government (with 59 of 125 seats in Queen's Park). Patterns of vote switching in these two elections are shown in Table 4.10. Although the 1979 survey data indicate the total amount of switching in Quebec was twice as great as that in Ontario (26% v. 13%), there was enough voter movement in the latter province to produce a result very different from the actual outcome.[40] Moreover, as Table 4.10 shows, in both provinces, voter migration was highly concentrated among the flexible partisans. The real difference in the two contests was the *pattern* of switching. As columns two and three of the table show, in Quebec very few voters in any partisan political interest category abandoned the PQ and for every category, except the durable low and moderate interest types, sizable numbers (in excess of 20% in each case) switched to the PQ. In contrast, in Ontario, although the Tories enjoyed a net advantage in exchanges with other parties in four of the six partisan political interest categories, these advantages were relatively small, a pattern quite in keeping with the overall election result.

TABLE 4.10
Incidence and Patterns of Vote Switching by Partisan
Type in Two Provincial Elections

A. Quebec, 1976 Partisan Type	% Switching	% Leaving PQ	% Moving to PQ
Durable high interest	17	0	14
Durable moderate interest	6	1	4
Durable low interest	7	0	2
Flexible high interest	31	0	22
Flexible moderate interest	41	2	29
Flexible low interest	44	0	34

B. Ontario, 1977 Partisan Type	% Switching	% Leaving PCs	% Moving to PCs
Durable high interest	0	0	0
Durable moderate interest	6	1	2
Durable low interest	0	0	0
Flexible high interest	17	6	9
Flexible moderate interest	26	4	10
Flexible low interest	16	4	7

These two elections also demonstrate the varying effects of transient and new voters. In Quebec, nearly two-thirds of the latter as opposed to only one-third of the former voted Péquiste. In contrast, over half of the transients but only one-third of the new voters chose the Liberals. Clearly, the PQ cause was aided by the presence of the newly eligible voters (the vast proportion of whom were young Francophones who had reached the age of majority since the 1973 election). On the other hand, the party would have won a more convincing victory had the transients decided to remain outside the active electorate. On balance, since the two groups were of approximately equal size, the *combined* effect of these two types of electoral replacement (i.e., variable turnout and demographic change) was small.

In Ontario, the distribution of transient voter support closely paralleled that given to various parties by the entire electorate. New voters, in contrast, manifested a distinct bias in favour of the Liberals, but the effect of their support was minimal since there were relatively few of them in the 1977 electorate. The paucity of new voters was partially a result of holding two provincial elections in a 21-month period (demographic and immigration trends being other relevant factors determining this type of electoral replacement). Thus, in Ontario, the circumstances of the election impinged on the ability of the new voter group to affect the election outcome. The transient group, given its size, potentially was a much more important force. As an instrument of political change, its force was blunted, not by countervailing tendencies among new voters as in the Quebec case, but by the pattern of voting decisions by transient voters themselves.

SUMMARY: VOTING, ELECTIONS AND REPRESENTATIVE DEMOCRACY

As the analyses of recent provincial elections in Ontario and Quebec illustrate, electoral outcomes are the product of a complex process. The way in which this process operates does much to determine the extent to which the provincial political systems approximate the model of representative democracy. This model requires that citizens choose their governors by selecting rationally among alternative groups of public office-seekers pledged to implement differing, well-defined policy agendas. Evidence presented in this chapter suggests that provincial electorates contain sizable numbers of people who are sufficiently flexible in their partisanship and sufficiently interested in politics to behave with at least a "rough and ready" rationality in the electoral arena. However, these people coexist in provincial electorates with others whose partisan attachments and/or political interest levels are such that it is unlikely that their voting decisions represent much more than the (re)affirmation of group loyalties or affective responses to parties and the personalities of their leaders and candidates. Complicating the situation further, electorates are not static entities. Rather, demographic processes and variations in political participation ensure that the mix of voters is never precisely the same in successive elections. Entering into and exiting from the electorate at any time are varying proportions of flexible and durable partisans with differing levels of political interest and knowledge. The composition of electorates thus ensures that provincial electoral processes will approximate only very imperfectly the requirements of representative democracy.

There are other limiting factors as well. Even the most interested voter will be constrained by available resources (e.g., time, energy, money) when searching for pertinent information. In fact, what most voters know about the political world is presented to them by the mass media. To the extent that the quality and quantity of political information presented by the media are influenced by politically irrelevant criteria (e.g., available time or space, the perceived need to maximize audience size or subscriptions), the potential for rational political action is diminished.[41] Moreover, even if all voters did have all the information needed to make informed choices, these choices still must be translated into election outcomes by the operation of provincial electoral systems. Present systems have strong tendencies to distort the expressed preferences of the electorate when translating votes into seats since the number of the latter, not the former, is the criterion by which governing parties are selected.

Additionally, serious limitations on the achievement of representative democracy are imposed by the behaviour of political parties and the inability of citizens to influence this behaviour. Specifically, unless parties provide voters with alternative policy options, options which reflect the issue concerns of large segments of the electorate, voters will not be able to behave in accord with the norms of representative democracy. Choosing wisely is impossible if relevant choices are not offered. In this regard, two considerations are pertinent. First, there are the kinds of choices presented to citizens when they vote. Although some critics have argued that Canadian parties do not offer "real" choices to voters, majorities (ranging in size from 57% in New Brunswick to 88% in British Columbia) in every province *believe* that which party is in power does make a difference. Analyses of governmental responsiveness to public needs to be presented in Chapter 8 indicate that these beliefs may be reality-oriented. When in office, various provincial parties have responded somewhat differently to different public needs. These differences, and the fact that most citizens in all parts of the country vote in provincial elections, suggest that although they may operate imperfectly, parties and electoral systems have combined to move the provinces at least some distance toward representative democracy.

However, regardless of the nature of the choices presented by parties, voting is "not enough." Even if parties do present real alternatives to the electorate, the goals of representative democracy cannot be approximated unless citizens play a role in determining the content of the alternatives that will be offered them. At this point the very limited amount of citizen participation documented earlier in this chapter assumes significance. By failing to involve themselves in party activity or other types of political action that might influence the options provided by parties, the vast majority of people in every province condemn themselves to a purely reactive posture. Rather than shaping electoral alternatives, most people simply choose among those presented to them. Even if party elites try to take voter reactions into account when selecting their electoral platforms, citizens relying on such a "law of anticipated reactions" still will have had no direct involvement in determining the content of the political agenda. Without this involvement, it is possible, indeed likely, that policy options of potential interest to many voters will be ignored by *all* parties. Moreover, by confining themselves to voting and occasionally discussing politics with friends and family, most citizens forfeit the psychological payoffs such as enhanced political and personal efficacy, greater political knowledge and awareness and the growth of a sense of community that derive from extensive political participation. As a consequence, many of the individual and collective benefits of representative democracy will remain unrealized.[42]

NOTES

1. For a more detailed exposition of these two arguments and references to the scholarly literature see William Mishler, *Political Participation in Canada* (Toronto: Macmillan, 1979), ch. 1.
2. *Ibid.*, p. 18.
3. On different types or "modes" of political participation see Sidney Verba and Norman H. Nie, *Participation in America* (New York: Harper and Row, 1972), ch. 3; Sidney Verba *et al.*, *Participation and Political Equality* (London: Cambridge University Press, 1978), ch. 3; and Samuel H. Barnes and Max Kaase *et al.*, *Political Action* (Beverly Hills: Sage Publications, 1979).
4. These percentages are based on data for the 1949–1965 period in John C. Courtney, ed., *Voting in Canada* (Scarborough: Prentice-Hall, 1967), Appendix A, and for the 1968–1979 period in the *Report of the Chief Electoral Officer* (Ottawa: Ministry of Supply and Services).
5. Viewed in cross-national perspective, these federal turnout rates are higher than comparable figures for the United States, but lower than those for several other countries such as the German Federal Republic or Australia. For example, measuring turnout as a percentage of the adult (age 20 and over) population, Taylor reports the following for a series of national elections in the mid-1970s, Australia — 87%, Great Britain — 75%, Canada — 68%, the United States — 52%. Charles L.

Taylor, *Changing Nations in a Changing World* (New Haven: Yale University Press, 1982), forthcoming.

6. Howard A. Scarrow, "Patterns of Voter Turnout in Canada," in Courtney, ed., *Voting in Canada*, pp. 104–114; Mishler, *Political Participation*, pp. 28–32.

7. Mike Burke, Harold D. Clarke and Lawrence LeDuc, "Federal and Provincial Political Participation in Canada: Some Methodological and Substantive Considerations," *The Canadian Review of Sociology and Anthropology* 15(1978), pp. 61–75; Allan Kornberg, Joel Smith and Harold D. Clarke, *Citizen Politicians — Canada* (Durham, N.C.: Carolina Academic Press, 1979), ch. 3.

8. 1974 national survey data also suggest that most people have the same activity levels in federal and provincial politics. See Burke *et al.*, "Federal and Provincial Political Participation," p. 69.

9. Susan Welch, "Dimensions of Political Participation in a Canadian Sample," *Canadian Journal of Political Science* 8(1975), pp. 553–559.

10. A useful compendium of many of these findings is Lester Milbrath and M.L. Goel, *Political Participation* 2nd ed., (Chicago: Rand McNally, 1977).

11. Milbrath and Goel, *Political Participation*, chs. 2–4.

12. Kornberg, Smith and Clarke, *Citizen Politicians*, p. 45.

13. *Ibid.*, pp. 76–77.

14. Information regarding the construction of the several variables used in these analyses are available from the authors upon request.

15. A brief guide to positions taken in this debate is provided in Harold D. Clarke, "The Ideological Self-Perceptions of Provincial Legislators," *Canadian Journal of Political Science* 11(1978), pp. 617–618.

16. This is essentially the thrust of many of the early voting studies conducted in the United States and elsewhere. See, for example, Bernard Berelson *et al.*, *Voting* (Chicago: University of Chicago Press, 1954) esp. ch. 15; Angus Campbell *et al.*, *The American Voter* (New York: Wiley, 1960), *passim*.

17. Recently, a number of authors have advanced this argument. See, for example, Samuel Popkin *et al.*, "What Have You Done for Me Lately? Toward An Investment Theory of Voting," *American Political Science Review* 70(1976), pp. 779–805.

18. Mishler, for example, argues that " ... the composition of Canada's political leadership has contributed to the changing content of public policy and the responsiveness of policies to public interest." Mishler, *Political Participation*, p. 135. Similarly, Simeon and Miller conclude: "The ideology of the party in power *does* make a difference." Richard Simeon and E. Robert Miller, "Regional Variations in Public Policy," *Small Worlds*, eds. David J. Elkins and Richard Simeon (Toronto: Methuen, 1980), p. 281, emphasis in original. In their study of policy outputs by the federal government over a 100-year period Kornberg *et. al.* find limited, but discernible, differences between Liberal and Conservative governments. Allan Kornberg, David J. Falcone and William T.E. Mishler II, "Legislatures and Societal Change: The Case of Canada," *Sage Research Papers in the Social Sciences: Comparative Legislative Studies Series*, 1 (1973), pp. 33–34. In contrast, Winn and McMenemy state that "there are few systematic differences to distinguish the output of one party from another." Conrad Winn and John McMenemy, *Political Parties in Canada* (Toronto: McGraw-Hill Ryerson, 1976), p. 267. Chandler and Chandler find some cases where it appears that the party in power was a significant variable influencing public policy but conclude that " ... in general change in governing party does not necessarily portend policy change," *Public Policy and Provincial Politics* (Toronto: McGraw-Hill Ryerson, 1979), p. 293.

19. On electoral systems in Canada see T.F. Qualter, *The Election Process in Canada* (Toronto: McGraw-Hill, 1970).

20. The major argument in favour of plurality electoral systems is that they are conducive to political stability because they tend to produce majority governments. Canadian data indicate the strength of this tendency is open to question.

21. In general, Canadian parties at both the federal and provincial levels have been extremely reluctant to form coalition governments. If no single party wins a majority of seats in an election the norm is for the party with the largest number of seats to form a minority government.

22. At the provincial level good recent examples of the emphasis on relationships between societal cleavages and voting can be found in several of the chapters in Elkins and Simeon, eds., *Small Worlds*. See also Chandler and Chandler, *Public Policy*, ch. 3. A listing of some of the better known studies at the federal level can be found in Harold D. Clarke *et al.*, *Political Choice in Canada* (Toronto: McGraw-Hill Ryerson, 1979), p. 129, fn. 15.

23. Most of these generalizations are based on observations of federal voting behaviour. See Clarke *et al.*, *Political Choice in Canada*, ch. 4 for an analysis of relationships between sociodemographic variables and voting in recent federal elections.

24. See, for example, Robert R. Alford, *Party and Society* (Chicago: Rand McNally, 1963), chs. 2, 11; and Seymour Martin Lipset and Stein Rokkan, "Cleavage Structures, Party Systems, and Voter Alignments: An Introduction," *Party Systems and Voter Alignments*, eds. S.M. Lipset and S. Rokkan, (New York: The Free Press, 1967), pp. 1–64.

25. On the weakness of class voting in Canada, see, for example, Alford, *Party and Society*, ch. 9; Clarke *et al.*, *Political Choice*, ch. 4.

26. Alford, *Party and Society*, ch. 4.

27. Regarding the debate about the position of Canadian parties on a left-right continuum see Clarke, "Ideological Self-Perceptions," *passim*.

28. Alford, *Party and Society*, chs. 5–7; David Butler and Donald Stokes, *Political Change in Britain*, 2nd college ed. (New York: St. Martin's Press, 1976), chs. 4, 9.

29. For additional information on partisanship in Canada see ch. 5. See also Clarke *et al.*, *Political Choice*, ch. 5.

30. Again, Popkin "What Have You Done for Me Lately?" provides a lucid discussion of the notion of partisanship and voting as investments. For a discussion of these ideas in the Canadian context see Jane Jenson, "Party Strategy and Party Identification: Some Patterns of Partisan Allegiance," *Canadian Journal of Political Science* 9 (1976), pp. 27–48; and Richard Johnston, "Federal and Provincial Voting: Contemporary Patterns and Historical Evaluation," *Small Worlds*, eds. D.J. Elkins and R. Simeon, pp. 164–166.

31. For data regarding the relative importance of family influence on acquisition of initial partisan attachments see Kornberg *et al.*, *Citizen Politicians*, pp. 47–50.

32. A more detailed analysis of cross-level consistency in partisanship may be found in Clarke *et al.*, *Political Choice*, ch. 5.

33. Data presented in ch. 3 (p. 85) documented that large majorities of voters obtain political information by watching TV news broadcasts, newspaper reading, etc.

34. The strength of orientations to provincial politics is examined in more detail in ch. 2, pp. 37–40.

35. The analysis developed here closely parallels that in ch. 10 of Clarke *et al.*, *Political Choice*. In that chapter a typology of the federal electorate is presented using data from the 1974 national election study.

36. The wording of the sequence of questions asked is virtually identical to that in Clarke *et al.*, *Political Choice*, pp. 418–419.

37. It is impossible to press the analysis of issue effects on provincial voting further because of the failure to ask about voters' perceptions of the most important issue in the most recent provincial election, how important that issue was in their vote decision and which party was closest to them on the issue. This sequence was asked at the federal level. An example of the sequence may be found in Clarke *et al.*, *Political Choice*, pp. 408–409.

38. Issue effects on federal voting in 1974 and 1968 are analyzed in Clarke *et al.*, *Political Choice*, ch. 11. A similar analysis for 1979 is contained in Harold D. Clarke *et al.*, "Processes of Political Change in Canada: Issues and Leaders in the 1979 Election," unpublished paper presented at the 1980 Annual Meeting of the American Political Science Association, Washington, D.C., August, 1980.

39. Similar countervailing patterns can be found at the federal level. See Clarke *et al.*, *Political Choice*, pp. 372–80.

40. The 1979 survey data are based on a sample of the national electorate as it existed then. As such, they cannot provide a fully accurate picture of provincial electorates in Quebec and Ontario as those electorates existed in 1976 and 1977 respectively.

However, the relative proximity of the dates of these elections to the time when the 1979 study was conducted and the large size of the Quebec (N = 753) and Ontario (N = 757) samples suggest the utility of the 1979 data for present purposes.
41. On the impact of the mass media on political orientations in Canada see Allan Kornberg and Judith D. Wolfe, "Parliament, the Media and the Polls," *Parliament, Policy and Representation*, eds. Harold D. Clarke *et al.* (Toronto: Methuen, 1980), ch. 3; and Richard G. Price and Harold D. Clarke, "Television and the House of Commons," ch. 4 of the same volume.
42. It is not necessarily in the interests of party elites that levels of public participation in party organizations increase. See Kornberg *et al., Citizen Politicians*, ch. 9.

FOR FURTHER READING

Clarke, Harold D., Jane Jenson, Lawrence LeDuc and Jon Pammett. *Political Choice in Canada*. Toronto: McGraw-Hill Ryerson, 1979, chs. 10, 11, 12, 13. These chapters contain analyses of the composition of the electorate, voting behaviour and the outcomes of the 1974 and 1979 federal elections which parallel the provincial level analyses presented in this chapter.
Drummond, Robert J., and Frederick J. Fletcher. "Political Communication and Orientation to Legislators among Ontario Voters," *Parliament, Policy and Representation*, eds. Harold D. Clarke, *et al.* Toronto: Methuen, 1980, pp. 103–123. Based on data gathered in their survey of the Ontario electorate, the authors analyze various factors influencing provincial voting behaviour. Particular attention is given to the impact of local candidates on voting behaviour and election outcomes.
Mishler, William. *Political Participation in Canada*. Toronto: Macmillan, 1979. The author reviews the role of citizen participation in democratic theory and examines the extent and correlates of various modes of participation in the Canadian political system. The book concludes by considering how participatory opportunities might be expanded.
Pinard, Maurice and Richard Hamilton, "The Parti Québécois Comes to Power: An Analysis of the 1976 Quebec Election," *Canadian Journal of Political Science* 11 (1978), pp. 739–776. In this detailed analysis the authors argue that the PQ was able to gain power by disassociating the election from the party's proposed referendum on sovereignty-association.
Wilson, John. "The Decline of the Liberal Party in Manitoba," *Journal of Canadian Studies* 10 (1975), pp. 24–41. The argument is made that the increasing strength of social class cleavages in Manitoba politics can explain the demise of the provincial Liberals and the growth of the NDP.

5
Political Parties
and Interest Groups

The origins of modern political parties can be traced to the first experiments with representative government and for obvious reasons. Political parties perform a number of important functions for representative democratic government such as helping to regularize and constrain societal conflict, recruiting candidates to run for public office, simplifying voter choice, organizing government and helping to generate public policy. Perhaps more importantly from our perspective, political parties contribute to the effective representation of public opinion. They do so, in theory, through a two-stage process: by aggregating or forming coalitions of related public interests and by articulating or promoting these interests through the political process.[1] Interest groups have more venerable origins than political parties. Like parties, however, their development in Western countries was spurred by constitutional struggles to secure fundamental civil liberties such as freedom of assembly and the right to petition government as well as by the industrial revolution and the resulting increase in both the number and complexity of social and economic institutions.

Given these commonalities it is not surprising that interest groups and political parties perform many of the same functions. The principal difference between them is that parties are integral to and operate primarily through the electoral systems of democratic countries. They try to win elections in order to organize and control governments. Interest groups, in contrast, are concerned principally with influencing the policies of governments rather than organizing and administering their several departments. This is not to say that interest groups are disinterested spectators in the electoral process. On the contrary, they often undertake a variety of activities intended to facilitate the victory of favoured parties or candidates. Occasionally, interest groups even offer candidates for elective offices. Although the latter practice is relatively rare in Canada, persons intimately associated with particular interest groups have become candidates for parliament or provincial legislative seats. However, they usually have run as candidates of one of the established parties.

Although many interest groups are formed to protect and enhance the economic interests of their members, there are many other types of groups as well: ethnic, religious, sports, veterans, professional, consumer, women, gay, and native peoples are but a few that come to mind. Some interest groups are highly political, others considerably less so. In this chapter we will try to describe the principal organizational features of the former, delineate their political activities and note some of the tactics they employ in attempting to reach their goals. Previous chapters already have suggested why interest groups should be a major concern in a book on provincial government. Because of federalism and the economic and political importance of the provinces, interest group leaders are encouraged to address many of their demands to provincial governments. For their part, legislators often feel it is in their self-interest to facilitate these demands, while provincial bureaucrats at times treat groups as clients rather than as objects of regulation. As a consequence interest groups not only are able to apprise provincial governments of their members' concerns, they also are able, under certain conditions, to influence both the content and administration of provincial public policy. These matters will be discussed in detail shortly.

Given the many critically important functions ascribed to political parties, it hardly requires that we justify examining their operation. Accordingly, we will begin with brief overviews of the origins and development of the Liberal, Progressive Conservative, Social Credit and New Democratic parties and follow these with sketches of the Union Nationale and Parti Québécois. We will then discuss salient attributes of parties' legislative and extralegislative organizations and consider some of the ways in which these affect and are affected by the millions of voters who have formed psychological attachments with provincial parties.

Since historically several other parties have played important roles in provincial politics and since the significance of the above parties in electoral politics has varied greatly — both across provinces and over time — the reader may ask why we are not pursuing a conventional descriptive approach. That is, why are we not providing histories of the several parties in each of the provinces? There are three reasons. First, relatively detailed studies of the histories of the party systems of the ten provinces or of individual parties within particular provinces or regions already exist.[2] Second, economies of space in a general text of this kind make such an undertaking impracticable. Third, and most important, we are concerned with attributes of party structure and process that either facilitate or impede progress toward representative democracy. This also is the case with respect to the operation of interest groups. Consequently, we emphasize those attributes and in the concluding section of this chapter we compare political parties with interest groups in these regards.

PARTY ORIGINS AND DEVELOPMENT: AN OVERVIEW

Most descriptions of major political parties in Western democracies emphasize their voluntary character and the fact that they contest elections in order to control governments. Similarly, we view Canadian parties as voluntary associations with three key attributes. The most visible and best known of these are parties' legislative officeholders and candidates. A second is parties' extralegislative organizations. These organizations include persons holding formal party positions that are hierarchically organized and which have associated with them various kinds of activities, as well as persons who are not officeholders but nevertheless exercise considerable influence in party affairs. A third is the "party in the electorate," those segments of the public who have formed psychological attachments with parties (i.e., who think of themselves as Liberals, Conservatives, and so forth) but who neither hold positions in their organizations nor have formal affiliations with them.

Explanations of the origins and development of Anglo-American and Western European political parties are of two types: "inside" and "outside" theories.[3] The former argue that political parties have their origins in legislative bodies. They begin as factional groupings loosely organized around influential political leaders. As issues arise whose resolution extends over a generation or more, factional lines begin to harden, internal organizations develop and cohesive group actions increase. Concomitant with the democratization of the electorate, the losing side(s) (the "outs") in such protracted controversies generally begin to develop ties with supporters in the electorate in an effort to become the "ins." In time they expand and develop these ties into formal electoral organizations. Since organization generally stimulates counter-organization, opposition parties begin to develop their own extraparliamentary structures. "Outside" theories of the origins of parties emphasize that some parties begin as mass social movements outside of legislatures rather than as factional groupings within them. These movements often are responses to severe social and economic dislocations caused by cataclysmic events such as wars or major depressions. Given the proper circumstances, some of these movements become increasingly institutionalized, develop organizational structures and begin to compete for control of a government by recruiting and trying to elect their own candidates to a legislature.

The origins of Canada's political parties are congruent with both the inside and outside explanations. The Liberals and Progressive Conservatives can be thought of as inside parties. Their beginnings are rooted in the early 19th century legislative struggle to achieve responsible government.[4] The Conservative party grew out of a pre-Confederation coalition of business–professional and Anglican Church elites who held sway in Ontario, and ultramontane French Catholic and Anglo-Scottish business and financial oligarchies in Quebec. Sir John A. Macdonald, the architect of this coalition, used its support to make himself Canada's first Prime Minister. The ancestors of the present Liberal party were rural and small town, non-established church and moderate reform groups in Ontario, and anti-business, anti-clerical, relatively radical reform elements in Quebec. Under the leadership of Alexander Mackenzie, they were able to oust Macdonald and his Tory colleagues in the federal election of 1874. However, 22 years were to pass before the Liberal party won its second national election.

The Social Credit and the New Democratic (until 1961, the Cooperative Commonwealth Federation) parties developed according to the outside theory. Both parties have roots in the short-lived Progressive Party which, in turn, developed out of a number of provincial United Farmers parties. The Progressive Party, it is argued, was a response to the exploitation of the Western provinces by the concerted actions of political and economic elites in Ontario and Quebec. Western farmers felt their interests not only were not adequately represented but, in fact, that they and their region were being exploited by the legislative policies of the Eastern-oriented and -led Liberal and Conservative parties. For example, Western farmers pointed to the fact that they had to sell their principal product, wheat, competitively in world markets whereas goods manufactured in Ontario and Quebec were protected from outside competition by tariffs. Attempts by Western MPs to ameliorate this situation or to protest against other kinds of discriminatory treatment either were ignored or overridden by the much larger delegations of Ontario and Quebec MPs in the Liberal and Conservative parliamentary caucuses.

The Progressives were able to elect 65 members to Parliament in 1921, the first national election in which they competed. Nonetheless, by the end of the decade their national organization largely was moribund. This was not true, however, of their organizations in provinces such as Manitoba and Alberta. In the latter, the newly formed Social Credit party included several of the former leaders of the Progressive Party and the United Farmers of Alberta. Many of the adherents of these two parties also shifted their electoral support to Social Credit legislative candidates. William Aberhart, a high school teacher and evangelical minister, was able to parlay this and other support into victory at the polls in the provincial election of 1935. The party was to govern Alberta continuously for the next 36 years.

Regarding the inside explanation of party development, it can be argued that the issue(s) that contributed to the hardening of parliamentary party lines was Macdonald's National Policy. It will be remembered that this policy called for the building of a transcontinental railroad, the creation of an industrial infrastructure in Ontario to be nurtured by protective tariffs, the exploitation of the primary resources of the Maritime and Western regional hinterlands and the development of interprovincial east–west trade carried primarily by the new railroad. The popularity of this policy enabled the Conservatives to weather a number of political storms and to remain in office continuously from 1878 to 1896. Additionally, it has been argued that the introduction of secret ballots and simultaneous elections in Ontario, Quebec and the Atlantic provinces in the election of 1878 increased the cohesiveness of parliamentary parties because these innovations made it impossible for candidates for Parliament to use the tactic of not declaring their support for a party until they had seen who would win an election. As a result, they no longer could be "ministerialists," supporting whichever party gained power in order to maximize benefits to their constituencies.[5]

Also consistent with the inside explanation, the opposition party, the Liberals, began to organize their supporters in the electorate in an effort to gain power and were able to build a strong provincial organization in Ontario in the decade following Confederation. By the 1890s the party in Quebec had made peace with the Catholic church and had purged itself of more radical elements. The Liberals were so successful they received an average of 58% of the popular vote and captured 81% of the Assembly seats in 11 provincial elections between 1897 and 1935. During the heyday of the Union Nationale (between 1936 and 1960) the Liberal party won only one election, but it continued to receive, on average, some 45% of the popular vote. Returning to power in 1960, it won three of four elections during the next 16 years but was badly beaten in 1976 by the Parti Québécois. Although the Liberals' share of the popular vote increased from 34% to 46% in the election of 1981, it captured only a third of the seats in the National Assembly.

Until very recently, Liberal fortunes almost always have been high in the Maritimes. They were the governing party in Nova Scotia at Confederation and, other than the period 1878–82, they held power continuously until 1925. Returning to office in 1933, they governed another 23 years and despite winning only two of seven elections since 1956, they have maintained the support of some 44% of the electorate in each provincial election. In New Brunswick the Liberals were victorious in the first four elections after Confederation, were out of office briefly, and then won four more successive elections. They governed continuously from 1935 to 1952 and from 1960 to 1970 but were defeated in each of three elections held in the 1970s by a resurgent Conservative party. In Prince Edward Island the Liberals were less successful in the generation after Confederation. As was the case in other provinces, however, the party began a period in office in 1935 that lasted approximately a quarter of a century (1935–1959). The party continues to be successful, having won three of the last four provincial elections and an average of 52% of the popular vote. Joey Smallwood was the principal architect of Confederation in Newfoundland. Smallwood-led Liberal governments were in office from 1949 to 1971, winning an average of almost 62% of the popular vote in each of six elections during this period. After narrowly losing to the Frank Moores-led Conservatives, a badly divided Liberal party was decisively defeated in the election of 1972. Although it has recovered some of its strength since then, it remains in the electoral wilderness.

In the West the Liberals also were able to govern for long periods of time: from 1888 to 1899 and from 1945 to 1958 in Manitoba; from 1905 to 1929 in Saskatchewan; from 1905 to 1921 in Alberta; and from 1916 to 1928 in British Columbia. However, since the late '50s, electoral support for Liberal candidates in federal as well as provincial elections has declined sharply. Since the mid-'70s only a handful of Liberals have been elected to the assemblies of the four Western provinces. The party has fared somewhat better in Ontario. The impetus provided by Mowat's leadership enabled Liberal administrations to govern from 1871 through 1905. Although the Liberals have not governed Ontario since 1943, the party still has managed in nine of 11 subsequent elections to hold its own against a strong and persistent NDP challenge for the position of Official Opposition.

Despite the challenge from both Liberals and New Democrats, for most of this century Ontario has belonged to the Conservatives. Coming to power in 1905, the party governed until 1919. It was returned to office in 1923 and governed until 1934. In 1943 the party began a period of stewardship which continues to this day. As indicated above, Conservative provincial parties also were victorious in every provincial election held during the 1970s in both New Brunswick and Newfoundland. They also have been victorious in recent elections in Nova Scotia (1978) and Prince Edward Island (1979). In 1958 the strong leadership of Duff Roblin propelled the party into a decade of office in Manitoba. After losing successive elections (1969, 1973) to the New Democrats, the party again formed the government in 1977, capturing 49% of the vote and 33 of the province's 57 legislative seats. Conservatives also have made a modest comeback in Saskatchewan, party candidates having won 17 legislative seats and 38% of the vote in the 1978 election. The party's greatest Western success, however, has come in Alberta. In 1963 it received only 13% of the vote and won not a single legislative seat. Eight years later it replaced the seemingly perennially governing Socreds. The party continues to dominate Alberta politics and, despite periodic speculation that he will enter federal politics, Peter Lougheed remains the party's leader and the province's First Minister.

Regarding the two outside parties, the New Democrats have enjoyed a considerably broader base of public support over the years than has Social Credit. Both, however, essentially are regionally-based parties. In fact, it might be more accurate to describe Social Credit as a provincially-based party. During the first quarter-century of its existence Social Credit gained control of the government of Alberta in 1935 and of British Columbia 17 years later, but fared very poorly elsewhere.[6] In contrast, although during its first quarter century the CCF-NDP captured power in only one province (Saskatchewan), the party became a strong electoral force in Manitoba, British Columbia and Ontario. In Manitoba, party standard-bearers won a total of 53 seats and an average of almost 25% of the vote in seven elections held between 1936 and 1959. Ten years later they came to office in the province, governed until 1977 and were reelected in 1981. In British Columbia, the party won a total of 96 seats and received, on average, slightly over 32% of the vote in eight provincial elections during the years 1937–1960. It finally won an election in 1972 and, although defeated three years later, the party continues to elicit the support of approximately two-fifths of the electorate. In Ontario, the party won a total of 74 legislative seats and received an average of 18% of the vote in eight elections between 1934 and 1959. Since 1960, the proportion of the party's popular vote and the number of its legislative seats have increased (25% of the vote and 23 legislative seats, on average). Only once (1975), however, has the party managed to duplicate its earlier feat (1943–1948) of winning enough seats to become the official opposition in Queen's Park. Elsewhere, during the post-World War Two period CCF-NDP candidates have received an average of approximately 13% of the popular vote in Alberta, 8% in Nova Scotia, but only once have exceeded 5% in Newfoundland and Prince Edward Island.

Despite its considerable electoral success, the NDP has been plagued by several factional conflicts over the years. The most serious occurred during the late 1960s and early 70s. A group of disaffected younger party activists labelled the "Waffle" questioned the direction the party had taken since 1961, the year in which the CCF formalized its close ties to organized labour and changed its name to the New Democratic Party. The Waffle was especially critical of the conservative "bread and butter" philosophy of provincial labour leaders who were influential in the NDP and tried to redirect the party toward the achievement of its initial socialist goals. The Waffle combined traditional socialist rhetoric with strong nationalist appeals and although its challenge to the party leadership failed, internal divisions based upon age and ideology continue to trouble the NDP both nationally and in several of the provinces.[7]

In one sense, two Quebec provincial parties, the Union Nationale and Parti Québécois, have had as great and, in some respects, a greater impact on Canadian political life than have either the New Democratic or Social Credit parties. The Union Nationale (like Social Credit and the CCF-NDP) has its origins in the Depression. Formed in 1936 as an alliance of Conservatives and dissident Liberals (the Action Liberale

Nationale), the Union Nationale exploited a combination of economic discontent and charges of political corruption to sweep the Liberals from provincial office after the latter party had held power continuously for 39 years. The Union Nationale quickly established its dominance over Quebec provincial politics and, under the leadership of Maurice Duplessis, governed for 19 of the next 24 years.

Party scholars have offered several explanations of the party's quarter century-long attractiveness to Quebec voters.[8] It has been argued that the suffering of the Depression years induced large numbers of disadvantaged people to look for an alternative to the governing Liberals. The Union Nationale was and long remained the only one available. The party's success also has been attributed to Duplessis' persistent efforts to present it as the defender of French Canadian culture which he claimed was threatened by the expansionist policies of Liberal governments in Ottawa. Duplessis was able to identify Quebec provincial Liberals with the policies of their federal namesake, policies then opposed by large numbers of Québécois. Yet another explanation rests on the astute and unscrupulous ways in which Duplessis and his party organizers were able to use patronage and the pork barrel to build an extensive network of patron-client relationships, particularly in rural areas that were disproportionately favoured by the electoral system of the time.

The modernization of Quebec society eroded much of the party's appeal. To the extent that its electoral strength rested on its reputation as the defender of French Canadian culture, societal transformations attendant upon modernization set in motion a reorientation in Québécois nationalist ideology that tended to make the party appear somewhat irrelevant. Under Duplessis the UN had attempted to minimize state intervention in society. In contrast, the Liberals and subsequently the Parti Québécois relied heavily on government intervention to advance both the socioeconomic and cultural interests of Québécois. Although Daniel Johnson was able to lead the UN back to power in 1966, his victory appears to have been a "last hurrah." In the past four provincial elections (1970, 1973, 1976, 1981) party candidates managed to capture only a handful of seats. More than ever, the UN finds itself ground between the opposing forces of federalism and separatism. As the debate over the future of Quebec has unfolded, the polarization of political forces has obliterated more and more of its support (e.g., in the 1981 election UN candidates received only 4% of the vote and no assembly seats). Electoral failure and a continuing inability to find a leader in tune with the times provide very little cause for optimism about the party's future.

The Parti Québécois, which was formed in 1968, rallied disparate separatist elements, including members of small parties such as the Rassemblement pour L'Indépendance National (RIN) and the Ralliement National (RN).[9] Both of these parties utilized a political style and rhetoric that were quite different from the technocratic approach favoured by many of the ex-Liberals who had rallied to the standard of René Lévesque, a former cabinet minister in the "Quiet Revolution" government of Premier Jean Lesage. Nonetheless, neither ideological nor stylistic differences prevented these several groups from offering their enthusiastic support to Lévesque's new party, the Parti Québécois. Under the dynamic leadership of Lévesque, the party came to the forefront of Quebec politics within eight years, its almost meteoric rise culminating in the November, 1976 election of a majority PQ government. In the April 13, 1981 election it renewed its mandate garnering 80 National Assembly seats and 49% of the popular vote.

Despite Lévesque's promise during the 1981 campaign to put the issue "on ice" for the next three or four years, political sovereignty for Quebec continues to be viewed by Péquistes as the *sine qua non* for the realization of Québécois economic, political and cultural aspirations. In this respect, the party differs from earlier nationalist parties which were content to defend the interests of Québécois within the framework of federalism. In emphasizing the positive role of the state in advancing nationalist goals, the PQ appears to have completed the ideological reorientation of Quebec political thought first manifested in the Quiet Revolution of the early 1960s. In essence this reorientation has been two-fold. In addition to a commitment to transform Quebec into an economically and technically advanced urban, secular society, it defines the province as the true homeland of French Canadians. Only within a sovereign Quebec it is argued, can French Canadians become "maîtres chez nous."

In striving to attain sovereignty, the PQ has consciously pursued a policy of *étapisme*, that is, it has tried to proceed in a "step by step" fashion. This strategy frankly recognizes that a majority of the Quebec population presently is not in favour of outright independence. However, party leaders calculate that over time public opinion may swing their way if they can allay fears regarding Quebec's ability to survive and prosper as an independent entity. To this end the party has stressed two principal themes. First, it has developed the concept of "sovereignty-association." In brief, this concept, if it were implemented, would make Quebec a sovereign state with economic ties to Canada. Second, the party has tried to project an image of competence and rationality in an attempt to persuade voters that its leaders have the ability to govern a modern industrial state.

To establish its good government image and propagate the wisdom of a sovereign Quebec, the PQ has proceeded slowly and cautiously, deferring, for example, the referendum on sovereignty-association for almost four years. Even this was not enough. On May 20, 1980, voters denied the PQ a mandate to negotiate sovereignty-association by a decisive margin (60% voted "no"). Analyses of the vote suggest that the result was not merely a byproduct of overwhelming Anglophone opposition, but rather that even among Québécois a majority rejected the proposition.[10]

Still, as the April, 1981 provincial election demonstrated, the party's future prospects are bright. Public opinion polls consistently have shown it to be more popular than the idea of sovereignty-association. Despite this, if the Prime Minister and provincial government leaders outside of Quebec fail to negotiate a renewed federalism deemed satisfactory by Québécois, Lévesque may yet be able to convince a majority of his fellow citizens of the wisdom of the PQ option. This judgment rests on evidence suggesting that support for the party and its policies will continue to grow both relatively and absolutely. The core of PQ support comes from young, well-educated professionals, many of whom currently occupy key positions in the media and various educational and cultural institutions. These young professionals are committed to the goal of a sovereign Quebec and can be expected to continue their support for both the party and its *indépendantiste* goals. Thus, over time, political socialization and the attrition that affects any electorate as older voters die and are replaced by younger generations may yet give the PQ the majority needed to create a sovereign state of Quebec.

This overview of the origins and development of these six parties was intended to introduce three of the more important features of the party system. The first is that the system's operation is exceedingly complex. Indeed, it can be argued that there really is not a single-party system, but several. In great part this is a consequence of the critical role the provinces play in Canadian political life. Whatever the reason(s), the reality, as the last chapter revealed, is a system in which support for parties and electoral competition can vary sharply from province to province. Moreover, within provinces, party competition at one level of government may be related only very loosely to competition at the other.

Consider some examples: interparty competition in Nova Scotia, Manitoba, and British Columbia is of the classic two-party variety. However, the identities of the contesting parties differ as one moves from east to west. In Nova Scotia, the electoral struggle is waged between the old-line center-left and center-right parties, the Liberals and Conservatives. In Manitoba, the fight is between the Conservatives and the NDP and in British Columbia it is between the NDP and its ideological opponent, Social Credit. Consider also the differences in the ideological climates of the several provinces. According to Martin Robin, a strong ideological and class component underlies the struggle between Social Credit and the New Democratic Party in British Columbia.[11] In Alberta, in contrast, Social Credit under the leadership of former Premiers Manning and Strom, shed much of its more radical ideological baggage. It became a conventional conservative party which used to point with pride to the stability and responsibility of its administration, while at the same time reminding Albertans of the well-funded array of social services a Socred government was providing. Consequently, the electoral struggle between the current Conservative government and the opposing Socreds pits two essentially conservative parties against one another.

Quebec and Ontario, in some respects, provide the best examples of the complex nature of party politics in Canada. In Quebec, the afore-mentioned provincial parties, Union Nationale and Parti Québécois, have governed for 60% of the post-World War Two period despite the fact that the province historically has been the federal Liberal party's principal bastion of electoral strength. Of course, provincial Liberals in Quebec have fared far better than their counterparts in Ontario. Millions of Ontarians were not even born in 1937, the year a Liberal party last formed a government in their province. As for the Conservatives, the well-named "Big Blue Machine," as noted above, has governed Ontario continuously since 1943 and also has been a formidable force in Ontario federal politics.[12] In Quebec, however, despite repeated efforts, the party has been a virtual non-starter in elections at both levels of the system. In short, the positions of Liberals and Conservatives in the two provinces containing some two-thirds of the Canadian population are dramatically different.

A second point about the party system already noted is that for almost a half century both the federal and provincial levels have tended toward one-party dominance. The Liberals have formed the national government for approximately 40 of the past 46 years (1935–1957, 1963–1979 and 1980 to the present) and the tendency toward one-party dominance is at least as pronounced at the provincial level. The long periods of hegemony exercised by the Liberals over Newfoundland, Prince Edward Island, Nova Scotia, Quebec, Saskatchewan and Alberta, by the Conservatives over Ontario, by the CCF-NDP over Saskatchewan and by the Social Credit over Alberta and British Columbia are examples that come readily to mind.

Third, tendencies toward one-partyism notwithstanding, when a party falls from grace, its decline, as noted earlier, is often precipitous. After governing for a generation, the Liberal party of Newfoundland suffered substantial losses[13] and the Social Credit party of Alberta virtually disappeared from the provincial legislature during the '70s. In Quebec, the Union Nationale has suffered equally grievous losses. As was observed in Chapter 4, these sharp swings in party electoral fortunes strongly suggest that the attachments of many Canadians to their political parties are unstable. Furthermore, the tendency of parties within a province to fare much differently in federal and provincial elections indicates many people split their partisan attachments, identifying with one party at the provincial and a second at the federal level.

LEGISLATIVE PARTIES

The institution of parliament and virtually all of its procedures initially were transported from Great Britain via the legislative bodies of the four provinces that united in 1867 to form the new Canadian state. Since that time the memberships of the House of Commons and the several provincial legislatures have changed from loose factions organized around one or more popular legislators into disciplined, cohesive parties carrying out their perceived mandate of either supporting or opposing government-initiated legislation. As has been the case in other countries with British-model parliamentary governments, the memberships of the House of Commons and provincial legislatures have increased as the population has grown. Concomitant with the growth in the size of legislative bodies have been changes in the procedures under which they operate. The principal thrust of such changes, which will be discussed at greater length in the next chapter, has been to limit opportunities available to non-cabinet members to participate in the process of drafting and evaluating legislation. The reasons for this are complex. Greatly simplified, the justification offered is that in order for legislatures to serve as effective instruments of representative government, victorious political parties must have the opportunity to carry out their policies and programs. This requires that members of a governing party act cohesively; i.e., they must work and vote together in support of the legislative programs introduced by party leaders in the cabinet. This, in turn, has forced opposition parties to unite against the government of the day in order to defeat it. Opposition parties also feel the need to act cohesively because they must project an image of being capable of governing if the public should turn to them in a future election.

The principal means of achieving cohesive action in both governing and opposition parties is caucus. When a provincial legislature is in session, the members of each legislative party generally caucus weekly. Caucus provides party members with an opportunity to discuss strategies and tactics to be employed in pursuing their legislative program. It enables members to hammer out positions on policy issues. It provides party members with opportunities to express grievances and exchange information about grass-roots opinions. Finally, caucus socializes members to accept a division of labour in which party leaders play the principal role in legislative debates while non-leaders give significant proportions of their time and attention to the performance of services on behalf of constituents.[14]

As important as it is for promoting the cohesion of legislative parties, caucus may constrain the ability of a party organization to maintain national unity by limiting opportunities for the effective expression of provincial opposition to national policies. The observation that there is no single party system suggests that the task of keeping the political system intact (i.e., the integrative function) has been performed with less than conspicuous success over the years. In a thoughtful essay, John Meisel has indicted the parties for their failure in this area and also has argued that their ability to perform functions such as political mobilization, interest aggregation and policy formulation has declined markedly since World War Two. He attributes this decline to long-term factors such as the rise of a bureaucratic state, increased interest group activity, incipient corporatism, federal-provincial diplomacy, the dominance of economic interests and the rise of electronic media and investigative journalism.[15]

Of particular interest is Meisel's claim that the ability of legislative parties to mobilize and to accurately represent public opinion has been seriously affected by the rise of electronic media (especially television) and the tendency of print media figures to ascribe to themselves the role of official opposition — not only to the government of the day but also to its opposition. With regard to electronic media, both government and opposition party leaders make statements and engage in other activities that are intended to attract media attention and, through them, the attention of the millions who daily watch television and listen to radio. In order to attract media attention, party leaders have had to accommodate themselves to media needs, the principal one being the need to entertain the widest possible audience. Consequently, with the encouragement and active collaboration of party officials, political issues, rather than being represented accurately and in all their complexity, instead frequently are represented in ways that will catch and hold the attention of mass audiences. Although such tactics may produce short-term gains for particular parties, there also is evidence to suggest that the overall impact in the long run is to contribute to the negative attitudes many people display toward political parties and their leaders,[16] and to limit public understanding of crucial issues.

EXTRALEGISLATIVE PARTY ORGANIZATIONS

In a number of Western countries one of the consequences of party officials' reliance on electronic media to project favourable images of themselves and their policies to the public has been a decline in the strength of party organizations generally and a diminution in the importance of their roles in electoral campaigns in particular. There is reason to assume that this also may be the situation in Canada. Studies of party organizations indicate that their officials currently are very much attuned to and make use of the latest campaign technology.[17] This is especially true of the Liberal and Conservative parties. Although the Liberals took the lead in building extralegislative organizations in the 19th century, as late as 1880 only about 50% of the constituencies had even paper party associations. Liberals did not hold their first national convention until 1893 and did not establish a national office until 1912. The Conservatives lagged behind them in both these areas (e.g., they did not hold their first national leadership convention until 1927)[18] and not until the 1920s did either party make concerted and systematic attempts to organize their supporters into viable extralegislative organizations capable of competing in federal and provincial elections. Their efforts were spurred by the expansion of the electorate that occurred at the time and the need to keep at least some of their promises to newly enfranchised groups. The Social Credit and the CCF-NDP generally have followed the lead of the two older parties.

It is difficult to generalize about parties' extralegislative organizations because their structures are so amorphous and variable. Consider, for example, the different kind of relationships federal and provincial components of the same party can have in different provinces or even within a single province. The Canadian brand of federalism, as has been indicated a number of times, is one in which the provinces play important political roles — more important, in fact, than in most federal countries. One might assume, therefore, that the organizations of the national and provincial units of each of the parties might be relatively separate and distinct entities or, at the very least, more separate and distinct than party organizations of other federal countries. A good example of such federal-provincial organizational distinctiveness is the Liberal party in Quebec. In fact, however, the extent to which the federal and provincial organizational components of each party actually *are* separate and distinct not only can differ dramatically from province to province, but also from riding to riding within a particular province. By way of illustration, a study of party organizations in metropolitan Vancouver and Winnipeg found that in each party a single person might occupy the same position in both the federal and provincial constituency organizations. Alternatively, one individual can occupy different positions in both, or two people can occupy the same position, or at least believe they do.[19]

As for their amorphousness, consider that which surrounds even so fundamental an act as joining a party. For some people, in some provinces and in some parties, affiliation involves the taking of an oath, the payment of dues, the signing of a membership card, or some other clear-cut action. For others, affiliation is a more complex process involving enhanced political interest and activity associated with increased participation in more-or-less formally structured party organizations. And, for still others, party membership, without being sought or accepted, can be conferred on the basis of having been present at the most routine annual meeting of a provincial party's constituency association.[20]

Despite their diversity and amorphousness, it is possible to make several general statements about extralegislative party organizations.

The first is that historically they have tended to be controlled by people whose principal goals have been to select and elect candidates for public office. This is not to say that those in control have not had other objectives, only that recruitment and election goals usually have taken precedence. Second, the tasks associated with the performance of the recruitment-election function virtually have been monopolized by officials in constituency level units of the several parties. They are the units most active in federal or provincial organizational hierarchies that generally are skeletal, decentralized and loosely related to one another. The Liberals, Progressive Conservatives and NDP have national offices in Ottawa. In some provinces they also have provincial offices with minimum staffs that can be expanded immediately before an election.[21] These offices may provide financial assistance, speakers, campaign materials and other forms of assistance to constituency organizations and their candidates. Such support is welcomed, since under certain conditions it may provide the margin between electoral success and failure. Despite this assistance and the periodic parachuting of candidates into constituencies in national and provincial elections, generally candidate recruitment and electioneering remain the prerogatives of constituency party leaders.

Third, the organizational form of most provincial constituency parties tends to be a truncated pyramid[22] with a maximum of four levels of organization. From smallest to largest these are variably termed the "poll," "area," "zone," and "constituency." The less fully organized constituencies generally dispense with the two intermediate layers. Fourth, most organizations are populated almost entirely by "amateurs," that is, party officials who have other occupations and statuses (e.g., teacher, lawyer, mother) which take precedence over party work if there are conflicting demands on their time and attention. Although in many areas of the country some party workers are paid either directly or indirectly for their services, in most cases payments are modest and are almost entirely restricted to individuals holding positions at the bottom level of a party's hierarchy. An overwhelming majority of a party's activists in upper echelon positions are unpaid. Their rewards are of a different kind, as will be indicated below. Fifth, democratic norms and customary practices as well as party constitutions usually require that the parties adhere to an open-door recruitment policy. Although they are not legally required to admit anyone, the need to maintain and broaden the base of their electoral support is a strong inducement for current leaders to accept and actively recruit representatives of major social groups in a riding. Recruitment is not always an easy task and party officials proceed with the business of acquiring new members much as do other voluntary associations. Personal friendships often are used to persuade people to work for a party and in some instances the prospect of holding a high party position or engaging in interesting and exciting work may be preferred as an inducement to join.[23]

Sixth, people usually join parties during periods of heightened political activity such as the month or two preceding an election. If asked what prompted them to join, party workers customarily offer several reasons. Of these the most frequently cited as being "most important" are: (a) a desire to improve government generally; (b) loyalty to a party or candidate; (c) the desire to expand one's social life and meet interesting people; and (d) pressures from family members, friends or co-workers.[24] Seventh, although there is some inter-party variation in the rate at which people volunteer, people entering party organizations more often volunteer their services than have them solicited by party officials. The great majority of volunteers seemingly are willing to do whatever work is required of them, whereas a majority of those who are recruited, join to perform a specific task.[25]

All in all, an examination of the reasons officials give for joining party organizations and the conditions under which they enter suggests that as a group they are not really committed politicians consumed with ideological fervour. Some join of their own accord. Others join to accommodate a friend or acquaintance already in a party. People who join parties as a convenience to others rarely develop intense political ambitions. However, they also do not expect to work very hard. Consequently, such officials are at best marginally active in carrying out the task of electing their candidates to public office. In this regard, however, Canadian party workers probably are no worse than their counterparts elsewhere.

Analyses of the social and political backgrounds of Vancouver and Winnipeg party officials, the circumstances surrounding their entry into organizational work and the development of their subsequent careers within parties were highly suggestive. Despite differences in parties' historical origins, ideologies and competitive statuses in federal and provincial politics, the officials of each party could be divided into three relatively distinct types, which we term "Stalwarts," "Insiders" and "Elites."[26]

Stalwarts generally occupy the middle-level positions of the truncated structures of constituency parties. They engage in a variety of routine record-keeping tasks and they apprise upper echelon position-holders and candidates for elected office of the distribution of partisan sentiments among voters, information collected in face-to-face canvassing and other forms of social interaction with the public. The principal tasks of Insiders, holders of high-level positions in formal party hierarchies, are to coordinate and supervise the work of Stalwarts. Insiders not only coordinate activities, they also perform some of the same tasks as Stalwarts. However, they generally have done them longer and more effectively. Elites usually occupy the highest organizational positions and they, more often than others, are a party's standard-bearers in electoral contests or its appointees to non-elective public offices. Elites more frequently than Insiders or Stalwarts come from middle and upper-middle class backgrounds, more often report being reared in politicized childhood and adolescent environments, having parents who were politically active, and most often come into contact regularly with other politically involved individuals. Although the exact proportions may vary somewhat by party and province, approximately 60% of the officials of every party can be classified as Stalwarts, about 30% as Insiders and the rest as Elites.

Studies of political participation in a number of Western countries indicate men participate more than women. Not unexpectedly, then, women are a distinct minority in provincial extralegislative organizations generally and they are even more underrepresented in their Insider and Elite ranks.[27] Because there are so few layers in a constituency party hierarchy through which officials can move upward, the pinnacle of a successful party career for men and women officials alike is to move out of the organizations proper by receiving nominations as party candidates in federal and provincial elections, and appointments to the judiciary or to one of the numerous boards, commissions and advisory groups which are integral parts of federal and provincial bureaucracies. These positions, rather than direct or indirect monetary compensation, are the principal payoffs to middle and upper-middle class individuals for their organizational work in contemporary political parties.[28]

PARTIES IN THE ELECTORATE

Few aspects of an individual's psychological profile are as revealing of political attitudes and behaviour as is partisan identification, a feeling of oneness with a party. In Chapter 4 it was noted that party identification has been employed to explain such diverse phenomena as public perceptions of political candidates, attitudes toward issues, cross-national differences in political behaviour, stability and change in electoral systems and the frequency and direction of individual voting. Research also has indicated that: party identities develop early in life; parents and other members of the nuclear family are the principal agents involved in the formation of an initial identification; identification, if it occurs early in life, tends to take the form of an affective attachment to a party symbol; and identifications, although firmly held by many people, are not immutable and can change as a consequence of a variety of personal experiences and environmental conditions.

Studies cited in Chapter 4 reveal that only about one Canadian in ten does not have a partisan identification and that more than a third have changed their identifications at the federal and provincial levels one or more times. Moreover, people apparently shift their partisan allegiances because of factors that are part of the normal political process. Comparisons with British and American studies suggest that ties between the electorate and parties may be less stable in Canada. For one thing, Canadians not only change party identifications more often, they also tend to shift between identification and non-identification. In the United States, people shift between a Democratic or Republican identification on the one hand and an Independent identification on the other, but they less often switch from a Democratic to a Republican identification or *vice versa*. In Great Britain, people may switch from a Labour to a Conservative identification but they are not inclined to change their Labour, Conservative, or Liberal identifications and become non-identifiers.[29]

It has been noted that Canadians not only change their partisan identifications, but, at one and the same time, they can identify with one party federally and another provincially. In the Atlantic provinces the provincial Liberal and Conservative parties tend to be the principal beneficiaries, respectively, of the affections of federal Conservatives and Liberals with divided party loyalties. In Manitoba and Saskatchewan, however, identifiers with the federal Liberal and Conservative parties tend to give their provincial loyalties to the NDP, whereas in British Columbia, the provincial Social Credit party, as well as the NDP, are the recipients of the affections of federal Liberals and Conservatives. In Ontario a greater percentage of disaffected federal Liberals than federal New Democrats think of themselves as provincial Conservatives, but the opposite condition obtains in Quebec. In that province, whereas 19% of federal Liberals (and 40%, respectively, of federal Conservatives and Créditistes) identify with the Parti Québécois, fully 88% of those identifying with the federal NDP give their provincial loyalties to the Péquistes.

With respect to the direction of partisan attachments, the Liberal party claims the loyalties of more people than any of its competitors, but it is much stronger in the eastern than the western half of the country and shows more strength federally than provinciallly. Conservative party strength is somewhat better balanced in that there are substantial numbers of Conservative identifiers in all but Quebec and British Columbia. Further, in five of the provinces (Prince Edward Island, Nova Scotia, New Brunswick, Ontario and Alberta) the party has more provincial than federal identifiers, while the opposite is the case in the other five provinces. As previously noted, the New Democratic and, particularly, Social Credit are regional parties with the latter currently being a significant force only in British Columbia. In contrast, the New Democrats have large numbers of identifiers at both levels of the federal system in Saskatchewan, British Columbia, and Manitoba, and a lesser but still appreciable body of identifiers in Ontario and Nova Scotia. The party has negligible strength in the remaining provinces, however. Particularly striking in this regard is NDP's failure to develop a body of provincial and federal identifiers in Quebec comparable in size to that which identifies with the party in neighboring Ontario (See Table 5.1).

The strength as well as the direction of partisanship have been shown to affect political attitudes and behaviour. Voting studies usually determine both the direction and strength of people's attachments to a party by asking them whether they think of themselves as Liberals, Conservatives, and so forth; and whether they feel they are very strong, fairly strong, not very strong, or a little closer to the party they have just named. In response to the latter question, in 1979 more people described themselves as fairly strong than either very strong or not very strong party identifiers. Overall, each party's proportions of very, fairly, and not very strong identifiers are relatively similar in magnitude. There are, however, variations in their size by province and by party within provinces. Identification with provincial Liberal parties is strongest in Newfoundland and New Brunswick and weakest in Manitoba and British Columbia. The latter is the home of the country's staunchest group of Socreds, whereas Alberta is the locus of the strongest Conservative sentiment in the country.

The 1979 national election study also provides information on the attributes of people who identify with provincial Liberal, Conservative, New Democratic and Social Credit parties and of Quebecers who identify with the Parti Québécois and Union Nationale. Complicating attempts to generalize about the socioeconomic and demographic correlates of provincial partisanship, however, is the fact that in different regions, indeed, in neighboring provinces, the attributes of identifiers with a particular party may differ considerably. Table 5.2, which presents what may be regarded as key attributes of provincial party identifiers within each province, illustrates this point. The table shows, for example, that the small group of NDP identifiers in New Brunswick is younger, more strongly identified with the party and more inclined to think of themselves as members of the lower class than fellow partisans in neighboring Nova Scotia. In the West more often than in the East they (NDP identifiers) are: older, strongly identified with the party, and of other than French or Anglo-Celtic origins. They also are less affluent and less often possessed of formal religious affiliations. Similarly, identifiers with the Conservative party in the Atlantic provinces are younger, more often are Catholics and are less affluent than Ontario Conservatives. They are also more frequently Catholic and less affluent than Conservatives living in the Prairies or British Columbia. Differences of varying magnitudes also distinguish Liberal and Social Credit identifiers. Compare, for example, some of the attributes of Quebec Créditiste identifiers with those of British Columbia Socreds or the attributes of Newfoundland and Alberta Liberals.

TABLE 5.1

Distribution of Federal and Provincial Party Identifications, 1979*

| | Liberal | | Conservative | | New Democratic | | Social Credit | | Union Nationale | | Parti Québécois | | No Identification | | N = |
	Province	Federal	Province	Federal	Province	Federal	Province	Federal	Province	Federal	Province	Federal	Province	Federal	Federal
Newfoundland	44%	53%	47	38	6	6	—	—	—	—	—	—	4	4	112
Prince Edward Island	50%	52%	35	32	1	1	—	—	—	—	—	—	15	15	109
Nova Scotia	38%	36%	40	35	12	11	—	—	—	—	—	—	11	17	195
New Brunswick	40%	40%	33	30	5	8	1	1	—	—	—	—	22	20	144
Quebec	50%	60%	2	9	—	6	3	7	4	—	30	—	11	18	724
Ontario	33%	42%	40	31	14	16	—	—	—	—	—	—	14	11	747
Manitoba	14%	25%	38	40	33	18	2	2	—	—	—	—	14	15	131
Saskatchewan	17%	17%	19	35	45	26	—	—	—	—	—	—	19	21	108
Alberta	7%	18%	73	61	4	5	5	4	—	—	—	—	10	11	197
British Columbia	6%	29%	5	29	42	25	40	3	—	—	—	—	8	13	277

*Table entries are percentaged horizontally (federal and provincial identifications separately).

TABLE 5.2
Social Profile of Provincial Party Identifiers

	Liberals	Conservatives	New Democrats	Social Credit
NEWFOUNDLAND				
Age	older (56+)	younger (18–35)	younger	—
Subjective social class	middle	working and lower	middle	—
Annual income	lower ($0–14,999)	lower and middle ($15,000–24,999)	lower and middle	—
Religious affiliation	upper status Protestant	Catholic	Catholic and high status Protestant	—
Mother tongue	English	English	English	—
Intensity of identification	very strong	fairly strong	fairly strong	—
PRINCE EDWARD ISLAND				
Age	middle (35–55)	younger (18–35)	—	—
Subjective social class	middle	middle and working	—	—
Annual income	lower ($0–14,999)	lower ($0–14,999)	—	—
Religious affiliation	Upper status Protestant & Catholic	Catholic	—	—
Mother tongue	English	English	—	—
Intensity of identification	very and fairly strong	fairly strong	—	—

NOVA SCOTIA

Age	younger (18–35) & older (56+)	younger (18–35) & older (56+)	younger (18–35) & middle (36–55)	—
Subjective social class	middle & working	middle	middle	—
Annual income	lower ($0–14,999)	lower ($0–14,999)	lower ($0–14,999)	—
Religious affiliation	Upper status Protestant	Catholic & Protestant	Catholic & Protestant	—
Mother tongue	English	English	English	—
Intensity of identification	fairly strong	fairly strong	fairly strong	—

NEW BRUNSWICK

Age	younger (18–35) & older (56+)	younger (18–35) & middle (36–55)	younger (18–35)	—
Subjective social class	middle and working	middle and working	lower	—
Annual income	lower ($0–14,999)	lower ($0–14,999)	lower ($0–14,999)	—
Religious affiliation	Upper status Protestant	Catholic & Protestant	Low status Protestant	—
Mother tongue	English	English	English	—
Intensity of identification	fairly strong	fairly strong	very strong	—

QUEBEC

	Liberals	Union Nationale	Parti Québécois	Parti Créditiste
Age	middle (36–55) & older (56+)	older (56+) and middle (36–55)	younger (18–35)	younger (18–35)
Subjective social class	middle	working	middle	middle
Annual income	lower ($0–14,999) & middle ($15,000–24,999)	lower ($0–14,999) and middle ($15,000–24,999)	evenly distributed	lower ($0–14,999)
Religious affiliation	Catholic	Catholic	Catholic	Catholic
Mother tongue	French	French	French	French
Intensity of identification	fairly and very strong	fairly strong	fairly strong	not very strong

ONTARIO

	Liberals	Conservatives	New Democrats	Social Credit
Age	younger (18–35) & middle (36–55)	older (56+) & middle (36–55)	younger (18–35)	—
Subjective social class	middle	middle	working	—
Annual income	middle ($15,000–24,999) & upper ($25,000+)	upper ($25,000+) & lower ($0–14,999)	middle ($15,000–24,999) & upper ($25,000+)	—
Religious affiliation	Upper status Protestant & Catholic	Upper status Protestant	Upper status Protestant & Catholic	—
Mother tongue	English	English	English	—
Intensity of identification	fairly strong	fairly strong	fairly strong	—

MANITOBA

Age	older (56+)	younger (18–35) & middle (36–55)	younger (18–35) & older (56+)	—
Subjective social class	working	middle & working	working	—
Annual income	lower ($0–14,999)	evenly distributed	lower ($0–14,999) & middle ($15,000–24,999)	—
Religious affiliation	Upper status Protestant & Catholic	Upper status Protestant	Protestant & Catholic	—
Mother tongue	English	English	English & other	—
Intensity of identification	fairly strong	fairly strong	very strong	—

SASKATCHEWAN

Age	older (56+)	older (56+)	older (56+) & younger (18–35)	—
Subjective social class	middle	middle	middle & working	—
Annual income	lower ($0–14,999) & middle ($15,000–24,999)	upper ($25,000+)	middle ($15,000–24,999) & upper ($25,000+)	—
Religious affiliation	Catholic and upper status Protestant	Upper status Protestant	Upper status Protestant & none	—
Mother tongue	English	English	English	—
Intensity of identification	fairly strong	fairly strong	fairly strong and very strong	—

ALBERTA

	Liberals	Conservatives	New Democrats	Social Credit
Age	middle (36–55)	younger (18–35)	younger (18–35) & older (56+)	older (56+)
Subjective social class	middle	middle	working	middle & working
Annual income	upper ($25,000+)	middle ($15,000–24,999) & upper ($25,000+)	middle ($15,000–24,999) & upper ($25,000+)	evenly distributed
Religious affiliation	Catholic	Upper status Protestant	Upper status Protestant & Catholic	Protestant & Catholic
Mother tongue	English & French	English	English & other	English
Intensity of identification	fairly strong	fairly strong	very strong	very strong & fairly strong

BRITISH COLUMBIA

	Liberals	Conservatives	New Democrats	Social Credit
Age	middle (36–55) & younger (18–35)	middle (36–55) & younger (18–35)	middle (36–55) & younger (18–35)	middle (36–55) & younger (18–35)
Subjective social class	middle & working	middle	middle & working	middle
Annual income	middle ($15,000–24,999) & lower ($0–14,999)	upper ($25,000+)	middle ($15,000–24,999) & upper ($25,000+)	upper ($25,000+)
Religious affiliation	Upper status Protestant	Upper status Protestant	Upper status Protestant & none	Upper status Protestant
Mother tongue	English	English	English	English
Intensity of identification	fairly strong	very strong	fairly strong	fairly strong

The image most Canadians have of the social composition of the parties — of who is a Liberal, Conservative, New Democrat, or Socred — is a simplified one that largely is conditioned by stereotypic conceptions of the group basis of federal party support.[30] It would probably come as quite a surprise to many Canadians to learn that these conceptions and the actual social composition of each party's cohort of provincial identifiers are far from identical. Thus, rather than being predominately Protestant, in three of the four Atlantic provinces the Conservative party in the electorate has a distinctly Catholic flavour. Similarly, substantial percentages of identifiers with the provincial NDP (nominally the party of organized labour) in Newfoundland, Nova Scotia, British Columbia, Ontario and Manitoba, think of themselves as members of the middle or upper-middle class rather than as a part of the working class. Conversely, literally thousands of low income, blue-collar workers in each province identify with the supposedly middle-class Liberal party. These complex patterns of partisan allegiance are testimony to the importance of provinces as political communities and the success of each province's party leaders in appealing to social groups who are important within their particular province even though they may not be "traditional" supporters of their party.

One reason for this success may be because party appeals in part are based on the personalities of party leaders and on historical considerations divorced from rational political interests. Another may be that party leaders articulate distinctly provincial rather than national needs and interests (e.g., "Nova Scotia needs jobs"; "Saskatchewan must sell its wheat"). Because they appeal to provincial rather than national interests, leaders of a party in one province may take different and, at times, opposite positions on particular issues from their counterparts in another province. A good example is the different positions on energy policy that have been taken by Messrs. Davis and Lougheed, leaders of the Conservative party governments of Ontario and Alberta, respectively. The need to respond to specifically provincial interests also can lead to differences between the leaders of the provincial and federal wings of the same party. Illustrative are the current differences in the positions of federal and provincial Liberal leaders in Quebec respecting issues pertaining to the division of jurisdiction and relative powers of the federal government and the provinces, and the differing stands on constitutional issues taken by Messrs. Broadbent and Blakeney, the national New Democratic leader and the First Minister of the New Democratic government of Saskatchewan, respectively.

Such differences in issue positions make it difficult for the parties, *as parties*, to convey clear, overall images of who they are and what they are about. In turn, an inability to project clear and reasonably well-defined public images may explain why approximately one of every five Canadians finds it possible to identify psychologically with one party provincially and another federally, and why, as well, between successive elections approximately one of every three voters switches party identification, or goes from identifying to not identifying with a party or *vice versa*. Since changes in party identification and direction of voting frequently go hand in hand,[31] both the volatility of the electorate and the periodic sharp rises and declines in party fortunes noted previously become more comprehensible. The inability of parties competing in both federal and provincial elections to project clear and sharply differentiated images and their tendency in both types of elections to respond to specifically provincial concerns also lend force to the charge of party scholars such as John Meisel. Meisel, as noted previously, has criticized the parties for a variety of failures, not the least of which is their inability to facilitate national unity by mobilizing their supporters behind issues whose scope and importance transcend the interest of a particular province or region.[32]

INTEREST GROUPS: FUNCTIONS

Interest groups are organizations of people making claims on others and upon government, national, provincial and local. Although the benefits that interest groups provide their members and the tangible and intangible rewards which interest group leaders receive in return are worthy of study in their own right, our principal concern here is the role interest groups play in the operation of provincial political systems. Provincial governments receive a great deal of attention from organized groups because of the jurisdiction they have over areas in which some of the greatest economic growth has occurred during the past quarter century. Interest groups also are encouraged to direct attention to provincial governments because there usually is less competition for access to provincial cabinet ministers and key bureaucratic officials than there is at the federal level. Where an interest group may be one of many competing for the attention of federal officials, it may be a singularly powerful contender for the attention of officials in a particular province.

The role that interest groups play in the operation of provincial political systems is three-fold: they communicate politically relevant information to and from provincial governments; they generate public support for them and their policies; and they carry out certain regulatory and administrative activities on their behalf. These activities are not mutually exclusive. Support for provincial governments and involvement in the regulatory process in a very real sense are byproducts of the "communicating politically relevant information" function. It is argued that interest group leaders are willing to actively support provincial governments as well as certain of their policies because they frequently see themselves as partners of government in the policy process. Governmental officials may use the information interest groups provide to generate a new policy, amend an existing one, or defer action on some matter. The linkage between provincial governments and interest groups is reciprocal, however. Provincial governments may make advantageous use of the information interest groups provide but, obviously, the latter also use governments to get consideration, if not acceptance, of their particular positions on issues in question. This mutual back-scratching has led scholarly observers to term the relationship between them a symbiotic one.

This symbiosis, as just indicated, extends even to the involvement of interest group leaders in the administration of certain regulatory policies of provincial governments. In various ways regulatory policies limit the freedom of action of important social and economic groups. Consequently, leaders of affected groups try either to resist regulation or, much more often, to limit its effects by convincing governmental officials that they (the group leaders) possess special knowledge, information, or expertise which enables them to regulate their members more effectively and efficiently than can government. The leaders of professional groups such as doctors, dentists, lawyers and engineers have been particularly successful in this respect. In every province they are integrally involved in regulating the professional standards and ethical conduct of their members. Their ability to do so rests principally on their power (with provincial government acquiescence) to license and thus control entry into their professions, as well as to impose sanctions on those who violate professional canons and ethics. Self-regulation is an important power. It enables interest group leaders to facilitate the development of their members' careers, establish highly favourable working environments for them and secure higher fees for their services. Relatedly, the willingness of group members to reward and provide support for their leaders is a function of the latter's ability to secure favourable treatment for them from government.

Of course, interest groups are not all of a piece. Not every group has the power medical and legal interest groups enjoy. They vary, at times dramatically, not only with respect to their power, but also with regard to motives, the size of their membership, their status and prestige in a community, the resources they command, the fullness and form of their organizations, the political sophistication of their leaders and their ability to act cohesively. Paul Pross terms interest groups which are large, well organized, cohesive, led by individuals with easy access to public officials and knowledgeable about how government works, "institutionalized" groups. Groups having limited organizational continuity, a small and fluid membership, leaders with a minimal knowledge of how government works, and limited access to governmental decision-makers, he terms "issue-oriented" groups.[33]

Institutionalized groups are better able than issue groups to influence both the day-to-day actions and the long-term policies of provincial governments but, in order to do so, they must act "responsibly." They must communicate their demands and try to influence governmental decisions while abiding by certain rules of the game: a cardinal one being not to draw unfavourable attention to or publicly embarrass governmental officials with whom they are dealing. There are, of course, times and issues when willful violation of these norms may be useful to a group, if for no other reason than to demonstrate the intensity of its concerns. As will be observed in Chapter 7, the doctors of Saskatchewan violated one of the basic rules of the game when they went public in their controversy with the CCF government over health policy. Despite such periodic departures from the norm, both the immediate and long-term influence of institutionalized groups, even those as powerful and prestigious as doctors, derives from the maintenance of harmonious relationships with provincial governmental officials. In contrast, the principal assets of issue-oriented groups are their unpredictability, flexibility, and willingness to bring the kind of pressure to bear on governments which institutionalized groups are unwilling to use for fear of losing access. Issue-oriented groups facilitate the representation of interests by mobilizing highly visible public support for or opposition to governmental officials contemplating particular policy actions, thereby providing them with instant feedback. However, they often do so in ways that embarrass and anger those officials, but since they generally are not primarily concerned with influencing long-term governmental policy, this is a matter of little concern to them.

Institutionalized and issue-oriented groups alike try to identify their objectives with community values such as freedom, prosperity, good health and the sanctity of private property. Doing so makes it easier to achieve their goals because it helps secure the support of other groups and avoids the charge of selfishness. Beyond this generalized attempt, the precise tactics employed by specific groups and the likelihood of their success will depend upon the issue at hand and the group's attributes. Let us illustrate: (1) A provincial medical association is more likely to persuade a health minister to raise fees for certain medical services than an anti-vivisectionist group is to persuade that same minister to order a halt to all medical experiments with animals because the former group has far more prestige and status in the community and with the minister than has the latter. (2) The medical association is more likely to succeed in raising fees if its leaders enter into discreet negotiations with the minister and his bureaucratic subordinates than if doctors picket hospitals and dress in rags to dramatize their need for larger incomes. (3) Weekly newspaper advertisements and television and radio commercials that extol the virtues of free enterprise and the insurance industry may establish a favourable climate of public opinion for the industry, but they are unlikely to defeat a government's bill "provincializing" the sale of automobile insurance. (4) A letter-writing campaign directed at members of a provincial legislature may be effective if a group has 10,000 members and its leaders can get all or most of them to write. The tactic is both inappropriate and unlikely to succeed if, instead, the group has only 100 members and half of them will not participate. To repeat, factors such as the issue at hand and the attributes of a group such as its prestige, size, organizational form and the sagacity of its leaders will significantly affect both the effective representation of interests and the tactics employed by groups.

INTEREST GROUPS, POLITICAL PARTIES, AND REPRESENTATIVE DEMOCRACY

Do the activities of interest groups contribute to representative democracy? Students of democratic politics frequently raise this question. Interest group advocates argue that they *do* because in a variety of ways they supplement constitutional procedures designed to implement popular control of government. Unlike the provincial legislator representing a particular constituency, an interest group can articulate the interests of its members without regard to their geographic locations. Groups thereby supplement the official geographically-oriented system of legislative representation. They also encourage popular participation in provincial politics. Group leaders encourage their members to vote, express themselves on political issues and join in collective efforts to influence provincial governments; efforts that can supplement but, obviously, need not replace individual political action. Interest groups are also linkage mechanisms. As was indicated previously, one of their principal activities is to inform governmental officials of their members' needs and interests and apprise their members of governmental policy proposals and actions that might affect them. They thus give large numbers of people the feeling that they affect the actions of provincial governments in ways they regard as desirable. By enhancing politically efficacious feelings in the public, interest groups can make a significant contribution to the achievement of more representative and democratic provincial political systems — or so it is argued.

Those who contend that the activities of interest groups do not facilitate the good health of representative democracy underscore the fact that their representational activities are highly selective. They bring the social, economic and political concerns of *particular* group interests to the attention of governmental officials. Consequently, they bias the provincial representational process so that it favours some and penalizes others. Those who are penalized include the great majority of unorganized citizens, whereas those favoured usually also are the best educated, most affluent and well-organized people in a province.[34]

Also, the ability of interest groups to supplement other vehicles of representation is limited by the operation of the cabinet system of government which places a premium on group access to cabinet members and, through them, senior civil servants. Institutionalized groups have the best access to cabinets because of their more elaborate organization, affluence, status and cohesion and because they also employ "functional accommodative, consensus-seeking techniques of political communication, rather than conflict-oriented techniques that are directed toward the achievement of objectives through arousing public opinion."[35] Less-favoured groups (e.g., those with limited financial resources, skeletal organizations, politically unsophisticated leaders, poor or limited access to the cabinet and the bureaucracy) simply are out of luck because "the system presents great impediments to those who want to raise new issues and who lack either the knowledge or the power to command access."[36]

Interest group critics further observe that it is precisely the institutionalized interest groups having the greatest access to provincial decision-makers whose internal organizations are the most likely to be undemocratic. They tend to be controlled by small cadres of well-paid, full-time professional leaders. These leadership oligarchies identify problems and define the issues their groups will pursue. The roles they assign to their members are to pay their annual dues and support what they (i.e., the professional leaders) tell them to support. Such restricted roles hardly are congruent with the claim of interest group champions who argue that group activities increase political participation on the part of the public.

Finally, critics contend that at best the public can exact only indirect accountability from interest groups. Certainly, it cannot exact the kind of accountability from major interest groups that it can from legislators or even from officials of party organizations. Regarding the latter, it is noted that both parties and interest groups are private organizations who periodically are authorized to perform certain public functions. For example, party officials recruit candidates for provincial legislatures and leaders of professional groups such as doctors, lawyers and dentists regulate the ethics and professional conduct of their colleagues. Tasks such as these are extremely important to the public; very few people would dispute the need for either legislative candidates or competent and ethical doctors, dentists and lawyers. The problem is that whereas the public can hold parties accountable for their selections by refusing to elect or re-elect their candidates, it cannot pass analogous judgments on how satisfactorily professional groups regulate their members' conduct.

Interestingly, although in many countries interest groups have increased in power and number, political parties appear to have grown weaker. Students of politics hesitate to ascribe a causal relationship to these two events because other conditions — the growth in size and power of bureaucracies and the influence of the media, for example — also have accompanied any decline of political parties. There is agreement, however, that even if political parties and interest groups are viewed as complementing rather than competing with one another in the representational process, any decline in the power and importance of parties is regrettable.

It is not that political parties in Canada and other Western countries have performed in exemplary fashion. Indeed, criticisms of them are legion and a number were referenced in the concluding section of the last chapter. To these can be added the criticism that, notwithstanding rhetoric to the contrary, officials of extralegislative party organizations do little to encourage people in any province to participate in party affairs. In addition, if the findings of a study of party organizations in Vancouver and Winnipeg can be generalized to other provinces, it appears that influence among party officials tends to be highly concentrated among leaders whom we have termed "Elites." The latter act as gatekeepers and largely determine "who gets in, who moves up and who moves out."[37] Within provincial legislatures, the adversary relationship in which government and opposition parties are habitually cast often makes it appear that interparty conflict is an end in itself, rather than a means of arriving at policies in the public interest. The media contribute to this appearance because in their coverage of legislative debates they tend to present provincial legislatures as "bear pits."[38] The media also can be faulted for depicting elections as athletic contests between contending party leaders and for focussing much of their day-to-day coverage on the strategies party leaders employ rather than on the content of their public speeches.[39]

For their part, party leaders exacerbate the problem of informing and educating the public by stressing issues during (and in the interim between) electoral campaigns on which there is no real distribution of public opinion. Classic examples are issues such as inflation, unemployment or a strong economy. Who, it may be asked, is in favour of unemployment or inflation, or opposed to a strong provincial economy? Electorates do not need to be told such "issues" constitute important public problems. What they require, and what parties frequently fail to provide, are clearly delineated policy proposals designed to ameliorate these problems. Moreover, even when the public is divided on an issue, the need to win elections (the so-called "electoral imperative") induces party leaders to take vague centrist positions, where, it is alleged, the largest proportion of voters are located. Consequently, a recurring complaint among scholarly observers of party politics is that party positions, especially those of Liberals and Conservatives, are ill-defined and overlapping, a condition which at once confuses voters and deprives them of meaningful choices. When one adds to this the tendency of federal and provincial leaders of the same party to take different, even diametrically opposite positions on an issue, it is not surprising that large numbers of people in every province lack the kinds of political knowledge, interest and sophistication a representative democracy requires of its citizens.

Despite their manifest deficiencies, the evidence presented previously indicates that political parties represent a much broader spectrum of provincial publics than do interest groups. Analyses of the social correlates of provincial party identifiers that were presented above indicate that in every province the competing parties have the loyalties (albeit, in some instances, only temporarily) of large numbers of voters in virtually every social and demographic category. In contrast to the social composition of voters identifying with their parties, the members of legislative parties and the leaders of their extralegislative organizations disproportionately are well-educated members of the middle and upper middle classes. Although people with similar attributes also comprise the membership and, especially, the professional leadership of most interest groups, there is a major difference between elites who lead parties and those who lead interest groups. The former must make at least an effort, even if only symbolic, to represent the public interest whereas the latter only are required to effectively articulate the interests of their members. Since the principal objective of political parties is to gain control of the instruments of government, it could hardly be otherwise. In short, the argument that any decline in the importance of political parties is regrettable because their activities are more congruent with the formalistic and responsiveness conceptions of what representation entails, is well-founded.

SUMMARY

We began this chapter by noting that the Liberals and Conservatives are inside parties which began as factions in the legislative assemblies of the four provinces that in 1867 joined in Confederation. The New Democratic and Social Credit parties, in contrast, are outside parties whose origins are rooted in the social dislocations that accompanied the settlement of the Prairie provinces and the Great Depression of the 1930s. The Liberals were the first to establish an extralegislative organization, but neither they nor the Conservatives developed a broad network of constituency-level parties until well into the present century. The CCF-NDP and Social Credit followed suit. Constituency-level parties largely monopolize the recruitment of candidates for provincial legislative offices. They are populated almost entirely by amateurs, people who have other occupations and statuses which normally take precedence over demands of party work. Because of the episodic nature of party work and the peculiar organizational structure (i.e., a truncated pyramid) of most extralegislative parties, the pinnacle of a career for most party officials is the attainment of either an appointive or an elective public office. In this regard, Canadian party organizations, irrespective of the level of government to which they are oriented, are not unlike those of other Western countries.

Canada does differ from many of these countries, however, in that it does not really have a single party system. The number of contesting parties, their identities and patterns of electoral competition between and among them can vary sharply from province to province. Moreover, within a particular province the competitive statuses and, at times, the identities of parties participating in national and provincial elections also may differ. This complexity is both a consequence and a cause of the importance of provinces as political communities and the distribution of partisan psychological identifications among members of the general public.

Further complicating party politics is the fact that about one person in five tends to split his or her identification, identifying with one party provincially and with another federally. Comparisons of Canadian data with information derived from surveys in other federal systems suggest that the tendency of large numbers of voters to divide their partisan attachments in this way is an aspect of party identification that is uniquely Canadian. Other comparisons indicate that the partisan loyalties of Canadians seemingly are less enduring than are those of voters in Anglo-American democracies such as the United States and Great Britain. As argued in Chapter 4, split and unstable partisan identifications likely reflect a substantial, if "rough and ready," rationality among portions of provincial electorates. Relatedly, these characteristics of partisanship are indicative of the weakness of Canadian parties — in particular, their frequent inability to formulate and adhere to clearly defined policy positions that transcend provincial and regional particularisms.

Irrespective of any weaknesses, it nonetheless has been argued that political parties are more appropriate vehicles of democratic representation than are interest groups. Defenders of interest groups argue that they supplement constitutional procedures designed to implement popular control of government because their leaders encourage greater participation and provide important feedback to governmental officials on the effects their policies are likely to have on people who will be most strongly affected by them. Interest group critics argue that these activities distort the representational process and they really do not significantly enhance popular participation in politics. More important, the public as a whole cannot exact the kind of accountability from interest groups that it can from political parties. Thus, the latter, despite their manifest deficiencies, are more appropriate representational vehicles and can contribute more to the achievement of representative democracy in the provinces than can interest groups.

NOTES

1. Most books on political parties, especially parties in democratic political systems, begin with a definition of party, an overview of the origins and development of political parties, and a list of the functions they perform in political systems. See, for example, Giovanni Sartori, *Parties and Party Systems: A Framework for Analysis* (London: Cambridge University Press, 1976), ch. 1; and Leon D. Epstein, *Political Parties in Western Democracies* (New York: Praeger, 1967), pp. 3–45.

2. See for example, J.A. Irving, *The Social Credit Movement in Alberta* (Toronto: University of Toronto Press, 1959); L.G. Thomas, *The Liberal Party in Alberta* (Toronto: University of Toronto Press, 1959); Herbert Quinn, *The Union Nationale* (Toronto: University of Toronto Press, 1963); Seymour Martin Lipset, *Agrarian Socialism: The Cooperative Commonwealth Federation in Saskatchewan* (New York: Doubleday, 1968); David E. Smith, *Prairie Liberalism*, (Toronto: University of Toronto Press, 1975); Martin Robin, ed., *Canadian Provincial Politics: The Party Systems of the Ten Provinces*, 2nd ed. (Scarborough: Prentice-Hall, 1978).

3. Joseph LaPalombara and Myron Weiner, "The Origin and Development of Political Parties," in Joseph LaPalombara and Myron Weiner eds., *Political Parties and Political Development* (Princeton: Princeton University Press, 1969), pp. 3–42.

4. See Escott M. Reid, "The Rise of National Parties in Canada," Papers and Proceedings of the Canadian Political Science Association 4 (1932), pp. 187–200.

5. See Frederick C. Englemann and Mildred A. Schwartz, *Canadian Political Parties: Origin, Character, Impact* (Scarborough: Prentice-Hall, 1975), p. 33.

6. For example, in Manitoba party candidates won a total of 11 seats and received an average of less than 5% of the vote in seven provincial elections held between 1936 and 1959. In Saskatchewan party candidates won a total of five seats and received less than 9% of the vote in six provincial elections held between 1938 and 1960.

7. Robert A. Hackett, "The Waffle Conflict in the NDP," in Hugh G. Thorburn, ed., *Party Politics in Canada*, 4th ed. (Scarborough: Prentice-Hall, 1979), pp. 188–205.

8. See, for example, Herbert F. Quinn, *The Union Nationale* (Toronto: University of Toronto Press, 1963); Maurice Pinard, "Working Class Politics: An Interpretation of the Quebec Case," *Canadian Review of Sociology and Anthropology* 7 (1970), pp. 87–109; and Kenneth McRoberts and Dale Posgate, *Quebec: Social Change and Political Crisis*, revised ed., (Toronto: McClelland and Stewart, 1980), ch. 5.

9. On the rise of the Parti Québécois see McRoberts and Posgate, *Quebec: Social Change and Political Crisis*, chs. 8, 9. See also Richard Hamilton and Maurice Pinard, "The Bases of Parti Québécois Support in Recent Quebec Elections," *Canadian Journal of Political Science* 9 (1976), pp. 3–26; Maurice Pinard and Richard Hamilton, "The Independence Issue and the Polarization of the Electorate: The 1973 Quebec Election, *Canadian Journal of Political Science* 10 (1977), pp. 215–260; Maurice Pinard and Richard Hamilton, "The Parti Québécois Comes to Power: An Analysis of the 1976 Quebec Election," *Canadian Journal of Political Science* 11 (1978), pp. 739–776; and Harold Clarke, "Partisanship and the Parti Québécois: The Impact of the Independence Issue," *The American Review of Canadian Studies* 8 (1978), pp. 28–47.

10. Jon Pammett, Harold D. Clarke, Jane Jenson and Lawrence LeDuc, "Political Support and Voting Behaviour in the Quebec Referendum," in A. Kornberg and H.D. Clarke, eds. *Political Support in Canada: The Crisis Years* (Durham, N.C.: Duke University Press, 1982), ch. 12.

11. See "British Columbia: The Politics of Class Conflict" in Martin Robin, ed., *Canadian Provincial Politics*, 2nd ed., pp. 28–60.

12. John Wilson and David Hoffman, "A Three Party System in Transition," in Martin Robin, ed. *Canadian Provincial Politics* 1st ed., (Scarborough: Prentice-Hall, 1972), pp. 198–239; Robert J. Drummond, "Voting Behaviour: Casting the Play," in Donald C. MacDonald, ed. *The Government and Politics of Ontario*, 2nd ed., (Toronto: Van Nostrand-Reinhold Ltd., 1980), pp. 272–290.

13. The Newfoundland Liberals won 98% of the provincial legislative seats in the 1966 election, 48% of the seats in the following election (1971), but only 19% in 1972.

14. Allan Kornberg, "Caucus and Cohesion in Canadian Parliamentary Parties," *American Political Science Review*, 60 (1966), pp. 83–92; Harold D. Clarke, Richard G.

Price and Robert Krause, "Constituency Service Among Canadian Provincial Legislators: Basic Findings and a Test of Three Hypotheses," *Canadian Journal of Political Science* 8 (1975), pp. 520–542; and Allan Kornberg and William Mishler, *Influence in Parliament: Canada* (Durham, N.C.: Duke University Press, 1976), pp. 177–181.

15. John Meisel, "The Decline of Party in Canada," in Hugh G. Thorburn, ed., *Party Politics in Canada*, 4th ed., (Scarborough: Prentice-Hall, 1979), pp. 121–135.

16. Harold D. Clarke, Jane Jenson, Lawrence LeDuc and Jon Pammett, *Political Choice in Canada* (Toronto: McGraw-Hill, Ryerson 1979), chs. 1, 7.

17. Allan Kornberg, Joel Smith and Harold D. Clarke, *Citizen Politicians — Canada* (Durham, N.C.: Carolina Academic Press, 1979), pp. 142–159.

18. Allan Kornberg, "Parliament in Canadian Society," in A. Kornberg and L. Musolf, eds., *Legislatures in Developmental Perspective* (Durham: Duke University Press, 1970), pp. 73–82. See also, John C. Courtney, *The Selection of National Party Leaders in Canada* (Toronto: Macmillan, 1973), pp. 59–81; and Donald Smiley, "The National Party Leadership Convention in Canada: A Preliminary Analysis," *Canadian Journal of Political Science* 1 (1968), pp. 373–379.

19. Kornberg *et al.*, *Citizen Politicians*, p. 143.

20. *Ibid.*, chs. 4, 5.

21. See Conrad Winn and John McMenemy, *Political Parties in Canada* (Toronto: McGraw-Hill Ryerson, 1976), ch. 10.

22. The use of this metaphor reflects our experience with the reality of local party structures. Party positions are hierarchically organized; hence, the use of the term "pyramid." Although their paper tables of organization suggest that they can be fuller and more vertically developed than the metaphor implies, in fact, the majority of officials occupy positions at lower levels of these organizations (i.e., the base and middle of the pyramid). Finally, there are relatively few levels of office between the base and the apex of the pyramid, prompting us to describe them as "truncated."

23. Kornberg *et al.*, *Citizen Politicians–Canada*, pp. 96–104.

24. *Ibid.*, p. 88.

25. *Ibid.*, p. 90.

26. *Ibid.*, chs. 7, 8.

27. *Ibid.*, ch. 9.

28. The Governor-General-in-Council (i.e., the federal cabinet) appoints all federal judges and all judges of superior provincial courts. Appointments to judgeships of lower provincial courts are made by Lieutenant-Governors-in-Council (i.e., provincial cabinets).

29. There are, however, important trends toward a weakening of traditional Conservative and Labour party ties in contemporary Great Britain. See, for example, Ivor Crewe "Britain's New Party: Can It Make It?" *Public Opinion* 4 (June/July 1981), p. 52.

30. Allan Kornberg, William Mishler, and Joel Smith, "Political Elite and Mass Perceptions of Party Locations in Issue Space: Some Tests of Two Positions," *British Journal of Political Science*, 5 (1975), pp. 161–185.

31. Clarke *et al.*, *Political Choice in Canada*, pp. 145–155.

32. See, for example, John Meisel, "Recent Changes in Canadian Parties," in Hugh G. Thorburn, ed., *Party Politics in Canada*, 2nd ed., (Scarborough: Prentice-Hall, 1967), pp. 41–42.

33. See A. Paul Pross, "Pressure Groups: Adaptive Instruments of Political Communications," in A. Paul Pross, ed., *Pressure Group Behaviour in Canadian Politics* (Toronto: McGraw-Hill Ryerson, 1975), pp. 9–18.

34. Repeated studies of the social composition of interest groups indicate their active and influential members disproportionately are well-educated, affluent professionals and business people. See, for example, Robert Presthus, *Elite Accommodation in Canadian Politics* (Toronto: Macmillan, 1973), ch. 10.

35. Pross, *Pressure Group Behaviour*, p. 19

36. *Ibid.*

37. Kornberg *et al.*, *Citizen Politicians*, p. 233.

38. On the media's treatment of legislators and legislative debates see Allan Kornberg and Judith D. Wolfe, "Parliament, the Media and the Polls"; and Richard G. Price and Harold D. Clarke, "Television and the House of Commons," in Harold D. Clarke *et al.*, *Parliament, Policy and Representation* (Toronto: Methuen, 1980), pp. 35–57, 58–83.

39. Clarke *et al.*, *Political Choice in Canada*, ch. 9.

FOR FURTHER READING

Clarke, Harold D., Jane Jenson, Lawrence LeDuc and Jon Pammett. *Political Choice in Canada*. Toronto: McGraw-Hill Ryerson, 1980, ch. 5. This chapter presents a detailed analysis of the characteristics of voters' psychological attachments to parties in federal and provincial politics.

Englemann, Frederick C. and Mildred A. Schwartz. *Canadian Political Parties: Origin, Character, Impact*. Scarborough: Prentice-Hall, 1975. The authors provide a wide-ranging analysis of relationships between parties and other important political actors such as socioeconomic elites, interest groups and the mass media.

Kornberg, Allan, Joel Smith and Harold D. Clarke. *Citizen Politicians–Canada*. Durham, N.C.: Carolina Academic Press, 1979. In this study of political party activists in Vancouver and Winnipeg, Kornberg *et al.* argue that socioeconomic, demographic and political socialization factors all are important for understanding who joins parties and who exercises influence within party organizations.

Robin, Martin, ed. *Canadian Provincial Politics* 2nd ed. Scarborough: Prentice-Hall, 1978. This book contains essays on the history and current status of the party systems in all 10 provinces.

Presthus, Robert. *Elite Accommodation in Canadian Politics*. Toronto: Macmillan, 1973; *Elites in the Policy Process*. London: Cambridge University Press, 1974. These two volumes present the results of a large-scale empirical study of the role of interest groups in federal and provincial politics. The author argues that the elitist nature of Canadian politics provides interest groups with broad scope to exercise influence in the policy process.

Pross, A. Paul, ed. *Pressure Group Behaviour in Canadian Politics*. Toronto: McGraw-Hill Ryerson, 1975. Although focussed primarily at the federal level, this book provides valuable insights into relationships between interest groups and government in Canada.

6
Legislatures, Bureaucracies and Judiciaries

It will be recalled that political theorists have different views on how the interests of citizens of a democratic society can best be represented. One view is that effective representation requires a set of institutions and processes that not only enable governmental officials to act on behalf of a public but also provide the latter with the means to hold officials accountable for their actions. Hanna Pitkin terms this conception of representation "formalistic." A second view is that irrespective of the effectiveness of the operation of its formal institutions and processes, a government is representative if the social characteristics of its major positionholders reflect, more or less accurately, the distribution of politically relevant characteristics in the population at large. This has been termed the "descriptive" conception of representation. A third view, the "responsiveness" conception, contends that a government is representative to the extent that the policies of its political leaders respond to the needs and demands of the citizens they govern. In Chapter 5 we focussed on the two principal informal institutions of representation, political parties and interest groups. In Chapters 7 and 8 we will consider the extent to which and the conditions under which provincial governmental leaders have responded to the needs of their publics. In this chapter we will focus on the composition, operation and effectiveness of three formal mechanisms of authorization and accountability in the provinces — their legislative assemblies, bureaucracies, and judiciaries.

MINISTERS AND FIRST MINISTERS

Cabinets are legislative, executive and administrative bodies composed of a select number of members of a governing legislative party, the party which has been victorious in the most recent election. These legislators, called ministers, are the political heads and administrators of the several departments of government. Collectively, the cabinet decides upon the content of the legislative program a provincial government pursues during any particular legislative session and executes any decisions made. In addition to their legislative, executive and administrative responsibilities, cabinets also make certain judicial and other appointments to public office. Traditionally, the head of the cabinet in a British model parliamentary system has been described as *primus inter pares*, first among equals. In fact provincial premiers currently are much more than simply first among equals. Their enhanced status *vis-à-vis* their cabinet colleagues (not to mention other members of a legislature) in great part is a consequence of the expansion of the electorate and the tendency of the media, especially since the end of World War Two, to present elections as contests between or among party leaders. Because they have, the public increasingly has focussed its attention on the party leaders rather than local candidates or the parties themselves. Relatedly, party officials, irrespective of the level at which they are competing, prefer leaders who promise them a reasonable chance of success at the polls. To enhance the probability of success, parties emphasize their leaders. They advertise their leader's status, achievements, personalities and families and generally try to project as favourable an image of the leader as possible. Their campaign tactics are structured around the leader's comings and goings and since the print and electronic media report campaigns in similar terms,[1] it is not surprising that for many people, provincial governments are synonomous with their first ministers.

A number of structural changes also have contributed markedly to the exalted status first ministers currently enjoy. Like their counterpart in Ottawa, they have acquired personal staffs whose principal tasks are to enhance their political stature in every area and with every major group. Effective staff work has helped to increase the visibility of first ministers, giving them a variety of advantages over cabinet colleagues. For example, their staffs have helped first ministers to centralize and coordinate the efforts of cabinet colleagues. In addition, with differences in detail, all provinces have instituted formal mechanisms to coordinate the work of cabinet ministers. These include cabinet committees concerned with substantive policy areas, treasury boards dealing with government finances and priorities and planning committees charged with ordering policy priorities and longer-term policy planning. The latter are chaired by first ministers. Informally, first ministers long have relied on "inner cabinets" consisting of cabinet colleagues whose advice is deemed especially valuable for coordinating the activities of their governments and maintaining and enhancing their political power. First ministers, with the advice of trusted staff, decide which of their colleagues will sit on which committees, who will chair them and with what matters they will be concerned.

As the scope of provincial governmental activity has increased, so has the proportion of time individual ministers must allocate to the basic concerns of departmental administration. Although first ministers at times make themselves the administrative heads of one or more operating departments, more often they leave themselves free of such responsibilities so that they can consider broad policy goals and try to influence the conditions that bear on the successful achievement of those goals. This task leads them to evaluate the contributions cabinet colleagues make toward their achievement, thereby placing them in a superior-subordinate relationship with the latter. Finally, although constitutional convention prescribes that cabinets are collectively responsible to the legislatures of which they are a part for their conduct and administration of the several departments of government, each minister, in practice, is personally responsible to the first minister. In short, he is the boss, and other ministers, although colleagues, are his agents.

This does not mean that a first minister is unconstrained insofar as behaviour toward other ministers is concerned. Although some may have been or, in fact, are, normally there are three important constraints upon them. First, the growth in provincial populations, the provinces' increased economic development, and the social and occupational differentiation that are consequences of economic modernization have led to the "provincialization" of most cabinets. Just as federal prime ministers have had to "federalize" their cabinets by including party colleagues who represent individual provinces, so provincial first ministers have had to include in their cabinets representatives of well-defined geographic regions (e.g., Northern Ontario, Southern Alberta) and major social groups (e.g., ethnic, religious and economic). Provincial cabinets, then, like their federal counterpart, have become forums for the representation and articulation of the interests of major regional and sociodemographic groups, although their membership is tempered by first ministers' personal preferences and natural inclinations to select colleagues whose ideological and policy positions are relatively congruent with their own.

Second (as has been the case at the federal level), rivals for the position of first minister generally have had to be included in provincial cabinets, if for no other reason than that their inclusion provides first ministers with an opportunity to "keep an eye on them." Although a premier's ability to dismiss potential rivals (or, for that matter, any other colleagues) is taken for granted, frequent or wholesale dismissals of ministers and colleagues threaten a first minister's own tenure. Such dismissals supposedly project an image of a divided government and governing party — an image, according to conventional wisdom, that may have deleterious consequences in a future election.

Third, relations between first ministers and their cabinet colleagues are affected by their respective personalities. Some first ministers are more astute politically than their colleagues, others are not. Some may be able to dominate and manipulate their colleagues, others may not. In brief, not all first ministers are "heavyweights," politically or otherwise, and even those who are may find it difficult on occasion to control the actions of independently-minded cabinet members, particularly if the latter have strong political bases of their own.

PROVINCIAL LEGISLATURES:

Composition.   Research has shown that the political recruitment processes bring to the national parliament individuals who are highly atypical of Canadian society — well-educated, middle-aged males who are successful professionals or businessmen. Studies also have demonstrated that MPs who hold leadership positions in the governing and opposition parties comprise an "elite within an elite." Data gathered in 1977 indicate that similar processes are at work at the provincial level (see Table 6.1). Across the country as a whole almost three quarters of all provincial MLAs had attended a university and a third had gone beyond the baccalaureate and received graduate or professional training. More than half were members of professions (17% were lawyers) and approximately a third were proprietors or managers of businesses. Cabinet ministers in the several provinces were more of an elite group in that, in addition to longer tenure, they were somewhat better educated and more often enjoyed prestigious occupations than did ordinary members. Moreover, all provincial legislative assemblies and cabinets, like their federal counterpart, are dominated by men — less than one in 20 of the members of provincial legislatures or cabinets in 1977 were women (see Table 6.2).

The paucity of women in provincial legislatures should not lead one to infer that there are no differences in the sociodemographic characteristics of MLAs in various provinces. For example, the proportion of lawyers in 1977 provincial cabinets ranged from 6% in Newfoundland to 33% in Ontario. In Saskatchewan almost a quarter of the ministers listed their occupations as farmers, but there was not a single person listing this occupation in the cabinets of Newfoundland, Prince Edward Island, Nova Scotia, Quebec and British Columbia. With regard to education, although 44% of British Columbia ministers ended their formal education in high school, almost two-thirds of the Prince Edward Island cabinet and over half of the Quebec and Alberta ministers attended a graduate or professional school. With respect to religious affiliation, the most heavily Protestant cabinets were those of British Columbia, Ontario and Alberta while, not surprisingly, all of the Quebec ministers were Roman Catholics.

What is true of cabinets also is true of non-cabinet MLAs. Thus, although there were large proportions of members in both the Saskatchewan and Prince Edward Island legislatures who in 1977 listed their occupations as farmers, the former were substantially better educated than the latter. Further, although a majority of the members of all provincial assemblies (other than Quebec) were members of Protestant religious denominations, the proportion of Protestants ranged from 51% in New Brunswick to 86% in British Columbia. However, what is more impressive than differences among legislators (cabinet and non-cabinet alike) in different provinces are the relative similarities in their socioeconomic backgrounds and current life statuses. In every province, provincial MLAs, like federal MPs, are a socioeconomic and demographic elite. This fact can provide precious little comfort for proponents of descriptive representation.

TABLE 6.1
Demographic and Socioeconomic Characteristics of Provincial Legislators and National Population

	Provincial Legislators*	National Population**
	(%)	(%)
Sex		
Men	96	48
Women	4	52
Age		
40 or less	30	46
41–50	35	19
51–60	25	15
61 and over	10	19
Religious Affiliation		
Protestant	57	39
Roman Catholic	38	46
Jewish	3	1
Other	2	11
None	0.5	4
Formal Education		
Secondary school or less	30	90
College or university to bachelor's degree	38	10
Professional or graduate school or other professional qualification	33	†
Occupation		
Lawyer	17	†
Other professional, business and managerial	68	17
Farmers	10	6
All others, including not classifiable	5	77

*Source — *Canadian Parliamentary Guide*, 1977
**Source — 1971 *Census of Canada*, Statistics Canada (Bulletins 1.1–3.3)
†less than 0.5%

TABLE 6.2
**Demographic and Socioeconomic Characteristics of
Provincial Backbenchers and Cabinet Ministers**

	Backbenchers*	Cabinet Ministers*
	(%)	(%)
Sex		
Women	4	4
Men	96	96
Age		
40 or less	33	25
41–50	31	44
51–60	25	24
61 and over	11	7
Religious Affiliation		
Anglican, Presbyterian, United	38	48
Other Protestant	16	15
Roman Catholic	41	34
Jewish	4	2
Other	1	2
None	†	0
Formal Education		
Primary or less	0	1
Some secondary or completed secondary	32	24
College or university to bachelor's degree	40	33
Professional or graduate school or professional qualification	28	42
Occupation		
Lawyer	15	22
Other professional, business and managerial	67	69
Farmers	13	5
All others, including not classifiable	5	4
Place of Birth		
In province	81	80
Elsewhere in Canada	13	15
Foreign born	6	5
Number of Times Elected as MLA		
Once	49	26
Twice	25	35
Three or more times	26	39
Mean # of times elected	2.0	2.4
Number of Years in Legislature		
0–4	53	29
5–8	25	38
9 or more	23	33
Mean # of years	5.9	7.5

*Source — *Canadian Parliamentary Guide*, 1977
†less than 0.5%

Change and Development. British model parliamentary government and its rules of procedure were quite appropriate for pre- and post-Confederation provincial legislatures for many of the same reasons that they had suited the "mother of parliament" a century earlier. Provincial populations were relatively small and until well into the current century large numbers of people in every province lived in rural areas. Further, the electorate was limited; an approximation of universal adult suffrage was not achieved until the 1920s. Perhaps most important, the activities with which provincial governments initially were charged were rather sharply constrained by the BNAA. Consequently, annual meetings of provincial assemblies were short and, when in session, they operated under a set of rules that permitted, at least in theory, broad member participation. The introduction and discussion of locally oriented private bills consumed a great deal of an assembly's time and cabinets made few serious efforts either to control the content of deliberations or hasten the rather leisurely pace at which they customarily proceeded.

We already have documented some of the ways in which the country changed during this century. Not the least of these has been the enhancement of the political importance of provincial governments and the great increase in the scope of their activities. Many practicing politicians and scholarly observers have argued that these changes have led legislatures and their members to change both *what* they do and *how* they do it. Among the most frequent justifications offered in defense of such changes are:

A. In a democracy the public chooses those whom it wishes to govern from among competing party candidates in free elections.

B. The victorious party must be given the opportunity to implement its policies and programs, although the opposition also must be able to criticize them and place its own policy views and perspectives before the legislature and the public. This requires that a government's legislation take calendar and time precedence over private members' proposals. It further requires that a legislature be in session almost continuously and that it be organized into subject matter committees in which both policy and budgetary proposals can be adequately and effectively scrutinized.

C. The problems with which current legislators must contend are extremely complex. Consequently, the task of formulating legislation to deal with them should be left largely to cabinet and its administrative bureaucracy, since they alone possess the requisite information and technical expertise to effectively handle them.

D. The principal task of non-cabinet members of a governing party and of opposition backbenchers is to represent their constituencies by taking action on their problems and apprising party leaders of the distribution of public opinion within their districts on major issues coming before the legislature.

   E. The representational tasks of current legislators are time and
      energy consuming, so much so, that the job of legislator is now
      a full-time one. Consequently, legislative salaries must reflect
      this reality and individual members must be provided with the
      human and material resources, staff and clerical assistance,
      office space, travel allowances and so forth, which will enable
      them to perform their representational functions effectively.

The late John Mackintosh[2] observed, in discussing the situation in
Great Britain, that not all legislators nor, for that matter, members of the
public share this perspective, which he terms "modern." He notes that
the traditional view is that parliaments are periodic gatherings in which
the "best and the brightest" come together to express their individual
views on the great issues of the day. The policy positions of those who
argue their views most cogently and persuasively prevail and are
implemented. Members then are free to return to their normal occupational pursuits. Thus, according to traditionalists, occupancy of a parliamentary position should not be a full-time job. Moreover, members
should not be welfare officers, ombudsmen or errand boys for their
constituents and party leaders. It follows, therefore, they have no need
for large salaries, travel allowances, expense accounts, private offices,
secretarial assistance, personal staffs or various other such privileges
and paraphernalia. Both of these essentially contradictory perspectives
have their advocates, and because they do, Mackintosh claims, "We are
in a first-class muddle about our politicians, about the kind of people we
want and the way they ought to behave."[3] Although he may be correct,
it appears that the modern rather than the traditional perspective
currently is ascendant. The increasing tendency to view the job of MLA
as an onerous, if not full-time, occupation is reflected in their salaries,
perquisites and staff assistance. For example, a nationwide survey[4] of
the administrative structures of provincial legislatures indicates that in
1980 the Ontario Legislature budgeted $19 million for "housekeeping"
expenses, including those required to pay a staff of nearly 300 people
(218 regular employees, 23 sessional employees, and 50 on special
contract). Moreover, in addition to an annual salary of $32,500 ($8,000 of
which was non-taxable), members of the Ontario Legislative Assembly
also received an allowance of some $6,500 if they represented a constitu-
ency outside of metropolitan Toronto. They were provided with as
many as 52 free economy air roundtrip fares between their constituences
and Toronto annually; allowed unlimited free travel by bus or train
within the province, as well as unlimited travel by car compensated at 13
cents per kilometre. They were provided offices in Queen's Park and
their constituencies and allocated approximately $36,000 per year for
staff assistance in these two offices. Nor was that all. In addition to
receiving group and hospital insurance, dental coverage, unlimited
franking privileges, and the use of unlimited amounts of office supplies,

a member even had the use of the recreational facilities of the University of Toronto under a special arrangement made by the Assembly. Members of the Quebec National Assembly fared even better: a $38,736 salary ($7,500 of which was tax free); an additional allowance of $4,600 for those representing constituencies outside of Quebec City; an office in both Quebec city and the constituency; and an allowance of up to $7,900 for constituency office expenses; up to $28,300 for constituency staff salaries; up to $16,008 for staff in legislative office; and so on.[5]

Nor are these emoluments availably only to the legislators of the two largest provinces. For example, in 1980 even Newfoundland provided a tax free allowance of $6,723 and a sessional allowance of $19,000 to its members. Although some of the other perquisites available to legislators in provinces such as Manitoba and Nova Scotia were not as grand as those available to their colleagues in Quebec and Ontario,[6] still, it is safe to assume that what they did have would make them the envy of parliamentarians in a number of European democracies, not to mention those in Third World countries. Of course, these conditions have not always obtained. As recently as 1977, only Ontario, Quebec and British Columbia paid their MLAs more than $15,000 a year and even in these provinces the trend toward professionalization is a relatively recent one. Nonetheless, despite interprovincial variations, the careers of provincial legislators are considerably more professionalized now than they were even a decade ago.[7]

Perhaps the most dramatic indicator of the trend toward the professionalization of the legislative career is the attention that MLAs give to constituency "casework," the problems of individual constituents. A nationwide survey of provincial legislators[8] reveals that although British Columbia MLAs spend the most and Prince Edward Island legislators the least amount of time on service and ombudsmen-like work, large numbers of members in every province are heavily engaged in constituency service tasks (see Table 6.3). Nationwide, 40% of the MLAs stated that they spend more than half their "working time" on constituency work. An additional 41% spend between a quarter and half their time and only 19% reported spending less than a quarter of their time this way.

The amount of time spent on constituency service work is related to how legislators conceptualize their representational roles. Two aspects of such role orientations may be distinguished — *focus* and *style*.[9] Representational role focus refers to "what" legislators see themselves representing. In Anglo-American countries, representational role focus is usually defined in geographic terms. Some legislators see themselves as representatives of the constituency that elected them, while for others, the primary focus of representation is the province or country as a whole. In some cases, legislators try to represent a combination of these spatial entities. Representational role style is concerned with the

TABLE 6.3
**Percentage of "Working Time" Provincial Legislators Spend
on Constituency Service Activities**

Province	Percentage of Time				
	0–25	26–50	51–75	76–100	(N)
Newfoundland	12%*	50	26	13	(8)
Prince Edward Island	50%	17	17	17	(12)
Nova Scotia	32%	26	32	11	(19)
New Brunswick	28%	33	39	0	(18)
Quebec	13%	57	17	13	(30)
Ontario	7%	46	44	3	(59)
Manitoba	31%	44	13	13	(16)
Saskatchewan	17%	42	33	8	(36)
Alberta	27%	43	30	0	(30)
British Columbia	15%	30	35	20	(20)
Canada	19%	41	31	9	(247)

*horizontal percentages

way legislators decide issues: whether they ascribe greater weight to their own judgment or to the wishes of constituents, party colleagues or other groups. It will be recalled that a preference for different representational roles is one of the criteria distinguishing representative and elitist theorists. In the provincial context it might be assumed that elitists would regard an entire province rather than a constituency as the appropriate geographic unit of representation and that they would prefer that MLAs rely on their own judgments rather than the preferences of constituents or other groups when making decisions.

The previously mentioned study of provincial legislators indicates that MLAs prefer what might be termed "mixed" representational role orientations: a majority (56%) stated they tried to represent both their province and constituency. An even larger proportion (60%) said they tried to combine their personal judgment with what they perceived to be the preferences of constituents when making decisions. Only a quarter of the MLAs said they tried to represent the interest of their entire province, while an identical proportion stated they relied primarily on their own judgments when making decisions. However, even smaller proportions (20% and 16%, respectively) were oriented primarily toward their constituencies. The tendency to deemphasize constituency in favour of mixed representational role styles and foci was evident among MLAs in most provinces. Indeed, only in Prince Edward Island and Nova Scotia did pluralities favour constituency delegate styles and in no province did a plurality opt for a constituency-oriented focus of representation. (See Table 6.4)

TABLE 6.4
Provincial Legislators' Representational Role Styles and Foci

Province	Emphasis in Representational Role Style				Emphasis in Representational Role Focus			
	Own Judgment	Mixed	Constituency	(N)	Province	Mixed	Constituency	(N)
Newfoundland	63%*	38	0	(8)	50%	38	13	(8)
Prince Edward Island	8%	42	50	(12)	18%	55	27	(11)
Nova Scotia	32%	32	37	(19)	0%	63	37	(19)
New Brunswick	33%	62	5	(21)	20%	60	20	(20)
Quebec	27%	50	23	(30)	38%	41	21	(29)
Ontario	24%	70	7	(59)	17%	57	26	(58)
Manitoba	25%	63	13	(16)	38%	44	19	(16)
Saskatchewan	11%	72	17	(36)	27%	68	6	(34)
Alberta	17%	70	13	(30)	21%	62	17	(29)
British Columbia	35%	55	10	(20)	35%	50	15	(20)
Canada	24%	60	16	(251)	24%	56	20	(244)

*horizontal percentages

As just indicated, the proportion of time legislators spend on constituency service and ombudsman-like tasks is related to both role style and focus.[10] Thus, whereas one-half of the MLAs with a constituency representational role focus spent over 50% of their time doing service work, only one-fifth of those with a provincial focus did so. Further, nearly one-half of the MLAs who ascribed the greatest weight to constituent opinions in their representational role styles spent more than 50% of their time on service work as opposed to only one-quarter of those who accorded greater importance to their own views than to those of their constituents.[11]

No one argues that the representation of constituencies begins and ends with the performance of services for individual constituents. There are other ways of discharging the representative function. A major one is to obtain group benefits such as public work projects, government buildings and related jobs for a constituency as a whole. However, in both parliament and provincial legislatures the ability to allocate group benefits largely rests with cabinet, a condition which can be of great benefit to constituencies which are fortunate enough to be represented by a member of a governing party, but one which brings only limited joy to districts whose voters have been unwise or stubborn enough to insist upon electing opposition party members. Moreover, legislative parties are strong and legislative committees are weak even in the Ontario and Quebec assemblies where the role of committees in the legislative process is most fully developed. Consequently, MLAs can make only very limited use of their committee positions to obtain favourable consideration for the group benefits they desire for their constituencies.[12]

It is difficult to specify precisely how much use MLAs are able to make of their committee assignments or any other positions because there have been few empirical studies of provincial legislatures and how their members go about their business. One such study, comparing Nova Scotia and Ontario MLAs, revealed that members adopt one of three principal orientations toward the policy process, becoming "initiators," "critics," or "facilitators."[13] The first of these three orientations seems the most popular; approximately 40% of the backbenchers of both legislatures considered it central to their policy roles. Policy initiators are disproportionately well-educated and speak out about their concerns on the floor of the Assembly and in committee, as well as lobby behind the scenes (although more in Ontario than in Nova Scotia). In doing so, they utilize a variety of techniques because their task is not an easy one.

Policy critics, in contrast (particularly in Ontario), primarily react to government initiatives and try to "maintain and define the differences between the governing party and the opposition."[14] Although, in Ontario policy critics tend to sit on the opposition benches, in Nova Scotia a suprisingly large number of the then governing Liberal party's own backbenchers were critics. Critics concentrate on suggesting alternative policies to their cabinet colleagues hoping to prevent them "from making costly mistakes and alienating voters."[15]

The third group, facilitators, try to play a kind of honest broker role.[16] On the one hand, they bring representatives of groups with a point of view to express on a particular bill together with an appropriate minister or bureaucratic official so that their positions can be made known. On the other, they apprise groups within their constituencies of governmental actions or intended actions that are likely to have a significant impact on them. They do so on the assumption that most of what governments do escapes public attention. Facilitators work primarily behind the scenes and derive their gratification whenever "announcements are made regarding new agreements or programmes that facilitators have had a part in creating."[17]

In short, existing studies of provincial assemblies and the roles legislators play therein indicate that although the great majority of any assembly's time is spent on the government's legislative program, large proportions of government and opposition members alike make an attempt to represent their constituents' policy interests. They introduce private bills and debatable resolutions and bring the interests and needs of their constituencies to the attention of colleagues in plenary sessions and in committee. They lobby ministers and bureaucrats on behalf of individuals and groups in their constituencies and facilitate constituents' lobbying efforts by providing them with access to appropriate governmental officials. Moreover, they inform constituents of current and intended governmental actions and suggest ways of taking advantage of such actions. As will be indicated below, for a variety of reasons, efforts to represent their public most often fall short when MLAs try to oversee the actions of cabinets and bureaucracies. If their efforts are not entirely successful, of even if they are entirely unsuccessful, the mere fact that MLAs have tried, and their constituents know that they have tried, is important. Such efforts symbolize the position of centrality the representational function occupies in a representative democracy.

PROVINCIAL BUREAUCRACIES

Overview. *Webster's Seventh Collegiate Dictionary* offers three definitions of bureaucracy: "i) a body of nonelective governmental officials; ii) government characterized by specialization of functions, adherence to fixed rules and a hierarchy of authority; and iii) a system of administration marked by officialism, red tape, and proliferation."[18] In this century, bureaucratic institutions have grown and become extremely powerful in all advanced industrial societies. The reasons why are readily apparent. First, bureaucracies exercise what have been termed quasi-legislative, judicial and executive powers. Second, as the scope of governmental activities has increased, there has been a concomitant increase in the size and importance of bureaucracies because so much of the authority of legislative and executive bodies must be delegated. Third, bureaucracies possess specialized information and expert skills that other branches of government and the public require. Fourth, elected officials tend to be preoccupied with other matters, principally their need to be reelected. Fifth, bureaucracies have the strong political support of important social groups within their societies.

Provincial bureaucracies exercise legislative powers in various ways. Senior bureaucratic officials identify problem areas requiring the action of cabinets. They marshall the information ministers require to decide among competing priorities, sometimes termed the "agenda-setting" function of bureaucracies,[19] and they either draft or assist in the drafting of legislation. More important, perhaps, they formulate general and specific rules having the force of law as part of the process of implementing legislation which assemblies have enacted. Simply stated, they fill in the details of pictures that legislators paint with very, very broad strokes.

Politics has been defined as "who gets what, when, how,"[20] and government as "the authoritative allocation of values for society."[21] Governments, in other words, legitimate political decisions benefiting some more than others. This is also the case with the allocation of costs. These, particularly if they adversely affect groups which are well-organized, are likely to be disputed. Disputes frequently involve appeals to bureaucratic officials who exercise what are, in effect, judicial powers when they dispose of specific cases on the basis of general rules. An excellent example is when bureaucrats make decisions in cases in which individuals, corporations or even entire industries are contesting income tax rulings. Bureaucrats also exercise judicial powers when they adjudicate between the claims of contending parties, as, for example, when they decide which of two claimants has the right to develop a particular parcel of land. Yet another illustration of the exercise of judicial power is when a bureaucratic official decides whether a person can claim a particular benefit such as a pension. There are numerous departmental and non-departmental boards and commissions engaged in work of this kind in every province.

The executive function of bureaucracies is said to entail "administrative activities aimed at increasing the efficiency of government in budgeting and disbursement, planning, personnel, and so on."[22] It can be argued that the most impressive change that has occurred in the conduct of public affairs during the past 20 years has been the enhanced ability of provincial governments to perform these several activities in as efficient a manner as the federal government. Until the 1960s it generally was agreed that the federal bureaucracy enjoyed a decided edge in this respect. Indeed, the ability of the federal government to extend its authority into areas that putatively were provincial concerns during the era of cooperative federalism might be attributed in part to the superior administrative abilities of federal officials. In the past decade, however, every province has recruited substantial numbers of officials expert in areas such as budgeting, planning, and policy coordination and skilled in the techniques (e.g., modeling, simulation and econometrics) upon which these rely. Some provinces (Alberta, Newfoundland, Ontario, Quebec and Saskatchewan) also have established departments of federal-provincial relations which employ graduates of programs in economics, political science and public and business administration. They help make up the platoons of expert advisers accompanying premiers and financial ministers to first ministers' conferences.

The executive function of bureaucracies includes the power to enforce public policy — to see that laws passed by provincial assemblies are faithfully executed. The activities of officials engaged in enforcement procedures vividly illustrate the manner in which governments impinge upon our daily lives. Enforcement activities include matters such as agricultural officials regulating acreage allotments, inspectors monitoring curriculum content in schools and clerks selling fishing and hunting licenses or administering driving tests to citizens wanting to exercise these privileges. In performing these and other activities thousands of civil servants engage in a phase of administration that regularly brings them into contact with large numbers of people. Finally, the executive function of bureaucracy also includes the administration of various government enterprises and corporations. Their intervention is a consequence of provincial governments having moved into economic areas in which private entrepreneurs, for whatever reasons, have been reluctant to enter. Government corporations also compete with private enterprises in other fields, or they may even preempt a field for themselves, as, for example, provincial governments have in generating and marketing hydroelectric power.

The expansion of the regulatory, judicial and entrepreneurial functions of provincial governments, particularly during the past 30 years, obviously has increased not only the size but also the power of provincial bureaucracies. Another important reason for their increased size and power is that cabinets, not to mention individual MLAs, have been willing to delegate powers to them. Ministers often lack the time, specialized information and expertise to define with any precision matters such as objectives, standards, tests and so on that a particular piece of legislation may require if it is to be fairly and effectively implemented. Nor do ministers always have the planning and related skills which would enable them to coordinate the implementation of new with existing programs. Accordingly, discretion in such matters is left largely to bureaucratic personnel who do have these skills and resources at their disposal. For their part, backbench legislators have been willing to leave planning, budgeting, general administration, managerial and enforcement tasks to bureaucracies because so much of their own time is taken up, as we noted above, in performing services, being ombudsmen, acting as communication links between their constituencies and legislative party leaders and campaigning for their own reelection.

Regarding the latter requirement, a truism of legislative politics in Canada and elsewhere is that "even statesmen have to be reelected." Reelection can be difficult for MLAs who, for whatever reasons, alienate bureaucratic officials because so much of their casework requires that they intercede with civil servants on behalf of constituents. To achieve a reasonable degree of success, MLAs must have not only civil servants' cooperation but also their active assistance. Indeed, one of the ways a freshman member of an assembly can acquire the status of an "old hand" is to learn whom in the bureaucracy to contact for specific purposes and how to cultivate these officials so that they will be forthcoming when their assistance is solicited. Given this dependence, it is not difficult for MLAs to perceive a harmony of interests among their constituents, the bureaucracy, themselves and, indeed, the whole province.

MLAs also can injure their chances of reelection if they create difficulties for civil servants or agencies administering programs having the support of important organized groups in members' constituencies. A number of students of Canadian politics have identified symbiotic and mutually supporting relationships that often exist between organized interest groups and bureaucratic agencies.[23] This is because a bureaucratic unit generally comes into existence to administer programs created by legislation passed in response to a social or economic problem of some kind. Since organized groups benefit from such programs, they may become both clients and staunch supporters of the agencies administering them. Segments of the public not directly affected by particular programs, or by the activities of civil servants administering them, tend to be either unaware of or indifferent to their existence. At a minimum, therefore, the active support of what may be a numerically small but vitally interested group can help to maintain the continuation of a bureaucracy in what Cairns has termed "a steady state."[24] The combination of limited but intensive support on the one hand and large-scale public ignorance or indifference on the other, also helps to explain why certain bureaucracies tend to remain alive and well after the social problems that initially brought them into existence are no longer particularly pressing.[25]

For a variety of reasons civil servants generally are not content to see their organization merely exist or maintain a steady state. As will be indicated in Chapters 7 and 8, the period since World War Two has witnessed the steady growth of bureaucracy at both the federal and provincial levels. However, provincial civil services have increased much more than has their federal counterpart. The most spectacular increases have occurred in Nova Scotia and Ontario. However, even in Saskatchewan, where the bureaucracy has grown the least, the rate of growth has been substantially greater than at the federal level. Another indicator of the enormous development of provincial governments is the increased proportion of civil service employees in provincial work forces. In 1951, 7.5 of every 1,000 members of the Ontario labour force were employed in civil service positions. Ten years later, this increased to 14.4, and by 1971, 20 of every 1,000 members of the labour force were civil servants. Nor was Ontario the only province where this occurred. In Prince Edward Island the rate of increase was even more dramatic: from 12.3 per 1,000 in 1951 to 29.0 in 1961, to 49.9 in 1971. During this period, the number of Quebec civil servants increased from 9.1 to 21.0 per 1,000 workers; in British Columbia, from 18.5 to 32.0.[26]

The rate of increase in the employment of government workers who are not classified as civil servants because they do not fall under the respective civil service acts of their provinces[27] has been equally impressive. In part this increase "reflects the contemporary and still-growing reliance on nondepartmental boards, corporations and commissions required for regulatory, deciding (sic) and entrepreneurial functions of provincial governments."[28] In part, however, the tendency to avoid the restrictions of civil service acts and their requirements of merit reflect the fact that in every province "patronage is still far from dead."[29] In the early 1970s the governments of New Brunswick and Nova Scotia had the largest proportions of employees not classified as civil servants, those of Newfoundland and British Columbia the smallest.[30]

Composition and Role of Bureaucracies. Max Weber, perhaps the leading student of bureaucracy, contended that bureaucratic forms of organization are responses to population growth and the scientific and technological explosions that are characteristics of modernity.[31] The advantages of bureaucracies over traditional forms of organization are that they combine hierarchy and stability with specialization of function and the application of rational and consistent procedures. Bureaucratic authority ultimately rests on the ability of its members to command and utilize scientific knowledge and its various technical applications. Not surprisingly, then, studies of bureaucracies in the United States and Western European countries indicate that higher civil servants are atypical of the societies of which they are a part in a variety of ways, the most notable being the level at which they are educated. This is also the case in Canada. Robert Presthus's comparative study of interest groups in the United States and Canada reveals that Canadian bureaucrats, federal and provincial, constituted far more of an elite group than either federal or provincial parliamentarians or leaders of organized interest groups. Fully 85% of his sample of bureaucratic officials, many of them deputy and assistant deputy ministers, had completed university and acquired graduate or professional training, as opposed to 58% of the parliamentarians.[32] Indicative of Canada's system of social stratification, Presthus found that a substantial proportion (31%) of the senior civil servants were reared in high status families. However, they also included a large number of "self-made men" who had experienced significant intergenerational social mobility.[33]

Not all civil servants are "mandarins" occupying commanding positions at the apex of bureaucratic hierarchies. According to Hodgetts and Dwivedi,[34] upwards of one-third of the thousands of civil service employees in every province are clerks and it is safe to say that the routine, repetitive nature of their work adds substantially to each province's annual production of red tape. Nor, contrary to the popular image of them, do all civil servants work behind desks in multi-storied office buildings in provincial capitals. Thousands of those whose occupations are described as "operational" in government employment manuals perform jobs of varying complexity "out in the field," far from provincial capitals. Nonetheless, the proportion of clerical and operational employees in provincial bureaucracies is growing smaller for two reasons: mechanization and electronic data processing which obviate the need for manual clerical labour; and the high degree of professional, scientific and technical knowledge required today to perform many managerial, administrative, executive and judicial functions effectively. Consequently, it is estimated that in some provinces persons engaged in the performance of tasks requiring a high level of skill or professional training now make up about half of all government employees. Although highly trained professionals and minimally skilled clerks alike are employed in the entire complex of bureaucratic units that are responses to both the public's and governments' desire for an expanded state role, the bulk of the increase that has occurred has taken place in long established departments such as health, highways, public safety, education, public works and welfare. According to Hodgetts and Dwivedi, "the growth in provincial public service employment is not so much related to the assumption of new functions but to the provision of a higher level of service [in existing areas]."[35]

Has the growth of provincial bureaucracies enabled them to respond effectively to the needs, interests and demands of the great mass of citizens? Although we cannot answer that question with certainty, we can delineate conditions that affect bureaucratic responsiveness. The best known are formal conditions which hold, *inter alia*, that members of all bureaucratic units encompassed by a particular department of government are responsible to a minister, the political head of that department, for their actions. Ministers, in turn, are responsible to other cabinet colleagues and to all other members of the legislative assembly for actions of officials in their departments. Ministers must explain and defend these actions and indeed, they must even be prepared to resign if a subordinate commits an error of omission or commission serious enough to warrant such a course of action. The process is not asymmetrical, however. In return for accepting responsibility, ministers expect subordinates to carry out their policy decisions irrespective of personal political views and to refrain from criticizing them publicly. Ministers also expect the officials of their departments to offer them their best professional advice, regardless of their personal feelings. In this manner all public employees become responsible to the cabinet, which is responsible to the assembly which, in turn, is responsible to the public.

There is, however, considerable disjunction between the formal theory of bureaucratic accountability and actual practice. First, ministers at times are unwilling to accept responsibility for the actions of officials in their departments. Second, bureaucrats do not always play their assigned roles. They are not always loyal to their ministers, not always content to remain politically neutral, and they do not always maintain an uncritical public silence. Nor do they always choose or are they permitted to choose the luxury of remaining anonymous. Third, a legislature's ability to check the exercise of ministerial and bureaucratic power largely depends on the capacity and inclination of opposition members and, to a lesser extent, on government backbenchers.[36] MLAs traditionally have not had the capacity and frequently they also have lacked the inclination to check ministerial and bureaucratic power. Since this also has been the case with federal MPs, concern over the inability of parliaments to secure the accountability of governments and bureaucracies has led royal commissions and academicians to suggest structural and procedural reforms that might strengthen the accountability process. These include strengthening and invigorating standing committee systems; changing legislative procedures to enable committees to perform the oversight function more effectively and providing expert staff assistance to legislative committees, party caucuses, and individual legislators.

Although some of these suggestions have been implemented, students of legislatures and bureaucracies are not entirely convinced that structural and procedural changes in legislative bodies are sufficient to secure accountability. They point out (as we also have) that there are excellent political reasons for MLAs wanting to establish and maintain good relations with civil servants, not the least of which is that failure to secure their good will can have a negative effect on a member's chances of reelection. It also is suggested that even with the assistance of staff, MLAs still lack the intellectual capacity and technical knowledge either to ask the right questions of bureaucrats or adequately evaluate their responses. This is true of many federal MPs as well. Further, many MLAs and MPs probably find the oversight function, especially as it relates to finance, boring and politically unprofitable.[37]

Legislative scholars further observe that ministers sometimes are unwilling to accept responsibility for the actions of bureaucratic underlings because to do so might adversely affect their careers.[38] Junior ministers want to hold more important portfolios and senior ministers want to be first ministers. Additionally, ministers must be concerned with the political fortunes of their party. Their own careers are not likely to be advanced by the defeat of the government of which they are a part — a distinct possibility if the actions for which they are expected to accept responsibility are sufficiently grave. Moreover, it can be argued (and it has been) that a minister ought not to be required to accept responsibility for the actions of civil servants implementing or administering policies or programs that he or she did not author. That responsibility should be placed on the shoulders of a preceding government or a previous incumbent of the position. Yet another reason offered is that ministers are human and come equipped with a full set of human emotions. Thus, they periodically can be as angry, chagrined or outraged by bureaucratic negligence, inflexibility or outright stupidity, as the proverbial man in the street. Why should they be asked to accept responsibility for acts of this kind? Finally, ministers cannot be expected to know what everyone in their department is doing and how well they are doing it. They depend upon their deputy and assistant deputy ministers for information and expert advice who, in turn, depend upon the information and expertise of individuals lower in a departmental hierarchy. If requisite information or expertise is not made available, ministers can hardly be blamed if things go awry in their departments. In this regard, it has been recommended that ministers should have available to them a staff of experts who are *not* civil servants but rather political appointees. Such a staff could provide supplementary information and advice that could help ministers to make independent evaluations of the actions of officials in their departments.[39]

Regarding bureaucratic contributions to the shortcomings of formal ministerial responsibility, it is contended that civil servants are not political eunuchs. Conventional norms regarding civil service neutrality notwithstanding, they do have political opinions.[40] And, like their political bosses in cabinet, they also have personal and collective ambitions. If these are threatened, or if they believe that they or their organizations are to be made public scapegoats, they will not always remain silent or uncritical of their political superiors' policies and programs. Civil servants, like legislators, sometimes resort to what is termed "leaking," divulging what is essentially self- or organization-serving information to the media.

More generally, it is argued that bureaucratic responsiveness is determined by the structure of relations of public officials with other actors in the political system and by the internal structures, procedures and norms of their own political units.[41] To facilitate good relations with other actors in the system, bureaucrats work hard to establish a favourable climate of opinion. Creating such a climate may involve them in establishing elite advisory groups,[42] cooperating with legislators and interest group representatives, organizing clientele groups if none exist,[43] identifying their roles with highly visible and valued political and societal symbols, making their administrative decisions seem objective and technically based, striking a balance among contending groups trying to influence their decisions, and allocating costs and benefits in ways that please their supporters and neutralize their opponents.[44] Over time, civil servants establish close and congenial relations with outside actors who can assist them in maintaining and enhancing their organizations. Not surprisingly, the most helpful outsiders are also those whose interests bureaucrats often appear to be representing.

The responsiveness patterns of bureaucratic units are further shaped by the nature of their tasks and the manner in which these are performed. Regarding the nature of their tasks, in addition to operating a variety of businesses in the guise of Crown corporations, bureaucracies, as noted above, exercise quasi-legislative, judicial and executive powers in the course of administering what have been termed regulative, distributive and redistributive policies as enacted in law by provincial legislatures. Of these, the administration of distributive policies normally generates the least controversy among members of the public since it involves the provision of public goods that are almost universally highly regarded and which people feel they have a relatively equal chance of receiving. Examples include the distribution of goods such as education, health care and public works. Since, other things being equal, distributive policies generate the least controversy and negative affect, bureaucracies appear to be most responsive to and representative of broad public interests when they are administering such policies.

As previously noted, the administration of regulative policies often generates controversy because the legislation that brought them into existence was intended to control and in some way limit the freedom of action of an important group or sector of a province. Resistance to such policies tends to take three forms: attempts by regulatees to demonstrate that they can and should be permitted to largely govern themselves; attempts by regulatees to demonstrate that they have expert knowledge in the affected area and hence should help determine which regulations should be applied; and attempts to demonstrate that regulators and regulatees have common values and interests and hence their relationship should not be adversarial but rather mutually supporting. The success of particular professions, such as law and medicine, and entire industries in achieving a very substantial degree of self-regulation or solicitous and sympathetic treatment from regulating agencies leads to charges that bureaucracies more often are responding to and representing special interests than the public at large.

Redistributive policies are by their nature controversial since they take resources or values from one category of people and give them to another. The passage of redistributive legislation often is fiercely resisted and the emotions aroused tend to manifest themselves periodically during the implementation and especially the administration phases of the policy process in arguments over "entitlements." Examples of such arguments include those generated by questions regarding the conditions under which individuals or groups are entitled to benefits such as public housing, medical care and workmen's compensation. The public scrutiny to which their actions are subjected and the affective feelings these arouse lead civil servants administering redistributive policies to be extremely cautious and precise. They try to project an image of being neutral, fair and of always "going by the book." These understandable tendencies, however, lead members of the public affected by them to complain that bureaucracies are slow, inflexible and bogged down by red tape: in short, that they don't respond to anyone.

The norms of bureaucracies, their recruitment and socialization practices, decision-making structures and standard operating procedures are internal factors that strongly affect their patterns of responsiveness and hence the representational images they project. The internal norms of bureaucratic organizations are important because they help to set standards of professional conduct. The use of objective and scientific standards and of professional work routines helps shield civil servants from outside interference by the non-professional public. Their use also creates strong ties with and feelings of empathy for other professionals. For example, lawyers in an attorney-general's office invariably enjoy excellent relations with members of the provincial bar. This usually is true of bureaucratic officials who are members of other recognized professions. Although these good relations may increase the responsiveness of civil servants to individuals who are members of the same professions, they may not be (or, at any rate, *appear* not to be) as responsive to citizens who are not lawyers, doctors, engineers, educators and so forth. Thus, the dramatic trends toward professionalism in bureaucracies which have been documented may have raised the standards of bureaucratic task performance, but they also may have made civil servants appear less responsive to segments of the public who do not share their professional values, interests and norms.

Professional norms are further reflected in the recruitment, socialization and career patterns of bureaucratic officials. It is true that central personnel agencies in some provinces are engaged in the recruitment of applicants for bureaucratic positions. They also may help monitor promotions and transfers within particular agencies. However, it is the officials of individual departments who largely determine the kinds of people they need, and who convey their personnel needs to the central agencies. Departmental officials are responsible for generating the standards and procedures that will be employed in moving people systematically upwards through a series of positions in bureaucratic hierarchies. As a person moves through the bureaucratic ranks, part of his or her socialization process involves the learning of professional and organizational "dos" and "don'ts." Adherence to these norms may facilitate interpersonal relationships and morale among departmental officials, but it may also create an impression that civil servants march to the beat of their own rather than the general public's drum.

One of the principal attractions of a parliamentary system is the opportunity it provides for the centralization and coordination of public policy administration in cabinet. However, even in a parliamentary system, there is a countervailing strain towards autonomy within the several sub-units of government. This strain is most evident in boards and commissions, many of which are only nominally under the direction of a minister. But it also exists within units of line departments, and for good reason. The more autonomous a unit is, the greater the control its officials will exercise over internal processes and matters such as promotions and the allocation of highly valued perquisites (e.g., clerical and other types of staff assistance, office size and location, and quality of office furnishings). This strain for sub-unit autonomy tends to weaken both centralized administration and coordination and, accordingly, the responsiveness of the units in question to their organizational and political leaders (i.e., assistant deputy ministers, deputy ministers and ministers.)

Finally, the generation and adoption of standard operating procedures enable provincial bureaucracies to process large amounts of often complex work quickly and routinely. This ability is their great strength and one of the principal reasons why bureaucracies are the great "doers" of a political system. Rigid adherence to these procedures and their santification through identification with neutral, objective, scientific and technical standards, however, help make bureaucracies appear unresponsive to individuals and groups in the public who try to circumvent standard procedures on the grounds that their particular problems constitute a "special case." The tendency of civil servants to resist the particularistic demands generated by special cases and to follow standardized procedures may well have inspired definitions such as that offered by Webster (e.g., of bureaucracy as "government administration characterized by adherence to fixed rules, officialism, and red tape.").

JUDICIARIES

Structure. In a representative democracy the authoritative actions of government putatively are grounded in and derived from law and are constrained by a public's civil rights and liberties. To the extent that judicial bodies ensure that members of the public have equal access to the legal process, receive equal treatment from court officers and enjoy equal protection of and from the law, judiciaries help to determine the extent to which a political system, in its day-to-day operations, approximates the ideals of representative democracy.

J.R. Mallory notes that it is important to understand that despite federalism and the division of jurisdiction over various parts of the judicial function between federal and provincial governments, "the effect has been to produce a single level of courts."[45] The constitutional base on which the court structure rests is set out in Articles 91(27), 92(14), 96, 97, 98, 99 (1 and 2, amended in 1960), 100, 101, and 129 of the BNAA. The Act, which left intact the existing system of provincial courts, also provided that the provinces were to be given the authority to establish and maintain courts within their boundaries — the judges for these courts to be selected from their respective bars. However, the appointment and tenuring of all judges of superior, district and county courts were to be made by the federal government, which also was to pay judges' salaries. To ensure the independence of the judiciary, judges were to serve during "good behaviour" with retirement at age 75; they could not be removed except by a joint resolution of both houses of parliament; and their salaries and other perquisites could not be diminished during their tenure of office.

Mallory divides provincial courts into three categories depending upon the method of appointment and tenure of their judges. The first category includes all judges of superior courts whose tenure is defined in section 99 of the BNAA as amended in 1960. The second includes judges of district or county courts who may be removed for cause by the federal government without resort to a joint address of parliament. Category three is made up of judges of the several provincial lower courts. They are usually appointed by provincial governments and serve during good behaviour.

Category one courts (Superior Courts) have different names in the several provinces but they have two principal divisions. The first is an appeals court made up of several judges sitting together. The second is a court of original jurisdiction in which a single judge sits, at times with a jury, at times without. The second category includes county and district courts originally established to provide a relatively inexpensive process for adjudicating minor disputes. Each of the provinces has created a series of lesser courts, such as magistrates' courts, which hear petty offenses, conduct preliminary hearings and so forth. Quebec courts are somewhat different, having two separate superior courts, the Court of Queen's Bench and the Superior Court. The first is both a court of original jurisdiction in criminal matters and a court of appeal in civil and criminal proceedings. It is presided over by the provincial Chief Justice and a panel of associate justices. The superior court, which has its own Chief Justice and 40 *puisne* judges, is a court of civil jurisdiction in which a single judge presides. Although Quebec does not have a system of county or district courts, it does have an equivalent in its Provincial Court which is staffed by judges appointed by the provincial government. It also has a system of courts whose judges are provincially appointed and which deal with welfare, family and other matters.[46]

Administration.   Unlike the United States, in which the administration of court systems is directed and carried out by judges themselves, in Canada the organizational, procedural and support systems of judiciaries are the responsibility of Ministers of the Crown — the federal justice minister, his or her Quebec counterpart, and the nine provincial attorneys general. The theoretical assumption underlying the allocation of administrative responsibilities to these ministers and their departmental subordinates is that it enables judges to perform their adjudication function without fear or favour. They are relieved of administrative chores and hence freed from the possibility of making decisions that in part might be based upon their administrative feasibility. Judicial scholar Carl Baar contends that, in practice, judges are directly involved in some aspects of administration and are also in a position to strongly affect the direction of administration in areas in which they may not be directly involved: specifically, those that affect the maintenance and enhancement of the judiciary as an organization.[47] He offers a three-fold explanation of their ability to influence the course of administrative affairs. First, departments of justice and offices of the attorneys general generally have not been deeply interested in administrative matters. Second, judges have successfully pursued a strategy of "encapsulation" and, third, they have forged very strong alliances with the legal communities of the several provinces. The latter two explanations require additional discussion.

Baar points out that Canadian judges have not tried to enhance their organizational status by increasing the size of the judicial bureaucracy since the principal result probably would be to strengthen departments of the attorney general rather than themselves. Encapsulation, instead, tries to *minimize* the number of public officials involved in judicial administration by emphasizing the distinctive characteristics of judges, courts and the judicial process. By focussing attention on their own importance and by arguing that they need to be insulated from non-judicial tasks, judges have been able to enhance their own rather than a bureaucratic role in the judicial process.

However, pursuing a strategy that deliberately attempts to minimize the number of public officials involved in the administration of justice requires that judges, who are relatively few in number, seek outside allies. They find them in provincial legal communities: provincial law societies, attorneys practicing before the courts, staffs of lawyers and crown prosecutors in attorney general offices, and, the attorneys general themselves. Their alliance with provincial legal communities is more gratifying, congenial and symmetrical than are the alliances which bureaucratic officials tend to form with interest groups. For a variety of reasons the latter often have values, norms and goals which differ in certain respects from those of bureaucrats, whereas the values and norms of judges and lawyers are almost always fully congruent. Given this congruence and the status and importance of lawyers in Canadian society, the legal community is in a position to support and defend the judiciary before the public and political decision-makers, thereby reducing the need of judges to step outside their adjudicative role and engage in self-serving pleading.[48] Thus, the simultaneous pursuit of encapsulation and alliance strategies both enhances the role the judiciary plays in the political system and contributes to the popular image of judges as public officials superior to those in other areas of government. Indeed, it reverses the conventional representational process, for instead of the judiciary representing the legal community, the latter represents the judiciary.

Function.   Since provinces have responsibility for property and civil rights and since they also are charged with administering criminal justice, the dockets of provincial courts generally are very busy. Although there have been relatively few systematic studies of the operation of the courts, it would appear that lesser courts, those established by provincial governments, not only are busy, but also are often overcrowded. Further, more than one court within a province can exercise concurrent jurisdiction in an area (e.g., juvenile and family matters) and both the structure of provincial court systems and the procedures they employ can vary substantially from province to province. More fundamental problems of access to the legal process and equal treatment of individuals and groups by the courts also have been noted.[49]

To their credit, most of the provinces have recognized these problems and there have been a number of calls to simplify and standardize the structure and procedure of provincial courts, to increase public access to them in cases of minor claims and to provide legal aid services to those in need of such services. These reforms, if implemented, would make a significant contribution to the achievement of genuine equality before the law — a goal to which democracies historically have aspired, but which has proven inordinately difficult to achieve. These reforms also would complement the performance of a function — the protection of the public from government itself — which the courts have had to assume as governmental activities have increasingly impinged on people's daily lives.

All governments, even the most democratic, rely on a mixture of voluntarism and the threatened application of sanctions backed by force to secure compliance with their authoritative edicts. The latter, whether they are passed by legislatures or formulated by bureaucratic officials, at once limit our freedom and enhance it since without laws we would have neither public order nor the freedom and security needed to enjoy our lives and property. In applying the law, judges, federal and provincial, enjoy an unparalleled degree of power and authority — more, in practice, than any other group of public officials. In part, this is a consequence of reliance, other than in Quebec, on English common law principles which assign fundamental importance to judges' interpretations of what particular laws mean. Even in Quebec, where civil law is employed, judges enjoy extremely wide latitude and authority in finding and applying the law. In part the privileged status of judges also is a consequence of other factors: their salaries and benefits are constitutionally protected; they are not liable for anything they say or do while carrying out their judicial assignments; they have powerful patrons and allies within and outside of government; and they enjoy virtually lifetime tenure since it is so difficult to remove them from office. As a consequence, judges enjoy the luxury of exercising virtually unlimited authority unencumbered by any of the mechanisms through which accountability to the public is sought from officials in other areas of government.

Their privileged status is justified on several grounds.[50] It is assumed, the absence of accountability notwithstanding, that judges are cognizant of public opinion and, in applying the law, they act in ways that neither are markedly in advance of the opinion nor markedly in arrears of it. It also is observed that, with few exceptions, the probity of their conduct more than fulfills the expectations the public has of them. It further is argued that judges must be able to apply the law equitably to even the most powerful groups in society without fear or favour, and they cannot do this if they are concerned with matters such as the necessity of reelection or the possibility of imminent removal from office. Finally, and most importantly, as the scope of governmental activities expands and the actions of legislative and bureaucratic officials impinge on virtually every aspect of people's lives, there is a concomitant increase in the potential for arbitrary and capricious governmental action. The judiciary, it is asserted, is a powerful countervailing force with the authority and prestige to interpose itself between a potentially arbitrary government and the citizen. Paradoxically, because judiciaries are responsible to no one, they are able to represent us all.

SUMMARY

In every provincial legislature educated men from the professional and business communities predominate. Although the social characteristics of persons elected to provincial legislatures have not changed much in the past several decades, their activities and the style in which these are performed have altered significantly. The modernization of provincial societies has led to the professionalization of provincial assemblies. As a result, annual legislative sessions have been greatly extended, the salaries and perquisites enjoyed by provincial legislators are substantially greater than in the past and MLAs have been provided with personal and committee staffs to facilitate the performance of their legislative, representational and bureaucratic oversight activities.

Despite these changes, the ability of provincial legislators to represent the policy interests of constituents is constrained by the fact that the formulation of policy is almost entirely in the hands of provincial cabinets and senior bureaucratic officials. Individual MLAs who are members of a governing party can try to influence policy formulation in caucus and members of all parties can try to exert behind-the-scenes influence on the implementation of legislation through discussion and negotiation with ministers and civil servants. They also can apprise the public and other legislative colleagues of their own and constituents' positions on policy by participation in assembly and committee debates and by introducing private members' bills and debatable resolutions. In great part, however, this kind of representation, like the legislators' performance of the oversight function, is symbolic rather than substantive. However, in a democracy, no less than in other political systems, symbols can be important. In the context of provincial legislatures, symbolic representational activities dramatize the concern legislative elites have for the interests of the public on whose behalf they are authorized to govern.

The social composition of provincial bureaucracies, especially since the end of World War Two, has changed dramatically. The proportions who are highly educated professionals and technicians have increased so much that in some provinces they currently constitute half or more of a work force that traditionally has been the repository of clerks and other semi-skilled white-collar workers. Bureaucratic officials exercise quasi-executive, legislative and judicial powers in the course of implementing and administering the enactments of provincial legislatures. Both the degree to which they are responsive to the public and the groups to whom they respond are determined by many factors. At the most general level, responsiveness patterns are a function of three variables: the kind of relations bureaucratic officials enjoy with other actors in the political system, the internal norms, decision-making structures and standard operating procedures of their organizational units and the kinds of policies that are being implemented.

Provincial bureaucracies tend to be most responsive to the general public when they are implementing distributive policies such as health and education. They tend to be less responsive and more "bureaucratic" when implementing redistributive policies such as welfare since these frequently involve questions of "who is entitled to what and under what conditions?" Somewhat paradoxically, bureaucracies give the appearance of being least responsive when they are administering regulatory policies. The explanation for this is two-fold. On the one hand, a number of groups (especially professional groups) have secured the right to largely regulate themselves. On the other hand, these groups often provide the strongest support for the policies of provincial governments. They have excellent rapport with bureaucratic officials and, not surprisingly, the latter often seem to regard them as clients rather than as objects of regulation.

The judiciary is a powerful and in many respects the most autonomous of provincial political institutions. Judges enjoy what amounts to lifetime tenure with excellent salaries and other benefits which cannot be reduced during their term of office. Nor can judges be held liable for anything they do or say in the course of applying the law. They enjoy the strong support of the provincial legal communities. Indeed, so strong is this support, and so free are members of the judiciary from the constraints under which other public officials, elected and appointed, operate, that judges appear to have reversed the representational process. Instead of representing others, they are themselves represented. However, precisely because they are not accountable in practice to even the most powerful individuals and groups in or out of government, judges are able to maintain the vitality of the rule of law upon which rests the political order and security of a democratic society.

NOTES

1. Harold D. Clarke, Jane Jenson, Lawrence LeDuc and Jon Pammett, *Political Choice in Canada* (Toronto: McGraw-Hill Ryerson, 1979), ch. 9.
2. John F. Mackintosh, "How Much Time Left for Parliamentary Democracy?" *Encounter* 43 (August 1974), pp. 48-52.
3. *Ibid.*, p. 48.
4. Robert J. Fleming, *A Comparative Study of Administrative Structures of Canadian Legislatures* (Toronto: Queen's Park, 1980).
5. It might also be noted that in Ontario and Quebec formal recognition is given to the position of parliamentary secretary. The position carries with it an indemnity of $5,460 in Ontario and $8,340 in Quebec. Additional financial compensation is given to committee chairmen, house leaders, whips and deputy whips.
6. Atkinson and White state that provincial legislatures may be divided into three groups on the bases of members' salaries and emoluments. Group one is made up

of the legislatures of Quebec and Ontario. Group two includes British Columbia and Saskatchewan. The remaining legislative assemblies are in group three, with Nova Scotia at the bottom of the list. Michael M. Atkinson and Graham White, "The Development of Provincial Legislatures," in Harold D. Clarke, Colin Campbell, F.Q. Quo, and Arthur Goddard, eds., *Parliament, Policy and Representation* (Toronto: Methuen, 1980), pp. 255-275.

7. *Ibid.*, p. 265.
8. For details concerning this study see Harold D. Clarke, Richard G. Price, and Robert Krause, "Constituency Service Among Canadian Provincial Legislators," *Canadian Journal of Political Science* 8 (1975), pp. 525-526.
9. For an elaboration of the distinction between representational role focus and style see Allan Kornberg, *Canadian Legislative Behavior* (New York: Holt, Rinehart and Winston, 1967), ch. 6.
10. Clarke, Price, and Krause, "Constituency Service Among Canadian Provincial Legislators;" and Harold D. Clarke, "Determinants of Provincial Constituency Service Behaviour: A Multivariate Analysis," *Legislative Studies Quarterly* 3 (1978), pp. 601-628.
11. Clarke, Price, and Krause, "Constituency Service Among Canadian Provincial Legisiators," p. 534.
12. The opposite condition obtains in the Congress and American state legislatures. For a recent comparative study of the legislative process in Canada and the United States see Norman C. Thomas, "An Inquiry into Presidential and Parliamentary Government," in Clarke *et al.*, eds., *Parliament, Policy and Representation*, ch. 16.
13. Michael Atkinson, "Comparing Legislatures: The Policy Role of Backbenchers in Ontario and Nova Scotia," *Canadian Journal of Political Science* 13 (1980), pp. 55-74.
14. Twenty-five percent of Ontario MLAs and 42% of those in Nova Scotia regard this orientation as "central." Atkinson, "Comparing Legislatures," p. 63.
15. *Ibid.*
16. This orientation is central to the roles of 34% of the Ontario but only 15% of the Nova Scotia MLAs. *Ibid.*
17. *Ibid.*
18. *Webster's Seventh New Collegiate Dictionary* (Springfield, Mass: G. & C. Merriam, 1970), p. 112.
19. Richard J. Van Loon and Michael S. Whittington, *The Canadian Political System: Environment, Structure & Process* 1st ed. (Toronto: McGraw-Hill Ryerson, 1971), pp. 414-446.
20. Harold D. Lasswell, *Politics: Who Gets What, When, How* (New York: McGraw-Hill, 1936).
21. David Easton, *A Systems Analysis of Political Life* (New York: John Wiley & Sons, 1965).
22. Peter Woll, *American Bureaucracy*, 2nd ed. (New York: Norton, 1977), p. 16.
23. See, for example, Robert Presthus, *Elites in the Policy Process* (London: Cambridge University Press, 1974), ch. 8; S.J.R. Noel, "Leadership and Clientelism," in David Bellamy, Jon Pammett and Donald Rowat, eds., *The Provincial Political Systems* (Toronto: Methuen, 1976), pp. 197-213; Alan C. Cairns, "The Governments and Societies of Canadian Federalism," *Canadian Journal of Political Science* 10 (1977), pp. 712-714; Garth Stevenson, *Unfulfilled Union* (Toronto: Macmillan, 1979), ch. 4.
24. Cairns, "The Governments and Societies of Canadian Federalism," pp. 695-726.
25. See the argument of James Q. Wilson, "The Rise of the Bureaucratic State," *The Public Interest* 41 (1975), pp. 77-103.
26. J.E. Hodgetts and O.P. Dwivedi, *Provincial Governments as Employers* (Montreal: McGill-Queen's University Press, 1976), Statistical Appendix, pp. 186, 190, Tables E-G.
27. British Columbia passed the first civil service act in 1917. Ontario, Alberta, and Manitoba followed in 1918. Saskatchewan did not pass such an act until 1930, Nova Scotia not until 1935. Quebec and New Brunswick passed their acts in 1943, Newfoundland in 1953. Prince Edward Island did not pass a civil service act until 1962.
28. Hodgetts and Dwivedi, *Provincial Governments as Employers*, p. 7.

29. Hodgetts and Dwivedi, *Provincial Governments as Employers*, p. 8. See also Noel, "Leadership and Clientelism," in Bellamy, Pammett and Rowat, eds., *The Provincial Political Systems, passim*.

30. In the other provinces 40% of Prince Edward Island, 33% of Quebec, 44% of Ontario, 56% of Manitoba, 60% of Saskatchewan, and 47% of Alberta governmental employees were not covered by civil service regulations.

31. Max Weber, *The Theory of Social and Economic Organization*, trans. by A.M. Henderson and Talcott Parsons, edited with introduction by Parsons (New York: Oxford University Press, 1947). See also "Bureaucracy" in H.H. Gerth and C. Wright Mills, translators and editors, *From Max Weber: Essays in Sociology* (New York: Oxford University Press, 1946), pp. 196-244.

32. Robert Presthus, *Elites in the Policy Process* (London: Cambridge University Press, 1974), p. 343.

33. Presthus, *Elites in the Policy Process*, pp. 341-342.

34. Hodgetts and Dwivedi, *Provincial Governments as Employers*, pp. 13-14, and p. 191, Table H.

35. *Ibid.* p. 11.

36. Kenneth Kernaghan, "Power, Parliament and Public Servants in Canada: Ministerial Responsibility Re-examined," in Clarke *et al.*, eds., *Parliament, Policy and Representation*, pp. 124-143, especially p. 125.

37. Paul G. Thomas, "Parliament and the Purse Strings," in Clarke *et al.*, eds., *Parliament, Policy and Representation*, pp. 160-180.

38. On this point see John Meisel, "The Decline of Party in Canada," in Hugh G. Thorburn, ed., *Party Politics in Canada*, 4th ed. (Toronto: Prentice-Hall, 1979), pp. 131-132.

39. Blair Williams, "The Para-Political Bureaucracy in Ottawa," in Clarke *et al.*, eds., *Parliament, Policy and Representation*, pp. 215-229. On the difficulty ministers have in comprehending problems, facing them and selecting appropriate actions see also John Meisel, "The Decline of Party in Canada," in Thorburn, ed., *Party Politics in Canada*, pp. 119-136.

40. See C. Lloyd Brown-John, "Membership in Canadian Regulatory Agencies," *Canadian Public Administration* 20 (1977), pp. 514-533. For a comprehensive discussion see Brown-John, *Canadian Regulatory Agencies* (Toronto: Butterworths, 1981).

41. The most forceful and comprehensive argument has been made by Salamon and Wamsley in their analysis of the responsibility of the United States federal bureaucracy. See Lester B. Salamon and Garry L. Wamsley, "The Federal Bureaucracy: Responsive to Whom?" in Leroy Rieselbach, ed., *People vs. Government* (Bloomington: Indiana University Press, 1975), pp. 151-188.

42. Advisory agencies or committees are devices frequently used by both federal and provincial bureaucracies to obtain the specialized knowledge and advice of private groups and individuals in the course of formulating policies and developing and administering programs. The use of expert advisers also enables elected and appointed public officials to maintain good relations with important individuals and groups in a province and to make use of the latter to generate support for themselves and their ongoing policies and programs. Although the use of expert advisers permits a measure of public participation in the formulation and administration of public policy in virtually every area, it also introduces an element of bias into the representational process. It provides certain high status individuals and groups (e.g., physicians, scientists, corporate executives) with privileged access to middle and top level public officials. See C. Lloyd Brown-John, "Advisory Agencies in Canada: An Introduction," *Canadian Public Administration* 21 (1978), pp. 72-91. For comparative purposes, see Leon Dion, "The Politics of Consultation," *Government and Opposition* 8 (1973), pp. 332-353.

43. Van Loon and Whittington, *The Canadian Political System*, pp. 373-379.

44. Salamon and Wamsley, "The Federal Bureaucracy," *passim*.

45. J.R. Mallory, *The Structure of Canadian Government* (Toronto: Macmillan, 1971), p. 290.

46. *Ibid.*, pp. 295-298.

47. Carl Baar, "Patterns and Strategies of Court Administration in Canada and the U.S.," *Canadian Public Administration* 20 (1977), pp. 242-274.
48. *Ibid.*, pp. 257-264. With respect to self-serving pleas, for example, Baar notes provincial judges traditionally have negotiated salary increases with attorneys general, leaving it for them to justify increases to their cabinet colleagues.
49. See, *inter alia*, Myron Debicki, "Courts," in David Bellamy, Jon Pammett, and Donald Rowat, eds., *The Provincial Political Systems* (Toronto: Methuen, 1976), pp. 369-380; J.C. Smith, "Regina v. Drybones and Equality Before the Law," *Canadian Bar Review*, 49 (1971), pp. 163-187; H.W. Arthurs and Pierre Verge, "The Future of Legal Services/Juridiques de L'avenir" *Canadian Bar Review*, 51 (1973), pp. 15-31; R.N. McLaughlin, "Comments: Regina v. Smythe — The Canadian Bill of Rights — Equality Before the Law — The Meaning of 'Discrimination'," *Canadian Bar Review* 51 (1973), pp. 517-523; D.G. Kellough, S.L. Brickey and W.K. Greenway, "The Politics of Incarceration: Manitoba, 1918-1939," *Canadian Journal of Sociology* 5 (1980), pp. 253-271; John Hagen, and Nancy O'Donnell, "Sexual Stereotyping and Judicial Sentencing: A Legal Test of the Sociological Wisdom," *Canadian Journal of Sociology* 3 (1978), pp. 309-319. See also the criticism by K. Wayne Taylor, Neena L. Chappell, and Stephen Bricke and the rejoinder by Hagen and O'Donnell in *Canadian Journal of Sociology* 5 (1980), pp. 55-61 and 62-63.
50. For a more extended discussion on the role of the judiciary in maintaining Canadian democracy see Mallory, *The Structure of Canadian Government*, pp. 303-324.

FOR FURTHER READING

Atkinson, Michael M. and Graham White. "The Development of Provincial Legislatures," *Parliament Policy and Representation*, eds. Harold D. Clarke *et al*. Toronto: Methuen, 1980, ch. 15. In their comparative analysis of provincial legislatures Atkinson and White argue that these bodies are gradually acquiring the structural characteristics and resources which will enable them to play more creative roles in policy processes.

Brown-John, C. Lloyd. *Canadian Regulatory Agencies*. Toronto: Butterworths, 1981. The author considers problems of accountability as these relate to the activities of regulatory agencies.

Kernaghan, Kenneth. "Power, Parliament and Public Servants in Canada: Ministerial Responsibility Re-examined;" and Audrey Doerr, "Parliamentary Accountability and Legislative Potential," *Parliament, Policy and Representation*, eds. Harold D. Clarke *et al*. Toronto: Methuen 1980, chs. 7 and 8. Although the authors are writing about the federal political system, their treatments of bureaucratic accountability and ministerial responsibility raise issues which apply equally well at the provincial level.

Mallory, J.R. *The Structure of Canadian Government*. Toronto: Macmillan, 1971, ch. 8. This chapter contains a succinct description of the place of courts in the Canadian judicial system.

Noel, S.J.R. "Leadership and Clientelism," *The Provincial Political Systems,* eds. David J. Bellamy, Jon H. Pammett and Donald C. Rowat. Toronto: Methuen, 1976, ch. 14. The author argues that clientelism is a pervasive feature of Canadian political culture and that patron-client networks involving "bureaucrat-patrons" and "bureaucrat-brokers" are key features of contemporary provincial political systems.

7
The Policy Process

The policy process holds the key to understanding provincial government. As the final product of the process by which government allocates its scarce resources among competing interests, public policy is a reflection of some of the underlying values of a society and provides important insights into the extent to which the provinces approximate the ideals of representative democracy. Examining how policies are made enables us to observe the dynamics of provincial politics and the interplay of the various political institutions, groups and processes discussed in previous chapters. This chapter provides an overview of provincial policy-making. It integrates previous discussions of the structure and functions of political institutions, describes the interactions of the various participants at each stage of the policy process and evaluates their influence on the content of public policy. A concluding section examines the process in practice through a case study of the evolution of health policy in Saskatchewan.

THE MEANING OF PUBLIC POLICY

Public policy has many meanings.[1] A provincial party leader's commitment to provincialize a natural resource industry, a decision taken by a provincial cabinet to reduce government spending on agriculture, a law enacted by a provincial assembly to satisfy public demands for expanded health care, a regulation adopted by a government department to reduce air and water pollution, even the unforeseen consequences of any or all of these actions have been labeled public policies. Given the diversity apparent in these few examples, it is important to clarify what we mean by "public policy" at the outset. Most simply stated, public policy is what government does. If, in Harold Lasswell's colourful phrase, politics is concerned with "who get what, when, how," then public policy is the "what" of politics. More specifically, public policy is the course of action government takes in response to public problems. Several aspects of this definition require elaboration.

First, policies are actions. Although policies frequently are intentional and result from governmental decisions, there may be important differences between what a government hopes to do (its intentions), what it determines to do (its decisions), and what it actually does (its policies). Similarly, because policies may have both intended and unintended consequences, it is important to distinguish what government does (policy) from the results (outcomes or consequences) those policies produce.[2]

Second, public policy refers to the course of action taken in response to a problem. Governments frequently attack a problem from several directions simultaneously. These actions may be coordinated or disjointed, compatible or contradictory. A provincial government may attack the energy problem by providing subsidies to homeowners who improve the energy efficiency of their homes. At the same time, however, it may be lobbying the federal government to hold down the domestic price of gasoline. Although the first action is likely to promote oil conservation, the second is likely to have the opposite effect. And even though the attempt to hold down the price of gasoline may be intended to control inflation, or to ease the financial burden on low wage earners, both actions, however contradictory, disjointed, or even unintended, in fact, are parts of the broad course of governmental action constituting that province's energy policy.

Third, "public" policies are distinguished from "private" policies by the scope of the activity and the authority of the policy-maker. Public policies are those that are broad in scope and are formulated through a process that citizens accept as legitimate. Although the actions of a private corporation or a labour union may have a significant impact on the people of a province or on the policies of its government, they are not formally *public* policies. At the same time, however, not all actions by governmental officials are public, either in the sense of being highly visible, or directly affecting large numbers of people. We noted in Chapter 6, for example, that provincial MLAs spend considerable time and energy helping individuals or groups with their specific, and frequently idiosyncratic, needs and demands. Such actions are legitimate and can be extremely important to those on whose behalf they are taken. However, they generally do not affect large groups of people and thus have only limited direct public consequences.[3]

STAGES OF THE POLICY PROCESS

Public policies generally develop gradually as a result of long and at times complex and conflicting interactions among a variety of individuals, groups and institutions. Although it is fashionable to refer to these interactions as the policy process, there is, in fact, no single process by which policies take shape. Differences in the substance of public problems, the structures of provincial bureaucracies, the dynamics of political conflict, the nature of the combatants and the tenor of the times, combine to ensure that each policy evolves through a somewhat different combination of circumstances and events. In Ontario welfare policy may be forged through different processes than agricultural policy; economic policy may develop differently in Manitoba than in New-foundland; current educational policy in Quebec undoubtedly is shaped by a different configuration of forces than 30 years ago. Notwithstanding this diversity, however, it is possible to identify several common stages through which most policies pass in the course of their evolution.[4]

Identifying Public Problems.   Since public policy is a course of action which a government takes in response to a public problem, it is logical that the development of policy begins with perceptions of a problem requiring governmental action. Unfortunately, there is little agreement on what a public problem is or how one should be defined. There are, however, two competing perspectives. The first, or "citizen demand" perspective, holds public problems to be whatever the public says they are. According to this view, public problems are identified by public opinion; they are subjective and usually result from public dissatisfaction with the status quo. The alternative "public need" perspective defines a public problem obejctively as the existence of widespread deprivation of basic human values. Thus, poverty, hunger, chronic unemployment and disease are viewed as public problems because they deprive significant segments of the population of fundamental human rights. Moreover, they constitute public problems irrespective of the public's awareness of them, or of demands for governmental action. Although it is sometimes argued that citizen demands provide a more democratic basis for identifying public problems whereas public needs provide a more rational basis, in fact, the two are related and because they are, governments recognize the legitimacy of both perspectives and strive to maintain a balance between them.

In every province there exists a very large number of problems, only a tiny fraction of which ever come to the attention of the government. Those that do typically are raised by one of several sources. Public problems may be communicated directly to government by individual citizens. Most often this is not the case because, as observed in the discussion of political participation in Chapter 4, the political resources of most people are limited and restrict effective opportunities for direct communication between them and government. As a consequence, the identification of public problems is a task most frequently performed *outside* of government by political parties, interest groups, government-created task forces and royal commissions, the mass media and policy experts in universities and private research institutes. *Inside* government the principal agents are legislators and bureaucrats.

Because of the size and diversity of their memberships, the extensive-ness of their organizations and the strength of their presence in government, political parties are well-equipped, in theory, to link citizens to government by identifying problems requiring governmental action. Parties, it was observed in Chapter 5, may identify public issues by forging coalitions of individuals with similar interests, developing platforms which embrace these common concerns and nominating candidates for public office who, if elected, will articulate and defend the party's commitment to these concerns. In practice, however, parties provide only imperfect channels of communication. The ephemeral nature of most party organizations in the interim between elections, the diverse and, at times, conflicting interests which comprise party coalitions, as well as the parties' frequent inability or unwillingness to formulate clearly defined policy alternatives, seriously undermine their ability to effectively identify problems and propose policy actions. Notwithstanding these factors, parties can make a contribution to the identification of public problems through the network of personal contacts which develop between local party activists and elected public officials. Even where the formal party machinery is limited or rusty from disuse, local activists have a vested political interest in keeping abreast of emerging public concerns and communicating them to party members in government. This is an important aspect of the representational process.

As governmental activities have increased and the problems with which governments deal have grown more complex, there has been a concomitant increase in their need for specialized knowledge and information. The latter enable governmental officials to manage their available resources more rationally and to develop policies and programs that can effectively address problems at hand. As was indicated in Chapter 6, interest groups and various advisory commissions provide governmental officials with precisely such specialized knowledge and information. Institutionalized interest groups have specific goals, enjoy stable organizational structures and maintain close and mutually beneficial contacts with both elected and appointed governmental officials. From the perspective of the latter, interactions with interest group leaders and expert advisors have the additional merit of securing group cooperation and support. What have been termed issue-oriented groups, although less important political actors, also can identify problems, as well as provide feedback on the manner in which current policies are affecting their members. Indeed, because many of the principal social and economic divisions of provincial societies are reflected in their interest group structures, such groups traditionally have been the principal vehicles, outside of government, for identifying public problems.

More recently, the mass media have played an increasingly important role in identifying public problems. The media, for example, may bring to the attention of the public and its governmental officials the fact that an industry is polluting the atmosphere and thereby endangering public health. Similarly, the media pride themselves on their ability to bring to light cases of governmental or bureaucratic mismanagement, inefficiency, waste or even corruption. The media's conception of their role as guardians and representatives of the public interest is a broad one. When they feel it is incumbent upon them to do so, they are perfectly willing to assume the position of unofficial opposition to both the government of the day and the official opposition; to criticize both for their presumed sins of commission and omission, what they have done and failed to do. Indeed, in their editorials, in their choice of subject matter and in the treatment they accord issues, print and electronic media often show their willingness to challenge a federal or provincial government's right to define what the public interest entails.

Nevertheless, it is at least arguable that most problems provincial governments address are identified within governments by legislators and bureaucrats. Legislators, as observed in Chapter 6, are public opinion specialists. Backbench members of provincial assemblies are especially sensitive to currents of opinion within their constituencies and spend large amounts of time reading and answering constituent mail, meeting citizens individually and in groups, reading local newspapers, keeping their political fences mended with local party officials, talking with interest group representatives and, generally, taking the "political pulse" of their districts.[5] Even though backbench MLAs possess little power to respond to public problems directly, they are well-placed to serve as conduits of constituent opinion to government ministers. They do so by raising matters of public concern either formally in caucus, question period and debate, or informally through private communications. This is a major component of their representational roles.

The bureaucracy also plays an important role in the identification of public problems. Where legislators are public opinion specialists, bureaucrats are expert in delineating interest group opinions and incorporating them in specific policy outputs. As the day-to-day administrators of public policy, they are in a position to assess the success or failure of existing policies and determine the need for new initiatives. At times this may lead them to promote and defend the interests of client groups in return for which the latter defend the powers and prerogatives of their particular patrons in intragovernmental struggles.[6] Finally, because cabinet members typically are not expert in every aspect of the policy areas they administer, they are highly dependent on the information their civil servants provide in identifying problems for cabinet action.

Setting Priorities. The identification of public problems is only the first stage in the evolution of public policy. Since the number of problems brought to the attention of a government invariably exceeds its available resources, a provincial government must establish priorities among competing interests and decide which problems are urgent and require prompt and serious attention and which can safely be postponed or ignored. Formally, a cabinet determines the government's policy agenda, establishes its budget priorities, sets the assembly's legislative agenda, and directs the bureaucracy's regulatory and administrative actions. In practice, however, the full cabinet usually delegates to cabinet committees responsibility for establishing priorities among competing claims. The structure and operation of these committees vary among the provinces. In the larger provinces at least, priorities are determined through a process of negotiation and compromise involving three principal sets of actors. However named, these are a priorities and planning committee, a treasury board, and a small number of subject matter committees. The latter coordinate programs and establish priorities among problems within their domain. They are guided in their decisions by broad policy objectives established by the priorities and planning committee and are constrained by financial and resource considerations imposed by the treasury board. Although the full cabinet routinely reviews all decisions taken in committee, it customarily becomes directly involved in agenda-setting only in those relatively few cases in which the committee process fails to produce an acceptable compromise between or among competing interests.[7]

Predictably, the process of agenda-setting is highly political. Although united by a common interest in the survival of the governments they head and a concern for their individual status and authority, cabinet ministers may be divided by personal and departmental rivalries. In fact, the former often become intertwined with the latter because personal ambitions may lead ministers to vigorously promote their department's programs and thus to compete for a high priority position in the resource allocation process. As the preeminent members of their cabinets, provincial premiers have the greatest impact on the content of the policy agenda. Premiers not only are responsible for charting the course governments will follow, they also can insure that their particular policy concerns will receive highest priority.[8] Nevertheless, the power of premiers is far from absolute. Their discretion is constrained by cabinet colleagues, some of whom are powerful political figures in their own right, who may regard themselves as current or future challengers for the premier's mantle of leadership. Consequently, the process of agenda-setting is fundamentally a political exercise in which members of a cabinet will trade support in order to build coalitions which maximize the priority accorded the policies of their respective departments. In establishing governmental priorities, ministers also must be sensitive to myriad external political and economic pressures. These pressures derive from many of the same sources involved in identifying public problems. Thus, one indication of the political sagacity of a cabinet is its ability to forge acceptable policy compromises among competing interest groups while remaining within the limits imposed by public opinion and limited resources.

Although we previously noted that MLAs, particularly those in a governing party, have periodic opportunities to influence a government's agenda, senior bureaucrats have substantially greater influence because cabinet ministers routinely delegate to them authority for all but the most important issues. Even when selecting among competing priorities, ministers rely heavily on senior bureaucratic officials for information and advice. Civil servants in any department enjoy an added measure of influence because they largely determine the issues that will reach a minister's desk. Through their control of the information a minister receives, they can shape both a minister's perceptions of the relative importance of problems and his or her evaluations of the merits of policy alternatives.[9]

As self-interested participants in the policy process, political parties, like interest groups, are not content simply to identify public problems. The principal means by which parties attempt to influence the policy agenda are periodic elections — winning them and gaining control of government. As a rule, provincial parties are not highly programmatic. However, in at least some instances, they are distinguished by broad differences in political outlook which are reflected, to varying degrees, in the priorities they establish when in office.[10]

Although contrary to the ideals of representative democracy, provincial policy processes normally operate in environments devoid of direct public involvement. However, when public opinion does coalesce around an issue, a provincial government may continue to ignore the issue or postpone a response only at its peril. Even when public opinion is not purposely mobilized, if aroused, its volatility and potential impact are such as to command a government's respect. In setting the agenda, a government may not always be directly influenced by what the public wants, but it is likely to be conscious of what it will and will not accept.[11]

Other factors being equal, wealthier provinces are better able than are less prosperous ones to respond to citizen concerns that involve very substantial expenditures of public funds. Poorer provinces also are less often able to engage in policy innovation because "non-discretionary" policies lock them into expenditure patterns that consume a larger proportion of their budgets than is the case in wealthier provinces.[12] In short, wealthier provinces may have greater latitude in establishing their policy priorities. All provinces, however, continuously confront the vexing questions of whether it is possible to respond to a problem given available resources and, if possible, whether the expenditures required justify subsequent neglect of other, less important, but possibly less expensive problems.[13]

Finally, the determination of provincial policy priorities is affected by the federal system. The BNAA assigns the federal government exclusive or concurrent jurisdiction over several important policy domains. No matter how critical a provincial government considers the problem of unemployment, for example, it is limited in its ability to respond because a 1940 amendment to the Act assigns exclusive jurisdiction for unemployment insurance to the federal government.[14] In areas of shared jurisdiction, provincial governments are constrained by the necessity to compromise any conflicting priorities with federal authorities. Federal pressures on the content of a provincial agenda typically are applied through conditional grant and tax abatement programs. By offering to share the costs of certain programs but not others, the federal government is able to alter a provincial government's calculations of the relative costs and benefits of different policies, thereby also changing its priorities. Since 1965 provinces have had the right to opt out of such programs. However, even wealthy provinces find it exceedingly difficult to ignore the lure of "cheap" federal dollars.[15]

This discussion has emphasized that provincial policy agendas are determined through a process of negotiation, compromise and accommodation. Nonetheless, it is important to recognize that all too frequently provincial priorities are determined by the force of events. Under normal circumstances, policy agendas are highly stable. Priorities tend to change slowly and in incremental fashion. Once accommodation is achieved among competing interests, it is extremely difficult for new problems or concerns to force their way onto the agenda.[16] As a consequence, provincial governments may fail to respond to public needs or demands until a problem reaches crisis proportions and no longer can be ignored. Social welfare reform, for example, was undertaken in the 1930s only after the onset of the Depression. Similarly, the long-standing need for a more rational energy policy finally was accorded priority consideration in the late 1970s, largely as a result of the crisis precipitated by the Arab oil embargo of 1973-74.

Formulating and Adapting Policy.   The formulation of particular policies is a complex and amorphous process involving the generation of alternative solutions to public problems; evaluation of the technical, economic, and political feasibility of these alternatives; selection of a preferred alternative; and the alternative's development, refinement and formal adoption by a government. The search for a solution to a public problem generally begins before it reaches a government's agenda. Politicians, being pragmatists and loathe to tackle hopeless causes, usually must be convinced that a solution exists before they will place a problem on the agenda.

When a cabinet does decide to proceed with a particular policy, its decision may be expressed in the following ways: through adjustments in government revenues and expenditures; by developing new legislation or regulations; by manipulating symbols (such as by renaming or reorganizing existing programs); or by a combination of all three.[17] The choice of policy instruments depends on the form and substance of the proposal, on constitutional requirements and on cabinet's perceptions of the relative costs and benefits of alternative strategies. Whichever course it decides to follow, cabinet typically returns the proposal to the department of origin so that it may be drafted in proper legal form. Although the drafting stage involves routine and technical concerns, it may provide some latitude for bureaucratic discretion and influence. After a proposal has been formalized, attention shifts to its adoption. Although the immediate source of authority for proposals may vary, ultimately authority is vested in the provincial assembly. Constitutionally, provincial legislatures are responsible for enacting all laws and appropriating all monies spent by their governments. Many regulations are formulated in cabinet and in the various departments, but the right to issue regulations — whether in the form of Orders in Council or Statutory Instruments — depends on the delegation of legislative authority, either expressed or implied.[18] In practice the role of provincial assemblies in the legislative process is considerably more modest than constitutional theory implies. Party discipline, limited time and information, the paucity and weakness of standing committees and the relative lack of adequate staff are common features of parliamentary systems which limit effective backbench participation in the formulation of public policy. As a result, the policy role of provincial assemblies largely is restricted to review and ratification of government proposals.

Policy Implementation.   The true measure of any policy ultimately is the manner in which it is implemented. In most instances, the policy formulation and adoption stages provide the broad outlines of a program, leaving important details to be determined by those responsible for administering it afterwards. Even when a program is formulated in some detail, its substance and impact may be altered significantly at the implementation stage by administrative interpretation of its intent or by the selective application and enforcement of its statutory provisions.

The bureaucracy is preeminent in the implementation of policy but its prerogatives are not absolute. The cabinet and assembly can preempt some of the bureaucracy's discretionary power by adopting more specific regulations and legislating in greater detail. Dissatisfied client groups or individual citizens have recourse to law and can go to court to appeal administrative interpretations or applications of laws. Cabinet ministers have a variety of means of coping with recalcitrant subordinates (although probably less than they would like) and backbench and opposition MLAs can enforce a limited measure of bureaucratic accountability through question period, behind-the-scenes inquiries and committee investigations.[19]

Evaluating policy. The evaluation of policy is less a separate phase than a component of every phase of the policy process. Assessments of the impact, cost and effectiveness of policies are ongoing and continuous. Unlike other aspects of the process, evaluation is not the preserve of any particular institution or group. The bureaucracy has formal responsibility for monitoring the daily operation of the programs it adminsiters and for long-range forecasting and policy planning. However, political parties, interest groups, the cabinet, legislative committees, individual legislators, private research groups, the mass media and a bevy of interested citizens — indeed, virtually everyone who feels he or she has an interest in a public policy — may play some role in evaluating it. Since their perspectives often differ, the evaluation process largely is subjective, impressionistic and frequently based on incomplete or incompletely assimilated evidence.[20] Even in the most culturally homogeneous province, there may be substantial disagreement on specific policy goals and the most appropriate means of achieving them.

To improve policy evaluation, provincial governments have tried to make the evaluation process more rational by utilizing systematic policy analysis techniques such as Management by Objective, Planning, Programming, and Budgeting (PPB), and Cost-Benefit Analysis. Although their specific procedures vary, the purpose of these techniques is to enable policy evaluators to measure, as objectively as possible, the effectiveness of policies in achieving a set of explicitly articulated goals. The procedures employed in PPB are typical. According to the Planning, Programming, and Budgeting Guide, prepared by the Treasury Board for the federal government, the evaluation process proceeds through six steps:

(a) The setting of specific objectives;
(b) Systematic analysis to clarify objectives and to assess alternative ways of achieving them;
(c) The framing of budget proposals in terms of programs directed toward the achievement of the objectives;
(d) The projection of the costs of these programs a number of years into the future;
(e) The formulation of plans of achievement year by year for each program; and
(f) An information system for each program to supply data for the monitoring of achievement of program goals and to supply data for the reassessment of the program objectives and the appropriateness of the program itself. [21]

In part because of their smaller sizes and less complex administrative structures, the provinces have yet to commit themselves to rational planning and evaluation with the same enthusiasm as the federal government. Saskatchewan experimented with a form of PPB as early as the 1940s, but Ontario and Quebec have gone farthest in implementing formal planning and evaluation procedures, having begun in the early and mid-1970s. However, virtually all provincial governments currently are committed to the principle of rational planning, even if they have not embraced elaborate evaluation forms and procedures.[22]

THE POLICY PROCESS IN PRACTICE: HEALTH POLICY IN SASKATCHEWAN

The development of public policy does not fit a rigid formula or follow a single pattern. Although each phase of the process can be observed in the development of most policies, the phases typically are not separate and distinct but are mixed, marble cake fashion, with one phase blending into another. Having presented a very general overview of this process, let us now consider the development of a specific policy in a single province, health policy in Saskatchewan. Although no more typical than other policies, its development nicely illustrates both the commonality and individuality of provincial policy processes[23] and the extent to which these processes implement the ideals of representative democracy.

Origins and Early Development. It is always difficult to identify the origins of ideas. Section 92(7) of the BNAA vests authority over "The Establishment, Maintenance, and Management of Hospitals, Asylums, Charities and Eleemosynary institutions . . ." in the provinces, but the idea that provincial governments might assume responsibility for ensuring public access to quality medical care at reasonable cost did not emerge until the early years of this century. It sprouted during the 1930s and began to blossom in the 1940s and '50s.

In Saskatchewan, as in other provinces,[24] health care initially had been regarded by most people as a private responsibility, to be borne by the individual, his or her family, private charity or, as a last resort, by municipal government (and then principally for the indigent). In Saskatchewan, however, as in the prairies generally, the effectiveness of a *laissez-faire* medical system was severely strained by a combination of a small, scattered population and "boom or bust" agriculture. The vitality of the economy depended on the magnitude and quality of the province's wheat crop, a crop susceptible to the vicissitudes of weather and the vagaries of international wheat prices.[25] Consequently, many areas of Saskatchewan either were too small or too impoverished to sustain a hospital or even support a single doctor.

Illustrative of the argument that at times seemingly mundane events can have important, if unintended, policy consequences, an early stimulus to the development of provincial health policy occurred in 1914 in the tiny municipality of Sarnia, Saskatchewan. Faced with the loss of its only physician, the Sarnia municipal council tried to persuade the doctor to stay by using public funds to provide an annual salary. Unfortunately, Sarnia's initiative, although successful, was taken without provincial authority and technically was illegal. To rectify this situation, in 1916 the provincial assembly passed legislation enabling municipalities to subsidize doctors' salaries with public funds. This restored Sarnia to the ranks of law-abiding municipalities. More important, it provided the statutory authority for development throughout the province of municipal medical and hospital care programs during the next 30 years.[26] The municipal medical programs of this period had two important consequences for the evolution of provincial health policy. First, they resulted in the establishment of a network of professional medical or client groups dependent on public funds for their well-being. Second, they contributed to a climate of public opinion increasingly supportive of government involvement in the provision of health services. The importance of both developments was enhanced by the Depression when many of the municipalities with established programs (about one-third of all municipalities in Saskatchewan) simply were unable to sustain their costs. Apart from accelerating the departure of medical personnel from the province, the deterioration of municipal medical programs during the Depression focussed the attention of various medical interest groups on the idea that the burden of financing public medical programs ought to be shifted from the municipalities to the federal or provincial governments.[27]

The Depression had other important consequences. It effectively transformed Saskatchewan's populist and cooperative public philosophy into a considerably more radical and politically potent socialist movement. The movement provided an ideological foundation for increased governmental involvement in many areas and the emergence of the Co-operative Commonwealth Federation (CCF), a democratic socialist party with a strong commitment to social security programs, including socialized medicine.[28] Established in 1932, the CCF fought its first election in Saskatchewan in 1934, winning 25% of the vote but capturing only five of 55 assembly seats. Ten years and two elections later, the CCF more than doubled its share of the popular vote, captured 47 assembly seats and formed the provincial government. In essence, Saskatchewan's population, economy, interest group structure and political culture, together with the experience of the Depression and a tradition of municipal medical services, combined to create a climate conducive to substantial government intervention in the area of health. The CCF proved to be an appropriate political instrument for this purpose.

Formulation and Implementation.   Public policy can develop at an uneven pace, with long periods of gradual and incremental change interrupted occasionally by short bursts of policy innovation. The 1944 election of the CCF signaled an end to the 30-year evolution of Saskatchewan's municipal medical system and the beginning of a two-year revolution in provincial health policy during which Saskatchewan developed the first comprehensive hospital insurance program in North America. The CCF had won the 1944 election on a platform promising sweeping changes in social security programs and public ownership of the province's major industries, including agriculture. Once in office, however, it quickly became apparent to the new government that promises made during the campaign considerably exceeded the limited resources available for governmental action. Priorities had to be established.[29] The commitment to provincial health legislation was due principally to two factors: the generally favourable predisposition of Saskatchewan's medical interest groups and the strong, personal commitment to better public health care on the part of the new CCF Premier Tommy Douglas. Douglas revealed his personal priorities when, following the election, he assumed the Public Health portfolio.

Unlike many of its other policy commitments which engendered strong opposition from affected interest groups and organizations, CCF proposals for expanding government involvement in health were greeted with cautious support by medical professional and hospital groups.[30] Although opposed to the socialist philosophy of the CCF and to some of the more radical schemes for a system of "state medicine," the medical profession and ancillary groups such as hospital administrators had vested interests in the expansion of provincial support for existing municipal medical programs. Moreover, the medical establishment had endorsed the principle of comprehensive health insurance when it had been advanced by the Liberal government in the months immediately preceding the 1944 election.

To reassure the medical profession and to circumvent the possibility that CCF initiatives might be sabotaged by civil servants loyal to the previous Liberal government, Douglas and his cabinet decided to appoint an *ad hoc* planning commission composed of sympathetic experts and representatives of the medical profession to undertake the task of diagnosing provincial health needs and formulating appropriate policy responses. In August 1945, after more than a year of technical research, consultation with interested groups and internal negotiation and compromise, the planning commission recommended the government concentrate on developing universal hospital insurance. The decision to concentrate on hospital insurance rather than the more ambitious comprehensive health insurance program promised during the election was based on a combination of medical, economic and political considerations including the commission's conclusion that hospital care was the public's greatest need, the realization that provincial resources were inadequate to support a more ambitious program and the perception that political resistance to provincial action would be substantially greater if physician services were included in the insurance scheme.[31]

Having recommended adoption of a largely undefined program of provincial hospital insurance, the planning commission proceeded to work in concert with government ministers and civil servants to develop and evaluate detailed proposals for formulating and implementing comprehensive hospital insurance. Proposals deemed most feasible by the planning commission were submitted to the cabinet in the fall of 1945. The cabinet debated the commission's alternatives and made a decision. After a final round of consultations with interested groups, the cabinet introduced the Saskatchewan Hospital Service Plan into the Assembly in March, 1946. The size of the CCF majority assured the bill quick and easy passage and it received Royal Assent a month later.

The still formidable task of implementing the plan remained. Although the basic principles for administering hospital insurance had been decided by cabinet in consultation with the planning commission during the formulation stage, political considerations, together with the government's desire to move rapidly in order to have legislation in place before provincial elections were called in 1948, prompted the cabinet to defer decisions on important administrative details to the implementation phase. Among the important decisions the cabinet did make were to use existing administrative structures insofar as possible, decentralize responsibility for enrolling citizens and collecting premiums to existing municipal, town and city governments and, bypass the possibly hostile Department of Public Health by investing authority to administer the hospital plan in a specially created Health Services Planning Commission (HSPC). It was the HSPC which, following enactment of hospital insurance legislation, established the regulations controlling the provision of hospital services, determined the formula for reimbursing hospitals and negotiated the tax collection procedures to be used by local governments. With these details decided, the Saskatchewan Hospital Insurance Plan went into effect on January 1, 1947.[32]

Consolidating and Fine Tuning.   Implementation of the Hospital Insurance Plan marked both an end to the first stage in the development of Saskatchewan's health system and served as a prologue to its continued evolution. Predictably, however, given the enormity of the hospital insurance scheme and the substantial investments of political capital, provincial revenue and individual energy that went into the program's creation, the years immediately following its initiation were devoted to consolidating existing policy and fine-tuning its administrative structure. Reelected in 1948 with a reduced majority, the CCF had neither the political will nor the financial ability to undertake additional significant health policy initiatives. The responsibility of governing had tempered the socialist ideology of the CCF, prompting a more pragmatic and cautious approach to government.[33] At the same time, the hospital insurance program proved considerably more expensive than originally anticipated, draining provincial resources and forcing the government to shift its attention from social service legislation to promoting provincial economic development. The decision by Premier Douglas to relinquish the Public Health portfolio in 1949 signaled both the successful completion of hospital insurance and a reordering of government priorities.[34]

Notwithstanding this shift, Saskatchewan's health policy continued to develop during the 1950s, albeit in a more modest and slower fashion. Although the government had decided shortly after its initial election that an optimal health policy would require the establishment of regional health boards with responsibility for coordinating all medical services in their respective areas, resources constraints, in combination with organized medicine's firm opposition, forced the government to postpone a comprehensive program in order to concentrate on hospital insurance. Rather than abandon the more ambitious program entirely, the government decided to experiment with the regional concept, establishing health boards in two demonstration areas. The most dynamic of these, located in the city of Swift Current, quickly gained control of its development and proceeded within its boundaries to establish a program of comprehensive health insurance.[35] Further progress toward a comprehensive health system was made in 1945 when the government, with the encouragement of the medical profession, decided to subsidize comprehensive health care for citizens on welfare.[36] Government efforts during the 1950s to expand the number of regional health programs were defeated by the medical profession but the size and scope of the medical assistance program for welfare recipients increased throughout the decade.

Illustrative of the interplay between public policy and private initiatives — and perhaps the most significant development in Saskatchewan's medical system during the 1950s — was the growth of voluntary prepayment and mutual medical insurance plans. Voluntary medical insurance plans provided coverage for more than 300,000 people or about two-thirds of the province's population by the end of the decade.[37] This development was facilitated by legislation adopted in 1938 by the previous Liberal government. The two largest of these plans were operated by the province's medical practitioners. Despite the contribution these voluntary prepayment plans were making to the quality and availability of health care, in the waning months of 1959 the CCF government decided to proceed with the long delayed and controversial next step in provincial health policy: the enactment of Canada's first universal, comprehensive medical insurance plan.

Comprehensive Medical Insurance: The Second Policy Revolution.
The decision to proceed with comprehensive medical insurance despite
intense opposition from the medical profession appears to have been
prompted by a combination of gradually increasing political pressures
and sudden economic opportunity.[38] The CCF government had long
since abandoned its radical socialist rhetoric, but it had retained its
specific commitment to universal health insurance, having reiterated
that commitment in virtually every federal and provincial election
campaign since 1933. As in 1946, when the approach of a provincial
election spurred the govenment to speed enactment of hospital
insurance, the need to call a provincial election in 1960 placed mounting
pressure on the CCF to honour its commitment to comprehensive
medical insurance. Many party leaders were concerned that the CCF
was losing its distinctive image as the party of social justice and viewed
adoption of comprehensive medical insurance as a means of rekindling
the radical spirit that had carried the party to office in 1944 and
sustained it in power for 16 years. Reinforcing the party's concern was
the personal commitment of Premier Douglas, who was approaching
the end of his tenure as provincial leader and hoped to establish
comprehensive medical insurance as a monument to his years in office.

Of even greater importance than the political pressures within the
province was a 1958 decision by the federal government to implement
national hospital insurance. In addition to reviving public interest in
health policy, the federal decision to subsidize the costs of provincial
hospital insurance plans provided Saskatchewan with a $13-million
bonanza in 1959-60. Since the money freed by the federal subsidy
already had been committed to health, it seemed reasonable to the
provincial government to reinvest the savings in new health programs.
Thus, health again became a priority on the government's policy
agenda.

Reelected in 1960, CCF planning for the introduction of comprehensive medical insurance began in earnest with the creation of an interdepartmental planning committee, a common administrative device for
coordinating programs cutting across traditional bureaucratic boundaries. Charged with reviewing the operation of existing public and
private medical insurance schemes and evaluating their relative costs
and effectiveness, the committee concluded that a "substantial minority" of Saskatchewan's citizens lacked any form of medical insurance
and that many others were inadequately covered or excessively charged.
The committee recommended universal, comprehensive provincial
medical insurance as the solution and proposed the establishment of a
public advisory committee to promote cooperation on the planning of
such a program between government, the medical profession and other
interest groups, notably labour and the insurance industry. The cabinet
accepted these recommendations, authorizing the planning committee

to appoint the advisory committee and to proceed to draft appropriate legislation. The committee returned to cabinet in November with a completed draft of a comprehensive medical insurance bill. It had completed the formulation process in less than seven months but it had failed to secure the medical profession's support.[39]

Unlike the hospital insurance proposals of 1945 which were supported by the medical profession and adopted expeditiously, the government's medical insurance scheme encountered intense opposition and frequent delay. Perceiving the new proposals as a threat to the self-governing status, professional independence and economic self-interest of its members, the Saskatchewan College of Physicians and Surgeons opposed the government's initiatives from the start. The position of the College, greatly simplified, was that health care was the responsibility of the medical profession and that government should limit its involvement to subsidizing the participation of low income citizens in voluntary medical insurance plans. Since its members would constitute a minority on the government's advisory committee, the College refused to cooperate unless the government both abandoned its *a priori* commitment to comprehensive public health insurance and authorized the advisory committee to consider the entire range of health policy alternatives — in essence, to reconsider all of the questions previously resolved by the interdepartmental committee. Because the government considered the cooperation of the medical profession essential to the success of its plan, Premier Douglas eventually accepted the College's demands, thus returning the policy process to the planning stage. The medical profession had won the first round.[40]

As the doctors feared, the advisory committee, when it was finally constituted, was controlled by members sympathetic to the government's views. When released, the committee's report contained most of the same policy recommendations as the interdepartmental committee report of the previous year. Predictably, the representatives of the medical and insurance industries dissented strongly. However, the cabinet decided against further negotiations or delay, drafted comprehensive medical insurance legislation and steered it through the Assembly before the end of the year.

Enactment of the Saskatchewan Comprehensive Medical Care Act in 1961 ended the second round in the battle to develop comprehensive medical insurance — a clear victory for the government, but a somewhat Pyrrhic one. The battle was far from over and the medical profession, convinced that the government had acted without adequate consultation, was determined to continue the fight. As is frequently the case in the policy process, the Medical Care Insurance Act established the basic principles of the insurance program, but left important substantive and administrative details to be decided by program administrators during the implementation stage. In yet another attempt to win support from the medical profession, or at least to diminish their opposition, responsibility for the administration of the medical insurance program was given to a specially created commission of doctors and civil servants. Again, the medical profession refused to cooperate and threatened to withdraw its members' services — in effect, to go on strike — should the government implement the program.[41]

The medical profession was aided and encouraged in its resistance by a series of events occurring in rapid succession in the months preceding and immediately following enactment of the medical insurance plan. Although the CCF had been returned to office with an increased majority of two seats in the provincial election of June 1960, popular support for the party fell to 41%, the lowest level since 1938. Since the election had been fought principally on the issue of the government's medical insurance proposals, the medical profession interpreted the results as a majority vote against comprehensive medical insurance. More importantly, however, having won the election and fulfilled his personal commitment to enact health insurance, Premier Douglas resigned his post as provincial party leader shortly after the election in order to become national leader of the newly established New Democratic Party. Woodrow Lloyd replaced Douglas as provincial premier and immediately appointed a new Minister of Health. Thus, just at the moment that implementation of medical insurance was to begin, a new, less experienced provincial administration assumed control.

Due largely to the intransigence of the medical profession, the government had twice postponed the date when its insurance plan would take effect, but it finally set July 1, 1962 as the date. As the deadline drew near, negotiations between the government and College of Physicians and Surgeons continued, with the government eventually offering to permit physicians to practice outside the program. At this critical juncture, external events intruded once again. A federal election was held on June 18th, the first fought by the NDP and its new leader, Tommy Douglas. Douglas campaigned extensively on a commitment to develop federal medicare legislation similar to that he had enacted in Saskatchewan. The results were disastrous. The NDP lost by substantial margins in every one of Saskatchewan's 18 federal ridings. Douglas himself was defeated. More certain than ever that public opinion was on their side, the doctors rejected the government's policy concessions. When the Medical Care Insurance Act went into effect without amendment on July 1, Saskatchewan's doctors went on strike.[42]

The government responded to the doctors' actions with both carrot and stick. On the one hand, it invited a British physician, Lord Taylor, to come to Saskatchewan and serve informally as a mediator and, on the other, it began recruiting abroad for foreign doctors to replace those on strike. The latter effort was only marginally successful. However, the intervention of Taylor was an unexpected success. As a socialist and early advocate of the British Health Service, he was trusted by the CCF. As a physician, he quickly gained the confidence of Saskatchewan's medical profession as well. Arriving more than two weeks after the strike began, Taylor succeeded in persuading both sides — whose resistance had been weakened by the trauma of the previous weeks — to make major concessions and to agree to a compromise program. The government quickly amended the Medical Care Insurance Act, the doctors' resumed their practices and Canada's first universal, comprehensive medical insurance program commenced operation.[43]

The Aftermath: Policy Legitimation and Maturation. To function effectively, public policies must be perceived as legitimate. In a democracy, a government can use its enforcement powers to compel compliance with unpopular policies only for limited periods. In the long run, successful implementation of governmental programs requires the voluntary compliance of the public generally and affected interest groups in particular. Although Saskatchewan's medical profession grudgingly acceded to the modified insurance plan, many doctors remained opposed to the program in principle and committed to its repeal. The legitimation of public policies, which normally occurs as a byproduct of the representation of dissenting views during the formulation and enactment phases of the policy process, did not occur in the case of medical insurance. Saskatchewan's doctors, as we have seen, did not believe they had been represented adequately and, based on their interpretation of election returns, they were convinced that the government had exceeded its mandate by forcing its minority views on a reluctant public.

The provincial election of 1964 ended 20 years of CCF government. Although popular support for the party remained relatively constant between 1960 and 1964, coordinated efforts by the opposition parties resulted in the election of a Liberal government with a small majority. Far from threatening the survival of hospital or medical insurance, however, the Liberals contributed substantially to the legitimation of the existing health policy. Political considerations had prompted them to oppose enactment of medical insurance in the Assembly in 1961, but their opposition was not ideologically based. To the contrary, the Liberals had endorsed the idea of comprehensive health insurance as early as 1943 and they supported the federal Liberal party's commitment to national medical insurance during the 1963 federal election campaign.

Despite the medical profession's several attempts to persuade the newly elected provincial Liberal government to repeal or at least substantially modify the Medical Care Insurance Act, their efforts were largely in vain. Not only did the Liberals decline to make significant changes in existing health programs, they greatly expanded provincial involvement, increasing spending on health by more than 90% during eight years in office. In effect, by supporting programs that had been associated so closely with the CCF-NDP, the Liberals effectively removed the principle of universal, comprehensive health insurance from partisan politics. By so doing they established the legitimacy of the government's continued and expanded involvement in the regulation and financing of health care.

* * *

This case study of the formulation and implementation of health policy in Saskatchewan and the programs that resulted have focussed on some of the similarities of the provincial policy process, providing an overview of its principal stages, essential features and the interplay of the several participants at each stage. Among the similarities are: 1) the incremental nature of the process — in the case of Saskatchewan, the movement from municipally subsidized physician services, to provincial hospital insurance, to a comprehensive provincially insured health program; 2) the preeminent influence of a premier over both the content and priorities of a provincial policy agenda; 3) the inclusion of representatives of interest groups affected by a potential policy or program in planning and other committees to ensure their support during the problem identification phase; 4) the relatively continuous consultation among public officials (elected and appointed) and representatives of affected groups during all phases of the policy process; 5) the disjunction between the demand and need for a particular policy and the resources available to a provincial government to fund it during the priority-establishment phase of the policy process; 6) the development and winnowing of alternative programs during the formulation phase; 7) the sketching of broad outlines of a policy in legislation approved by cabinet and assembly during the formulation phase and the filling in of details by the bureaucracy during the implementation phase; 8) the tendency of federal government actions to affect the calculations of provincial policy-makers; 9) the utilization of professional associations (e.g., the College of Physicians and Surgeons) to help administer policies and resulting programs; and 10) the use of rational planning and systematic evaluations of ongoing programs to monitor their impact.

The Saskatchewan case study also has demonstrated some of the many ways in which the policy process may vary. With regard to the evolution of health policy in Saskatchewan, these differences include: 1) the use of regional demonstration programs for innovating policies; 2) the decision of a cabinet to formulate and implement a controversial policy despite substantial opposition from key interest groups affected by the policy; and 3) the willingness of a powerful institutionalized interest group to "go public" in their opposition to a proposed policy and subsequently to refuse to cooperate in its implementation. In short, the study of the evolution of health policy in Saskatchewan, although it illustrates common patterns, also underscores the fact that each provincial policy may be shaped by a somewhat different combination of dynamics and constraints.

SUMMARY: PROVINCIAL POLICY-MAKING AND REPRESENTATIVE DEMOCRACY

The struggle for political representation in the provinces is waged principally in the policy arena. Important conclusions about the representative character of the provinces can be drawn from examining the opportunities the process provides competing interests to influence the distribution of provincial resources. Although it could encompass a number of variations, the *ideal* policy process in a representative democracy is one in which the several groups most likely to be affected by a particular policy have ample and relatively equal opportunity to communicate with and influence the decision of public policy-makers on the issue at hand. There are obvious risks involved in generalizing from a single case, but the analysis of the development of health policy in Saskatchewan affords an opportunity to evaluate the extent to which the provincial policy process approximates the ideal.

Analysis suggests the provinces have travelled some distance on the road to becoming representative democracies. By way of illustration, we may note the respective roles played by the CCF opposition and the governing Liberals during the 1930s. The CCF identified and focussed attention on the existence of unmet health needs and mobilized public pressure for governmental action, while the Liberal government played its part by placing health on the provincial agenda in the early 1940s. Evidence of the representative character of the policy process is further reflected in the operation of the electoral process, which, on several occasions, enabled the public to influence the direction of policy and hold the government accountable for its actions.

Another indication of the representative character of provincial policy-making is the extensive participation of organized interest groups in every phase of the formulation and implementation of two major health programs. Even at the height of their confrontation with the government, the leaders of the medical profession and private insurance industry still enjoyed regular access to and were in frequent contact with government leaders, civil servants and opposition members of the Assembly. Although opposition groups were unable to prevent implementation of the medical insurance plan, their influence was substantial. They succeeded in postponing any form of medical insurance for 20 years and secured important concessions from the government when legislation finally was approved. At the same time the ultimate inability of opposition groups to prevail illustrates another aspect of the representative character of the policy process. This is that although affected groups must be accorded extensive opportunities to express their views and participate in the development of policy, in the end a government must be capable of honouring its commitments and putting programs into effect. In short, in a representative democracy the will of the public, as expressed through its freely elected government, must prevail.

The Saskatchewan case also illustrates some of the ways in which provincial policy-making departs from the ideals of representative democracy. Access to government and influence over policy are far from equally distributed among contending groups. Particularly striking in the Saskatchewan case was the relative absence of involvement of groups opposing the doctors and the insurance companies, especially those representing the interests of disadvantaged members of society, the poor, the aged and the infirm. Another indication of the gap between democratic ideals and the reality of provincial policy-making concerns the political role played by the bureaucracy. It was noted in Chapter 6 that the *formal* theory of representation assigns the bureaucracy the role of anonymous, neutral and responsive servant of government. In Saskatchewan, however, certain senior civil servants were hostile to the policies of the newly elected CCF government and were able to use their strategic positions to oppose the government's health insurance plans. Finally, although Saskatchewan's party and electoral systems functioned effectively in identifying and responding to public health needs, parties and elections are imperfect instruments of accountability. In the Saskatchewan case, the CCF committed itself to a broad range of new social and economic programs, in addition to health, during the 1944 campaign, but was able to fulfill only a portion of its promises during the following term. It was not so much a matter of the CCF acting in bad faith as it was an illustration of how the electoral process encourages parties to promise more than they possibly can deliver as governments. In Canada, as in other democracies, voters tend to support parties which promise the most, but rarely punish those which promise too much. Consequently, parties often are encouraged to tell voters what they want to hear, but seldom what they need to know.

To recapitulate, an analysis of the process through which two major health programs were formulated and implemented in Saskatchewan reveals that the provincial policy process manifests a degree of openness and provides substantial opportunities for *organized* interests to influence the content of public policy. However, it also makes clear that important aspects of the process are not congruent with the ideals of representative democracy. In light of this, it can be argued that greater openness in government, more equal access to policy-makers by a large number and variety of interest groups, more responsible political parties, more responsive bureaucracies and more informed, active and responsible electorates all would facilitate the progress of the provinces toward greater representative democracy.

NOTES

1. For elaboration of these arguments see Charles O. Jones, *An Introduction to the Study of Public Policy* (North Scituate, Mass.: Duxbury Press, 1977), pp. 2-5; and James E. Anderson, *Public Policy-Making* (New York: Praeger Publishers, 1975), pp. 1-6.
2. It is important to note in this regard that inaction also is a form of policy. A government's decision to respond to a problem by doing nothing represents a negative form of action and tacit acceptance of the policy already in effect. See, in this regard, the provocative discussion of the concept of non-decisions in Peter Bachrach and Morton Baratz, "Decisions and Nondecisions," *American Political Science Review*, 57 (1963), pp. 632-642.
3. It is possible, however, that the performance of such constituency service tasks (or the failure to do so) may have indirect consequences, as, for example, by affecting public support for the legislature and other aspects of the political system. See John C. Wahlke, "Introduction," in Samuel C. Patterson, Ronald D. Hedlund and G. Robert Boynton, *Representatives and Represented* (New York: Wiley, 1975), pp. 12-17; and Allan Kornberg, Harold D. Clarke and Lawrence LeDuc, "Some Correlates of Regime Support in Canada," *British Journal of Political Science* 8 (1978), pp. 199-216.
4. The outline of the policy process developed in this section is adapted from Anderson, *Public Policy-Making, passim*; and Jones, *An Introduction to the Study of Public Policy*. Our discussion also parallels in most respects the treatment of the federal policy process in Richard J. Van Loon and Michael S. Whittington, *The Canadian Political System: Environment, Structure, and Process* 2nd ed. (Toronto: McGraw-Hill Ryerson, 1976), chs. 14-17.
5. Harold D. Clarke, Richard G. Price, and Robert Krause, "Constituency Service Among Canadian Provincial Legislators: A Test of Three Hypotheses" *Canadian Journal of Political Science*, 8 (1975), pp. 520-542.
6. See in this regard, S.J.R. Noel, "Leadership and Clientelism" in David J. Bellamy, Jon H. Pammett, and Donald C. Rowat, eds., *The Provincial Political Systems: Comparative Essays* (Toronto: Methuen, 1976), pp. 197-213.
7. An excellent description of the structure and operation of cabinet committees in Ontario is provided by George J. Szablowski, "Policy-Making and Cabinet: Recent Organizational Engineering at Queen's Park," in Donald C. MacDonald, ed., *Government and Politics in Ontario* (Toronto: Macmillan, 1975), pp. 114-134.
8. Illustrative of the influence of a premier on the shape of a provincial agenda was the role played by Premier Douglas in Saskatchewan in persuading his CCF government to give highest priority to the development of provincial hospital insurance during the 1940s. See in this regard, R.F. Badgley and S. Wolfe, *Doctors' Strike: Medical Care and Conflict in Saskatchewan* (Toronto: Macmillan, 1967), *passim*; and Malcolm G. Taylor, *Health Insurance and Canadian Public Policy* (Montreal: McGill-Queen's University Press, 1978), pp. 69-104. The development of Saskatchewan's health policy is discussed in detail below.
9. An interesting discussion of the relationship between ministers and civil servants, viewed from the perspective of a provincial premier, is Allan E. Blakeney, "The Relationship Between Provincial Ministers and Deputy Ministers," *Canadian Public Administration*, 15 (1972), pp. 42-45. A more general discussion of this relationship at the federal level is provided in Colin Campbell and George J. Szablowski, *The Super-Bureaucrats* (Toronto: Macmillan of Canada, 1979), pp. 146-208.
10. Considerable controversy surrounds the question of the policy impact of Canadian parties. A summary of the arguments and evidence is provided by Marsha A. Chandler and William M. Chandler, *Public Policy and Provincial Politics* (Toronto: McGraw-Hill Ryerson, 1979), pp. 66-69.
11. It might be argued, for example, that the demise of the federal Conservative government of Prime Minister Clark in 1979 — after less than one year in office — occurred in large measure because Clark failed to appreciate the depth of public opposition to his proposed tax increases. More generally, it has been argued that the greater emphasis placed on public ownership of natural resources in Saskatchewan compared to Alberta, has been possible because of a more permissive attitude

toward public ownership. An excellent elaboration of this is provided in John Richards and Larry Pratt, *Prairie Capitalism: Power and Influence in the Canadian West* (Toronto: McClelland and Stewart, 1979), *passim*.

12. Non-discretionary spending results from long-term government commitments that are difficult to change or can be changed only over long periods. For example, although government spending on health can be changed in the long run through legislative amendments to provincial health acts, in the short run such spending is relatively uncontrollable. Changes in the cost of provincial health programs, year to year, are determined more by inflation or changes in public medical utilization patterns than by governmental decisions.

13. For discussions of the impact of resource constraints on provincial spending in the areas of health, education, and welfare, see William Mishler and David Campbell, "The Healthy State: Legislative Responsiveness to Public Health Needs in Canada, 1920-1970," *Comparative Politics*, 10 (1978), pp. 479-497; and William Mishler and Allan Kornberg, "Evaluating Legislative Performance in Canada: Preliminary Tests of a General Theory," paper presented at the World Congress of the International Political Science Association, Moscow, USSR, August, 1979.

14. Even in areas in which federal government has primary jurisdiction, however, the provinces still have the ability to bring pressure to bear on the federal government, thus indirectly shaping federal priorities. See, for example, Leslie Bella, "The Provincial Role in the Canadian Welfare State: Influence of Provincial Social Policy on the Design of the CAP," *Canadian Public Administration*, 22 (1979), pp. 439-454.

15. The literature on the economic aspects of Canadian federalism is voluminous. For an introduction to the subject see Richard W. Phidd and C. Bruce Doern, *The Politics and Management of Canadian Economic Policy* (Toronto: Macmillan, 1978), pp. 492-507; Marsha A. Chandler and William M. Chandler, *Public Policy and Provincial Politics* (Toronto: McGraw-Hill, Ryerson, 1979), ch. 5; and Donald V. Smiley, *Canada in Question: Federalism in the Eighties* 3rd ed. (Toronto: McGraw-Hill Ryerson, 1980), ch. 6.

16. A classic description of the incremental nature of the policy process is Charles Lindblom, "The Science of Muddling Through," *Public Administration Review*, 19 (1959), pp. 79-88.

17. Some of the differences in the various instruments of public policy are discussed in Chandler and Chandler, *Public Policy and Provincial Politics*, pp. 121-137.

18. James McNally, "The Supervision of Delegated Powers" in Donald C. Rowat, ed., *Provincial Government and Politics: Comparative Essays* (Ottawa: Department of Political Science, Carleton University, 1973), 2nd ed., pp. 245-256.

19. On the limitations of these devices see ch. 6.

20. Van Loon and Whittington argue that the problem confronting policy-makers is not too little information but too much. Because of the wealth of information generated by bureaucrats, interest groups, independent research institutes, and individuals, policy-makers are confronted by "information overload " — they simply cannot digest, assimilate, and properly interpret the volumes of complex and often contradictory evidence which they receive. Van Loon and Whittington, *The Canadian Political System*, p. 337.

21. Canada Treasury Board, *Planning, Programming, and Budgeting Guide* (Ottawa: Queen's Printer, 1969), p. 8.

22. R.M. Burns, "Budgeting and Finance" in Bellamy *et al.*, eds., *The Provincial Political Systems*, pp. 327-330.

23. Another and perhaps equally important reason for focussing on health policy in Saskatchewan is the wealth of previous research on the subject. Few other provincial policy areas have benefited from as much research and probably none is better understood. Among the excellent treatments of the topic are Badgley and Wolfe, *Doctors' Strike* and Taylor, *Health Insurance and Canadian Public Policy*. Taylor's work is especially valuable and provides the basis for much of the discussion that follows.

24. Note, however, that governmental concern with provincial health insurance developed relatively early in British Columbia. Royal Commissions in 1919 and 1929 both recommended provincial initiatives in health. British Columbia also

enacted hospital and medical insurance legislation in 1936, but opposition from the medical profession prevented its implementation. Thus Saskatchewan's Hospital Services Plan was the first provincial health insurance program actually implemented. On British Columbia's early efforts see, Donald Swartz, "The Politics of Reform: Conflict and Accommodation in Canadian Health Policy" in Leo Panitch, ed., *The Canadian State: Political Power and Political Economy* (Toronto: University of Toronto Press, 1976), pp. 311-343. On early federal and provincial health efforts, more generally, see Taylor, *Health Insurance and Canadian Public Policy*, pp. 1-68.

25. On the impact of environment on the political development of the prairie provinces see, Seymour Martin Lipset, *Agrarian Socialism* (New York: Doubleday, 1968). See also C.B. MacPherson, *Democracy in Alberta: Social Credit and the Party System* 2nd ed. (Toronto: University of Toronto Press, 1962).
26. Taylor, *Health Insurance and Canadian Public Policy*, pp. 69-73.
27. *Ibid.*, pp. 78-79.
28. Lipset, *Agrarian Socialism, passim.*
29. Richards and Pratt, *Prairie Capitalism*, pp. 126-129 and 135-147.
30. Compare, for example, the role of interest groups in opposing CCF proposals to acquire public ownership of natural resources with the role of the medical profession in the development of hospital insurance in Richards and Pratt, *Prairie Capitalism*, pp. 93-147; and Taylor, *Health Insurance and Canadian Public Policy*, pp. 82-86.
31. Taylor, *Health Insurance and Canadian Public Policy*, pp. 78-80.
32. *Ibid.*, pp. 97-101.
33. Richards and Pratt, *Prairie Capitalism*, pp. 126-147.
34. Taylor, *Health Insurance and Canadian Public Policy*, pp. 104 and 264-270.
35. *Ibid.*, pp. 245-252.
36. *Ibid.*, p. 252.
37. *Ibid.*, pp. 252-257.
38. *Ibid.*, pp. 266-267.
39. *Ibid.*, pp. 270-276.
40. The role of the medical profession in opposing comprehensive medical insurance is admirably detailed in Badgley and Wolfe, *Doctors' Strike*.
41. Taylor, *Health Insurance and Public Policy*, pp. 297-98.
42. *Ibid.*, pp. 287-307.
43. *Ibid.*, pp. 316-327.

FOR FURTHER READING

Chandler, Marsha A. and William M. Chandler. *Public Policy and Provincial Politics*. Toronto: McGraw-Hill Ryerson Ltd., 1979. An excellent introduction and general overview of the structures of provincial policy-making and the substance of social service and resource development policies in the provinces.

Doern, G. Bruce and V. Seymour Wilson, eds. *Public Policy in Canada*. Toronto: Macmillan, 1979. A well-chosen collection of essays on various aspects of the policy process in Canada. The concluding chapter provides an especially valuable discussion of some of the principal aspects of the policy process which bear upon government's capacity for political accountability and responsiveness.

Jones, Charles O. *An Introduction to the Study of Public Policy*. North Scituate, Massachusetts: Duxbury Press, 1977. A standard in the field, this short and very readable volume sketches the basic stages of the policy process and describes the principal actors, institutions and processes involved at each stage.

Simeon, Richard. "Studying Public Policy," *Canadian Journal of Political Science* 9 (December, 1976), pp. 548-580. A critical summary and synthesis of recent developments in the study of public policy, this insightful essay identifies the strengths and weaknesses of existing theories and approaches in the field and proposes an ambitious agenda for future research.

Taylor, Malcolm G. *Health Insurance and Canadian Public Policy.* Montreal: McGill-Queen's University Press, 1978. The definitive case study of the development of Canada's hospital and health insurance policies.

8
Policy Responsiveness

As observed in Chapter 1, for some theorists the acid test of the representativeness of any government is the extent to which its policies are responses to the needs and demands of its citizens. Accordingly, an assessment of provincial political systems as representative democracies requires that we try to determine the extent to which the policy outputs of provincial governments reflect public needs and demands. Our investigation will focus exclusively on needs for two reasons. One, because, while conceptually, needs and demands can be distinguished from one another, empirically there is a strong correlation between the two. Demands are grounded in social and economic realities. For example, demands for better health care are related to the high incidence of health problems of various kinds and accompanying judgments that better health services are required. Demands for post-secondary education reflect the fact that the kinds of knowledge and skills needed in a complex industrial society can only be obtained in institutions of higher learning. Demands for a wide range of social services such as aid to dependent children, daycare and assistance to the elderly reflect needs not adequately met by families, churches and traditional providers of social assistance. In a real sense, then, needs and demands are two sides of the same coin. A second reason for focussing on needs rather than demands is the absence of adequate data on public policy preferences in each province during the post-World War Two era, the time period we wish to consider.[1] Happily, we do have data that permit us to gauge public needs in each province during this period. Our assessment of relationships between policy outputs and public needs will focus on three major policy areas: health, education and social welfare.

In analyses of this kind, expenditures are perhaps the best indicator of governmental priorities because political decision-makers are inevitably constrained by finite resources. Typically, as the case study of health policy-making in Saskatchewan revealed, the demand for provincial resources exceeds the supply. Accordingly, when a provincial government funds a program or alters its level of spending for an existing one, it is revealing a policy commitment. Consequently, in this chapter we will employ expenditure data as the major indicator of provincial policy. After examining patterns of expenditure in the three areas during the post-World War Two period, we measure the responsiveness of provincial governments to public needs in these areas, trace changes in responsiveness since 1945 and consider how political and environmental factors have influenced these changes. We demonstrate that although patterns of provincial government responsiveness have varied over time, the dominant pattern is one of overresponding to health needs while underresponding to educational and social welfare needs. Both environmental and institutional factors have played an important part in explaining how provincial governments have responded to public needs.

THE GROWTH OF PROVINCIAL GOVERNMENT

The history of Canadian government has been one of relentless growth. As indicated in the discussion of bureaucracies in Chapter 6, the size and scope of governments at all levels of the political system have increased dramatically and almost continuously during this century.[2] The increasing size and complexity of provincial economies and societies discussed in Chapter 3 partially account for this expansion. So too does the shift in public philosophy to a more positive view of the role of the state. Given these economic, social and ideological changes, it is perhaps inevitable that over the years the distinction between public and private interests has become blurred. Thus, many problems considered individual responsibilities 50 years ago are today viewed as public concerns to which government is expected to respond.[3] Spurred by opportunities to enhance their power and prestige, as well as by a genuine desire to be of assistance, provincial officials have responded, often eagerly, to public demands for increased governmental services. Frequently, when demands have not developed spontaneously, officials have encouraged citizens to articulate them.[4] Provincial governments are not unique in these regards, however. The growth of the public sector has characterized virtually all western countries, especially since the end of the Second World War.[5]

In Canada, most of the growth in the public sector has occurred at the provincial and municipal levels. Evidence of this can be seen in the growth of governmental expenditures diagrammed in Figure 8.1. Although there has been a dramatic rise in spending by all governments, growth in provincial expenditures has been the most substantial, increasing by more than 1,000% since 1950, even discounting the effects of inflation. Federal spending, by comparison, has grown at less than half this rate. The extraordinary growth in provincial spending cannot be explained simply by pointing to the increased size and affluence of the population. Whereas federal spending, as a proportion of the gross national product, has remained relatively constant at about 20% over the past three decades, the proportion of the GNP spent by provincial governments has tripled. Similarly, although the level of federal per capita spending has doubled since 1950, provincial per capita spending has increased nearly six-fold and now exceeds that of the federal government.

An analogous although less dramatic pattern can be observed in the growth of government employment (Table 8.1). Since 1959, the first year when comparable data are available, provincial employment has grown almost twice as rapidly as federal employment. Municipal employment has grown even faster, increasing by well over 150% during this period. By 1971, approximately 50 of every 1,000 persons in the labour force were civil servants and about 50% of these were employed by the

FIGURE 8.1   The Growth of Spending by All Levels of Government 1950-75 (Gross Expenditures in Millions of 1971 Dollars)

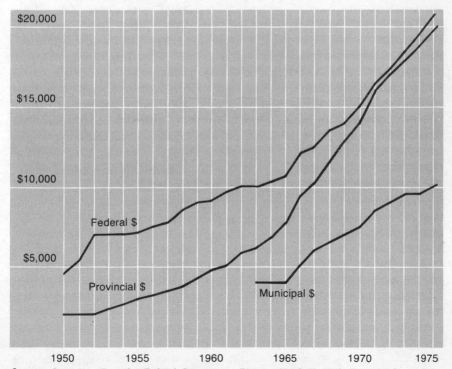

Sources: Statistics Canada, *Federal Government Finance* (DBS 68-211); *Provincial Government Finance* (DBS 68-207); and *Local Government Finance* (DBS 68-203).

provinces. Counting everyone on public payrolls, nearly three-quarters were employed by the provinces or municipalities. These persons constituted approximately 15% of the entire labour force.[6]

Spending and employment are highly visible indicators of governmental activity. Regulation, sometimes termed the "hidden side" of government, although less salient, is also important.[7] In fact, regulation has borne much of the brunt of criticism by those who argue that government has grown too large, too fast. Government regulations are more difficult to catalogue and quantify than levels of expenditures and employment. Therefore, hard data on trends in regulatory activity are less plentiful and those which are available should be interpreted with caution. Nonetheless, the evidence suggests the growth of governmental regulation has been more modest than some observers have contended (see Table 8.1).[8] At the federal level it appears that the pace of regulatory growth since 1950 has approximated that of population increase. Comparable data are available for only five provinces for the period 1960-1975. They indicate that provinces annually issue about eight times as many regulations as the federal government, but that the provincial rate of increase in the number of regulations issued is roughly parallel to that at the federal level.

A somewhat different pattern characterizes increases in legislative activity. Consistent with Parkinson's Law that "work expands to fill the time available," legislative activity in the provinces has increased at approximately the same pace as legislative sessions have lengthened. Currently, the 10 provincial legislative assemblies annually enact 10 to 20 times as much legislation as the federal parliament. Nevertheless, the number of new statutes enacted each year has increased only very slightly and, unlike other areas of provincial activity, has not kept pace with the growth of population. However, since existing laws and regulations rarely are rescinded when new legislation and regulations are enacted, it is at least arguable that the patterns of provincial regulatory and legislative growth approximate those characterizing provincial expenditures and employment.

THE SCOPE AND SUBSTANCE OF PROVINCIAL POLICY

Both subtle and dramatic changes in the substance of provincial policies and the ordering of political priorities underlie the expansion of provincial governments. In Chapter 2, it was noted that within broad limits the BNAA defines the policy jurisdiction of provincial governments. Section 92 of the Act gives the provinces exclusive jurisdiction over a list of subjects that includes most classes of public works, hospitals and charitable institutions, public lands and resources, the administration of justice and the protection of property and civil rights. Section 93 endows

TABLE 8.1
Growth of Federal and Provincial Government Employment and Statutory and Regulatory Enactments for Five Year Intervals, 1950-74

Years	Mean Number of Govt. Employees[1] (and as % of Civilian Workforce)		Mean Yearly Number of New Statutes Enacted[2] (and per million capita)		Mean Number of New Regulations[3] (and per million capita)	
	Federal	Provincial	Federal	Provincial	Federal	Provincial
1950-54	NA	NA	69 (4.9)	797 (56.9)	576 (41.1)	53[a] (66.2)
1955-60	NA	NA	57 (3.5)	746 (46.6)	468 (29.2)	97[a] (114.1)
1960-64	335,355 (5.1%)	215,145 (3.3%)	46 (2.6)	819 (45.5)	519 (28.8)	993[b] (254.6)
1965-69	363,722 (4.8%)	291,570 (3.8%)	43 (2.2)	876 (44.9)	594 (30.5)	1465[c] (248.3)
1970-74	407,147 (4.7%)	345,632 (4.0%)	55 (2.6)	915 (42.5)	633 (29.4)	1526[c] (238.4)
% Growth in Govt. Across period	+21% (-7%)	61% (+21%)	-20% (-46%)	+14% (-25%)	+9% (-28%)	NA

Sources:
[1]Statistics Canada, *Federal Government Employment*, (4th Quarter) 1959-1974, DBS 72-004; and Statistics Canada, *Provincial Government Employment* (4th quarter) 1959-1974, DBS 72-007.
[2]Statutes of Canada
[3]Data compiled and provided by Mary Faulkner, Information and Reference Services Division, Legislative Library, Queen's Park.

[a]Figures based on data from only one province, Manitoba
[b]Figures based on data from three provinces, Manitoba, Alberta, British Columbia
[c]Figures based on data from six provinces, Manitoba, Alberta, British Columbia, Saskatchewan, New Brunswick and Quebec

the provinces with jurisdiction over education and Section 95 provides concurrent jurisdiction with the federal government over agriculture and immigration. In practice, the scope of provincial policy has been determined as much by social, economic and political developments as by constitutional mandate. Historically, the principal concerns of provincial governments have been the social and economic development of their respective societies. To create the infrastructures required to develop their economies, the provinces have committed substantial resources to building transportation networks. To encourage social and economic development they have invested heavily in public education. Although education and public works continue to be major concerns, the direction provincial policies have taken since the Depression has been influenced by at least two policy "revolutions" and by a substantial degree of evolutionary change.

The first revolution, in social welfare policy, took place during the early 1930s and was precipitated by the Depression. Until then, the provision of welfare services largely had been left to private institutions. Governments limited themselves to exercising minimal supervision over these institutions and to providing them and municipal welfare programs with modest subsidies. For example, prior to World War One barely 8% of provincial budgets were spent on welfare services, broadly defined. However, the social dislocation and suffering caused by the Depression proved too great a burden for private charities and local governments to bear. The provincial response was immediate and substantial; between 1929 and 1934 provincial spending on welfare more than tripled and the proportion of expenditures devoted specifically to "relief" increased from less than 1% in 1929 to nearly 25% in 1934.[9] The federal response was equally impressive, so that by the end of the '30s a large, complex, but largely uncoordinated welfare system involving the three tiers of government had been established. Subsequently, a series of federal initiatives intended to consolidate authority and coordinate responsibility for existing programs in Ottawa led to a decline in the emphasis provinces accorded welfare needs. Consequently, although there has been a five-fold increase in real per capita provincial spending on welfare since 1950, until quite recently, the proportion of total provincial expenditures devoted to welfare has remained relatively constant at about 10% (see Table 8.2). Even the passage of the Canada Assistance Plan of 1966, which required the federal government to pay half of a province's welfare costs, failed to stimulate more than a modest increase in provincial welfare spending.

A second revolution in provincial policy occurred during the decade following World War Two when health emerged as a major concern. The idea that the provinces might play a significant role in providing health and hospital care was not widely accepted until the 1930s. As indicated in the case study of Saskatchewan health policy in Chapter 7, it was not

TABLE 8.2

Average Percentage of Gross Provincial Spending by Policy Area for Selected Intervals, 1950–1977

Years	Health	Welfare	Education	Transportation	Natural Resources	Protection of Persons and Property	General Govt.	All Other
1950–54	19%	12%	19%	26%	7%	4%	3%	10%
1955–59	18	10	18	29	6	4	4	11
1960–64	24	10	25	21	6	3	4	7
1965–69	23	10	26	17	5	3	4	12
1970–74	24	11	25	10	4	4	5	17
1975–77	25	14	24	8	3	4	5	17
Percent Growth in Real Per Capita Spending (1971 $) 1950–77	978%	544%	945%	150%	203%	483%	970%	Total Govt. Spending 640%

Source: Statistics Canada, *Provincial Government Finance: Revenues and Expenditures 1950–1978*, DBS 68–207

until the CCF gained control of the Saskatchewan government in 1944 that the health policy revolution began in earnest. The implementation of a hospital insurance program by Saskatchewan was followed by the adoption of similar programs by the governments of British Columbia, Alberta and Newfoundland. Between 1945 and 1950 provincial spending on health nearly quadrupled and, by 1951, it had emerged as the second largest item in provincial budgets (Table 8.2). Further impetus to provincial emphasis on health was provided by the 1957 federal decision to share the costs of provincial hospital insurance programs. Anticipating federal legislation, Ontario enacted hospital insurance in 1955 and the remaining provinces followed suit by 1961.

Almost immediately another related change ensued. The CCF in Saskatchewan enacted comprehensive medical insurance in 1961, as did Social Credit governments in Alberta and British Columbia two years later. Again, anticipating federal assistance, Ontario enacted medical insurance in 1965, the year before federal legislation was adopted. Federal subsidies of up to 60% of provincial costs enticed the remaining provinces to establish comprehensive medical insurance programs by 1971.[10] Together, these changes brought about a dramatic expansion of the role provincial governments play in providing health services to their citizens.

More recently, federal and provincial authorities have initiated efforts to limit the growth of health spending.[11] In 1975, the federal government, alarmed by steady and rapid cost increases in the early 1970s and acting on the assumption that divided federal-provincial responsibility was at least partially responsible, imposed a three-year ceiling on its contribution to health care and tied further expenditures to increases in the gross national product. Discussions followed between appropriate federal and provincial officials and in 1977 new funding arrangements were initiated. Very briefly, the federal government provided a per capita block grant amounting to approximately one-half of its 1975 contributions to the provinces, with provisions for annual escalations based on population and gross national product increases. It was estimated that this block grant would cover approximately 25% of the costs of the most popular health programs.[12] Ottawa also agreed to yield an additional 13.5 percentage points of personal and 1 percentage point of corporate tax revenues to the provinces and to equalize these new revenues in the same way as other income taxes. The understanding was that the yield from these taxes, at a minimum, would equal the value of the block grant. In addition, each province was to receive an unconditional per capita payment of $20 to help support its extended health care services such as home nursing and long-term institutional care for the elderly.

Indications are that the provinces have become more cost conscious and have attempted to impose ceilings on their health expenditures because of these arrangements. Some provinces also have sought greater control over the disposition of their block grants by not complying with certain of the conditions (i.e., that provincial health programs be comprehensive, universally available, portable and that access to health facilities be unencumbered by any financial barriers) under which federal funds for health purposes traditionally have been made available to the provinces. Interestingly, despite the fact that Ottawa initiated the most recent changes because of concern over escalating federal contributions to provincial health programs, the federal contribution as a percentage of total health expenditures actually increased between 1975 and 1980. In part this increase was a consequence of continuing inflation and slow economic growth. These required the federal government to make up the difference between the yield from the additional tax points and the 25% block grant. In 1980-81 the difference amounted to approximately $1 billion and, given the magnitude of this sum, Ottawa may well seek additional changes in the mechanisms for funding health care. Still, any definitive predictions about either the level or conditions of federal and provincial funding for health care in the 1980s would be premature.

Changes in the emphasis accorded other policy areas have taken place more gradually but some of them have been substantial. A good example is the increase in the proportion of provincial spending devoted to education. Propelled at least partially by demand created by the post-World War Two baby boom and the ensuing growth of the school age population, as well as by the tendency of students to remain in school for longer periods of time to acquire higher levels of formal education, per capita spending on education has grown approximately twice as rapidly as overall provincial spending since 1945. Between 1950 and 1977, total provincial increases in real per capita spending on education averaged 945% and, today, education consumes an average of 25 cents of every dollar the provinces spend.

Growth in one sector of a budget usually requires a concomitant reduction in other sectors. Specifically, the rapid expansion of provincial spending on health and education has been achieved largely by proportional reductions in expenditures on transportation. With the completion of the Trans-Canada Highway and basic networks of intraprovincial roads, new highway construction in the provinces became a less pressing concern to provincial officials. More generally, transportation needs traditionally have received lower priorities when additional resources have been required for social policy concerns. Thus, transportation bore the brunt of provincial budget cutting during the Depression and transportation also suffered disproportionately when provincial spending was curtailed to support the 1939-45 war effort. Placing transportation needs on a back burner also has been made easier by the fact that the federal government has jurisdiction over and funds railroad, aviation and related programs.[13] It is not surprising, then, that the emphasis accorded transportation policy over the last 20 years has declined in the face of increases in provincial spending on health and education. What is suprising is the extent of this decline. In absolute terms, real per capita spending on transportation has increased by 150% since 1950. However, the *proportion* of provincial spending on transportation has fallen from a post-war high of 32% in 1948 to less than 10% during the late 1970s.

None of the remaining areas of provincial jurisdiction ever has claimed more than 10% of provincial budgets. Therefore, although very substantial increases have been registered in real per capita spending for activities such as the protection of persons and property, these increases have had relatively little impact on the overall structure of provincial expenditures. For example, despite the concern certain provincial governments recently have shown for securing total control of their natural resources, spending in this area never has exceeded 10% and has declined steadily throughout the post-war period. This decline is attributable in part to the fact that in several resource-rich provinces, Alberta in particular, development largely has been left to private enterprise.[14] Whatever the explanation, less than 5% of provincial budgets currently are devoted to natural resource development: approximately half the proportion expended for this purpose 30 years ago.

During the past decade provincial policy agendas appear to have stabilized. The magnitudes of expenditures in most policy areas have continued to increase but the priorities accorded them, as reflected in the budgetary proportions they enjoy, have remained relatively constant (see Table 8.1). Thus, education and health are firmly established as major policy concerns, together consuming at least two-fifths of all provincial budgets. Despite the fact that expenditures on transportation and welfare have undergone substantial real growth during the decade, they remain secondary concerns. Resource policy, the protection of persons and property and general governmental administration are accorded the lowest priority, consuming, in total, less than 15% of provincial expenditures.

PROVINCIAL VARIATIONS

Constitutional constraints and the lure of federal money have combined to foster a considerable degree of similarity in the policies provincial governments pursue and the priorities they accord them. As noted, health and education currently are the largest items in provincial budgets. The proportion of funds allocated to them ranges from 42% in Prince Edward Island and Saskatchewan to 51% in Ontario. Social welfare expenditures consistently rank third, although allocations for this purpose are steadily increasing in all but the Atlantic provinces.

Everywhere, transportation is accorded less emphasis. Over time the extensive use of federal cost-sharing mechanisms has helped to narrow interprovincial differences in several policy areas. The tendency is perhaps most evident in health, the area in which federal cost-sharing efforts have been greatest. In fact, since 1950, variations in provincial spending in this area have been reduced by more than 50%.[15]

Notwithstanding growing similarities in provincial spending patterns in several areas, certain differences are evident (see Table 8.3). These differences reflect the fact that the provinces vary greatly in the size of their populations, their wealth and the partisan forces operating within them. The western provinces, the historic birthplace of several of Canada's most significant social protest movements and radical third parties such as the Progressives, CCF and Social Credit, traditionally have led the way in health and social welfare reform. The development of health policy in Saskatchewan has been discussed in the previous chapter. With respect to social welfare, Alberta, British Columbia and Manitoba established workmen's compensation programs after World War One; they pioneered the development of mother's allowance programs in the same era; and they were among the first provinces to join the federal old-age pension program during the 1930s.[16] Later, during the 1950s and '60s, when the emphasis accorded welfare generally declined, British Columbia and Manitoba were less affected by the trend. They also were among the first to reemphasize welfare measures by increasing expenditures for these purposes in the early 1970s.

In contrast, Quebec and the Atlantic provinces consistently were "last and least" in the provision of social services. It has been argued that poverty, the weakness of protest movements and programmatic parties, a tradition of patronage politics and the value ascribed to thrift and self-reliance combined to retard the development of progressive health and welfare policies in the latter provinces.[17] Their relative poverty made it difficult for them to take full advantage of federal cost-sharing programs since these required substantial provincial contributions. There was a tendency to view social services as luxury items, not as important as education and transportation programs, both of which presumably contributed more to social and economic development. Still another factor that may explain the relative emphasis the Atlantic provinces have placed on transportation policy is that federal subsidies have provided up to 90% of the costs of some of these programs, but only 50 to 60% of health and welfare costs.

Although a partial exception to this pattern, Newfoundland illustrates the constraints that poverty may impose on ideological or programmatic intent. Elected in 1949 on a platform promising a "social revolution" in the province, Joey Smallwood's Liberal government began by investing heavily in social services.[18] Newfoundland was the only province east of Saskatchewan to develop any form of hospital

TABLE 8.3
**Percentage of Provincial Spending by Major Policy Area
for Selected Intervals, 1950-77**

Province/Year	Policy Area				
	Health	Welfare	Education	Transpor-tation	All Other
Newfoundland					
1950-54	22%	21%	16%	21%	20%
1960-64	21	14	22	22	21
1970-74	19	11	25	12	33
1975-77	19	10	25	10	36
Prince Edward Island					
1950-54	16	10	13	38	23
1960-64	19	9	18	30	24
1970-74	18	10	26	13	33
1975-77	18	10	26	10	36
Nova Scotia					
1950-54	13	12	20	30	25
1960-64	26	8	21	22	23
1970-74	25	9	25	12	29
1975-77	24	9	24	9	34
New Brunswick					
1950-54	12	12	16	30	30
1960-64	25	8	14	27	26
1970-74	21	10	29	11	29
1975-77	20	13	27	11	29
Quebec					
1950-54	16	14	17	26	27
1960-64	21	15	25	16	23
1970-74	25	15	25	10	25
1975-77	24	16	27	8	25
Ontario					
1950-54	16	10	19	28	27
1960-64	26	6	26	20	22
1970-74	29	10	27	9	25
1975-77	27	14	23	7	29
Manitoba					
1950-54	14	12	17	23	34
1960-64	27	10	19	16	28
1970-74	27	12	25	8	28
1975-77	27	17	20	6	30
Saskatchewan					
1950-54	32	11	14	18	25
1960-64	30	9	21	14	26
1970-74	26	12	23	12	27
1975-77	23	13	20	7	37
Alberta					
1950-54	16	10	17	31	26
1960-64	23	9	28	18	22
1970-74	26	12	28	8	26
1975-77	24	10	23	8	35
British Columbia					
1950-54	24	12	15	18	31
1960-64	21	12	20	21	26
1970-74	27	14	20	12	27
1975-77	27	16	18	9	30

Source: Statistics Canada, *Provincial Government Finance: Revenues and Expenditures*,
1950-1978, DBS 68-207.

insurance before 1950. Throughout the '50s it ranked first in the proportion of public funds allocated to social welfare and trailed only Saskatchewan and British Columbia in the proportion of its budgetary expenditures on health. Despite a continued commitment to social services, however, Newfoundland's poverty restricted its ability to participate in federally funded programs. Thus, the government fell behind wealthier provinces when they expanded social services throughout the 1960s and '70s. Smallwood's defeat in 1971 and the election of a Conservative government under Frank Moores contributed further to a trend which has seen Newfoundland fall from first to ninth in the proportion of its budget devoted to health and social welfare.

Because of their size, wealth and distinctive social and political conditions, Ontario and Quebec have moved in somewhat different directions from the above provinces and from one another. Ontario, governed by successive Conservative administrations since 1943, has never played an innovative role in the social service field. It has been quick to respond to federal initiatives, however, and has expanded its social programs whenever the federal government has been willing to share the costs. For example, Ontario's General Welfare Assistance Act of 1958 was adopted to take advantage of the benefits provided by the 1956 Federal Unemployment Assistance Act. The government enacted the Family Benefits Act of 1966 in response to the Canada Assistance Act of the same year and the province's hospital and comprehensive health insurance programs were passed in anticipation of federal cost-sharing schemes.[19] Thus, economic well-being and an ability to anticipate federal initiatives have enabled successive Tory governments to allocate large proportions of their budgets to health and welfare programs. Finally, because of its affluence, its deemphasis of transportation programs after federal subsidies were reduced, and its ability to take advantage of health and welfare contributions from the federal government, Ontario has been able to spend somewhat more of its budget on education than have some other provinces.

Historic differences in the social, economic and political development of Quebec have led that province to adopt a distinctive pattern of priorities. The importance of the Roman Catholic Church and the belief that health and welfare assistance for the needy were church responsibilities forestalled provincial health and welfare innovations and impeded participation in shared-cost health and welfare programs.[20] The Quiet Revolution of the early 1960s at once signalled the willingness of Québécois to have their provincial government intervene more extensively and forcefully in many areas of social life and further contributed to pressures for provincial policy autonomy.[21] As a consequence of the latter, Quebec was the last province to develop programs to take advantage of federal hospital and comprehensive medical insurance subsidies. Moreover, following the federal government's enactment of the Established Programmes Act in 1965, Quebec was the only province to take advantage of the opportunity to "opt out" of federal programs by ceasing to participate in schemes such as unemployment assistance, the Canada Assistance Plan and the Canada Pension Plan.

This is not to say that Quebec has neglected the health and welfare needs of its citizens. Although it was among the last to undertake significant health policy reforms, in the past two decades successive governments have increased the proportion of their budgets devoted to health. Quebec currently occupies a middle position with respect to expenditures in this area. Similarly, despite the lingering view that welfare is a private concern, the province ranks among the leaders in the proportion of public funds spent on welfare.

Although not reflected in provincial spending patterns, education is the policy area where Quebec has been most distinctive and contributed most to policy innovations. Because of the strength of religious institutions in the province and the traditional ties between religion and education, Quebec historically maintained a highly decentralized school system with separate Roman Catholic and Protestant authorities. A major philosophic tenet of the architects of the Quiet Revolution was that education could bring about social changes that were both fundamental and highly desirable. Thus, they initiated a series of changes intended to impose more centralized and secular control over educational policy. In rapid succession, Quebec established its first Ministry of Education in 1964, initiated a comprehensive system of secondary education, provided kindergartens and a system of community colleges and assumed responsibility for universities.[22] In brief, Quebec has moved further and faster in these directions than other provinces and its reforms have established a pattern some elements of which (e.g., community colleges) have been followed in other provinces during the past 15 years.

POLICY RESPONSIVENESS TO PUBLIC NEEDS

Responsiveness to public needs and demands is a critical measure of the representative character of government.[23] An evaluation of provincial political systems as representative democracies requires that we assess the extent to which provincial policies correspond to public needs and demands.[24] As noted above, attention here is restricted to needs. One means of assessing congruence between policies and needs is to compare changing patterns of provincial expenditures with public needs in several policy areas.[25] We focus here on education, health and welfare for two reasons. First, these are the areas in which provincial activity is greatest, and public needs in these areas are critically, indeed, fundamentally important and are widely recognized as such. Second, programs in these areas account for one-half to two-thirds of total provincial spending.

That needs are widely recognized does not imply that they are easily measured. Our measure of needs assumes they can be ascertained by examining the objective conditions of society. Regarding educational needs, for example, the size of the population between the ages of five and 18 indicates the level of need for schools, teaching materials and teachers. Similarly, the number of destitute persons in a province provides an indication of the magnitude of social welfare needs. In health, the incidence of infant mortality reflects a population's need for care for mothers during pregnancy; recidivism rates for alcoholism and drug addiction reflect the level of need for care for alcoholics and drug addicts; and the number of working days lost because of illness reflects the need for health care generally. Several indicators such as the above are used to construct composite measures of the level of needs in each of the health, social welfare and education areas. A "need" score is assigned to each province for every year in each area.[26]

There also are a number of problems involved in measuring political responsiveness, one of the most difficult being to determine the amount of spending in each policy area appropriate to meet existing levels of public needs.[27] Although one might assume that the more a province spends on a problem the better it is responding, this overlooks the holistic character of public policy — that specific policies are interrelated segments of a single system. Since levels of public need almost invariably exceed the limited resources with which governments can respond, increased spending in one area usually necessitates reduced spending in one or more others. Accordingly, provincial governments may *overrespond* to certain needs, and commit such large proportions of available resources that they are forced to *underrespond* in other areas, thereby neglecting needs of equal or potentially greater importance. In the short run, particularly when it appears that intensive efforts may solve a chronic problem, there may be valid reasons for provinces to overrespond to certain needs. In the long run, however, provincial governments are judged responsive to the extent that they distribute available resources in a manner commensurate with public needs in all areas.

Given this perspective, we have measured provincial responsiveness in the areas of education, health and welfare by comparing the proportion of total spending allocated to each with relative needs in that area.[28] Thus, a province responding appropriately to public needs in an area will receive a score of 100%. A score greater than 100% indicates that a government is overresponding, whereas a score of less than 100% indicates it is underresponding. It should be emphasized, however, that this index measures *relative* responsiveness (i.e., the extent to which governments are responding to public needs in one area relative to others). It does not measure the responsiveness of provinces by any absolute standard.

Patterns of Provincial Policy Responsiveness: Figure 8.2 illustrates trends in average responsiveness scores for all provinces in the areas of education, health and welfare for the period 1946-1975. The most notable pattern in these data is the disjunction between education and welfare responsiveness on one hand and health responsiveness on the other. Regarding the former, the dominant pattern during most of the post-war period for both education and welfare is one of gradual decline. Since the provinces overresponded to educational needs during the early post-war years, the decline during the late 1950s brought expenditures and needs closer to equilibrium, and thus increased overall responsiveness. However, education responsiveness declined thereafter. Accordingly, by 1969, provincial expenditures on education were only about 60% of the funds required to meet relative needs. Worse, welfare spending was less than 40% relative to need.

In marked contrast, throughout most of the post-war period provincial spending on health increased at a rate substantially in excess of

FIGURE 8.2   Average Education, Health and Welfare Policy Responsiveness Scores (Expenditures as Percentages of Needs) for All Provinces, 1946–75

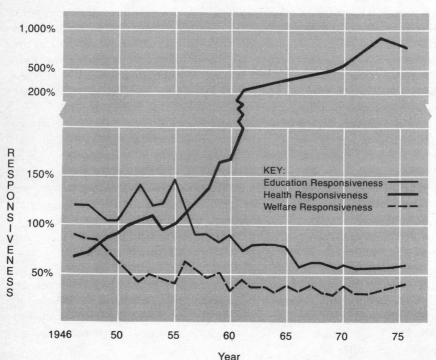

need. In 1945 health was the most neglected of the three policy areas. However, following the lead of Saskatchewan, the enactment of a series of provincial hospital insurance programs during the late 1940s and early '50s brought provincial expenditures and needs into relative equilibrium by 1953. There was a brief pause in the growth of health spending between 1953 and 1956. Then, enactment of federal hospital insurance precipitated the previously described explosion in health spending and substantially upset the balance between health expenditures and needs.

Four additional generalizations about provincial policy responsiveness are in order. First, there are notable differences in the manner in which the western provinces and Ontario, on one hand, and the Atlantic provinces and Quebec, on the other, have responded to the health needs of their respective populations (see Table 8.4, panel A). Consistent with their reputations for leadership in health, governments of the western provinces were first to recognize and respond to health needs. They also were first to overemphasize health. For example, in the early 1970s their expenditures exceeded existing needs by more than 1000%. Indeed, in Alberta health expenditures in 1972 exceeded needs by more than 2000%! Although never a leader in health policy, Ontario's pattern is similar, the principal difference being one of lagging a year or two and several percentage points behind the West. The response of Quebec and the Atlantic provinces to health needs has been more cautious. These provinces did not balance expenditures and needs until federal subsidies were made available in 1958 and only Newfoundland adopted a form of hospital insurance before the federal program was enacted. Constrained by limited resources and insulated from many of the partisan pressures at work in the West, the governments of Quebec and the Atlantic provinces were less tempted by federal subsidies to overspend on health.

Second, differences in provincial welfare responsiveness have been less pronounced. Since 1945 these differences have narrowed as the federal government assumed increasing responsibility for funding most welfare programs (Table 8.4, panel B). Although only Newfoundland has spent approximately as much as public needs require, Prince Edward Island and Quebec generally have made a more adequate response than have Ontario and the western provinces. Although the former provinces have not spent as many dollars on welfare programs as the latter, they have done a better job of *equitably* apportioning their limited resources among competing public needs. By overresponding to health needs, western governments have been forced to underrespond to welfare needs. Saskatchewan has been an exception, ranking among the top five provinces in welfare responsiveness, despite overemphasizing health. However, it has managed this feat by neglecting education, where it ranks last.

TABLE 8.4
Average Policy Responsiveness (Expenditures as a Percentage of Needs) for Five-Year Intervals, 1946-75

Panel A: Health

Province	1946-50	51-55	56-60	61-65	66-70	71-75	Total 1946-75
Newfoundland	80%	81%	92%	155%	246%	352%	167%
Prince Edward Island	72	98	129	161	253	588	217
Nova Scotia	59	76	145	196	347	479	217
New Brunswick	47	81	149	237	326	481	220
Quebec	70	77	96	160	252	347	168
Ontario	56	94	152	234	471	951	326
Manitoba	66	102	163	283	547	777	323
Saskatchewan	121	130	165	321	684	1653	512
Alberta	86	105	155	251	790	1769	526
British Columbia	76	131	177	257	530	847	536

Panel B: Social Welfare

Province	1946-50	51-55	56-60	61-65	66-70	71-75	Total 1946-75
Newfoundland	111	90	113	106	81	51	92
Prince Edward Island	95	63	58	55	62	39	62
Nova Scotia	104	53	34	31	29	31	47
New Brunswick	84	62	53	39	28	36	50
Quebec	101	71	67	46	46	41	62
Ontario	68	29	21	17	19	25	29
Manitoba	86	40	32	28	28	35	42
Saskatchewan	72	65	84	35	30	36	54
Alberta	73	39	29	30	31	35	40
British Columbia	58	30	27	27	29	36	34

Province	1946-50	51-55	56-60	61-65	66-70	71-75	Total 1946-75
Newfoundland	48	53	49	51	46	58	51
Prince Edward Island	65	77	65	67	52	71	66
Nova Scotia	79	116	92	76	57	54	79
New Brunswick	74	93	66	48	72	67	70
Quebec	79	97	86	81	63	60	78
Ontario	184	283	144	118	80	64	146
Manitoba	91	171	95	75	59	55	91
Saskatchewan	50	45	45	52	49	47	48
Alberta	79	109	102	94	56	52	82
British Columbia	322	273	134	110	65	47	158

TABLE 8.5

Index of Overall Political Responsiveness (and Rankings)
for Five-Year Intervals, 1946-75

Province	1946-50	1951-55	1956-60	1961-65	1966-70	1971-75
Newfoundland	28(6)	25(4)	24(2)	37(1)	73(1)	115(1)
Prince Edward Island	23(5)	21(2)	35(3)	46(3)	79(3)	196(5)
Nova Scotia	22(4)	29(6)	40(4)	63(4)	120(5)	165(4)
New Brunswick	32(7)	21(2)	43(5)	83(8)	109(4)	159(3)
Quebec	17(1)	18(1)	17(1)	44(2)	78(2)	157(2)
Ontario	53(9)	87(9)	58(9)	78(6)	157(6)	321(8)
Manitoba	19(2)	44(8)	45(7)	93(9)	187(8)	262(6)
Saskatchewan	33(8)	40(7)	45(7)	111(10)	235(9)	557(9)
Alberta	21(3)	25(4)	43(5)	76(5)	277(10)	594(10)
British Columbia	96(10)	91(10)	61(10)	80(7)	179(7)	288(7)

Third, the greatest discrepancies in policy responsiveness are evident in education (Table 8.4, panel C). Ontario and the western provinces (other than Saskatchewan) overresponded and the eastern provinces underresponded to educational needs at the beginning of the post-war period. After that, responsiveness in the former declined in direct proportion to their initial overemphasis. For example, provinces such as British Columbia and Ontario, in which expenditures exceeded needs by 200-300% in the 1940s, experienced the most precipitous decline. The pattern is somewhat different but no more salutary in Saskatchewan. Its government neglected educational needs in the 1940s and has continued to do so.

Fourth, by summing the extent of provincial over- and underresponsiveness to public needs across the different policy areas, we can rank the provinces on an overall index of political responsiveness. For example, if during the years 1966-70, Saskatchewan had overresponded to health needs by 100 points and underresponded to educational and welfare needs by 50 and 10 points respectively, its score on the overall index would be 160 points (100 + 50 + 10). In contrast, if during the same period the government of Newfoundland had been *perfectly* responsive to needs in all three areas its score would be 0 (0 + 0 + 0). Newfoundland's lower score would show that it ranks higher on overall responsiveness than does Saskatchewan. Scores such as the above and rankings of the provinces based on them for six five-year periods between 1945 and 1975 are displayed in Table 8.5. Table 8.6 presents responsiveness scores and a ranking of the provinces for the entire 30-year period.

Since the mid-1950s all provinces have suffered substantial reductions in overall responsiveness. Nevertheless, important differences exist with respect to both the extent and sharpness of this decline. The greatest distortions have occurred in the provinces and periods in which health concerns dominated the political agenda. As the provinces most insulated from federal pressures, Newfoundland (by virtue of its poverty) and Quebec (by insisting on its autonomy) have responded most equitably to competing public needs and rank first and second respectively in overall responsiveness (Table 8.6). The other Atlantic provinces' responses to health needs also were modest and they rank third (Prince Edward Island), fourth (Nova Scotia) and fifth (New Brunswick) in overall responsiveness. They are followed by Manitoba, whose initial, modest response to health needs was offset by an overemphasis on education. Because of their initial overresponse to education, their more recent overresponse to health, and their consistent neglect of social welfare, Ontario, British Columbia and Alberta suffered early and severe distortions and rank behind Manitoba, seventh, eighth and ninth respectively. Saskatchewan, the leader in health spending, stands at the bottom of the rankings. It consistently has underresponded to educational needs in order to maximize efforts in the health field.

When considering this ordering of the provinces, it must be remembered that the scores are *relative*. To observe that Newfoundland and Quebec have been more responsive overall than Ontario and British Columbia is not to say that the former either have spent more money or provided higher quality services to their citizens during the past 35 years than the latter. Rather, given their available resources, they have allocated these more rationally in the sense that their expenditures in each policy area have been more congruent with public needs therein.

EXPLAINING PROVINCIAL POLICY RESPONSIVENESS

Variations in provincial policy responsiveness are products of many factors. These include the social, economic and political environments in which provincial policies are made. An especially powerful influence in the political environments of the provinces is the omnipresent federal government with its transfer payments, conditional and block grants, and other fiscal and monetary instruments of influence and, at times, control. However, the relative affluence of provinces, the extent of their industrial bases, the magnitude and value of their natural resources, and the size and occupational structures of their populations are among economic and social factors that condition their ability to respond to federal initiatives and the needs and demands of their citizens.[29] In the political realm, cultural factors such as levels of trust, efficacy and interest, the direction and strength of partisan attachments, the character of beliefs about the appropriate role of government in social and

TABLE 8.6
Index of Overall Political Responsiveness
and Rankings of Provinces for the
Entire 1946–75 Period

Province	Responsiveness Index Score	Ranking of Province
Newfoundland	41	1
Quebec	43	2
Prince Edward Island	63	3
Nova Scotia	64	4
New Brunswick	67	5
Manitoba	97	6
Ontario	114	7
British Columbia	120	8
Alberta	168	9
Saskatchewan	170	10

economic life as well as orientations toward provincial and federal politics are important. Other relevant forces in the political environment include the strength of particular political parties and interest groups, the intensity of interparty electoral competition and the extent and nature of political participation.[30] In the Canadian context, these have been cited as factors conducive to the generation and implementation of policies with a pronounced "middle-class bias."

It also is argued that institutional factors are associated with policy responsiveness.[31] Although, as observed in Chapter 6, the formal political institutions of provinces are fundamentally similar, substantial differences in detail characterize their day-to-day operation. The size of provincial legislative assemblies varies greatly, as does the length of their sessions, the number and vitality of their committees and the quantity and quality of staff available to assist them. Also, to some extent relationships among first ministers and cabinet colleagues differ, as does the degree of control cabinet is able to exercise over bureaucratic subordinates. Again, the size of bureaucracies and the skills of bureaucratic officials differ greatly, as do relationships among bureaucrats, legislators, interest group representatives and other major political actors.

Other institutional factors may influence policy responsiveness as well. Perhaps one of the most important is the electoral system. As shown in Chapter 4, provincial electoral systems distort the translation of votes into legislative seats. How this occurs depends on the larger matrix of political forces at work in a province. For example, a party receiving 40% of the votes cast in a province where several parties offer candidates may be able to form a majority government, whereas in another, this level of popular support may result in a party being turned out of office. In short, electoral systems and the magnitude and distribution of partisan forces interact to influence the outcome of provincial elections and thereby affect the likelihood that particular parties will be able to gain office, form a majority government and, as a consequence of this, the length of time a party is likely to hold power. Finally, it has been contended that the interaction of environmental with institutional factors — particularly economic prosperity and a climate of increasing public expectations for governmental services in conjunction with interest group pressures and the internal dynamics of bureaucracy — combine to produce what has been termed policy momentum, a phenomenon to be discussed below. For now, let us consider how these several influences on policy have affected the responsiveness of the provinces in the fields of health, education and welfare.

As observed in Chapter 7, the revolution in health policy which began in Saskatchewan in 1946 largely was the product of the election two years earlier of a social democratic (CCF) government and the existence of a favourable climate of public and interest group opinion.

Partisan considerations also help explain the early emphasis given health in British Columbia, where the growing strength of the CCF during the 1940s induced a Liberal-Conservative coalition government to follow the Saskatchewan model in an attempt to stem the "socialist tide."[32]

Where partisan pressures have been less compelling, federal policies and the nature of the federal system itself have played a major role. Although the BNAA assigns the provinces jurisdiction over most categories of health policy, in practice the federal and provincial governments have shared responsibility. By enabling both levels of government to enjoy a dollar's worth of health benefits for every 50 cents either has had to spend on health, the division of responsibility encouraged each to invest heavily in order to maximize benefits received from limited resources. Additionally, the division of responsibility is said to have tempted both levels of government to claim credit for the benefits health programs produced and to assign blame for their costs to the other government. The argument is that the *de facto* division of authority for health created a situation in which neither level of government was held accountable for the distortions in provincial policy priorities produced by an overemphasis on health programs, whereas both were able to accumulate political capital from the benefits and general popularity of these programs. Consistent with this argument, the decline, since 1977, in the tendency of provincial governments to overrespond to health needs parallels the federal government's decision to transfer to the provinces much of its authority for health, thereby centralizing responsibility for this policy area at the provincial level and dramatizing for provincial authorities the fact that "a dollar spent [on health] is now just that and health spending must be viewed in the context of a consolidated budget."[33]

The varying impact of federal initiatives also is manifested in the education field. Education is an area of provincial responsibility, but one in which the federal government has demonstrated relatively less interest. Federal programs to aid post-secondary education and provide vocational training were established in the 1950s and '60s, but federal authorities played a relatively minor role in influencing the direction of these programs, despite the fact that they were and are expensive and have required substantial federal contributions.[34] Prior to 1977, the federal government provided block grants to the provinces equal to 50% of the operating costs of their post-secondary educational institutions. These funds were derived from 4.5 personal income tax points yielded to the provinces, plus cash payments where tax-derived revenues did not cover 50% of their operating costs. After 1977, an arrangement was entered into under which the provinces retain the yield from the 4.5 personal income tax points, and also receive a per capita grant tied to increases in the gross national product. At a minimum the latter grant must be equal to the value of the national average cash grant made to the provinces in 1975-76, under the previous funding formula.

In general, spending on education has not kept pace with spending on health. Moreover, because of the increase in the number of persons of school age and a growing tendency to remain in school until graduation, educational needs have increased and have more than offset increases in provincial spending, thus producing declining levels of educational responsiveness. Since education, especially post-secondary education, is such an expensive enterprise, it is not unexpected that responsiveness has been higher in affluent provinces such as Ontario and British Columbia than in poorer ones such as Newfoundland. Further, since concern about the content and level of demand for educational programs tends to be greater among citizens of higher socioeconomic status, variations in partisan support may influence educational responsiveness. Persons of higher socioeconomic status tend to support the candidates of more conservative parties. Perhaps not surprisingly, therefore, education has prospered most (or suffered least) in provinces which have had Conservative or (in the case of Alberta and British Columbia) Social Credit governments.

Welfare is a policy area in which the impact of partisan forces has been less obvious. Historically, the federal government assumed primary responsibility in this field. Not only has Ottawa paid the largest share of welfare costs, most federal spending has been in the form of direct assistance to individuals. In contrast to shared-cost programs (which have encouraged provincial spending), direct assistance seemingly encouraged the provinces to reduce their level of spending and thus to underrespond to public needs in the welfare area. Although the federal government began to utilize shared-cost welfare programs more often during the late 1960s and early '70s and continues to employ them today, these have not stimulated the same degree of provincial response as did earlier and similarly structured programs in health. We can only speculate why this should be the case, but it is plausible that provincial reactions can be explained in part by the different client groups served by health and welfare programs. Health problems, like the weather, affect the poor and not-so-poor, the powerful and the not-so-powerful alike and health care can be *extremely* expensive — constituting a serious financial threat to all but the very rich. In contrast, welfare assistance is needed by comparatively small and politically impotent groups in the population (e.g., the poor, the handicapped). Thus, from the perspective of narrow self-interest, welfare programs will be less attractive to provincial officials concerned with their political popularity than will be health programs that have near universal appeal.

Explanations of the determinants of public policy such as the above have considerable currency in the literature on provincial politics. Unfortunately, they seldom have been accompanied by rigorous empirical analysis, because, until recently, investigators have lacked the required data and statistical tools to do so. However, it is now possible to conduct such an analysis.[35] The results reveal that differences in the composition of provincial governments have been associated with changing patterns of responsiveness in all three policy areas. More specifically, increases in health responsiveness (or overresponsiveness) have been closely tied to the strength of the CCF/NDP party. Moreover, despite the belief of some observers that programmatic differences between the Liberal and Conservative parties are inconsequential,[36] welfare spending relative to needs has been greatest in those provinces and time periods in which the Liberal party has been strongest, whereas the emphasis on educational spending has been most pronounced in provinces and times in which Conservative and Social Credit parties have been strong.

Less important generally than partisan composition, several institutional characteristics of provincial governments are related to differences in their responsiveness. The most important of these are the professionalism of their legislative assemblies, the size of constituencies, the level of competition among parties in legislative assemblies and the majority or minority status of governing parties. Finally, variations in policy responsiveness are attributable as well to environmental factors. The most important of these are the strength of electoral support for various parties, voter turnout in elections and the relative economic affluence of provinces. On the whole, however, their impact is less marked than the first category of variables, the partisan composition of provincial governments.

SUMMARY: PROVINCIAL POLICY RESPONSIVENESS

Since 1945 the size and complexity of provincial governments have increased enormously as has the scope of their activities. Provincial governments currently are among the country's largest employers; they have broad powers that touch almost every aspect of our lives; and their expenditures consume more than 20% of the gross national product. Paradoxically, growth in the size and power of provincial governments during the post-war era has been accompanied by declines in the overall levels of their responsiveness to public needs. The strength and consistency of policy response patterns strongly suggest that the responsiveness of provincial governments has declined at an accelerating rate since the early 1950s and only recently has begun to recover. The disproportionate emphasis given health needs throughout most of the period bears principal responsibility for the general decline in overall policy responsiveness.

Although it is difficult to fully explain why health programs prospered at the expense of their educational and welfare counterparts, our investigation indicates that incentives provided by the federal government have played an important part. Federal money helped fuel the explosion in health in the mid-1950s and the division of responsibility between Ottawa and the provinces made it easier for both to avoid accounting to the public for any liabilities, while claiming credit for any and all benefits. Having a CCF/NDP government or even a large contingent of MLAs from this party also contributes to an emphasis on health programs at the expense of others such as those in the educational field. The latter have fared much better than welfare programs, however, especially in provinces where the Conservative or Social Credit parties are powerful political forces. It can be argued that the preferences of these parties reflect a more general middle-class bias in favour of education and health over welfare.

The possibility that a middle-class bias has affected policy responsiveness more generally is consistent with three well-known explanations of the weakness of class politics in Canada. The first is that the electorate rarely has been offered meaningful choices among policies rooted in distinctive party ideologies. The claim is that there always has been considerable overlap between the positions of the Liberal and Conservative parties on major policy issues.[37] Further, even if their ideologies remain distinguishable from those of the two older parties, it is frequently contended that for more than a quarter century both the CCF/NDP and Social Credit have been moving toward the centre of the ideological continuum in response to pressures to broaden their political support in the middle class. A closely related explanation for the middle-class tenor of Canadian politics also assigns responsibility to political elites. According to this explanation, upper and upper-middle class elites periodically have played on public fears of political instability by invoking the spectre of national disintegration to justify the lack of class-based and conflictual politics. The resulting weakness of class politics has enabled the elites both to maintain their hegemony and to avoid making substantial policy concessions to economically disadvantaged segments of the public.[38] A third explanation is that although social class has both an objective and subjective reality in Canada, seldom have large numbers of working class voters concluded that their class positions and interests can be furthered through political action.[39] Occasionally, however, parties articulating relatively distinct ideological positions have operated in a political environment in which levels of class consciousness have been heightened. Perhaps the most salient examples of this conjunction were Saskatchewan in the mid-1940s and British Columbia in the early 1970s. In both instances, a CCF/NDP government committed to major policy innovation was swept into power. The point remains, however, that such occurrences have been rare.

Finally, another type of explanation of the failure of provincial governments to be more responsive involves the notion of "policy momentum." The basic patterns of provincial expenditures on health, education and welfare were established shortly after World War Two. These were appropriate for the structure of needs at the time and increased the overall level of governmental responsiveness so that a reasonable balance between expenditures and needs was struck about 1950. Health programs largely were successful in achieving their goals. Thus, public need in this area declined, but expenditures on health not only were maintained, but increased continually. In contrast, welfare needs remained relatively constant and educational needs increased markedly because of the post-war baby boom and the ensuing growth in the school age population. Despite these needs, the pattern of provincial expenditures, once established, proved highly resistant to change.

The momentum sustaining existing patterns in the face of unmet needs is at least partially a consequence of the strength of the patron-client networks that developed in response to existing policies. Groups benefitting from these policies naturally wished to see them continue and bureaucrats administering them were only too happy to oblige! Mutual self-interest generated strong support for the status quo, or, more accurately, for more of the same.[40] Further, in the buoyant economic climate of the 1950s and '60s, relatively little concern was expressed about the cost of ongoing programs. Groups not benefitting directly from them could be convinced that their interests were not adversely affected by the programs and that new policy initiatives would be forthcoming shortly to provide the benefits they sought. In the 1970s and '80s, in an economic environment increasingly plagued by recurring inflation, unemployment and low productivity, the assumption of "more for all" has been severely challenged and governmental expenditures on costly programs have become matters of increasing concern. The momentum that carried health policy expenditures to seemingly ever-higher levels finally has halted. As a consequence, public needs in other policy areas and expenditures for them may be brought into better balance and total governmental responsiveness may actually increase in the near future.

NOTES

1. This is not to say there are no data on provincial differences in policy preferences. See, for example, Richard Simeon and Donald E. Blake, "Regional Preferences: Citizens' Views of Public Policy," in David J. Elkins and Richard Simeon, eds. *Small Worlds* (Toronto: Methuen, 1980), ch. 3.
2. Foremost among the numerous studies which catalog the growth of government in Canada are: Richard Bird, *The Growth of Government Spending in Canada* (Ottawa: Canadian Tax Foundation, 1970); and Bird, *The Growth of Public Employment in Canada* (Montreal: Institute for Research on Public Policy, 1979).

256 *Representative Democracy in the Canadian Provinces*

3. Changing attitudes regarding governmental responsibility for social welfare are the classic example. See Marsha A. Chandler and William M. Chandler, *Public Policy and Provincial Politics* (Toronto: McGraw-Hill Ryerson, 1979), pp. 180–182.

4. Robert Presthus, *Elites in the Policy Process* (London: Cambridge University Press, 1975), pp. 271–72.

5. For example, the growth of government in Canada has proceeded at approximately the same rate as in Great Britain, at a somewhat faster pace than in the United States, France, West Germany and Japan, but at a slower rate than in Sweden or other Northern European nations. David R. Cameron, "The Expansion of the Public Economy: A Comparative Analysis" *American Political Science Review* 72 (1978), pp. 1243–1261.

6. These figures include teachers, hospital and municipal employees. They are derived from J.E. Hodgetts and O.P. Dwivedi, *Provincial Governments as Employers* (Montreal: McGill-Queen's University Press, 1975), pp. 7, 13, 190.

7. An introduction to government regulation is G. Bruce Doern, "The Concept of Regulation and Regulatory Reform" in G. Bruce Doern and Seymour V. Wilson, eds., *Issues in Canadian Public Policy* (Toronto: Macmillan, 1975), pp. 8–35.

8. It is possible, of course, that our figures demonstrating the modest growth in the *number* of new regulations issued annually may mask substantial increases in the *scope* and *intensity* of regulation. Unfortunately, systematic evidence regarding the latter is unavailable for either the federal or provincial governments.

9. Percentages are based on data from M.C. Urquhart and K.A.H. Buckley, eds., *Historical Statistics of Canada* (Toronto: Macmillan, 1965), Table G318–329, p. 215.

10. On the history of the development of Canada's hospital and medical insurance system see Malcolm G. Taylor, *Health Insurance and Canadian Public Policy* (Montreal: McGill-Queen's University Press, 1978).

11. On recent developments in federal–provincial approaches to health policy see Richard Van Loon and David Falcone, "Canadian Public Attitudes and Intergovernmental Shifts in the Responsibility for Health Policy: Paying the Piper Without Calling the Tune," in Allan Kornberg and Harold D. Clarke, eds., *Political Support in Canada: The Crisis Years* (Durham, N.C.: Duke University Press, 1982), ch. 8.

12. *Ibid.*

13. For a brief introduction to Canadian transportation policy see J. Baldwin, "The Evolution of Transportation Policy in Canada," *Canadian Public Administration* 20 (1977), pp. 600–631.

14. An excellent discussion of the nature, causes, and consequences of Alberta's private enterprise approach to natural resource development is provided in John Richards and Larry Pratt, *Prairie Capitalism: Power and Influence in the Canadian West* (Toronto: McClelland and Stewart, 1979). For an interesting case study of the evolution of natural resource policy in one province see H.V. Nelles, *The Politics of Development: Forest, Mines, and Hydro Electric Power in Ontario, 1839–1951* (Toronto: Macmillan, 1975).

15. Richard Simeon and Robert Miller, "Regional Variations in Public Policy," in D.J. Elkins and R. Simeon, eds., *Small Worlds*, p. 255.

16. For a review of early provincial efforts in welfare see Henry Cassidy, *Public Health and Welfare Reorganization* (Toronto: Ryerson, 1955). See also the summary of the structure and development of provincial social development policies in Chandler and Chandler, *Public Policy and Provincial Politics*, pp. 178–252.

17. For elaboration of these points see David J. Bellamy, "The Atlantic Provinces" in Bellamy, Jon H. Pammett, and Donald C. Rowat, eds., *The Provincial Political Systems: Comparative Essays* (Toronto: Methuen, 1976), ch. 1. See also the sketches of the Atlantic provinces' political cultures in Martin Robin, ed., *Canadian Provincial Politics*, 1st ed. (Scarborough: Prentice-Hall, 1972).

18. Susan McCorquodale, "Newfoundland: The Only Living Father's Realm," in Robin, ed., *Canadian Provincial Politics*, p. 152.

19. A good illustration of Ontario's anticipation of a federal cost-sharing program can be seen in the development of its hospital insurance program which is described in Malcolm G. Taylor, *Health Insurance and Canadian Public Policy.*

20. Kenneth McRoberts and Dale Posgate, *Quebec: Social Change and Political Crisis*, revised ed. (Toronto: McClelland and Stewart, 1980), ch. 5.

21. *Ibid.*, ch. 6.
22. For a description of the structure of Quebec's educational system, see *The Review of Education Policies in Canada: Quebec*, (Toronto: Council of Ministries of Education, 1975).
23. The classic statement of this thesis is Hanna F. Pitkin, *The Concept of Representation* (Berkeley: University of California Press, 1967), pp. 209-250. See ch. 1, *supra.*, pp. 2-8.
24. Although formal and descriptive views of representation are valuable principally as means to ensure the responsiveness of government, certain political structures and processes also have intrinsic value for democratic government. Democratic theorists believe that widespread opportunities for citizen participation are important not only as means to hold government accountable, but also as necessary conditions for proper civic education and individual self-development. See William Mishler, *Political Participation in Canada: Prospects for Democratic Citizenship* (Toronto: Macmillan, 1979), ch. 1.
25. The rationale for restricting our analysis to public needs is discussed in the introduction to this chapter. In further limiting our analysis to provincial expenditures we recognize, as well, that government spending is only one dimension of public policy. Initially, we employed several indicators of policy in our analysis (including measures of legislation). However, because the different measures were highly related (in most cases the correlations exceeded .90), we have reported only the expenditure-based data.
26. Economies of space require that our discussion of the assumptions and limitations of our approach to measuring needs and of the specific procedures employed be kept both simple and brief. Suffice to say that multiple indicators of public needs in each of the three areas were subjected to factor analysis — a technique which isolates the common variation in a large set of interrelated measures and generates a single, weighted, composite measure of the relative position of provincial needs in each policy area for each of the 30 years covered by our analysis. More detailed discussions of these procedures are available in William Mishler and David Campbell, "The Healthy State: Legislative Responsiveness to Public Health Care Needs in Canada, 1920–1970," *Comparative Politics* 10 (1978), pp. 579–597; and William Mishler and Allan Kornberg, "Evaluating Legislative Performance in Canada: Preliminary Tests of a General Theory," paper presented at the International Political Science Association Meeting, Moscow, USSR, August, 1979. A very readable explanation of factor analysis is provided in R.J. Rummel "Understanding Factor Analysis," *Journal of Conflict Resolution* 2(1967), pp. 555-580.
27. These problems are discussed in Mishler and Campbell, "The Healthy State," and Mishler and Kornberg, "Evaluating Legislative Performance."
28. Expressed symbolically, for example, health policy responsiveness was defined by the equation:

$$Rh = (Eh/Et)/(Nh/Nt) * 100$$

Where: Rh = Health Policy Responsiveness
Eh = Health Policy Expenditures
Et = Total Spending on Health, Education and Welfare
Nh = Health Care Needs
Nt = Total Needs in Health, Education and Welfare.

Total expenditures were measured simply as the sum of gross provincial spending across the three areas. Similarly, a composite measure of total needs was constructed by adding provincial scores on three policy need variables that were constructed from factor analyses of multiple indicators of needs in each area. Because the individual need measures have standard, normal distributions (i.e., $\bar{x}$ = 0, sd = 1.0) the ratio of policy specific to total needs provides a standardized measure of the *relative* importance of each area by province and over time.
29. The importance of economic context in the policy process is well established. See, in particular, Thomas Dye, *Politics, Economics, and the Public* (Chicago: Rand McNally, 1966), *passim*; Richard I. Hofferbert, "The Relationship between Public Policy and Some Structural and Enivronmental Variables in the American States," *American Political Science Review*, 60 (1966), pp. 73–82; and in Canada, Allan

Kornberg, David Falcone, and William Mishler, *Legislatures and Societal Change: The Case of Canada*, Sage Research Papers in the Social Sciences (Beverly Hills: Sage Publications, 1973); and David Falcone and William Mishler, "Legislative Determinants of Health Policy in Canada," *Journal of Politics* 39 (1977), pp. 355–367. Regarding the social context of the policy process see Karl Deutsch, "Social Mobilization and Political Development," *American Political Science Review* 55 (1961), pp. 593–615; B. Guy Peters, "Social Change, Political Change and Public Policy: A Test of a Model," in Richard Rose, ed., *The Dynamics of Public Policy* (London: Sage Publications, Ltd., 1976), pp. 113–156; and Kornberg, Falcone and Mishler, *Legislatures and Societal Change*, pp. 15–19.

30. The classic statement of these relationships is V.O. Key, *Southern Politics in State and Nation* (New York: Alfred Knopf, 1951). See also, Jack L. Walker, "The Diffusion of Innovations Among American States," *American Political Science Review*, 63 (1969), pp. 880–899; Sidney Verba and Norman H. Nie, *Participation in America* (New York: Harper and Row, 1976); William Mishler, *Political Participation in Canada*, pp. 132–152; and William Mishler and David Campbell, "The Healthy State," pp. 579–597.

31. John Grumm, *A Paradigm for the Comparative Analysis of Legislative Systems*, Sage Research Papers in Comparative Politics, vol. 2, series No. 01-018 (Beverley Hills: Sage Publications, 1971), pp. 28–37; Edward Carmines, "The Mediating Influence of State Legislatures on the Linkage between Interparty Competition and Welfare Policies," *American Political Science Review* 68 (1975), pp. 1118–1125; and Mishler and Campbell, "The Healthy State," pp. 579–597.

32. Martin Robin, "British Columbia: The Politics of Class Conflict," in Robin, ed., *Canadian Provincial Politics*, p. 51.

33. Van Loon and Falcone, "Canadian Public Attitudes."

34. Simeon and Miller, "Regional Variations," p. 261.

35. The discussion that follows is a simplification of a methodologically more sophisticated analysis previously reported in Mishler and Kornberg, "Evaluating Legislative Performance."

36. For a brief review of the debate regarding ideological differences between Canadian parties see Harold D. Clarke, "The Ideological Self-Perceptions of Provincial Legislators," *Canadian Journal of Political Science* 11(1978), pp. 617–35.

37. A classic statement of this argument is John Porter, *The Vertical Mosaic* (Toronto: University of Toronto Press, 1965), ch. 13.

38. Porter, ch. 13. A recent exposition of the argument is M. Janine Brodie and Jane Jenson, *Crisis, Challenge & Change* (Toronto: Methuen, 1980), ch. 1.

39. For example, the reader will recall the data in Ch. 3 showing that large majorities of citizens in all classes in every province judged that differences in economic well-being were products of natural inequalities in character and ability.

40. Noel puts the argument succinctly: "Bureaucrat-patrons and bureaucrat-brokers tend to be concerned above all with system maintenance — which in practice amounts to the maintenance of their own security, affluence, power and privileges." S.J.R. Noel, "Leadership and Clientelism," in Bellamy *et al.*, eds., *The Provincial Political Systems*, p. 209.

FOR FURTHER READING

Bird, Richard. *The Growth of Government Spending in Canada*. Toronto: The Canadian Tax Foundation, 1970. The definitive, although now somewhat dated, description and analysis of the growth of public spending by all levels of Canadian government.

Butler, Dan and Bruce D. Mcnaughton. "Public Sector Growth in Canada: Issues, Explanations and Implications," *Canadian Politics in the 1980's*, eds. Michael S. Whittington and Glen Williams. Toronto: Methuen, 1981, pp. 84–107. A lucid discussion of the growth of government in Canada, this essay provides an excellent summary of some of the prevailing socioeconomic, political and organizational explanations of the growth of government.

Doern, G. Bruce. "The Concept of Regulation," *Issues in Canadian Public Policy*, eds. G. Bruce Doern and V. Seymour Wilson. Toronto: The Macmillan Company of Canada, Ltd., 1974, pp. 8–35. An overview of the "other half" of government activity, this essay examines the nature and dynamics of the regulatory functions of Canadian governments.

Mishler, William and David Campbell. "The Healthy State: Legislative Responsiveness to Public Health Care Needs in Canada, 1920–1970," *Comparative Politics* 10 (1978) pp. 579–597. An empirical examination of the determinants of provincial responsiveness to public health care needs, this study elaborates the underlying rationale for the measure of policy responsiveness used in this volume.

Simeon, Richard, and Robert Miller. "Regional Variations in Public Policy," in *Small Worlds*, eds. David J. Elkins and Richard Simeon. Toronto: Methuen, 1980, pp. 242–284. A detailed and methodologically sophisticated analysis of some of the social, economic, and political determinants of provincial spending in several policy domains.

9
Representative Democracy Reconsidered

We can still have a modern, viable theory of democracy which retains the notion of participation at its heart.

CAROLE PATEMAN,
Participation and Democratic Theory

REPRISE

It is doubtful if any real-world political system merits the designation "representative democracy." Indeed, only a small minority of the world's political systems even roughly approximate the model of representative democracy set forth in this volume and for very good reason. As noted in Chapter 3, such political systems rest upon particular configurations of economic, social and cultural conditions and constellations of institutions and processes not present or present to only a very limited extent in most countries. Throughout this book it has been argued that the provincial political systems are among the minority that have travelled *some* distance along the road to being representative democracies. At least part of the reason they have been able to do so is because in varying degrees they have been endowed with or have achieved many of the prerequisites for the establishment and maintenance of such a political order.

With respect to the social and economic bases of democracy, data were presented in Chapter 3 indicating that Canada, currently a country of some 24 million people, is one of the most industrialized, urbanized and affluent members of the international community. Canadians also are among the best-educated people in the world. Millions have graduated from secondary school and approximately one person in 10 has attended a college or university. Significant proportions of the population are members of the several professions or executives or proprietors of businesses. Millions of others pursue a variety of well-compensated blue- and white-collar occupations. Regarding political culture, large majorities of persons in all provinces have positive, if divided, political loyalties. Québécois excepted, most Canadians give very strong support to both the federal and their provincial political communities. Also, many citizens in all provinces combine reasonably high levels of social trust with positive views of the role of the state and what it can do to facilitate their general life satisfaction and, more specifically, their economic well-being. In terms of their political institutions, in every province citizens have the opportunity to vote for candidates for parliament, provincial legislatures and municipal councils. Millions regularly do so. At both the federal and provincial levels, large bureaucracies staffed by extremely well-educated public servants administer and independent judiciaries adjudicate the myriad rules and regulations of government. At both levels of the federal system there are political party organizations and interest groups in which people can participate to have their needs and interests brought to the attention of public decision-makers. Finally, occupants of and contenders for public elective offices long ago accepted the rules of the democratic political game. They abide by the results of elections, executive powers pass peacefully from one group of political actors to another and, with singularly rare exceptions, neither aspirants for various public offices nor current incumbents employ extra-constitutional means to achieve or maintain these positions.

In comparative perspective then, it is likely that Canada as a whole and each of the provinces more closely approximate the model of representative democracy than do a large majority of the other political systems in the world. Still, there are noteworthy differences in the degree to which the provinces exhibit some of the preconditions for representative democracy. Consider, for example, interprovincial differences in so fundamental a precondition of democracy as wealth. In the late 1970s Ontario alone contributed more than six times as large a proportion of the gross domestic product as the four Atlantic provinces combined. The per capita value of Alberta's gross provincial product was more than two and one-half times as great as Prince Edward Island's and per capita personal income rose sharply as one moved from Newfoundland westward to British Columbia. All in all, an examination of a variety of economic indicators reveals that there are three relatively distinct groups of provinces: the affluent (Alberta, Ontario and British Columbia); the moderately well-to-do (Quebec, Manitoba and, most recently, Saskatchewan); and the hard-pressed (New Brunswick, Nova Scotia, Prince Edward Island and Newfoundland).

The cultural environments in which provincial political systems operate also differ but the pattern of these differences is more complex and their extent should not be exaggerated. Consider, for example, the manner in which two of the most important psychological dimensions of political culture, trust in governmental elites and political efficacy, are distributed. In every province the level of the former seems higher than the latter, but the significance of the distribution of trust is more difficult to interpret. On the one hand, trust is reasonably high everywhere and some two-thirds of the populations of virtually every province believe that governmental officials are intelligent, honest and generally can be trusted to do what is right. On the other hand, similar proportions in every province feel that these same governmental officials waste a great deal of money, and people in every province frequently are not very complimentary in their evaluations of elected officials. In particular, they judge them to be poor managers of the economy. Consider, also, the findings that people in every province expect a great deal from governments, want them to do more of practically everything, but, at the same time, judge elected officials are unresponsive to their needs and demands and that they (the people) are incapable of doing much about this condition. Indeed, although provincial differences in political efficacy are discernible, the major determinant of efficacy clearly is not province of residence, but rather socioeconomic status.

The provinces also are characterized by limited variations in their underlying social cleavage structures. In his landmark study of social class and power, John Porter argued that Canadian society in the 1950s was marked by significant reinforcing cleavages.[1] This was especially the case in Quebec, where patterns of ethnicity, language, religion and socioeconomic status were such that Francophone Catholics tended disproportionately to be low-income, blue- and white-collar workers, whereas English-speaking Protestants of Anglo-Celtic origins pre-dominated in the professional and business classes. Porter maintained that these reinforcing cleavages not only affected the distribution of power among various social groups, they also influenced the potential for social conflict and political instability. Although Quebec and other provinces are now considerably different from the societies of the '50s described by Porter, some cleavages still strongly reinforce one another. In Quebec, for example, religion, language and ethnicity reinforce one another, but religion and language now tend to crosscut socioeconomic status divisions. That is, most Francophones still are Roman Catholic whereas most Anglophones are Protestant. However, no longer are Francophones disproportionately confined to lower status, poorly-paid occupations while Anglophones dominate the upper status, high in-come positions. On average, ethnicity, language, religious affiliation and socioeconomic status reinforce one another most strongly in New Brunswick and Prince Edward Island and least strongly in Alberta. However, provincial differences in the extent to which societal cleavages reinforce one another are not great. Moreover, the inferences to be drawn from these cleavage patterns for representative democracy are not clear. One might be that in every province there is enough crosscutting to provide a firm social base for representative democracy. In contrast, however, it may be that although every province provides a social environment conducive to the establishment and maintenance of representative and democratic institutions, the prospects for these would be enhanced further if the social and economic cleavages of the several provincial societies crosscut to a greater degree than they do at present.[2]

Similar to societal cleavage patterns, only limited provincial differences were observed in attitudes and behaviour relevant to the achievement of representative democracy. Generally, people in the several provinces do not vary greatly in the extent to which they manifest an interest in politics, use issues as the primary basis for making electoral choices, or participate politically in activities other than voting. Thus, for example, the proportions of citizens following politics at least "fairly closely" range from slightly over one-half in New Brunswick to slightly over two-thirds in British Columbia and the proportions who are moderately or very interested in politics and are sufficiently flexible in their attachments to political parties that they might exercise at least a rough and ready rationality when voting range from one-fifth in Nova Scotia to two-fifths in British Columbia. The number of such potentially rational voters in seven of the 10 provinces differs by 5% or less. There also is little variation in provincial standings in overall participation in electorally related activities. In every province most people confine their political participation to voting and one other activity, such as periodically discussing politics with friends and family — activities requiring little in the way of the commitment of time, energy or material resources.

To reiterate, it can be argued that every province is characterized by an economic, cultural and sociopolitical environment that provides some minimal basis for the achievement of representative democracy. However, it also can be argued that these enviroments are far from ideal and that the prospects for representative democracy would be enhanced if, in every province, material resources and educational opportunities were greater and distributed more evenly throughout the population, people felt more politically efficacious, were less ambivalent in their feelings about political officials, voted more often on the basis of informed and rational calculations, and made more and better use of the different types of political opportunities which are formally available to them.

When evaluating the tendency of people in all provinces to refrain from most kinds of political activity, it must be noted that some of the avenues for participation which are open in theory are less open in practice. With little difficulty people can try to convince family members, friends and associates that a particular party or candidate merits their electoral support. They can attend political rallies, listen to campaign speeches, put bumper stickers on their automobiles and signs on their lawns and, subject to the availability of funds, contribute to party coffers. But they may find it is more difficult to become involved in party organizational work on a sustained basis. Except when recruiting workers to perform mundane tasks such as stuffing envelopes, posting signs and canvassing, party officials are rather selective in their choice of people to whom they turn for assistance. Many of those who are asked and who do join parties often drop out, either temporarily, or permanently. In part, high levels of personnel turnover are a consequence of the routine and repetitive nature of most of the tasks associated with the principal goal of provincial parties, the election of candidates bearing their party labels. Turnover probably also is a function of the oligarchic nature of party organizations. Although parties perform critically important functions in provincial political systems, nowhere is the composition of parties' extralegislative organizations descriptively representative of cross-sections of the general public. Nor are these organizations' internal procedures fully democratic. Only a very small minority of rank-and-file party workers in any province participate in important activities such as the selection of candidates, the construction of the platforms on which candidates run, or the generation of the policies their legislative parties pursue when in office or opposition.

Regarding parties in the electorate, although data in Chapter 5 indicate that provincial parties frequently have been successful in building coalitions that cut across major sociodemographic cleavages within provinces, the existence of such coalitions is not evidence of widespread citizen influence over party affairs. In truth, the vast majority of persons identifying with a provincial party exercise no direct influence over either candidate and leader selection, or the formulation of positions on major policy issues. Further, as argued in Chapter 4, several provinces are characterized by tendencies toward one-party dominance. In these cases, it is doubtful whether electoral competition among parties gives voters generally, or party identifiers in particular, much in the way of indirect or *post hoc* influence over the governing party's candidate selection or policy formulation processes. Additionally, although it appears that many party identifiers may choose their parties on the basis of specific or more general policy concerns, many others evidently do not. From one quarter to slightly over one-half of party identifiers in every province have always identified with the same party and many of these persons have done so since childhood or adolescence. For many of these durable partisans, party attachments are largely affective, essentially irrational ties. It is highly unlikely that these persons are genuinely concerned about influencing the selection of party policies, candidates or leaders. Rather, party policies and candidates invariably are perceived as "good" simply because they bear the "right" party label. By fostering such positive perceptions, the unswerving allegiance of these durable partisans effectively negates their desire to influence the conduct of party affairs.

Limited participation and influence over the conduct of organizational affairs on the part of the rank-and-file is perhaps even more characteristic of major interest groups. Interest groups, like political parties, can perform important functions in a representative democracy. *Inter alia*, they can suggest policies and provide information to elected public officials. By so doing, they can help make those in positions of authority cognizant of the special needs and demands of particular segments of the public and provide them with data relevant to the design and implementation of responsive policies. By representing the interests of their members in this way, and by communicating the reactions of public officials to their members, interest groups help link individuals psychologically to government and the larger political system. They thereby can enhance the democratic nature of the polity and build support for the political community and regime as well as particular policies.

In practice, however, interest groups in every province function as highly biased channels of communication. Many elements of the public are not organized into interest groups at all or, if so organized, are enrolled in groups which lack effective access to political decision-makers. In fact, such access frequently is confined to business and professional groups. Membership in the most important of these is effectively restricted to persons who are affiliated with large corporations or are members of prestigious professions. Further restricting the representational utility of interest groups is their oligarchic nature. Even in (perhaps particularly in) "institutionalized" interest groups which are able to command the attention of party and bureaucratic elites, patterns of influence and control are such that only a minority of members has an effective voice — often only those who are full-time salaried officials at the very apex of the organization. "Issue" interest groups coalescing around a shared desire to communicate a specific, pressing need or demand to government provide more significant opportunities for rank-and-file participation. However, they also are generally less effective in influencing the conduct of public affairs than are the more institutionalized and resource-rich groups.

In Chapter 5 it was argued that although both political parties and interest groups can play important roles in making representational processes operate effectively, the former are more appropriate instruments of representation because they can articulate a wider range of group interests and are more accountable to the public for their actions. At present, however, the ability of provincial political parties to perform representational functions is constrained by a number of factors. One of them is the method by which candidates are elected to provincial legislatures. Single- or multi-member plurality electoral systems introduce an element of distortion into the representational process because the proportion of a party's legislative seats rarely is perfectly congruent with the proportion of the popular vote it receives. In the post-World War Two period, the largest distortions have occurred in Alberta, Prince Edward Island and Ontario; the smallest in Manitoba, New Brunswick and Saskatchewan. In all provinces the effect has been substantial. More important, perhaps, than the distorting effect of a first-past-the-post electoral system, but related to it, is the tendency for a single party to control the government of a province for relatively long periods of time. At some point in their histories all the provinces have experienced this phenomenon. Since 1945 the governments of Quebec, Manitoba and New Brunswick have been subjected least often to relatively long periods of one-party control; those of Ontario, Alberta, Newfoundland and Saskatchewan most often.

Long periods of governmental control by a particular party can distort the representational process in two ways. First, one-party dominance may lead to the generation and implementation of public policies which disproportionately reflect the interests of one or more major institutionalized interest groups. The latter, because of their organizational structures and bountiful resources, are well-positioned to develop and maintain intimate relationships with the cabinet ministers and bureaucratic officials who formulate and administer policies that are especially important to the groups. Second, given the British-model parliamentary systems and disciplined legislative parties operative in each of the provinces,[3] the policy positions of substantial proportions of the provincial electorates who have voted for opposition party candidates may be under- or unrepresented for lengthy periods. The policies advocated by opposition members of a legislature receive very short shrift from a governing party which feels itself securely ensconced in power.

The argument that domination of government by a single party can distort the representational process rests in part on the assumption that parties promulgate different policies when in office. Although there is a long and continuing debate regarding the extent of policy differences among various parties in several of the provinces,[4] there is some empirical support for the notion that it makes a difference who governs. Two types of data are relevant in this regard. First, analyses of aggregate data on the health, education and welfare policies pursued by the provinces in the post-war period indicate that Liberal governments are more responsive to public welfare needs than are other parties. Conservative and Social Credit governments tend to be more responsive to educational needs, and NDP governments tend to respond (indeed to overrespond) to health needs. Further, survey data indicate that substantial percentages of the general public in all provinces believe that the party in power makes a great deal of difference. The electoral strength of the NDP in a province seems particularly important in conditioning public views of the extent of policy differences among parties; the percentage of persons in a province reporting it makes a difference which party is in power is almost perfectly correlated with the magnitude of electoral support for the NDP in that province.

This is not to say that the NDP is unaffected by the kinds of political forces that influence the behaviour of other parties in particular provinces. As observed in the case study of health policy in Saskatchewan in Chapter 7, even New Democrats, when in office, have their policy decisions affected by the leaders of major interest groups and senior members of provincial bureaucracies. Bureaucracies share legislative and executive functions with cabinets and legislative assemblies as well as perform traditional administrative tasks. Unlike members of governing and opposition parties in provincial legislatures, bureaucrats accountability to the public cannot be secured by the threat of electoral defeat. Rather, relationships between the executive, the bureaucracy and the legislature are designed, in theory at least, to preserve the political neutrality and anonymity of civil servants.[5] As a result, the public depends on the formal procedures of parliamentary government and the more amorphous informal subjective norms operative in the bureaucratic units themselves to secure accountability.

Formal accountability through the cabinet and legislature may break down under a variety of conditions. Ministers may refuse to accept responsibility for the actions of bureaucratic subordinates. Legislators may lack the resources (e.g., standing committees, expert staff, specialized information) or the incentives to oversee the activities of public servants. For their part, bureaucratic officials neither are invariably neutral in their policy positions nor always willing to toil in silent anonymity. In this respect, members of provincial bureaucracies may be in a dilemma in the sense that strict adherence to the canons of expertise, neutrality, equality and other "standard operating procedures" at times makes them appear to be representing their own rather than the public's interests. At other times, when bureaucratic officials establish too close and continuous relationships with interest group leaders, or treat groups who nominally are the objects of their regulations as cherished clients, appearance may give way to reality![6]

Arguably, representative democracy in the provinces might be enhanced if bureaucratic accountability to the legislature and the public could be increased. As indicated, however, the utility of formal mechanisms of accountability is constrained because even the largest and most professionalized province legislatures (i.e., those of Quebec and Ontario) do not perform the oversight function effectively. Individual legislators and the institutions of which they are members are much better conveyors of authority than they are exactors of accountability. British-model parliamentary systems such as those operative in the provinces with their often weak and ineffectual standing committees, their dependence for information on the bureaucracies they are overseeing and their lack of expert staff and the specialized information which such staffs can generate, are not equipped to perform oversight activities in a vigorous and systematic manner.[7] When one adds to these structural deficiencies the strongly felt need of individual MLAs in all provinces to devote much of their time to ombudsman and other constituency service tasks widely assumed to increase their chances of being reelected,[8] small wonder that provincial legislative bodies are not known for their ability to ensure that bureaucratic officials are responsive to the general public rather than to well-organized and powerful interest groups.

More generally, backbench and opposition members of provincial legislative bodies are not especially noted for their ability to influence the policy process. The several stages of the process — the identification of problems requiring governmental response, the establishment of a policy agenda by deciding among competing priorities and the formulation and implementation of specific programs intended to achieve broad policy goals — are dominated by provincial premiers, their cabinet colleagues, senior civil servants and the representatives of powerful interest groups. At best, individual MLAs can influence the initial and concluding stages of the process (i.e., the identification of public problems and the evaluation of the effectiveness and appropriateness of specific programs). Even then their influence depends more on the effective use of informal contacts with ministers and senior civil servants than participation in the formal deliberations of provincial assemblies. In all provinces, institutional factors currently inhibit the ability of legislators to represent effectively the policy demands and needs of their constituents.

If, in comparative perspective, the provinces basically are similar in the way their political institutions operate both to facilitate and to limit the achievement of representative democracy, the same cannot be said of the resources which they can bring to bear to meet public needs and demands. In this respect, given the importance many social theorists ascribe to societal wealth as a prerequisite for the establishment of a democratic political order, it is ironic that there is an inverse correlation between the wealth of a province and its overall level of responsiveness to public needs in education, health and social welfare during the post-1945 period. In fact, were it not that Saskatchewan, until recently one of the least affluent provinces, ranks so low in *overall* responsiveness, the correlation between wealth and low responsiveness would be almost perfect. It must be emphasized, however, that responsiveness, as we have measured it, is not simply a surrogate for the magnitudes of governmental spending in the several policy areas. For example, in the mid-1970s, per capita expenditures on health, education and welfare by

Ontario and Alberta substantially exceeded those by Newfoundland and Nova Scotia. Yet, the latter two provinces ranked higher than Ontario and Alberta in overall responsiveness. It also will be recalled that the index of policy responsiveness does not measure the *quality* of public services a provincial government provides. Physicians in Newfoundland and Nova Scotia are no more skilled, nor are their hospitals better equipped than those of Alberta and Ontario. Nor do Newfoundland and Nova Scotia enjoy superior schools or more effective social welfare programs. However, Newfoundland and Nova Scotia do perform better than Alberta and Ontario in providing a more equitable distribution of their scarce resources among competing public needs. In this sense the index of responsiveness is a measure of a provincial government's rational and effective behaviour in responding to public needs — its ability to do the best with what it has available.

We have seen that the ability of provincial governments to do the best with the resources available to them is influenced by a number of factors, not least of which are the actions of the federal government. Over the years the federal government consciously has pursued a policy of redistributing some of the country's wealth to less prosperous provinces to help standardize the quality of governmental services. For example, in the mid-1970s, the value of the per capita transfer payments from the federal government to the less affluent provinces of Prince Edward Island and Newfoundland were 265% and 170% greater than the grant to Alberta, now one of the country's richest provinces. The manner in which the provinces choose to spend these funds affects their level of responsiveness.

Levels of responsiveness are also affected by participation in federal-provincial cost-sharing programs. In this respect, in 1977, a number of changes were made in the arrangements under which the federal government assists the provinces to fund major programs in fields such as health and post-secondary education.[9] The federal government had a two-fold objective in initiating these changes. The first was to try to control the continuously escalating federal contribution to these programs; the second, to centralize authority and responsibility for the disposition of funds for the management of these programs in the hands of provincial governments. Preliminary indications are that although, for a variety of reasons, the proportion of the federal contribution to such programs actually has increased rather than diminished since 1977, the provinces have become more cost conscious and have tried to impose ceilings on expenditures, at least in the health field. Consequently, their overresponse to health needs, as measured here, has declined somewhat. Although any prediction respecting the continuation of this trend would be premature, it does appear that a major determinant of the ability of provinces to respond to public needs — in the sense of making the best use of their available resources — is the extent to which they are free to dispose of the federal contribution to these resources.

TOWARD REPRESENTATIVE DEMOCRACY

Thus far in this discussion three points deserve emphasis. First, none of the provinces conform to the model of representative democracy set forth in Chapter 1. All fall short of meeting the specified conditions in a number of ways. Second, and equally important, however, all of the provinces come closer to meeting the requirements of this model than do a large majority of the world's political systems. Third, although it is doubtless true that the provincial political systems and the economies, societies and cultures upon which they rest differ in a variety of significant ways, with reference to the model, they are much more alike than different. This being the case, it is possible to entertain ways of enhancing the extent to which the provinces approximate the ideals of representative democracy in terms of a series of reforms that are applicable in varying degrees to all.

Proposals for Reform   Over the years, scholars and interested laypersons alike have offered a great many proposals designed to foster representative democracy. Although these proposals are too numerous to make a systematic analysis of their relative merits possible, fortunately, many can be reduced to variants on a few major themes. At the most general level, they approach the problem of bolstering democracy in two ways. The first focuses on altering the environment of a political system, that is, on changing economic, societal and cultural factors that condition the conduct of political life. Scholars with this perspective frequently argue that changes in the structure of and relationships among social classes are crucial if Western political systems are to move any substantial distance along the road to representative democracy. Specifically, they contend, social and economic inequalities among classes must be dramatically reduced.[10] Such reductions would increase the levels of political interest, efficacy and knowledge among currently disadvantaged members of the public and contribute to an enhanced sense of community within and among groups. These changes, in turn, would lead to both quantitative and qualitative increases in citizen participation in political life. Widespread, informed political participation would make political leaders more responsive to citizen needs and demands. Moreover, questions of its instrumental value aside, political participation is a defining characteristic of representative democracy.

The second approach to fostering representative democracy focuses on one key idea: the efficacy of institutional change. In the voluminous literature on democratic government and politics, those who share this perspective frequently advocate the reform of legislative institutions.[11] Recognizing the shortcomings of contemporary Western democracies, and assuming that legislatures are *the* key representative bodies in these polities, they contend that changes in legislative structures will improve prospects for representative democracy. Thus, literally thousands of proposals have been made to provide legislators with greater opportunities to participate more effectively in policy formulation, oversee the activities of the executive and the bureaucracy, and enhance their ability to communicate with constituents, interest groups, the mass media and extraparliamentary party organizations.[12] Normally, these proposals involve limited institutional reforms such as strengthened committees (more, fewer, bigger, smaller, with more general or more specific mandates), more staff (for individual legislators, for parliamentary committees, for party caucuses), or changes in the conduct of legislative business (longer sessions, shorter sessions, more time for the opposition to speak against government legislation, more time for the government to implement its legislative program, etc.).

Some of the proposed changes in legislatures amount to little more than institutional tinkering and whether they would add anything of real substance to the quality of political life is questionable. Other recommendations for structural changes, however, appear to have greater potential. In this latter category are proposals to change the method by which legislative representatives are chosen. A perennially popular, albeit controversial, suggestion is to abandon the current electoral system in favour of some form of proportional representation.[13] In Canada, a long-time favourite is to alter the structure and functions of the Senate and change the method by which senators are selected to provide more equitable and effective representation of regional or provincial interests in Parliament.[14] More far-reaching are proposals which concern the division of legislative powers between levels of government in the federal system or the grafting onto the parliamentary form of government certain features of the congressional system such as powerful legislative committees.[15]

Analytically, the environmental and institutional approaches to political change are easily distinguished. Empirically, it is likely that any meaningful alterations in important political institutions would require commensurate changes in the economy, society and culture in which institutions are embedded. Such *reciprocal* relationships between the way in which a political system operates and its environment raise the possibility of "vicious" circles of causality which could inhibit substantial movement toward greater representative democracy. As C.B. Macpherson recently observed:

> The reduction of social and economic inequality is unlikely without strong democratic action. And it would seem . . . that only through actual involvement in joint political action can people transcend their consciousness of themselves as consumers and appropriators. Hence the vicious circle: we cannot achieve more democratic participation without a prior change in social inequality and in consciousness, but we cannot achieve the changes in social inequality and consciousness without a prior increase in democratic participation.[16]

The questions are, then, can one break out of these circles and, if so, how? Our response to the first of these questions is positive. In part, progress toward greater representative democracy is possible precisely because at least some of the requisites for such a political order already are in place. Because they are, incremental but nevertheless meaningful reforms in existing political institutions are possible. These, in turn, can lead to changes in the social, economic and cultural environments of the provinces, thereby initiating a spiral of effects, the cumulative results of which will be to enhance the quality of political life. Let us consider some specific possibilities.

Of the multiple loci for possible institutional change, the federal system is particularly important. The federal and other provincial governments and the mechanisms of the federal system (e.g., first ministers and interprovincial conferences) constitute key institutional elements in the environments of every provincial political system. In particular, the capacity of any province, large or small, to respond to the needs and demands of its citizens is affected by the amount and type of resources available to its government. Federal–provincial fiscal arrangments thus assume critical importance. Both the magnitude of the funds and the manner in which they are made available to the provinces have important consequences. It can be argued that federal cost-sharing programs, by offering money "with strings attached," constrain provincial policy-making because they channel spending toward programmatic areas for which funds are available and lead to the neglect of others. As a consequence, one recommendation for enhancing provincial responsiveness is to replace shared-cost programs with a system of block grants. The latter would provide the provinces with the latitude and flexibility required to spend money most effectively to meet various public needs and demands and, thereby, facilitate their ability to be responsive.

From the perspective of maintaining the integrity of the Canadian political system, a potential pitfall of such a strategy is its manifest provincial bias. Former Finance Minister John Turner reportedly described it as "combining the federal right to tax with the provincial duty to spend."[17] A possible consequence of augmenting the federal taxing/provincial spending pattern would be the serious erosion of support for the federal government and, perhaps, even for the very idea of an overarching Canadian political community. Thus, another proposal is that rather than simply making block grants to the provinces, the federal government should share more of its taxing authority — permitting the provinces to raise and spend additional tax revenues as they see fit. The objection to this recommendation, however, is that it would perpetuate, in fact, exacerbate, existing provincial economic disparities. The contention is that without federal intervention in the form of an equalization mechanism, the value of tax revenues of a province such as Alberta always will significantly exceed those of a New Brunswick. Other factors being equal, the "have" provinces always will have greater financial capacity to be responsive to citizen needs and demands than the "have nots."

Yet another and quite different recommendation is to enhance *federal* fiscal powers, particularly the ability of the federal government to redistribute wealth among the provinces. The argument is that current arrangements have proven inadequate. The poorer provinces are losing ground and, if the trend continues, the long-term viability of the national political community itself will become problematic. Essentially this is one of the principal justifications political leaders such as Prime Minister Trudeau have offered for strengthening the economic power and authority of Ottawa in any renewed federal system.[18]

Clearly, there is an inconsistency between these latter two proposals. Maintaining or enhancing federal fiscal powers constrains the ability of richer provinces to maximize responsiveness to *their* citizens. As noted, however, emasculating federal fiscal powers would deny poorer provinces the resources required to respond effectively to the needs and demands of their citizens. In our view, a compromise position that enables the federal government to maintain considerable redistributive authority is the proper solution. Although such a compromise might result in modest alterations in the existing fiscal powers of the federal government, the real reform required in this area is not structural but rather attitudinal. There is a profound need for political leaders and the general public alike to recognize the implications of accepting the idea that people in *every* province are members of an overarching Canadian political community. All citizens of this community deserve the benefits of representative democratic government. As long as one is unwilling to abandon the concept of enhancing representative democracy in *all* parts of the country, the notion of ensuring that the less prosperous provinces have adequate resources to act responsively remains valid. That richer provinces inevitably will be unable to be as responsive as they might be is, in this perspective, a price that must be paid if advances in representative democracy are not to be restricted to the wealthy.

Irrespective of the possible impact these recommendations, if implemented, might have on the ability of provinces to move toward the achievement of representative democracy, the availability of adequate financial resources is a necessary but not sufficient condition for meeting this goal. In a full-blown representative democracy formal mechanisms of authorization and accountability encompassing legislators, bureaucrats and citizens are needed and would constitute an intricate and sensitive network of communication and control. In such a network provincial legislators would be more accurately apprised of the needs and demands of their constituents and would be able to hold their respective bureaucracies more accountable for the implementation of policy than is currently the case. Proposals such as freedom of information legislation which might open up government, and institutional reforms such as those recently proposed at the federal level by the Lambert Commission (the Royal Commission on Financial Management and Accountability)[19] provide a point of departure for constructing a more effective set of linkages between citizens' elected representatives and bureaucratic officials. The Lambert Report and various commentaries[20] on it are especially intriguing. Although differing in detail, they call for revamping legislative committees, the provision of additional staff and other resources for such committees and for individual legislators and, perhaps most importantly, a rethinking of traditional procedures used to ensure public service neutrality and anonymity.

A politically neutral and anonymous civil service is part and parcel of parliamentary government, as that process is currently understood. In fact, however, as Campbell and Szablowski,[21] Cairns,[22] and others have observed, senior civil servants currently are involved in making crucial *political* decisions. Moreover, they do so in an environment which effectively shields them and other important political actors such as cabinet ministers and interest group representatives from public scrutiny. As a result, the public's elected representatives, no matter how intelligent and sensitive to public needs and demands they may be, have neither the requisite information to analyze and comprehend the content of governmental programs, nor the ability to assess their possible consequences. Accordingly, structural and procedural changes which would make government operations more visible and amenable to public scrutiny, as well as changes which might improve the information-gathering and analysis capacities of legislators, could make a significant contribution toward the achievement of representative democracy generally and the accountability of bureaucrats to elected public officials in particular.

The chain of communication and control required to make authorization and accountability function more effectively has other weak links as well. Specifically, links between the general public and their MLAs need to be strengthened. The most obvious is the electoral connection, which enables an electorate to signal either pleasure or displeasure with an incumbent government by reelecting it or rejecting its candidates in favour of those of a competing party. In a democracy, this is a powerful and authoritative message. Nonetheless, as many political theorists have noted, electoral mechanisms, as they currently operate in Canada and other Western countries, constitute very imperfect communications channels and very blunt instruments of popular control.[23] Regarding the former, both in logic and in fact, elections frequently fail to convey clear signals about either the content of public policy preferences or the priorities voters assign to these preferences. Also, as noted previously, the plurality electoral systems employed in all provinces tend to distort the actual distribution of party votes when these are translated into legislative seats.

The ability of elections to serve as instruments of control in part is contingent upon the motives of political elites: more specifically, their political career aspirations. Other than a normative desire to adhere to the canons of representative democracy, elected officials who entertain no, or only modest political ambitions, have little incentive either to anticipate or to respond to public needs and demands.[24] For their part, there is very little voters can do other than render a *post hoc* negative judgment on the performance of such officials at the next election. Additionally, there are no guarantees that candidates of parties aspiring to power will be more responsive than the "rascals" whom the electorate may wish to "throw out," or that challenging parties will present policies which differ meaningfully from those currently being pursued.

Is there anything which can be done to improve the operation of the electoral system? Clearly, political parties cannot be forced by legislative fiat to offer clearly distinguishable policy alternatives. Nor is it possible to legislate officeholders' motives during their terms of office. However, it may be possible to minimize the distortion of election results that presently occurs when votes are translated into legislative seats. Some form of proportional representation, if adopted, might ensure that the composition of legislative assemblies would reflect more accurately the electoral strength of parties in a province.

Advocates of proportional representation long have argued that the major beneficiaries of such a system would be smaller, weaker parties which traditionally have had great difficulty either securing or maintaining a foothold in provincial legislatures.[25] Gaining greater legislative representation would provide them with continuing access to one of the most important platforms in a democracy for making their policy positions known. The adoption of proportional representation also would help to break the system of oligopolistic competition among dominant parties, thereby widening the range of policy choices available to the electorate and demonstrating that a vote for a small minority party is not necessarily wasted. Over time, the cumulative effects of proportional representation might well be the development of significantly more competitive and ideologically diverse provincial party systems. Increased competition among ideologically diverse parties, in turn, might have a salutary effect on responsiveness by encouraging electoral candidates to be more attentive to public opinion and facilitating the public's ability to make meaningful choices among clearly defined policy alternatives proffered by competing parties.

Opponents of proportional representation question both the validity of these claims and the appropriateness of the system for Canada. Regarding the former, they ask whether proportional representation would appreciably improve the competitive position of Liberals in Alberta and British Columbia, of Conservatives in Quebec and British Columbia, of the New Democratic Party in the Atlantic provinces, Quebec and Alberta, or of Social Credit in any province east of Alberta. The prospects of these provincial parties also would be impaired if, as seems probable, some version of a "five percent" regulation were adopted as part of a proportional representation package. As it operates in some European countries, the regulation requires that a party receive a minimum of five percent (or some other stipulated figure) of the total vote cast before its candidates can be seated in the legislature. Although this rule makes it difficult for fringe groups espousing anti-democratic sentiments to gain a legislative platform for their views, if used in Canada, it also probably would impair the electoral prospects of some of the provincial parties referred to above.

As for the claim that proportional representation would encourage political parties to present more meaningful policy choices to voters, critics point out that most parliamentary systems employing proportional representation have coalition governments. These coalitions are formed *after*, rather than before an election and it is often very difficult to forecast which coalitions might occur. Moreover, because of the politics of coalition building, voters casting their ballots for party "A" on policy grounds may receive something quite different in the way of policy if the party becomes part of a governing coalition.[26]

There are other criticisms of proportional representation. For example, it is argued that proportional representation is inappropriate for parliamentary systems of the kind found in Canada. These function best when a single party is able to achieve the parliamentary majority required to govern. Proportional representation, however, increases the probability of coalition governments which may be fractious and unstable. The possible results include continuing policy stalemate, more frequent elections and general political instability.[27] Additionally, although they need not, polities employing proportional representation frequently have list voting and multi-member legislative districts. Under these conditions, the likelihood of election is dependent upon a candidate's position on a party list; the higher the position, the greater the likelihood of election. These lists generally are prepared by small groups of upper-echelon, full-time, salaried, party organizational officials who, it may be assumed, are unlikely to slate candidates in favourable positions if their social and demographic characteristics or policy views differ markedly from their own (i.e., the list-makers'). In sum, list voting might make party organizations even more oligarchic and legislatures more unrepresentative than they are currently.[28]

These objections to proportional representation notwithstanding, it may be the case that in *some* provinces the claims of advocates of such systems might be realized without incurring problems such as those cited above. Given this possibility and the manifest need to eliminate, insofar as possible, the distorting effects of present provincial electoral systems, the pros and cons of proportional representation should receive more systematic and unbiased consideration than they appear to have to date.

In any event, neither proportional representation nor any other electoral mechanism will eliminate the need for political leadership. In this respect, representative democracies are no different than other political systems. In a representative democracy the division of political labour between governors and governed places an inescapably heavy burden on political leaders, irrespective of the process by which they are selected. Although generations of political theorists have spent a great deal of time and effort on the task, a permanent solution to the leadership recruitment problem remains elusive. Of course, a fundamental rationale for democracy is precisely that there are no foolproof means of ensuring that leaders will be responsive to the public. Leaders' internalization of democratic norms, their more general political ideologies, and their political ambitions all may make them adhere to public needs and demands, but ultimately citizens must assume responsibility for protecting their own interests by active involvement in political life.

Unfortunately, as observed a number of times in this book, one of the most salient characteristics of political behaviour in all provinces is that few citizens do anything political but vote and occasionally discuss politics with friends and family. The pervasiveness of low levels of participation might tempt one to infer that little or nothing can be done to enhance popular political involvement. Such an inference would be unwarranted. After all, in every province a minority of persons *are* politically active. In terms of attitudes and beliefs, they are people with high levels of political interest who believe that they have the competence to influence the behaviour of those who govern, and assume that "who governs" can and does make a difference. Sociologically, political activists tend to be well-educated, middle-aged, upper and upper-middle class men with prestigious professional or managerial occupations. Indeed, these are literally the defining characteristics of the most politically active and influential persons — leaders of parties and interest groups and holders of elective and appointive public offices. Knowing who they are enables us to suggest ways in which more extensive and intensive citizen participation can be achieved.

Our first suggestion flows from the observation that there is a causal chain linking socioeconomic status and political participation. Upper and upper-middle class persons frequently have the material resources and leisure time that lead to the development of psychological orientations (e.g., political interest, efficacy and knowledge) conducive to political activity. Although in a free society it is impossible to redistribute societal goods and services to ensure that everyone has the material and temporal resources currently available to the upper and upper-middle classes, greater efforts in this direction are possible. Particularly important is improved access to educational opportunities for lower socioeconomic status persons, minorities and women. As noted in Chapter 3, since 1960 every province (with the assistance of the federal government) has significantly expanded its system of secondary and post-secondary education. These systems are in place and constitute the structural basis for providing more citizens with the educational resources conducive to more extensive political involvement. Greater access to educational opportunities is merely a beginning. Studies of the relevance of secondary and higher education for political socialization in Canada have concluded that during the course of their formal schooling most people receive little or no information about how their political institutions and processes function.[29] Consequently, a second recommendation is that, at a minimum, people receive basic factual information about the nature of their political system and how it operates. Although this proposal might seem modest it can have significant effects if, as we believe, the knowledge people acquire will enhance both their interest in participating politically and the feeling that they can do so effectively.

A third suggestion is to provide opportunities and encouragement for greater participation in the governing of ostensibly "non-political" institutions such as schools, factories and offices. Advocates of this approach contend that for too long a time overly narrow conceptions of what is and is not political have discouraged participation by defining the political process almost entirely in terms of the operation of institutions such as legislatures, parties and bureaucracies. These are institutions which most people have little personal knowledge of or experience with and, hence, they have been unwilling to try to participate, assuming they could not do so effectively. A broader conceptualization of the political process, one that encompasses institutions such as schools and the workplace, is, therefore, desirable — both for its own sake and because it would encourage the development of attitudes conducive to participation in more manifestly political institutions. Regarding the desirability of a broader conceptualization of the political process, the argument is that societal institutions that organize work, education and leisure have a major impact on most people. It is within these structures that people spend substantial proportions of their daily lives. Consequently, widespread participation in their decision-making processes is desirable in and of itself.[30] Participation of this kind would enhance people's feelings of personal competence which, in turn, would stimulate even more intensive participation on their part. Equally important, what persons learn and experience within the confines of these institutions can be generalized and transferred to the political arena more narrowly defined.[31] The net result of greater participatory opportunities might well be an expanding spiral of political efficacy and participation. To reiterate, if people are given meaningful opportunities to participate in the decision-making processes of institutions such as workplaces and schools, they will acquire an enhanced sense of political competence. This will encourage them both to participate more intensively in such institutions and to extend their involvement to manifestly political institutions. The latter would produce strengthened feelings of competence, which would reinforce the desire to participate.

PROSPECTS FOR REFORM

Offering blueprints for political reform is not terribly difficult. Indeed, the construction of plans for utopian polities has been an intellectual pastime for political theorists since Plato. Unfortunately, attempts to put such reforms into practice generally have led to bitter disappointment. After suffering such disappointments, erstwhile reformers often have accepted the truth of the old adage that "the road to hell is paved with good intentions" and become political "realists." In recent times, among the most influential members of the realist school have been the elitist democrats who defend the status quo by arguing that only very limited reforms of the political systems of Western countries are either possible or desirable. From the vantage point of democratic theory, one can reject the normative thrust of these arguments.[32] However, their empirical aspects are more difficult to evaluate. A skeptic, reviewing the historial wreckage of so many of the schemes for political reform, is justified in asking just how likely it is that meaningful changes can be effected. The question is a valid one, but a precise response, unfortunately, is impossible.

As has been indicated throughout this book, a number of barriers exist to meaningful democratic reform. Most of these can be reduced to the observation offered earlier in this chapter of the strong circularities in relationships between societal change and political reform. Significant social changes require institutional reforms which are highly unlikely in the absence of thoroughgoing societal changes. Breaking out of these circles of causality through actions initiated by reform-minded political leaders is difficult since these leaders profit the most from existing political, social and economic arrangements. Accepting this reasoning, some critics would abandon Western liberal and democratic traditions entirely and place their hopes for achieving desired societal changes on violent revolution led by enlightened cadres of counter-elites.[33]

Evidence adduced in this and other studies of political attitudes and behaviour suggests, however, that we are not necessarily fated to be crushed between the "rock" of the status quo and the "hard place" of violent revolution. For one thing, considerable research has shown that political elites tend to be the strongest proponents of democratic norms in contemporary Western countries.[34] To conclude, therefore, that "when push comes to shove" political elites invariably will abandon these norms in favour of some version of a narrow class interest is unduly pessimistic. For another, our analysis of voting behaviour in Chapter 4 indicates that the burden of moving the polity in the direction of greater representative democracy need not rest entirely on the shoulders of political elites. Substantial numbers of persons in every province already demonstrate a capacity for effective participation in a representative democracy and presumably would be receptive to proposed reforms designed to improve the quality of political life. In short, there is no reason to accept the extreme pessimism of either radical critics of the motives and behaviour of political elites or elitist democrats who disparage the capacities and inclinations of average citizens.

Still to be answered, however, is the question of how we break out of the circles of causality which reinforce the status quo. Do we begin with the political elites and political institutions or with the general public and society at large when initiating processes of reform? One answer, we believe, is to attempt incremental but *non-trivial* modifications of existing economic, social and political institutions, using widespread perceptions of the need for change as a base on which to build a consensus regarding the desirability of specific reforms. Although such reforms probably will have to be initiated by political leaders, as noted, there are reasons to believe that both elites and the general public will be receptive to them. Moreover, there is reason to believe that this receptivity will increase concomitantly with a growing recognition that the social and economic foundations of the Canadian political system, like those of other Western polities, currently are being subjected to severe, perhaps unprecedented, stresses. These include pressures deriving from continuing high rates of unemployment and inflation, recurring shortages of various raw materials and foodstuffs, ever-shrinking supplies of fossil fuels with accompanying escalations of energy costs, massive environmental pollution and rapid technological changes that seriously disrupt traditional social patterns and threaten the survival of minority cultural groups. Within the Canadian context, some of these problems are felt acutely, others are more remote. On balance, however, these stressful conditions have profoundly shocked the Canadian political system and helped produce the continuing and widely recognized "Crisis of Confederation."

Paradoxically, this crisis may well provide an unprecedented opportunity to improve the quality of Canadian political life. The view that problems such as those cited above must be dealt with immediately and systematically already is widespread. This recognition has prompted numerous proposals for revamping different aspects of the political system. To date, with the exception of the federal government's attempts to entrench a charter of rights in a new constitution, virtually all of these proposals have focussed quite narrowly on the federal system. Altering the powers of the federal and provincial governments and changing the institutions of the former to increase the ability of the latter to voice their demands at the national level have been major topics of debate. By conceptualizing solutions to the problems facing Canadians in terms of relationships between the two levels of *government*, federal and provincial politicians and other participants (e.g., academics, journalists) in this debate have neglected the need to change institutions at *both* levels to enhance the responsiveness of the political system to popular needs and demands.

Although, as previous discussion has indicated, proposals to change the federal system are relevant to the task of building representative democracy, clearly, revamping federalism is not enough. More extensive and profound institutional, societal and cultural changes are required. Prospects for such thoroughgoing changes are uncertain, but not necessarily bleak. Since the systemic stresses which produced the ongoing crisis are unlikely to be eliminated (although they may be ameliorated) by altering the structures of federalism, pressures for additional reforms are likely to continue. It is possible that these pressures will be in the direction of representative democracy. In this regard, it is trite, but nevertheless true that much will depend on how elites and members of the general public react when it becomes apparent that changes in federalism provide only partial answers to the serious problems confronting the country.

Scholarly opinion regarding how the complex of problems facing Canada and other Western countries will affect the long-term prospects for democracy is sharply divided. Michael Margolis, for example, is quite pessimistic. In his opinion, despite their apparent discontent, neither elites nor the general publics in Western democracies want real reform. Rather they support the status quo and will continue to do so because they believe existing governmental institutions can deliver an ever-increasing abundance of the goods and services that they have come to take for granted. As a result:

> Only when the resources that have sustained this growth [in the economies of Western countries] have nearly run out will any radical adjustments in policy occur. For the citizens' own good these adjustments will be imposed upon them by experts from the

governing elite. The policies imposed may or may not be successful ... but the policy process will be neither liberal nor democratic.[35]

C.B. Macpherson, in another recent work on the future of democracy, is
even more critical of elites, but his high regard for the potential of
citizens to recognize the pressing need for change makes him guardedly
optimistic about the future of Western polities:

> So we have three weak points in the vicious circle — the increasing
> awareness of the costs of economic growth, the increasing aware-
> ness of the costs of political apathy, the increasing doubts about the
> ability of corporate capitalism to meet consumer expectations while
> reproducing inequality. ... [T]ogether, they conduce to a decline in
> consumer consciousness, a reduction of class inequalities, and an
> increase in present political participation.[36]

Both Margolis and Macpherson agree that the economic and social
catalysts for change are present; they disagree about the likely directions
of change. Margolis believes that citizens in Western countries are
unlikely to abandon what Macpherson has called "consumer consciousness" to emphasize values such as a sense of community, a clean,
healthy environment, a more equitable distribution of societal goods
and political participation itself. Macpherson, in contrast, judges that
the present crisis may have precisely this effect on people's values and
the result will be breaks in the reinforcing relationships of elite domination and mass apathy which heretofore have inhibited movement
toward greater democracy in all Western societies.

We do not know if either of these two rival hypotheses will be proven
correct. Social and political systems are complex entities and forecasting
the future is necessarily a risky business. Nevertheless, it is apparent
that significant social and economic changes are occurring and that these
probably will lead to equally substantial changes in Canadian political
life. It also is evident that it requires, for political elites and citizens alike,
a "leap of faith" to attempt to channel the processes of change in the
direction of representative democracy by working to institute political,
social and economic reforms such as those described in this chapter. But
this is nothing new. Democratic theory always has been predicated on
faith: faith in the capacity of people for self-government. To abandon
this faith is tantamount to denying the possibility of representative
democracy. To affirm it may be simply naive, but an alternative and
more generous interpretation is that such an affirmation is at worst a
secular analogue of "Pascal's wager." Granted, the stakes are not as high
as those which concerned the 17th century French philosopher. Still, the
possibility of achieving a genuinely representative democratic system in
a more humane and participatory society makes the game well worth
the candle.

NOTES

1. John Porter, *The Vertical Mosaic* (Toronto: University of Toronto Press, 1965), *passim*.
2. See, for example, Arend Lijphart, "Typologies of Democratic Systems," *Comparative Political Studies* 1 (1968), p. 12; Douglas Rae and Michael Taylor, *The Analysis of Political Cleavages* (New Haven: Yale University Press, 1970), p. 86.
3. For a succinct description of the properties of such systems see Nelson Polsby, "Legislatures," in Fred I. Greenstein and Nelson Polsby, eds., *Handbook of Political Science* 5 (Reading, Mass.: Addison-Wesley, 1975), ch. 4. On recent changes in the British parliament see John E. Schwarz, "Exploring a New Role in Policy Making: The British House of Commons in the 1970's," *American Political Science Review* 74 (1980), pp. 23–47; and Philip Norton, "The Changing Face of the British House of Commons in the 1970s," *Legislative Studies Quarterly* 3 (1980), pp. 333–358.
4. See Harold D. Clarke, "The Ideological Self-Perceptions of Provincial Legislators," *Canadian Journal of Political Science* 11 (1978), pp. 617–634.
5. For a recent discussion of these relationships see Kenneth Kernaghan, "Power, Parliament and Public Servants in Canada: Ministerial Responsibility Re-examined," in Harold D. Clarke *et al.*, eds., *Parliament, Policy and Representation* (Toronto: Methuen, 1980), ch. 7.
6. On the breakdown of bureaucratic neutrality and anonymity in Canada see Colin Campbell and George J. Szablowski, *The Superbureaucrats: Structure and Behaviour in Central Agencies* (Toronto: Macmillan, 1979).
7. A number of scholars have made this argument. See, for example, Audrey Doerr, "Parliamentary Accountability and Legislative Potential"; Paul G. Thomas, "Parliament and the Purse Strings"; and Colin Campbell and George Szablowski, "The Centre and the Periphery: Superbureaucrats' Relations with MPs and Senators," in Clarke *et al.*, *Parliament, Policy and Representation*, chs. 8, 9 and 11.
8. Harold D. Clarke, Richard G. Price and Robert Krause, "Constituency Service Among Canadian Provincial Legislators: Basic Findings and a Test of Three Hypotheses," *Canadian Journal of Political Science* 8 (1975), p. 534.
9. See David Falcone and Richard J. Van Loon, "Public Attitudes and Intergovernmental Shift in Responsibility for Health Programs: Paying the Piper Without Calling the Tune," in Allan Kornberg and Harold D. Clarke, eds., *Political Support in Canada: The Crisis Years* (Durham, N.C.: Duke University Press, 1982), ch. 8.
10. More radical exponents of the perspective have argued that this can *only* be accomplished if the present capitalist economic system is replaced by a socialist one.
11. This is not to say that concern for legislative reform is a recent phenomenon. Scholars long have been interested in the topic. See, for example, Gerhard Loewenberg, *Modern Parliaments: Change or Decline?* (Chicago: Aldine Alherton, 1971).
12. For a selection of proposed reforms in the Canadian Parliament and provincial legislatures see the several papers collected in Clarke *et al.*, *Parliament, Policy and Representation*.
13. See, for example, Report of the Task Force on Canadian Unity, v. 1 *A Future Together: Observations and Recommendations* (Hull: Canadian Government Publishing Centre, 1979), ch. 7.
14. Examples include E.D. Briggs, "The Senate: Reform or Reconstruction?" *Queen's Quarterly* 75 (1968), pp. 91–104; Government of Canada, *The Constitutional Amendment Bill* (Ottawa: Ministry of Supply and Services, 1978); Task Force on Canadian Unity, *A Future Together*, pp. 97–99; Colin Campbell, *The Canadian Senate: A Lobby From Within* (Toronto: Macmillan, 1978), ch. 7.
15. For arguments regarding the need for strengthening legislative committees see Thomas, "Parliament and the Purse Strings," and Campbell and Szablowski, "The Centre and the Periphery," chs. 9 and 11 in Clarke *et al.*, *Parliament, Policy and Representation*. Proposals for restructuring the federal system are legion. Recent examples include Task Force on Canadian Unity, v. 1 *A Future Together*, ch. 7; and The Constitutional Committee of the Quebec Liberal Party, *A New Canadian Federation* (Montreal: January 9, 1980). A concise exposition of the Parti Québécois'

proposal for sovereignty-association is contained in André Bernard, *What Does Quebec Want?* (Toronto: James Lorimer, 1978), ch. 4.

16. C.B. Macpherson, *The Life and Times of Liberal Democracy* (Toronto: Oxford University Press, 1977), p. 100.

17. Falcone and Van Loon, "Public Attitudes and Intergovernmental Shift in Responsibility for Health Programs."

18. Pierre Elliott Trudeau, *The Constitution and the People of Canada* (Ottawa: Queen's Printer, 1969).

19. Royal Commission on Financial Management and Accountability, *Final Report* (Hull: Canadian Government Publishing Centre, 1979).

20. See, for example, Kernaghan, "Power, Parliament and Public Servants in Canada"; Doerr, "Parliamentary Accountability and Legislative Potential"; and Thomas, "Parliament and the Purse Strings"; chs. 7, 8, and 9 in Clarke *et al.*, *Parliament, Policy and Representation*.

21. Campbell and Szablowski, *The Superbureaucrats*, chs. 7, 8.

22. Alan C. Cairns, "The Governments and Societies of Canadian Federalism," *Canadian Journal of Political Science* 10 (1977), pp. 695–726.

23. A succinct summary of these arguments can be found in Macpherson, *The Life and Times of Liberal Democracy*, pp. 82–92.

24. Joseph A. Schlesinger, *Ambition and Politics* (Chicago: Rand McNally, 1966), ch. 1; Harold D. Clarke and Richard G. Price, "Parliamentary Experience and Representational Role Orientations in Canada," *Legislative Studies Quarterly* 6 (1981), pp. 373–390.

25. For a recent argument to this effect see the Task Force on Canadian Unity, *A Future Together*, p. 105.

26. A.J. Milnor, *Elections and Political Stability* (Boston: Little, Brown, 1969), pp. 91–98.

27. *Ibid.*

28. For an expanded version of this argument with reference to the proposals of the Task Force on Canadian Unity see Allan Kornberg, Harold D. Clarke and Arthur Goddard, "Parliament and the Representational Process in Contemporary Canada," in Clarke *et al.*, eds. *Parliament, Policy and Representation*, p. 20.

29. T.H.B. Symons, *To Know Ourselves: The Report of the Commission on Canadian Studies* (Ottawa: Association of Universities and Colleges of Canada, 1975), p. 65.

30. Macpherson, *The Life and Times of Liberal Democracy*, pp. 103–105; Carole Pateman, *Participation and Democratic Theory* (Cambridge: Cambridge University Press, 1970), chs. 3, 4; Peter Bachrach, *The Theory of Democratic Elitism* (Boston: Little Brown, 1967), ch. 7.

31. Pateman, *Participation and Democratic Theory*, chs. 3, 4; Gabriel Almond and Sidney Verba, *The Civic Culture* (Princeton: Princeton University Press, 1963), ch. 12.

32. See, for example, Jack L. Walker, "A Critique of the Elitist Theory of Democracy," *American Political Science Review* 30 (1966), pp. 285–295; Lane Davis, "The Cost of Realism: Contemporary Restatements of Democracy," *Western Political Quarterly* 17 (1964), pp. 37–46; Graeme Duncan and Steven Lukes, "The New Democracy," *Political Studies*, 2 (1963), pp. 156–177.

33. The possible and desirable roles of elites in effecting political change has long been a topic of intense debate among radical critics of liberal democracies. See, for example, Henry B. Mayo, *Introduction to Marxist Theory* (New York: Oxford University Press, 1960), ch. 5.

34. Two classic studies documenting this point are Herbert McClosky, "Consensus and Ideology in American Politics," *American Political Science Review* 58 (1964), pp. 361–382; and James W. Prothro and Charles M. Grigg, "Fundamental Principles of Democracy: Bases of Agreement and Disagreement," *Journal of Politics* 22 (1960), pp. 276–294.

35. Michael Margolis, *Viable Democracy* (Markham: Penguin Books Canada Limited, 1979), pp. 186–187.

36. Macpherson, *The Life and Times of Liberal Democracy*, p. 106.

FOR FURTHER READING

Heilbroner, Robert L. *An Inquiry Into The Human Prospect*, revised ed. New York: W.W. Norton, 1980. Reading Heilbroner's lucid treatment of the crises confronting mankind in the late 20th century allows one to place the problems facing contemporary Canada in a global perspective.

Macpherson, C.B. *The Life and Times of Liberal Democracy.* Toronto: Oxford University Press, 1977, ch. 5. The author presents an argument for expanding citizen participation in political decision-making processes and examines the problems of and prospects for doing so.

Margolis, Michael. *Viable Democracy.* Harmondsworth, Middlesex: Penguin, 1979. The author presents a brief, readable analysis of the development of democratic theory and practice and a consideration of prospects for enhancing democracy in the face of unprecedented social and economic problems. Proposals for reform focus on expanded freedom of information and the use of new communications and data processing technologies.

Pateman, Carole. *Participation and Democratic Theory.* Cambridge: Cambridge University Press, 1970. After considering the role of participation in several influential statements of democratic theory, Pateman discusses how to expand opportunities for citizen participation in advanced industrial societies. Emphasis is placed on bolstering citizens' political efficacy through meaningful participation in the decision-making processes of important, albeit ostensibly nonpolitical, institutions such as factories and schools.

Smiley, Donald V. *Canada in Question: Federalism in the Eighties*, 3rd ed. Toronto: McGraw-Hill Ryerson, 1980. Chapters 8 and 9 consider dimensions of the crisis of Canadian federalism and discuss alternative possibilities for resolving the crisis.

Index

843